MODERN LEGAL

70 0174120 X

TELEPEN

LAW OF THE
COMMON
AGRICULTURAL
POLICY

CA

of the Series
. B. McAuslan

AUSTRALIA AND NEW ZEALAND
The Law Book Company Ltd.
Sydney : Melbourne : Perth

CANADA AND U.S.A.
The Carswell Company Ltd.
Agincourt, Ontario

INDIA
N.M. Tripathi Private Ltd.
Bombay
and
Eastern Law House Private Ltd.
Calcutta and Delhi
M.P.P. House
Bangalore

ISRAEL
Steimatzky's Agency Ltd.
Jerusalem : Tel Aviv : Haifa

MALAYSIA : SINGAPORE : BRUNEI
Malayan Law Journal (Pte.) Ltd.
Singapore

PAKISTAN
Pakistan Law House
Karachi

MODERN LEGAL STUDIES

LAW OF THE COMMON AGRICULTURAL POLICY

by

FRANCIS G. SNYDER
B.A. (Yale), J.D. (Harvard), Doct. Spéc. (Paris I)
Member of the Bar of Massachusetts (U.S.A.)
Reader in Law at the University of Warwick

LONDON
SWEET & MAXWELL
1985

Published in 1985 by
Sweet & Maxwell Limited of
11 New Fetter Lane, London.
Computerset by Promenade Graphics Ltd., Cheltenham.
Printed in Great Britain by
Page Bros. (Norwich) Ltd.

British Library Cataloguing in Publication Data

Snyder, Francis G.
Law of the Common Agricultural Policy.—(Modern
legal studies)
1. Agriculture and state—European Economic
Community countries   2 Agricultural laws and
legislation—European Economic Community countries
I. Title   II. Series
341.7'5471   HD1920.5.Z8

ISBN 0–421–31880–5
ISBN 0–421–31890–2 Pbk

© Francis G. Snyder
1985

PREFACE

The aim of this book, the first of its kind in English, is to provide a concise introduction to the legal aspects of the European Community's Common Agricultural Policy (CAP).

The economic and political importance of CAP law has constantly been reaffirmed by the continuing controversy that surrounds the CAP, especially in Britain. Its neglect by legal scholars is explained by the particular ways in which numerous strands of English intellectual history, the organisation of economic knowledge and the determinants of legal research are interwoven in late twentieth century western Europe.

Law teachers and researchers in the United Kingdom have paid relatively little attention to the legal issues involved in the formulation and implementation of agricultural and food policy. With regard to the CAP, legal scholars as well as economists and other social scientists have rarely dealt adequately with the intimate connection, yet real distinction, between policy and law. Common lawyers have often considered the CAP to be primarily a matter of administrative regulations. In the absence of a tradition of research on economic law or of well-developed theories of the state, they have therefore tended either to treat the CAP in isolation from economic policy or to view it as only occasionally raising questions of general legal significance. Agricultural economics have presented the best discussions of the principles, costs and controversies of the CAP. These economists are mainly concerned, however, with agricultural policy, of which legislation and judicial decisions are deemed to be merely an expression. Within the past decade, sociologists of law have focused closely on the state, and some theorists have recently begun to view European Community (EC) institutions through a similar lens. Yet up to now they have virtually ignored the range of policy instruments and legal measures involved in agricultural policy; the ways in which the legal framework and measures of the CAP have modified past relations between the production, processing and marketing of agricultural commodities; and the consequences of these continuing shifts for the role of the state. None of these approaches has given sufficient attention to the reciprocal relationship between policy and law, thus, in the event, over-emphasising policy and neglecting law.

By taking such contextual and theoretical issues implicitly into account, this book may help to lay a foundation for a broader study of the premises, the means and the consequences of supranational legal intervention in the European agricultural economy. Its main purpose, however, is not to describe EC agricultural policy or to analyse the political economy of European law, but rather to present the principal legal issues involved in the elaboration and implementation of the CAP. The text is organised so as to treat the major functional aspects of the CAP and, within each, the elements which raise important legal issues. Special emphasis is given to three central features of the CAP, which often appear unusual to lawyers and law students. First, the CAP, throughout its existence, has frequently been expressed in novel legal forms. Secondly, the regulation of agriculture on a European scale has posed familiar questions in unfamiliar terms and sometimes given rise to new legal issues. Thirdly, the resolution of complex questions of economic policy has continually been attempted by the European Court. Accordingly, the discussion concentrates mainly on the intra-community aspects of CAP law. The CAP's international legal aspects, though important, are for reasons of space discussed primarily in the context of other topics; so are "food law," fisheries policy and the numerous proposals by economists for reforming the CAP. Although special attention is given to the United Kingdom, CAP legislation and European Court decisions mentioned in the book refer to all Member States.

The book is intended primarily for university and polytechnic undergraduate students in law, who already have a basic knowledge of EC law and institutions. It should also be of direct interest to students in agricultural economics, politics and European studies. In addition, the book may be useful to teachers, researchers, or practitioners in law, agricultural economics or European studies, or to others who, by reason of their employment, are concerned in any way with the operation of the CAP. Finally, I hope that it may be of interest to all who wish to understand the operation of the CAP, especially its legal aspects, in order to contribute to the continuing debate about its future.

I wish to thank The Nuffield Foundation for its generous financial support of the research. I am grateful also to the EC Commission for facilitating research in Brussels; to numerous staff members of the Commission and the Council; and to a large number of people from the Ministry of Agriculture, Fisheries and Food (MAFF) in London, the Intervention Board for Agricultural Produce (IBAP) in Reading, the former Central Council for Agricultural and Horticultural Co-operation (CCAHC, now Food from Britain), the Centre for European Agricultural Studies (CEAS), Wye College, the Instituto Naçional de Administração, Oeiras, Portugal, Wye College of the University of London, and

the Universities of Reading, Exeter and Warwick. I am especially
indebted to Jolyon Hall, Lesley Cropper, C. K. Kuek, Ian Love-
land, Siân Miles and Jasper Snyder, to whom this book is dedi-
cated. The book does not, however, necessarily represent the
views of any of these organisations or individuals; I alone am
responsible for its contents.

The law is stated as of September 1, 1984, though it has been
possible at proof stage to take account of some later developments.

1985
University of Warwick   Francis G. Snyder

OTHER BOOKS IN THE SERIES

CONTENTS

TABLE OF CASES
BEFORE THE COURT OF JUSTICE

(in alphabetical order)

TABLE OF CASES
BEFORE THE COURT OF JUSTICE

(in numerical order)

TABLE OF CASES BEFORE NATIONAL COURTS

TABLE OF COMMUNITY TREATIES

TABLE OF
COMMUNITY SECONDARY LEGISLATION

TABLE OF U.K. LEGISLATION

TABLE OF U.K. STATUTORY INSTRUMENTS

ABBREVIATIONS

A.C	Appeal Cases
All E.R.	All England Reports
Bull. E.C.	Bulletin of the European Communities
C.D.E.	Cahiers de Droit Européen
C.M.L.R.	Common Market Law Reports
C.M.L.Rev.	Common Market Law Review
E.C.R.	European Court Reports
E.L.Rev.	European Law Review
I.C.L.Q.	International and Comparative Law Quarterly
J.A.E.	Journal of Agricultural Economics
J.C.M.S.	Journal of Common Market Studies
J.O.	Journal Officiel des Communautés Européennes
J.W.T.L.	Journal of World Trade Law
L.I.E.I.	Legal Issues of European Integration
N.I.L.Q.	Northern Ireland Legal Quarterly
O.J.	Official Journal of the European Communities
O.J. Sp.Ed.	Official Journal of the European Communities, English Special Edition
Q.B.	Queen's Bench Division
R.T.D.E.	Revue Trimestrielle de Droit Européen
W.L.R.	Weekly Law Reports

ACKNOWLEDGMENTS

THE author and publishers wish to thank the following for permission to reprint material from the books and periodicals indicated:

Basil Blackwell Ltd.:
Grant, *The Politics of the Green Pound, 1974–1979* (1981) 19 J.C.M.S.

Consumers' Association:
Common Agricultural Policy (1977) Money Which?

George Allen & Unwin:
J. S. Marsh and P. Swanney, *Agriculture and the European Community* (1980).

Hutchinson Publishing Group Limited:
M. Butterwick and E. Neville-Rolfe, *Agricultural Marketing and the EEC* (1972).

Pergamon Press Ltd.:
Butterwick, "Grain Marketing in Some Western European Countries" in D. K. Britton (Ed.), *Cereals in the United Kingdom* (1969).

Trade Policy Research Centre:
Heidhves, Josling, Ritson and Tangermann, *Common Prices and Europe's Farm Policy*, Thames Essay No. 14 (1978).

Chapter 1

INTRODUCTION

Agriculture, Law and the Common Market

Food production, state and law

Food is essential to life, and its production, distribution, exchange and consumption are of vital importance in any society. Every individual is implicated in the food economy, "the set of activities and relationships that interact to determine what, how much, by what method and for whom food is produced."[1] Until recently, however, political decisions regarding agriculture, the aspect of the food economy with which this book is concerned, have, especially in the United Kingdom, been mainly the province of farmers, politicians and technical specialists, and have remained invisible to ordinary people. Farm policy, moreover, has sometimes been conceived, formulated and implemented as if the agricultural sector existed in isolation, whereas in fact it is integral to the food chain and society as a whole. The agricultural sector's distinctive status perhaps reflects, historically, farmers' attempts since the late nineteenth century to assert and defend, sometimes in conjunction with the state, a measure of structural autonomy against industrialisation.[2] But today such claims to special treatment, however legitimate they may be as regards individual farmers or particular groups of producers, are being widely questioned in so far as they refer to an entire economic sector. Correlatively, farmers' political power in most European countries is on the decline. With the partial industrialisation of agriculture and the gradual internationalisation of capital in the food economy, farmers have become increasingly dependent on the mechanical

---

[1] Organisation for Economic Co-operation and Development, *Food Policy* (1981) at 10.

[2] See, *e.g.* M. Peterson, *International Interest Organizations and the Transmutation of Postwar Society* (1979) at 113–171; D. Irwin, *From Ploughshare to Ballotbox* (1980)

1

and chemical industries, food processors, distributors and retailers, and financial institutions and the state.[3]

The direction, means and consequences of state intervention in the food economy as a whole have rarely been analysed in any systematic way. Concerning the rather narrower domain of agricultural policy, however, three contrasting approaches may be distinguished. Each embodies a different view of the aims of agricultural policy, the nature of the state and the role of law.[4]

First, the neo-classical view considers agriculture to be an atomised industry, characterised by near-perfect competition but an inherently imperfect product market: agricultural prices tend to be unstable and demand for agricultural products is relatively inelastic. State intervention is, therefore, a necessary aberration, designed primarily to facilitate the operation of the market and restore equilibrium. The state represents the general will and it uses law, an expression of social consensus, to establish a neutral framework for economic activity.

Second is a predominantly institutional approach. It regards the market itself as the result of a complex process of bargaining among state agencies, farmers' organisations and companies which supply the means of agricultural production or process, distribute or market agricultural commodities. Agricultural policies similarly result from political bargaining, as the interests of different, often corporately organised groups shape and in turn are advanced or

---

[3] Useful reviews of these changes in agriculture include Newby, "Trend Report: Rural Sociology" (1980) *Current Sociology* 1; Newby, "Rural Sociology and Its Relevance to the Agricultural Economist" (1982) 33 *Journal of Agricultural Economics* 125; H. Newby and F.H. Buttel (eds.), *The Rural Sociology of the Advanced Societies* (1980); L. Malassis, *Economie agro-alimentaire, I: Economie de la consommation et de la production agro-alimentaire* (1973); "L'internationalisation du secteur agro-alimentaire en Europe. Recherche comparative sur douze pays de l'Est et de l'Ouest" (1982) 16 *Economies et Sociétés* 1117; "L'Etat et la politique agraire en Europe. Présentation des politiques agricoles de douze pays de l'Est et de l'Ouest," (1978) 10 *Economies et Sociétés* 1337; D. Goodman and M. Redclift, *From Peasant to Proletarian* (1981).

[4] This schematic summary is based on numerous sources on agricultural policy, of which the most important are; D.G. Johnson, *World Agriculture in Disarray* (1973); B. E. Hill, *The Common Agricultural Policy: Past, Present and Future* (1984); Josling, "Agricultural Policies in Developed Countries: A Review" (1974) 23 *Journal of Agricultural Economics* 229; Josling, "A Formal Approach to Agricultural Policy" (1969) 20 *Journal of Agricultural Economics* 175; C. Ritson, *Agricultural Economics; Principles and Policy* (1977); H. Newby and F.H. Buttel (eds.),*The Rural Sociology of the Advanced Societies* (1980); C. Clutterbuck and T. Lang, *More Than We Can Chew* (1982); see also Jessop, "The Capitalist State and the Rule of Capital: Problems in the Analysis of Business Associations" (1983) 6 *West European Politics* 139.

disadvantaged by state policies. Legal measures thus reflect specific, shifting configurations of interests. Law is both an instrument and an expression of policy, but generally it is not used consistently in favour of any single group.

A third approach emphasises the connections between the role of the state and the forms of class conflict in capitalist societies, based fundamentally on the accumulation of capital or the search for profit. Agricultural policy may thus be viewed as an instrument of the dominant economic class; as an attempt by ruling groups to implement measures favourable to capital within systematic, structural limits constraining state action; or as an exercise of state power which condenses, in a particular form, specific social forces. Law, as instrument and ideology, tends to express the dominant capitalist interests and to mediate class relations. At the same time, it imposes certain limits on state action and class power by virtue of its abstract, universalistic and apparently neutral form.

These contrasting approaches, for reasons of space, are presented here only in a highly schematic, simplified form. Even this brief summary, however, should suffice to suggest that the analysis of agricultural policy and law raises important questions, concerning not only everyday economics and politics but also social, political and legal theory. Although these different approaches are usually presumed to refer to the nation-state, each is also echoed at the level of the European Community (EC).[5]

The Common Agricultural Policy

The EC in 1982 had a total population of approximately 270 million people, of which about 8.2 million were employed in agriculture. Agriculture, forestry and fisheries in the EC Ten accounted for approximately 3.9 per cent. of gross national product at factor cost, 7.6 per cent. of employment (1981 figure), 8.9 per cent. of exports by value and 14.8 per cent. of imports by value.[6] The EC's ten Member States accounted for about 25 per cent. of world agricultural imports and between 8–10 per cent. of world agricultural exports.[7] The EC and the United States, with very different agricultural structures,[8] together accounted for about one-third of

---

[5] The singular form is, for the sake of convenience, used throughout this book.
[6] Commission of the European Communities, *The Agricultural Situation in the Community: 1983 Report* (1984) at 187.
[7] Agra Europe, "The Common Agricultural Policy and the Prospects for Reform" *Agra Briefing No. 2* (1984) at 6.
[8] Commission of the European Communities, *The Agricultural Situation in the Community: 1983 Report* (1984) at 15.

world agricultural trade and nearly 30 per cent. of world agricultural exports.[9]

The EC's Common Agricultural Policy (CAP) has influenced agricultural policy and law in the Community's Member States for over 25 years. The different forms of intervention by individual states in their national agricultural economies have gradually been supplemented, though by no means replaced, by the supranational legal regulation of agriculture on a Community level. In addition, the CAP has provided a partial legal framework and some legal measures for the internationalisation of the production and exchange of agricultural commodities. The EC has been accurately described as "less than a federation, more than a regime," but with respect to agricultural policy and law it has effectively established itself as another level of government.[10]

Today the CAP is the EC's major common policy; it is also the most costly and most controversial. Agriculture accounts for an extremely large share of Community legislation and judicial decisions. More than 83 per cent. of all EC legislation in 1976 and 1977, for example, concerned agricultural matters.[11] The latter accounted for a similarly large proportion of all cases before the European Court of Justice (see Chap. 3). Of the EC Commission's 20 administrative departments, the Directorate General for Agriculture (DG VI) is among the largest, with approximately 10 per cent. of all administrative staff.[12] Between 63 per cent. and 76 per cent. of the annual EC budget between 1979 and 1983 was agricultural expenditure.[13] Total net expenditure on the CAP in 1983 amounted to 14,194.9 million ecu (European currency units), or approximately £7956.2 million.[14] The 1984 cost (gross) of the CAP has been estimated to be in excess of 19 billion ecu, or £11.21 billion.[15] In assessing the economic costs of agricultural policy, the total budgetary cost is perhaps less important than the policy's effects on food prices, income distribution, resource transfers and world trade. In all of these respects, the CAP has been heavily

---

[9] *Ibid.* at 27.

[10] Wallace, "Less than a Federation, More than a Regime: The Community as a Political System" in H. Wallace, W. Wallace and C. Webb (eds.), *Policy Making in the European Community* (2nd ed., 1983).

[11] Commission Answer to Written Question 588/78 (O.J. 1978, C.282/56).

[12] Commission Answer to Written Question 1560/79 (O.J. 1979, C.110/56).

[13] Commission of the European Communities, *The Agricultural Situation in the Community: 1983 Report* (1984) at 155.

[14] *Ibid.* at 154.

[15] Agra Europe, "The Common Agricultural Policy and the Prospects for Reform" *Agra Briefing No. 2* (1984) at 3.

criticised for much of its existence,[16] and numerous proposals have been advanced for its reform.[17] It has been suggested, however, that major reforms are likely to result only from the prospect of the EC's financial ruin.[18]

Historical Background

Agriculture and the Rome Treaty

The Treaty of Rome, signed on March 25, 1957, is the European Economic Community's written constitution. Though virtually excluded from the Treaty's initial draft,[19] despite previous attempts at European-level co-operation,[20] the agricultural sector was eventually included in the common market.[21] The Six shared,

---

[16] See, *e.g.* H. Priebe, D. Bergmann and J. Horring, "Fields of Conflict in European Farm Policy," Trade Policy Research Centre, *Agricultural Trade Paper No. 3* (1972); S. Holland, *UnCommon Market*, (1980) at 27–33; A. Zeller, *L'Imbroglio agricole du Marché commun* (1970); Zeller, "European Agriculture in the World Economy," in M. Kohnstamm and W. Hager (eds.), *A Nation Writ Large?* (1973); C. Mackel, J. Marsh and B. Revell, "The Common Agricultural Policy" (1984) 6 *Third World Quarterly* 131; Butler, "EEC Agriculture after Athens" (1984) 40 *The World Today* 52; "The Infernal Food Machine" (1981) 85 *Agenor* 1. The controversy over the British budgetary contribution is discussed in Taylor, "The EC Crisis over the Budget and the Agricultural Policy: Britain and its Partners in the Late 1970s and Early 1980s" (1982) 17 *Government and opposition* 397. For a comparative study of the positions of the left in Britain and France, see M. Newman, *Socialism and European Unity* (1983).

[17] An early survey is R. Fennell, *The Common Agricultural Policy: A Synthesis of Opinion*, Centre for European Agricultural Studies, Wye College, Report No. 1 (1973). More recent proposals are cited in Pearce, "The Common Agricultural Policy: The Accumulation of Special Interests" in H. Wallace, W. Wallace and C. Webb (eds.), *Policy Making in the European Community* (2nd ed., 1983) at 174, n. 19.

[18] Agra Europe, "The Common Agricultural Policy and the Prospects for Reform" *Agra Briefing No. 2* (1984); Tangermann, "What is Different about European Agricultural Protectionism?" (1983) 6 *The World Economy* 39 at 47.

[19] A.D. Robinson, *Dutch Organised Agriculture in International Politics 1945–1960* (1961) at 103.

[20] On pre-EC attempts at agricultural co-operation, see *ibid.* at 78–91; M. Tracy, *Agriculture in Western Europe* (2nd ed., 1982) at 261–266; M. Peterson, *International Interest Organizations and the Transmutation of Postwar Society* (1979), *passim.*

[21] On the preparation and adoption of the CAP, see generally Robinson, *ibid.* at 92–139; Tracy, *ibid.* at 266–290; Peterson, *ibid.*, *passim*; W.F. Averyt, Jr., *Agro-politics in the European Community* (1977); L.N. Lindberg, *The Political Dynamics of European Integration* (1963) at 219–282; Heathcote, "Agricultural Politics in the European Community" Department of Political Science, Research School of Social Sciences, Australian National University, *Occasional Paper No. 7* (1971).

with regard to agriculture, a recent history of extensive govern-
mental intervention. The Netherlands, Italy and particularly
France strongly favoured including agriculture in any common
scheme. In any event, France would not have opened its market to
German industrial products without some counter-advantage,
which for France, with the largest agricultural area of the Six and
the greatest potential for expansion, lay primarily in increasing its
agricultural exports.[22] The exclusion of agriculture, by leading to
different food prices in the Member States and thereby influencing
wage levels, might also have hindered free trade in industrial
goods. In addition, it was argued that in agriculture, as in industry,
a larger market might result in a more efficient allocation of
resources, thereby benefiting both producers and consumers. In
the Six, moreover, agriculture then accounted for about 25 per
cent. of employment and 10 per cent. of gross national product[23]:
it was therefore of great political and economic importance. A
consensus thus emerged among the Member States that agriculture should be included in the Treaty.[24]

Importance of war

[22] See E. Kolodziej, *French International Policy under de Gaulle and Pompidou*
(1974) at 263–274, 284–291; A.S. Milward, *The Reconstruction of Western Europe 1945–51* (1984) at 460–461. French President de Gaulle, at a press conference on July 29, 1963, declared that the very existence of the EEC depended
solely on the realisation of its agricultural programme (Alting von Gesau, "Les
sessions marathon du Conseil des Ministres" in P. Gerbet and D. Pepy (eds.),
La décision dans les Communautés européennes (1969) at 102). This view should
not, however, have been surprising. In 1962 77.5 per cent. of the EC agricultural
fund's share of Member State expenditure for market intervention and export
subsidies went for the latter, and France, as the leading exporter, was the main
beneficiary, with 82.5 per cent. of the total (Riesenfeld, "Common Market for
Agricultural Products and Common Agricultural Policy in the European Community" (1965) *University of Illinois Law Forum* (Winter) 658 at 681–682); such
subsidies favoured mainly the large farmers and export traders. From 1958 to
1972 French cereals exports towards other EC Member States increased 22-fold
(see La Documentation française, "Les échanges agro-alimentaires de la
France" (1978) 4487 *Notes et Etudes documentaires* at 26. See also Dam, "The
European Common Market in Agriculture" (1967) 67 *Columbia Law Review*
209 at 213–214.
[23] Pearce, "The Common Agricultural Policy: The Accumulation of Special Interests" in H. Wallace, W. Wallace and C. Webb (eds.), *Policy Making in the European Community* (2nd ed., 1983) at 142; more complete figures may be found in
L.N. Lindberg, *The Political Dynamics of European Integration* (1963) at
220–226.
[24] See W. Wallace, "Less than a Federation, More than a Regime: The Community
as a Political System" in H. Wallace, W. Wallace and C. Webb (eds.), *Policy
Making in the European Community* (2nd ed., 1983) at 411, 418–419; A.S.
Milward, *The Reconstruction of Western Europe 1945–51* (1984) at 460–461. The
different interests of the contemporary Member States are analysed in Harvey,
"National Interests and the CAP" (1982) *Food Policy* 174.

A common agricultural policy was also clearly intended to be a main pillar of European economic and, potentially, political integration, at least if the Treaty is interpreted according to a contextual method.[25] Part One, "Principles," provides that the activities of the Community shall include "the adoption of a common policy in agriculture" (Art. 3(*d*); see also Art. 38(4)). Such a common policy was one of several means by which the Community aimed:

> "by establishing a common market and progressively approximating the economic policies of Member States, to promote throughout the Community a harmonious development of economic activities, a continuous and balanced expansion, an increase in stability, an accelerated raising of the standard of living and closer relations between the States belonging to it." (Art. 2)

Accordingly, together with the "four freedoms" concerning the movement of goods (Arts. 9–37), natural and legal persons (Arts. 48–58), services (Arts. 59–66) and capital (Arts. 67–73) and the projected common transport policy (Arts. 74–84), agriculture formed the "Foundations of the Community" (Rome Treaty, Part Two).

Agriculture is the subject of Treaty Articles 38–47 (see later chapters). Article 40(3) is the "powers" clause concerning common organisations of the market, whereas Article 43 provides the legal basis for most CAP legislation. The Treaty established a schedule for the implementation of measures regarding the common market in agriculture and a common agricultural policy. In order to evolve the broad lines of a common agricultural policy, the Commission was, immediately the Treaty entered into force, to convene a conference of the Member States with a view to making a comparison of their agricultural policies, in particular by producing a statement of their resources and needs (Art. 43(1)). This conference was held at Stresa, Italy, from July 3–12, 1958. Within two years of the Treaty's entry into force, the Commission was, taking into account the work of the conference and after consulting the Economic and Social Committee, to submit proposals for working out and implementing the common agricultural policy, including the replacement of national market organisations by one of the forms of common organisation provided for in Article 40(2), and also for implementing the measures specified in Title II— Agriculture. Such proposals were to take account of the inter-

---

[25] This method of interpretation is used extensively by the European Court: see L. Neville Brown and F.G. Jacobs, *The Court of Justice of the European Communities* (2nd ed., 1983) at 248–252.

dependence of the agricultural matters mentioned in the Title (Art. 43(2), paras. 1–2). The common market was to be established progressively during a transitional period of 12 years, divided into three stages of four years each (Art. 8(1)). Regarding agriculture in particular, the Member States constituting the Community were to develop the common agricultural policy by degrees during the transitional period and bring it into force by the end of that period at the latest (Art. 40(1)). Acting unanimously during the first two stages and by a qualified majority thereafter, the Council was, on a proposal from the Commission and after consulting the Assembly (Parliament), to make regulations, issue directives or take decisions, without prejudice to any recommendations it might also make (Art. 43(3), para. 3). Transitional rules were provided by Articles 44, 45 and 46.

Some major developments

The gradual establishment of the CAP, the adjustments required in Member States' trading arrangements including GATT,[26] and the different political forces concerned in the formation of the CAP[27] will not be described in detail here. In the light of the Stresa Conference and ensuing discussions, major decisions concerning agricultural policy were taken during marathon sessions of the Council in December 1961 to January 1962 and in December 1963. Each resulted in the establishment of common policies for the principal agricultural products: the former for cereals, pigmeat, eggs, poultry, fruit and vegetables and wine; and the latter for beef, veal, dairy products and vegetable oils and fats. At the 1961–62 session, agreement was also reached concerning the application of EC competition policy to agriculture and the basic financial regulations (see below). The move to the second stage of the transitional period was also approved. Largely

---

[26] See, however, M. Tracy, *Agriculture in Western Europe* (2nd ed., 1982) at 266–293; J. Marsh and C. Ritson, *Agricultural Policy and the Common Market* (1971); C. Constantinides-Megret, *La politique agricole commune en question* (1982) at 22–35. A chronology of major events through mid–1981 may be found in A. Ries, *L'ABC du Marché commun agricole* (2nd. ed., 1981) at 181–198. Some aspects of the CAP's historical development are also discussed briefly later in this book. On GATT in particular, see Steenbergen, "The Status of GATT in Community Law" (1981) 15 *J.W.T.L.* 337.

[27] On CAP politics, see, *e.g.* M. Peterson, *International Interest Organizations and the Transmutation of Postwar Society* (1979), passim; Delorme, "Le rôle des forces paysannes dans l'élaboration de la politique agricole commune" (1969) 19 *Revue française de Science politique* 356.

because of the difference between French and German prices, however, an agreement on the Community target price for cereals—the central commodity—was not reached until a marathon session in December 1964; its entry into force was postponed until July 15, 1967. In 1966 the Council reached agreement on prices for olive oil and oil seeds, sugar, milk, butter, beef, veal and rice.

> ". . . . In some cases—cereals, sugar beet and grain-fed livestock—the common prices were established at a level midway between the highest and lowest national prices; for other products, in particular dairy products, the eventual compromise lay towards the upper end of the range.
>
> The resulting common agricultural policy was more protectionist than the sum of the previous national policies for several reasons: (i) the high-price countries fought for comparatively high prices in order to avoid farm income problems; (ii) the range of products covered by protectionist measures was widened in some countries because special protectionist interests in individual countries were extended to Community-wide protection; and (iii) the supply-control policies, previously practised in exporting countries, were abandoned in the face of the opportunities provided by the Community's market and were replaced, in effect, by a policy of export push by developing the dormant potential of their agriculture."[28]

The price levels for these other products were therefore rather narrowly constrained by the previously agreed, relatively high common price for cereals as well as by the basic CAP principle that agricultural incomes were to be supported through market and price policy.[29] By July 1, 1968, the single market stage had been reached for almost all agricultural products. The main exceptions were wine, for which support arrangements were not adopted until April 1970; sheepmeat, for which a market organisation was established only in 1980; and potatoes and ethyl alcohol of agricultural origin, for which no common market organisation exists today. Thus, the shape of the CAP had already been established by the

---

[28] Heidhues, Josling, Ritson and Tangermann, "Common Prices and Europe's Farm Policy" Trade Policy Research Centre, *Thames Essay No. 14* (1978) at 7.

[29] See J. Marsh and C. Ritson, *Agricultural Policy and the Common Market* (1971) at 130–134. Market and price policies are discussed below in Chaps. 4 and 5. On cereals prices, see Delorme, "L'adoption du prix unique des cereales" in P. Gerbet and D. Pepy (eds.), *La décision dans les Communautés européennes* (1969).

formal end of the agreed transitional period on December 31, 1968.[30]

Acceptance of the *acquis communautaire* and solution of any difficulties by means of transitional procedures were, therefore, basic principles in the later negotiations between the Community of Six and subsequent applicants for membership. The Treaty and Act of Accession of January 22, 1972, concerned the accession of the United Kingdom, Denmark and Ireland.[31] For the United Kingdom in particular, accession to the Community required a revision of previous agricultural policy principles, such as relatively free trade in agricultural commodities, privileged ties with the Commonwealth and support of farmers' incomes by tax-financed deficiency payments.[32] The European Communities Act 1972 provided, *inter alia*, for the implementation of the CAP in the United Kingdom, and the transitional period for agriculture under

---

[30] On the factors influencing the development of the CAP, see S. Harris, A. Swinbank and G. Wilkinson, *The Food and Farm Policies of the European Community* (1983) at 37–38. The characteristics of the agricultural sector which facilitated the partial transfer of authority to EC level are discussed in W. Wallace, "Less than a Federation, More than a Regime: The Community as a Political System" in H. Wallace, W. Wallace and C. Webb (eds.), *Policy Making in the European Community* (2nd ed., 1983) at 418–419.

[31] On arrangements for agriculture, see Olmi, "Agriculture and Fisheries in the Treaty of Brussels of January 22, 1972" (1972) 9 C.M.L.Rev. 293. See also S.Z. Young, *Terms of Entry* (1973) at 58–102; Britton, "Problems of Adapting U.K. Institutions in the EEC" in S.T. Rogers and B.H. Davey (eds.), *The Common Agricultural Policy and Britain* (1973). Post-Treaty events and the 1975 referendum are described in M. Newman, *Socialism and European Unity* (1983); R. Jowell and G. Hoinville, *Britain Into Europe* (1976); D. Butler and U. Kitzinger, *The 1975 Referendum* (1976); Lasok, "Some Legal Aspects of Fundamental Renegotiations" (1976) 1 E.L.Rev. 375; Emerson and Scott, "The Financial Mechanism in the Budget of the European Community: The Hard Core of the British Renegotiations of 1974–75" (1977) 14 C.M.L.Rev. 209; Recent polls show a bare majority of people in Britain favour continuing EC membership, R. Jowell and C. Airey (eds.), *British Social Attitudes: The 1984 Report* (1984) at 36.

[32] As of the late 1960s and early 1970s, however, the U.K. was gradually shifting away from deficiency payments and towards a system of import levies, the cost of which would fall on the consumer: see Norton, "The Heart of the Matter: U.K. and the EEC, the Problem of Agriculture" (1971) 6 *Texas International Law Forum* 221 at 224; Josling, "The Agricultural Burden: A Reappraisal" in J. Pinder (ed.), *The Economics of Europe* (1971) at 75–76; T. K. Warley, *Agriculture: The Cost of Joining the Common Market*, PEP European Series No. 3 (1967) at 27–29. On U.K. agricultural policy generally, see J.H. Kirk, *The Development of Agriculture in Germany and the U.K. 2: U.K. Agricultural Policy 1870–1970*, Centre for European Agricultural Studies, Wye College, *Miscellaneous Study No. 3* (1979); a comparative study is M. Corti, *Politique agricole et construction de l'Europe* (1971).

the Act of Accession terminated at the end of 1977.[33] Greece
acceded to EC membership by virtue of the Treaty and Act of
Accession of May 28, 1979.[34] Spain and Portugal have also applied
for membership; among the most difficult issues in the continuing
negotiations is the implementation of the CAP.[35]

Basic Financial Arrangements

Establishment

Article 40(4) of the Treaty provides that one or more agricultural guidance and guarantee funds may be set up in order to
enable the common organisation of agricultural markets to meet
its objectives. The first financial legislation was not adopted, however, until the 1961–1962 marathon session. Regulation 25/62[36]
established the European Agricultural Guidance and Guarantee
Fund (EAGGF, often known by its French initials: FEOGA). It
was based on the principle that, since at the single market stage
agricultural markets would be organised at Community level, "the
financial consequences thereof shall devolve upon the Community" (Art.2(2), para.1). The Fund was to finance (a) refunds
on exports to third countries, (b) intervention measures aimed at
stabilising markets, including intervention purchases, private storage and production aids; and (c) "common measures adopted in
order to attain the objectives set out in Article 39(1) of the Treaty,

[33] See Case 231/78 *Commission* v. *United Kingdom* [1979] E.C.R. 1447.
[34] See Schloh, "The Accession of Greece to the European Economic Communities" (1980) 10 *Georgia Journal of Internaional and Comparative Law* 385;
Pepelasis, Yannopoulos, Mitsos, Kalamotousakis, and Perdikas, "The Mediterranean Challenge: IV: The Tenth Member—Economic Aspects" *Sussex European Papers No. 7* (1980). On agriculture and the second enlargement generally,
see Rollo, "The Second Enlargement of the European Economic Community—
Some Economic Implications with Special Reference to Agriculture" (1979) 30
Journal of Agricultural Economics 333; L. Tsoukalis, *The European Community
and its Mediterranean Enlargement* (1981) at 196–269; J. Marsh, "The Impact of
Enlargement on the Common Agricultural Policy" in W. Wallace and I. Herre-
man, *A Community of Twelve?* (1978); S. Harris, A. Swinbank and G. Wilkinson, *The Food and Farm Policies of the European Community* (1983) at 146–186.
[35] Negotiations concerning Spain are discussed in "Make or break" *The Economist*, August 18, 1984 at 47. On Portugal, see Jalles, "State Monopolies of a Commercial Character (Article 37 of the EEC Treaty) and Their Importance in
Connection with Portugal's Accession to the European Communities" (1980) 10
Georgia Journal of International and Comparative Law 411; Barends, *As Conse-
quências Económicas para Portugal da Adesão a Comunidade Económica Euro-
peia* (1983) 3 vols.
[36] J.O. 20.4.62, 991/1. See also Verges, "L'élaboration du système de financement
de la politique agricole commune" in P. Gerbet and D. Pepy (eds.), *La décision
dans les Communautés européennes* (1969).

including the structural modifications required for the proper working of the common market" (Art.2(2), para.1). This regulation applied through mid-1965, when it was supplemented by Regulation 130/66[37] after the Luxembourg compromise (see Chap.3).

In 1964 Regulation 17/64[38] divided the EAGGF into two sections: a Guarantee Section for the implementation of policies concerning agricultural markets, including intra-Community intervention and export subsidies; and a Guidance Section for financing structural policies. The Guidance Section, according to Regulation 25/62, Art.5(2), was initially to absorb up to one-third of total expenditure, but in practice the major proportion of CAP spending has been on the Guarantee Section (see Chaps.4–7).

The current system

The Council Decision of April 21, 1970,[39] based on Article 201, established the EC's current "own resources" system.[40] Community resources, instead of relying on national contributions according to a fixed "key" (Article 200), were henceforth to include (a) as from January 1, 1971, all levies on agricultural imports from third countries and levies charged to sugar producers; (b) a proportion (increasing to 100 per cent. by January 1975) of customs duties on imports from third countries; and (c), in principle as from January 1, 1975, but in fact as from January 1, 1979, up to 1 per cent. of the value added tax as applied by the Member States (excepting transitional measures applied to Greece). An increase in the VAT percentage to 1.4 per cent has been agreed in principle from January 1, 1986.[41] The April 1970 Council Decision was implemented by Regulation 2/71 of January 2, 1971.[42] All "own resources" are treated as Community revenue, with the portion spent on agriculture being channelled through EAGGF.

[37] O.J. 1966, 165/2965.
[38] O.J. Sp.Ed. 27.2.64, 586/103.
[39] O.J. 1970, L.94/224.
[40] See generally Sopwith, "Legal Aspects of the Community Budget" (1980) 17 C.M.L.Rev. 315; Usher, "The Financing of the Community" in Commission of the European Communities (ed.), *Thirty Years of Community Law* (1983); H. Wallace, *Budgetary Politics: The Finances of the European Communities* (1980); Pipkorn, "Legal Implications of the Absence of the Community Budget at the Beginning of a Financial Year" (1981) 18 C.M.L.Rev. 141.
[41] See (1984) 3 Bull.E.C. at 7–10, 77; (1984) 6 Bull.E.C. at 7–13, 88; and, on the proposed legislation, O.J. 1984, C.126/5.
[42] O.J. Sp.Ed. 1971, 3.

Regulation 729/70[43] established the current system for financing the CAP. Based on Article 201, it provided that EAGGF was to be part of the Community budget, thus underscoring the principle of financial solidarity (see Chap. 2). Necessary funds for EAGGF expenditure were to be advanced by the Community, but paid out by agencies designed by the Member States. The provisions concerning expenditure chargeable to EAGGF tend to be interpreted strictly by the European Court.[44] Regulation 1883/78 lays down general rules for the financing of intervention measures.[45]

The scope within the CAP for financial mismanagement and fraud is enormous, especially in connection with import duties, export subsidies and production aids.[46] From July 1, 1980 to June 30, 1981, for example, a total of 306 irregularities, amounting to 18,152,144 ecu, were reported by Member States. Of these, 257 concerned the Guarantee Fund and 52 the Guidance Fund; in only 90 (Guarantee) and 46 (Guidance) cases, a total of 1,806,367 ecu, had the expenditure been recovered.[47] Under Regulation 729/70, Member States are required to take the necessary administrative and judicial procedures to satisfy themselves that transactions financed by EAGGF are actually carried out and executed correctly, to prevent and deal with irregularities and to recover sums lost as a result of irregularities or negligence.[48] Regulation 283/72[49] establishes a system of co-operation between Member States and between Member States and the Commission. Directive 76/308[50] provides for mutual assistance for the recovery of claims; this was implemented by Commission Directive 77/794.[51] In prac-

[43] O.J. Sp.Ed. 1970, 218.
[44] See, *e.g.* Case 11/76 *Netherlands* v. *Commission* [1979] E.C.R. 245.
[45] O.J. 1978, L.216/1.
[46] See, *e.g. Re Fraud on Agricultural Levies* [1974] 1 C.M.L.R. 251; Case 125/75 *Milch-, Fett- und Eierkontor* v. *Hauptzollamt Hamburg-Jonas* [1976] E.C.R. 771; Case 44/76 *Milch-, Fett- und Eierkontor* v. *Council and Commission* [1977] E.C.R. 393; Commisson of the European Communities: Special Committee of Inquiry, "Report concerning the EAGGF Guarantee Section—Oilseed and Olive Oil Sectors" COM(75)37 (1975); Commission of the European Communities, "Report concerning the Guarantee Section of the EAGGF, Cereal Sector" COM(79)686 (1979). See generally Harding, "The European Communities and Control of Criminal Business Activities" (1982) 31 I.C.L.Q. 246; Delmas-Marty, "White-collar Crime in the E.E.C." in L.H. Leigh (ed.), *Economic Crime in Europe* (1980).
[47] Commission of the European Communities, *Fifteenth General Report on the Activities of the European Communities in 1981* (1982) at 174.
[48] See Joined Cases 178, 179 and 180/73 *Belgium and Luxembourg* v. *Mertens and Others* [1974] E.C.R. 383.
[49] J.O. 1972, L.36/1.
[50] O.J. 1976, L.73/18.
[51] O.J. 1977, L.333/11.

tice, however, these procedures may leave much to be desired, at least from the Commission's standpoint, since they depend largely on the institutions, procedures and staff of the Member States.[52]

---

[52] See also Case 267/78 *Commisson* v. *Italy* [1980] E.C.R. 31.

Chapter 2

PRINCIPLES AND OBJECTIVES

General Principles

Foundations

The law of the CAP derives, directly or indirectly, from the Rome Treaty. Its foundations consist of six general principles, which at least in theory underlie EC secondary legislation and European Court of Justice decisions concerning the CAP. Three basic principles stem from the Treaty. The first is the inclusion of agriculture in the Community scheme; "[t]he common market shall extend to agriculture and trade in agricultural products" (Art. 38(1)). Second, the provisions in Title II—Agriculture form to some extent an exception to general Treaty rules.[1] As Article 38(2) states, "[s]ave as otherwise provided in Articles 39 to 46, the rules laid down for the establishment of the common market shall apply to agricultural products." Third, agriculture, unlike industry, is subject to a common Community policy. "The operation and development of the common market for agricultural products must be accompanied by the establishment of a common agricultural policy among the Member States" (Art. 38(4); see also Art. 3(e)).

Three other principles were embodied in the important 1962 market and financial regulations, as subsequently interpreted.[2] The principle of the unity of the market is merely implicit in Article 38(1), but today it underpins EC price policy and the European Court's decisions on the free movement of goods. Community preference is stated in the Treaty even more indirectly;

---

[1] As such they are interpreted restrictively by the European Court: see Joined Cases 2–3/62 *Commission* v. *Luxembourg and Belgium* [1962] E.C.R. 425. On the extent of agriculture's exceptional status, see Usher (1978) E.L.Rev 305 and Neri, "La jurisprudence de la Cour de Justice des Communautés européennes relative à l'application de la législation agricole communautaire" (1982) 5–6 C.D.E. 507 at 508–517.

[2] Commission of the European Communities, "Stocktaking of the Common Agricultural Policy" COM(75)100 (1975), para. 12, published in (1975) 2 *Bulletin of the European Communities* (Supplement). See also M. Tracy, *Agriculture in Western Europe* (2nd ed. 1982) at 274–275.

Article 44(2) provides that the system of minimum prices, allowed by Article 44(1) during the transitional period, "shall not be applied so as to form an obstacle to the development of a natural preference between Member States." It was generalised, however, in Case 5/67 *Beus* v.

Hauptzollamt München, when the Court stated that in balancing interests in order to achieve CAP objectives "the Council must take into account, where necessary, in favour of farmers, the principle known as 'Community preference,' which is one of the principles of the Treaty and which in agricultural matters is laid down in Article 44(2)."[3] Financial solidarity is ultimately based on the notion, expressed in Regulation 25/62 establishing the European Agricultural Guarantee and Guidance Fund, that, since at the single market stage agricultural policy would be organised at Community level, "the financial consequences thereof shall devolve upon the Community."[4] Although criticised as "not properly speaking a legal principle,"[5] it is nonetheless an essential, albeit highly controversial, part of the CAP.

Scope

The common market thus extends to agriculture and trade in agricultural products, but the Treaty does not define either "agriculture" or "trade in agricultural products" precisely or consistently. Instead, Article 38(1), on the one hand, provides that " 'agricultural products' means the products of the soil, of stockfarming and of fisheries and products of first-stage processing directly related to these products." "[P]roducts of first-stage processing directly related" to basic products must be interpreted, according to the Court, as implying "a clear economic interdependence between basic products and products resulting from a pro-

---

[3] Case 5/67 *Beus* v. *Hauptzollamt München* [1968] E.C.R. 83 at 98; see also Case 72/69 *Hauptzollamt Bremen-Freihafen* v. *Bremer Handelsgesellschaft* [1970] E.C.R. 427 at 435; Case 55/72 *Getreide-Import* v. *EVst für Getreide und Futtermittel* [1973] E.C.R. 15. The purpose of Community preference is to protect EC producers against cheap imports, and it therefore has, in principle, no bearing on exports: Case 6/71 *Rheinmühlen Düsseldorf* v. *EVst für Getreide und Futtermittel* [1971] E.C.R. 823. Moreover, it does not prevent the granting of less favourable treatment to EC importers than to third country importers when their situations are not really comparable: Case 73/69 *Oehlmann and Co.* v. *Hauptzollamt Münster* [1970] E.C.R. 467. The principle is also embodied in the 1972 Act of Accession, Art. 55.

[4] Reg. 25/62, Art. 2(2), para. 1 (J.O. 1962, 992/62).

[5] Melchior, "The Common Agricultural Policy: Section I—The Common Organization of Agricultural Markets" in Commission of the European Communities, (ed.) *Thirty Years of Community Law* (1983) at 441.

ductive process, irrespective of the number of operations involved therein."[6] If, for example, the cost of the agricultural raw material were merely marginal in relation to processing costs, the processed product would be outside Article 38(1)'s scope. Article 38(3), on the other hand, states that

"The products subject to the provisions of Articles 39 to 46 are listed in Annex II to this Treaty. Within two years of the entry into force of this Treaty, however, the Council shall, acting by a qualified majority on a proposal from the Commission, decide what products are to be added to this list."

Three groups of products were added to Annex II by Council Regulation 7a/59.[7] In practice, therefore, Article 38(1) has been interpreted as merely indicative, and the definitive list of agricultural products covered by the CAP is contained in Annex II.[8]

Yet, for perhaps more political than logical reasons, Annex II includes such products as margarine and ethyl alcohol of agricultural origin, while omitting wool, cotton and wood. Regarding products thus excluded from the CAP, the Commission has used Article 235, for example, as the legal basis of specific regulations.[9] Moreover, the omission from Annex II of products of secondary processing potentially threatened the position of EC second-stage food processors as against their non-EC competitors. Consequently, in October 1966 a parallel trade system was introduced for certain "Non-Annex II products."[10] Provisions governing

[6] Case 185/73 *Hauptzollamt Bielefeld* v. *König* [1974] E.C.R. 607 at 618.

[7] J.O. 1961, 71; O.J. Sp.Ed. 1959–1962, 68.

[8] Joined Cases 2–3/62 *Commission* v. *Belgium and Luxembourg* [1962] E.C.R. 425; Case 16/69 *Commission* v. *Italy* [1969] E.C.R. 377.

[9] On wool, see Case 77/83 *CILFIT Srl, Rome and Lanificio di Gavardo SpA, Milan* v. *Ministero della Sanita*, not yet reported, (O.J. 1984, C.88/6). The omission of cotton required a special Protocol No. 4 of the Greek Accession Treaty in order to establish support arrangements for this product; see Reg. 2169/81 laying down general rules for the system of aid for cotton (O.J. 1981, L.211/12). The omission of wood from Annex II has delayed the introduction of an EC forestry policy, which in the event is based primarily on Art. 235 of the Treaty. For further discussion of the relation between Art. 38(1) and Annex II, see Gilsdorf, "La politique agricole commune (Die Gemeinsame Agrarpolitik)" JUR(81) D/ 00825, typescript, 17–20; Olmi, "Agriculture" JUR(79) D/01575, typescript 13–14.

[10] The basis of this system today is Reg. 3033/80 (O.J. 1980, L.323/1). See also Food Manufacturers' Federation, "The Impact of EEC Trade Policy upon UK Exports of Processed Products" in House of Lords Select Committee on the European Communities, *Agricultural Trade Policy*, 2nd Report, Session 1981–82, (1981) H.L. 29 at 94. For an economic analysis of the position of Non-Annex II products, see S. Harris, A. Swinbank and G. Wilkinson, *The Food and Farm Policies of the European Community* (1983) at 243–248.

secondary processed products thus mirror, to some extent, those concerning agricultural products included in Annex II and therefore in the CAP.

The territorial scope of the CAP is, in principle, the same as that of the Treaty, set forth in Article 227. The CAP applies to agricultural products originating in an EC Member State.[11] The Treaty's agricultural provisions, including Article 40(4) since the expiration of the two-year period provided in Article 227(2), and other CAP rules also apply fully to the French overseas departments, which according to the French constitution are part of the French Republic.[12] They also apply to the European territories for whose external relations a Member State is responsible (Art. 227(4)), though not to the Faroe Islands or the Sovereign Base Areas of the United Kingdom in Cyprus (Art. 227(5)(*a*), (*c*). The CAP applies only partly to the Channel Islands and the Isle of Man (Art. 227(5)(*c*)). As provided in Protocol No. 3 of the 1972 Act of Accession,

> "In respect of agricultural products and products processed therefrom which are the subject of a special trade regime, the levies and other import measures laid down in Community rules and applicable in the United Kingdom shall be applied to third countries.
>
> Such provisions of Community rules, in particular those of the Act of Accession, as are necessary to allow free movement and observance of normal conditions of competition in trade in these products shall also be applicable" (Art. 1(2)).

In addition, a wide variety of arrangements govern EC agricultural relations with third countries.[13]

Objectives

Article 39(1)

The objectives of the CAP are stated in Article 39(1) as:

> "(a) to increase agricultural productivity by promoting technical progress and by ensuring the rational development of agricultural production and the optimum utilisation of the factors of production, in particular labour;

---

[11] Case 14/74 *Norddeutsches Vieh- und Fleischkontor GmbH* v. *Hauptzollamt-Ausführerstattung Hamburg-Jonas* [1974] E.C.R. 899.

[12] See Case 148/77 *Hansen* v. *Hauptzollamt Flensburg* [1978] E.C.R. 1787.

[13] A convenient summary is given in S. Harris, A. Swinbank and G. Wilkinson, *The Food and Farm Policies of the European Community* (1983) at 252–287.

(b) thus to ensure a fair standard of living for the agricultural community, in particular by increasing the individual earnings of persons engaged in agriculture;
(c) to stabilise markets;
(d) to assure the availability of supplies;
(e) to ensure that supplies reach consumers at reasonable prices."

Resulting from prolonged negotiations, this statement of aims is necessarily general and inherently contradictory. It represents "nothing less than an encyclopedia of economic problems."[14]

Judicial interpretation

Since 1968 the European Court in cases of dispute has consistently held that "[t]hese objectives, which are intended to safeguard the interests of both farmers and consumers, may not all be simultaneously and fully attained."[15] Weighing the conflicting aims of the CAP is thus a political decision. In practice, therefore, the meaning of Article 39(1) depends, partly, on the ways in which the objectives have been interpreted by Community institutions. Such decisions are not the exclusive prerogative of the Commission and the Council. The resolution of complex questions of social and economic policy has also been undertaken by the European Court, especially in judicial review of CAP legislation.

In assigning priority to the different Article 39(1) objectives, the Court, according to one commentator,[16] has followed two approaches. With regard to the short-term, it has recognised the shifting priorities which the Commission and the Council have provisionally established among different aims according to changes in economic conditions and the gradual implementation of the CAP. As the Court pointed out in the first case concerning monetary compensatory amounts:

"In pursuing these objectives, the Community Institutions must secure the permanent harmonization made necessary by

---

[14] According to Professor Walter Hallstein, the first President of the Commission, in Commission de la Communauté économique européenne, *Recueil des Documents de la Conférence agricole des Etats membres de la Communauté économique européenne à Stresa du 3 au 13 juillet 1958* (1959) at 27.
[15] Case 5/67 *Beus* v. *Hauptzollamt München* [1968] E.C.R. 83 at 98.
[16] G. Druesne, *La politique agricole commune devant la Cour de justice des Communautés européennes 1958–1978* (1980) at 13–20. Similar conclusions may be gleaned from a more recent review in Neri, "La jurisprudence de la Cour de justice des Communautés européennes relative à l'application de la législation agricole communautaire" (1982) 5–6 C.D.E. 507.

any conflicts between these aims taken individually and, where necessary, allow any one of them temporary priority in order to satisfy the demands of the economic factors or conditions in view of which their decisions are made."[17]

In thus giving temporary priority to certain objectives, the Commission and the Council enjoy broad discretion, subject to marginal judicial review (see Chap. 3).

With regard to the longer-term, the Court has frequently appeared to consider certain priorities to be implicit in Article 39. The first is the priority of the maintenance of producers' incomes (Art. 39(1)(b)) over increased agricultural productivity (Art. 39(1)(a)), or, as it is sometimes expressed, priority of a "social" rather than an "economic" goal.[18] Article 39, taken literally, provides that the objective of ensuring a fair standard of living for agricultural producers is to be achieved by structural changes, increasing, through specified means, agricultural productivity. This causal connection was given special emphasis by Dr. Sicco Mansholt, the Commission's first Vice-President and *de facto* Commissioner for Agriculture, at the 1958 Stresa Conference.[19] Subsequently, however, it has rarely been stressed in Community policy. In 1977, for example, Advocate General Capotorti suggested that a strict interpretation of the Treaty might

"justify the conclusion that the whole of the market policy so far followed by the Community is illegal in view of the fact that . . . its essential basis is the fixing of prices to suit agricultural products in order to assure farmers an adequate income, whereas the policy favouring the modernization and structural improvements and, in consequence, the rational development of agricultural production has been late in gathering momentum and is now evolving slowly and with considerable difficulty."[20]

[17] Case 5/73 *Balkan-Import-Export GmbH* v. *Hauptzollamt Berlin-Packhof* [1973] E.C.R. 1091 at 1112. See also Joined Cases 63–69/72 *Wilhelm Werhahn Hansamühle* v. *Council* [1973] E.C.R. 1229; Case 29/77 *S.A. Roquette Frères* v. *French State-Administration des Douanes* [1977] E.C.R. 1835.

[18] This artificial distinction between "social" and "economic" goals is employed by Druesne, *op.cit.* at 13–20 and also by C. Constantinides-Megret, *La politique agricole commune en question* (1982) at 6; see also Advocate General Capotorti in Case 114/76 *Bela-Mühle Josef Bergmann KG* v. *Grows-Farm GmbH and Co. KG* [1977] E.C.R. 1211 at 1229.

[19] See Commission de la Communauté économique européenne, *Recueil des Documents de la Conférence agricole des Etats membres de la Communauté économique européenne à Stresa du 3 au 12 juillet 1958* (1959) at 105–106.

[20] Case 114/76 *Bela-Mühle Josef Bergmann KG* v. *Grows-Farm GmbH and Co. KG* [1977] E.C.R. 1211 at 1229.

Hence he rejected any mandatory link between farm income support and structural change. Instead, other means have been used to support farmers' incomes; the Court seemed thus to view the stabilisation of markets in at least two early cases.[21] More recently, the Court has emphasised the protection of producers' incomes and the stabilisation of markets as the main aims of the CAP.[22] In principle, however, a particular objective cannot be favoured to such an extent as to render impossible the achievement of others.[23]

Second, the Court has recognised the priority, often embodied in CAP legislation, of the interests of producers over those of consumers. Article 39 (1)*(e)* provides that an objective of the CAP is "to ensure that supplies reach consumers at reasonable prices." In Case 34/62 *Germany* v. *Commission*[24] the Court dismissed an application for the annulment of a Commission decision refusing to authorise Germany to suspend customs duties on imported oranges. It held that the expression "reasonable prices" in the Treaty must be considered in the light of the common agricultural policy and could not be taken to mean the lowest possible prices. Accordingly, in 1972 the Commission was permitted to favour producers as against consumers by preferring exports as against imports through differential monetary compensatory amounts.[25] Article 40(3), para. 2, of the Treaty states that common organisations of the market "shall exclude any discrimination between producers or consumers within the Community." In Case 5/73 *Balkan-Import-Export GmbH* v. *Hauptzollamt Berlin-Packhof* the Court interpreted this phrase to refer only to discrimination between producers or between consumers, while the balance between the conflicting interests of the two groups was to be dealt with by Article 39. The latter was not contravened, however,

---

[21] Case 34/62 *Germany* v. *Commission* [1963] E.C.R. 131; Joined Cases 106–107/63 *Alfred Toepfer and Getreide-Import Gesellschaft* v. *Commission* [1965] E.C.R. 405.

[22] See Case 113/75 *Frecassetti* v. *Amministrazione delle Finanze dello Stato* [1976] E.C.R. 983; Joined Cases 54–60/76 *Compagnie industrielle et agricole du comté de Lohéac* [1977] E.C.R. 645. The stabilisation of markets does not, however, necessarily require that pre-EC trading patterns be maintained: Joined Cases 63–69/72 *Werhahn* v. *Council and Commission* [1973] E.C.R. 1229; Joined Cases 56–60/74 *Kampffmeyer* v. *Commission and Council* [1976] E.C.R. 711.

[23] See Joined Cases 197–200, 243, 245 and 247/80 *Ludwigshafener Walzmühle Erling KG* v. *Council and Commission* [1981] E.C.R. 3211.

[24] [1963] E.C.R. 131.

[25] Joined Cases 9–11/71 *Compagnie d'Approvisionnement, de Transport et de Crédit* v. *Commission* [1972] E.C.R. 391.

unless a disputed measure led to consumer prices which were "obviously unreasonable."[26]

Evaluation

These priorities have been severely criticised, particularly in the United Kingdom. Prior to joining the Community the United Kingdom relied heavily on the world market for imports of comparatively low-cost food; British farmers have long been few in number and relatively efficient; and British consumer interests are well organised and articulate. The Consumers' Association in 1976 published a balanced, overall verdict on the achievement of the CAP's Treaty objectives:

"The CAP has gone a long way towards achieving two of its aims—stabilising food prices and achieving security of food supplies. But it hasn't succeeded in meeting its other aims: the CAP has done very little to increase productivity, many farmers' incomes are still low, food prices are higher than they could be if import taxes were cut and the EEC bought more of its food on the world market. What's more, surpluses are evidence that too much of some types of food are being produced within the EEC."[27]

This evaluation, with some modifications perhaps, still stands today. In determining priorities or the extent to which CAP objectives have been met, however, the European Court's role has been

[26] [1973] E.C.R. 1091 at 1112. At least one author considers that it is uncertain whether Art. 40(3), para. 2 includes the final consumer or is limited to consumers of primary agricultural products: see Vajda, "Some Aspects of Judicial Review within the Common Agricultural Policy—Part I" (1979) 4 E.L.Rev. 244 at 255. Compare, however, the definition of a consumer as a person to whom goods or services are supplied for a purpose which can be regarded as being outside his [sic] trade or profession: Convention on the Law applicable to Contractual Obligations (80/934/EEC), Art. 5(1) (O.J. 1980, L.266/1).

[27] Consumers' Association, "Common Agricultural Policy" (1977) *Money Which?* 334 at 339. For other evaluations of the CAP, see Commission of the European Communities, "Stocktaking of the Common Agricultural Policy," COM(75)100 (1975), published in (1975) 2 *Bulletin of the European Communities* (Supplement); MacKerron and Rush, "Agriculture in the EEC: Taking Stock" (1976) *Food Policy* 286; D. Dosser, D. Gowland and K. Hartley (eds.), *The Collaboration of Nations: A Study of European Economic Policy* (1982) at 134–153; J. Pearce, *The Common Agricultural Policy* (1981) at 31–36; J. Marsh and P. Swanney. *Agriculture and the European Community* (1980); J. Raux (ed.), *Politique agricole commune et Construction communautaire* (1984).

basically reactive. Any change in priorities therefore depends ultimately not on the Court, or even on the Commission, but rather
on the Council.

Relation to General Treaty Rules

A special sector?

To what extent are agriculture and trade in agricultural products
subject, like industrial commodities, to general rules of the
Treaty? The agricultural common market has been described as "a
separate subsystem with its own aims and implementing instruments, provided, however, that the basic elements of the Treaty
are respected."[28] Yet, since (and partly because of) the establishment of the Community, agriculture in the Member States

> "has become increasingly drawn into a food-producing
> complex whose limits lie well beyond farming itself, a com-
> plex of agro-chemical, engineering, processing, marketing
> and distribution industries which are involved both in the sup-
> ply of farming inputs and in the forward marketing of farm
> produce."[29]

Are any differences in the legal treatment of agriculture and industry still justifiable?

The special, ambivalent status of the agricultural sector is
enshrined in the Treaty. Article 38(2) states that rules for the
establishment of the common market shall apply to agricultural
products "save as otherwise provided in Articles 39 to 46." These
articles specify exceptions, of which the first is that:

> "In working out the common agricultural policy and the
> special methods for its application, account shall be taken of:
> (a) the particular nature of agricultural activity, which
>   results from the social structure of agriculture and from
>   structural and natural disparities between the various
>   agricultural regions;

---

[28] Schermers, "The Role of the European Court of Justice in the Free Movement
of Goods" in T. Sandalow and E. Stein (eds.), *Courts and Free Markets* (1982)
Vol. 1 at 267–268.
[29] Newby, "Trend Report: Rural Sociology" (1980) 28 *Rural Sociology* 1 at 61. See
also, *e.g.* "L'internationalisation du secteur agro-alimentaire en Europe.
Recherche comparative sur douze pays de l'Est et de l'Ouest" (1982) 16 *Economies et Sociétés* 1117; J. Bombal and P. Chalmin, *L'Agro-alimentaire* (1980);
M. Marloie, *L'internationalisation de l'agriculture française* (1984).

    (b) the need to effect the appropriate adjustments by
        degrees;
    (c) the fact that in the Member States agriculture consti-
        tutes a sector closely linked with the economy as a
        whole" (Art. 39(2)).[30]

Second, the common organisations established for agricultural
product markets according to the provisions of Articles 40 and 43
may include "all measures required to attain the objectives set out
in Article 39" (Art. 40(3)). In principle at least, such measures
may derogate from the general Treaty rules.[31] Third, the rules in
Part II, Title II, Chap. 3 on competition, which concern undertakings (Arts. 85–90), dumping (Art. 91) and state aids (Arts. 92–94),
apply to the production of and trade in agricultural products "only
to the extent determined by the Council within the framework of
Article 43(2) and (3) and in accordance with the procedure laid
down therein, account being taken of the objectives set out in
Article 39" (Art. 42). Fourth, during the transitional period Member States were authorised to apply, under specified conditions,
non-discriminatory import prices (Art. 44) and bilateral trading
arrangements *inter se* (Art. 45). Fifth, Article 226 enabled a Member State, following an application by the State and a determination by the Commission, to take, during the transitional period,
emergency protective measures which might involve derogations
from general Treaty rules. Such derogations were to be limited,
however, to the extent strictly necessary to attain specified objectives, and priority was to be given to measures which least disturbed the functioning of the common market (Art. 226).[32]
    With these exceptions, agriculture and trade in agricultural pro-
ducts have been subject, even during the transitional period, to
"rules laid down for the establishment of the common market"
(Art. 38(2)). These rules have not been judicially delineated in any
comprehensive way. Leaving aside transitional rules such as
Article 8, however, the most significant substantive rules for agriculture concern the free movement of goods; competition, including state aids; and general principles of law.

---

[30] At least one member of the Commission's Legal Service considers, however,
    that these elements are not the only ones to be taken into account; others include
    the protection of health, overseas development policy and protection of the
    environment: see Gilsdorf, "La politique agricole commune (Die Gemeinsame
    Agrarpolitik)" JUR(81) D/00825, typescript at 37–38.
[31] Case 17/67 *Neumann* v. *Hauptzollamt Hof/Saale* [1967] E.C.R. 441.
[32] See Case 72/72 *EVst* v. *Baer-Getreide* [1973] E.C.R. 377.

Free movement of goods

Article 3(*a*) of the Treaty provides for "the elimination, as between Member States, of customs duties and of quantitative restrictions on the import and export of goods, and of all other measures having equivalent effect." Part II, Title I of the Treaty contains more detailed provisions on the free movement of goods. Articles 12–29 concern the elimination of customs duties between Member States and charges having equivalent effect, while Articles 30–37 concern the elimination of quantitative restrictions and all measures having equivalent effect.

These provisions are the legal expression of the economic principle of a unified market and a basic element in the EC's mixed capitalist economy. Despite significant exceptions to free market principles, such as the agricultural price system and related financial mechanisms (see Chap. 5), they are therefore an important ideological reference point for the European Court, especially in relation to the agricultural sector.[33] Thus, in Joined Cases 90 and 91/63 *Commission* v. *Luxembourg and Belgium*,[34] the Court held that the "standstill" provision in Article 12 prohibited the introduction of new customs barriers to agricultural trade, even though agricultural products were dealt with in a separate chapter of the Treaty.

Article 8(7) of the Treaty provides that

> "Save for the exceptions of any derogations provided for in this Treaty, the expiry of the transitional period shall constitute the latest date by which all the rules laid down must enter into force and all the measures required for establishing the common market must be implemented."

Member States were required to bring the common agricultural policy into force by the end of the transitional period at the latest (Art. 40(1)). Trade in agricultural products lacking a common market organisation as of the end of the transitional period, however, was held by the Court to be subject to the free movement of

---

[33] See for example, Joined Cases 5, 7 and 13–24/66 *Kampffmeyer* v. *Commission* [1967] E.C.R. 245; Case 193/80 *Commission* v. *Italy* [1981] E.C.R. 3019; G. Druesne, *La politique agricole commune devant la Cour de justice des Communautés européennes 1958–1978* (1980) at 133, 178; Schermers, "The Role of the European Court of Justice in the Free Movement of Goods" in T. Sandalow and E. Stein (eds.), *Courts and Free Markets* (1982); P. Oliver, *Free Movement of Goods in the EEC* (1982) and *Supplement* (1984).
[34] [1964] E.C.R. 625.

goods provisions; no derogation was possible even if the sector was covered by a national market organisation.[35] After December 31, 1977, the end of the transitional period under the 1972 Act of Accession, this applied to the new Member States.[36] In establishing a common market organisation the Council might, in principle, derogate from these provisions,[37] but in practice such derogations would be justifiable only in exceptional circumstances.[38] As the Commission argued in Case 68/76 *Commission* v. *France,*

"the special rules on agriculture cannot, in principle, affect the rules of the Treaty concerning free movement of goods. These rules are binding upon the Community legislator in relation to the setting-up of the common agricultural policy. . . . Apart from the case of quite exceptional circumstances, the agricultural provisions of the Treaty do not allow the Community institutions the possibility of drawing up measures which do not conform to these rules."[39]

In the absence of enabling provisions in the Treaty, therefore, common market organisations established by EC legislation are subject, like national market organisations, to the provisions on free movement of goods.[40]

Among the most important provisions is Article 30, prohibiting quantitative restrictions on imports and all measures having equivalent effect. Equivalent measures, prohibited by Article 30 unless justified under Article 36, were defined by the Court in two leading cases. In *Dassonville,* the Court in 1974 considered them to include "all trading rules enacted by Member States which are capable of hindering, directly or indirectly, actually or potentially, intra-Community trade."[41] In the absence of a Community system, however, Member States could take such measures as were

---

[35] Case 48/74 *Charmasson* v. *Minister for Economic Affairs and Finance* [1974] E.C.R. 1383; see Paulin and Forman, "The French Banana Story and Its Implications" (1975) C.M.L.Rev. 399. See also Case 68/76 *Commission* v. *France* [1977] E.C.R. 515; Case 232/78 *Commission* v. *France* [1979] E.C.R. 2729.

[36] Case 118/78 *Meijer* v. *Department of Trade, Ministry of Agriculture, Fisheries and Food and Commissioners of Customs and Excise* [1979] E.C.R. 1387.

[37] Case 153/73 *Holtz and Willemsen* v. *Council and Commission* [1974] E.C.R. 675.

[38] Case 37/70 *Rewe-Zentrale* v. *Hauptzollamt Emmerich* [1971] E.C.R. 23.

[39] [1977] E.C.R. 515 at 523.

[40] See Joined Cases 80 and 81/77 *Commissionaires Réunies and Ramel* v. *Receveur des Douanes* [1978] E.C.R. 927; noted Usher (1978) 3 E.L.Rev. 305. But see Case 106/81 *Julius Kind KG* v. *Council and Commission* [1982] E.C.R. 2885.

[41] Case 8/74 *Procureur du Roi* v. *Dassonville* [1974] E.C.R. 837 at 852; see also Barents (1981) 18 C.M.L.Rev. 271.

"reasonable." In *Cassis de Dijon*, the Court in 1979 noted that, in the absence of common rules,

> "[o]bstacles to movement within the Community resulting from disparities between . . . national laws . . . must be accepted in so far as those provisions may be recognised as being necessary in order to satisfy mandatory requirements relating in particular to the effectiveness of fiscal supervision, the protection of public health, the fairness of commercial transactions and the defence of the consumer."[42]

With these exceptions, Member States must accept, following Article 30, the principle of equivalence: a product lawfully produced and marketed in one Member State must be admitted into another.

After 1978, the Community was marked increasingly by economic recession, centrifugal political trends and nationalist protectionism. Infringements of EC law grew sharply and steadily in number, became more sophisticated and were often deliberate. In this context, *Cassis de Dijon* offered a "minimalist" legal strategy for the free movement of goods. Though in many respects merely a logical development of previous judicial decisions, it contributed to a gradual change in policies pursued by the Commission towards so-called "technical barriers to trade." EC efforts to harmonise divergent food laws, for example, were increasingly based not, as before, on Council directives under Article 100 for the approximation of national laws, but rather on action under Article 30 against national quantitative restrictions on imports and measures having equivalent effect.[43] Partly for this reason, and partly because of the real increase in infringements, the number of infringements of Community law (excluding directives) detected

---

[42] Case 120/78 *Rewe Zentrale* v. *Bundesmonopolverwaltung für Branntwein* [1979] E.C.R. 649 at 662.

[43] See Gormley, "Cassis de Dijon and the Communication from the Commission" (1981) 6 E.L.Rev. 454; Welch, "From 'Euro Beer' to 'Newcastle Brown,' A Review of European Community Action to Dismantle Divergent 'Food' Laws" (1983) 22 J.C.M.S. 47; S. Harris, A. Swinbank and G. Wilkinson, *The Food and Farm Policies of the European Community* (1983) 305. For a summary of the most important EC measures regarding the harmonisation of provisions on the production and marketing of agricultural products, see European Parliament Secretariat, *Europe Today: State of European Integration 1982–1983* (1983), s.3(5). On harmonisation of laws, see Dashwood, "The Harmonisation Process" in C. Cosgrove Twitchett (ed.), *Harmonisation in the EEC* (1981); Dashwood, "Hastening Slowly: The Community's Path towards Harmonisation" in H. Wallace, W. Wallace and C. Webb (eds.), *Policy-Making in the European Community* (1983).

by the Commission's own enquiries or on the basis of complaints rose from 208 in 1980 to 591 in 1983. Most of these concerned the free movement of goods under Articles 30 and 95.[44] The number of actual infringements far surpassed that of detected infringements and only a small proportion of the latter were eventually taken to the Court. Nonetheless the *Cassis de Dijon* doctrine was applied and reaffirmed in numerous cases.[45]

Whilst thus making an important contribution to EC administrative practice and legal doctrine, the *Cassis de Dijon* principles have not always been implemented in practice. Indeed, four years after the celebrated decision, Dijon cassis was still not sold in Germany.[46] In November 1982 Dutch lorry drivers complained that no fewer than 300 rubber stamps were required to transport Gouda cheese into France. Suits for infringement of the free movement of goods provisions were then reported to be pending in the European Court against every Member State. France led the way as defendant in 40 cases, followed by Italy (28), Germany (17), Denmark (12), Belgium and the Netherlands (11 each), the United Kingdom (8), Ireland (7) and Luxembourg (5).[47]

The *Cassis de Dijon* doctrine embraces two kinds of measures: first, measures which apply only to imports and, second, measures which are "indistinctly applicable" to both foreign and domestic goods but which in fact discriminate against imports. This principle might be assumed to pertain not only to Article 30 but also, *mutatis mutandis*, to Article 34, which prohibits quantitative restrictions on exports and measures having equivalent effect.

---

[44] Commission of the European Communities, "First Annual Report to the European Parliament on Commission Monitoring of the Application of Community Law, 1983," COM(84)181 final (1984) at 5–7. On Art. 95, see Case 170/78 *Re Excise Duties on Wine: Commission* v. *United Kingdom* [1980] E.C.R. 417, noted Easson (1980) 5 E.L.Rev. 318; Case 170/78 *Re Excise Duties on Wine* (*No. 2*): *Commission* v. *United Kingdom* [1983] 3 C.M.L.R. 512, noted Easson (1984) 9 E.L.Rev. 57.

[45] See Case 152/78 *Commission* v. *France* [1980] E.C.R. 2299 (advertising of alcoholic beverages); Case 788/79 *Gilli and Andrés* [1980] E.C.R. 2071 (marketing of vinegar), noted Wyatt (1981) 6 E.L.Rev. 185; Case 27/80 *Fietje* [1980] E.C.R. 3839 (labelling of alcoholic beverages); Case 53/80 *Eyssen* [1981] E.C.R. 409 (additive in cheese); Case 130/80 *Kelderman* [1981] E.C.R. 527 (dry matter content of bread), noted Wyatt (1982) 7 E.L.Rev. 196; Case 261/81 *Walter Rau Lebensmittelwerke* v. *De Smedt* [1982] E.C.R. 3961 (packaging of margarine); Case 94/82 *De Kikvorsch Groothandel-Import-Export* [1983] E.C.R. 947 (labelling of beer). See also Dashwood, "The Cassis de Dijon Line of Authority" in St. John Bates *et al.* (eds.), *In Memoriam J.D.B. Mitchell* (1983).

[46] "Rules and Ruses in the Protection Racket" (1983) 1 *Europe Today* 9.

[47] "Urgent Brussels Scrutiny of French Controls" *The Times* (London), November 20, 1982, at 5.

Such an assumption was rejected, however, by the European Court in Case 15/79 *Groenveld* v. *Produktschap voor Vee en Vlees*. Considering Dutch legislation prohibiting sausage manufacturers from keeping or processing horsemeat, the Court held that Article 34

> "concerns national measures which have as their specific object or effect the restriction of patterns of exports and thereby the establishment of a difference in treatment between the domestic trade of a Member State and its export trade, in such a way as to provide a particular advantage for national production or for the domestic market of the State in question."[48]

This view was confirmed in Case 155/80 *Sergius Oebel*,[49] in which a ban on night baking that did not distinguish between products for domestic use and export products was held to fall outside Article 34. A similar conclusion was reached recently in Joined Cases 141–143/81 *Gerrit Holdijk and others*.[50] These cases arose from criminal proceedings against a farmer, a fodder dealer and a feedingstuffs producer accused of having kept calves for veal production in enclosures that did not meet Dutch legislative requirements for the protection of animals. About 90 per cent. of Dutch veal production was destined for export. Nevertheless, the Court held that neither Article 34 nor the relevant EC market organisation rules prevented a Member State from laying down minimum standards for animal protection, as long as the standards, though perhaps restricting exports, applied without distinction to animals intended for export and those intended for the domestic market.

Measures prohibited by Article 34, like those prohibited by Article 30, are generally considered to refer to national measures in relation to marketing. In Case 68/76 *Commission* v. *France*,[51] for example, the Court held inconsistent with Article 34 a purely formal requirement of a previously endorsed declaration for the export of potatoes. They have also, however, been held to include a production quota on hyacinth bulbs[52] and a slaughter quota on

[48] [1979] E.C.R. 3409 at 3415.
[49] [1981] E.C.R. 1993, noted Oliver (1982) 7 E.L.Rev. 118. See also Dashwood, "The Cassis de Dijon Line of Authority" in St. John Bates *et al.* (eds.), *In Memoriam J.D.B. Mitchell* (1983) at 155–158.
[50] [1982] E.C.R. 1299.
[51] [1977] E.C.R. 515. See also Case 29/82 *F.van Luipen en Zn BV* [1983] E.C.R. 151; compare Case 237/82 *Jongneel Kaas BV* v. *Holland and Stichting Centraal Orgaan Zuivelcontrole*, not yet reported (O.J. 1984, C.79/3).
[52] Case 190/73 *Officier van Justitie* v. *Van Haaster* [1974] E.C.R. 1123.

chickens.[53] In each of these last two cases, the national restriction on production was inconsistent with an EC common market organisation. It has accordingly been suggested that measures for products not covered by a common organisation may be prohibited by Article 34 only if they apply to the marketing stage. For other products, however, Article 34 may prohibit national restrictions on production, but only if they are inconsistent with the sector's common organisation.[54]

Exceptions to Articles 30 to 34 are provided in Treaty Article 36:

> "The provisions of Articles 30 to 34 shall not preclude prohibitions or restrictions on imports, exports or goods in transit justified on grounds of public morality, public policy or public security; the protection of health and life of humans, animals or plants; the protection of national treasures possessing artistic, historic or archaeological value; or the protection of industrial and commercial property. Such prohibitions shall not, however, constitute a means of arbitrary discrimination or a disguised restriction on trade between the Member States."

As a derogation from the fundamental free movement of goods provisions, Article 36 is to be strictly interpreted.[55] Thus the "mandatory requirements" set out in *Cassis de Dijon* are generally considered as exceptions to the *Dassonville* formula, not as additions to Article 36.[56]

The Article 36 public health exception to Article 30 was invoked by the United Kingdom in the recent controversy regarding the import of French ultra heat-treated (UHT) milk. A common organisation of the market for milk and milk products was originally established in 1968, but it (still) does not provide common

---

[53] Case 111/76 *Officier van Justitie* v. *Beert van den Hazel* [1977] E.C.R. 901.

[54] Wyatt (1977) 2 E.L.Rev. 281 at 284.

[55] Case 46/76 *Bauhuis* v. *Netherlands* [1977] E.C.R. 5.

[56] Compare Barents, "New Developments in Measures Having Equivalent Effect" (1981) 18 C.M.L.Rev. 271 at 284–291 and Dashwood, "Cassis de Dijon: The Line of Cases Grows" (1981) 6 E.L.Rev. 287 with Oliver, "Measures of Equivalent Effect: A Reappraisal" (1982) 19 C.M.L.Rev. 217 at 230–234. In Case 113/80 *Commission* v. *Ireland* [1981] E.C.R. 1625 the Court held that the list of exceptions in Art. 36 could not be extended: grounds such as consumer protection or the fairness of commercial transactions, which are not expressly included, could not therefore be relied upon under Art. 36. In a subsequent answer to a written Parliamentary question, the Commission stated that "mandatory requirements" apply "if (and only if) the measures in question applied equally to domestic and imported goods" (W.Q. 874/81; O.J. 1981 C. 295/95).

standards for the health and hygiene aspects of producing liquid milk for human consumption or for the quality and marketing of liquid milk.[57] In 1978, France's largest dairy co-operative, Union Laitière Normande, seeking to penetrate the large and potentially profitable United Kingdom market, twice sent its London subsidiary, French Dairy Farmers Ltd., a consignment of UHT milk which had been processed and packaged in litre containers in France. The first shipment was turned back, because an import licence, required under the United Kingdom Importation of Carcases and Animal Products Order 1972,[58] had not been obtained. The second could not be marketed, since it did not comply with United Kingdom requirements, laid down by the Milk and Dairies (General) Regulations 1959[59] and the Milk (Special Designation) Regulations 1977,[60] on the treatment and packaging of milk. French Dairy Farmers terminated the contract, whereupon Union Laitière Normande brought a suit for non-performance in the Paris Tribunal de Commerce. The Paris court immediately referred to the European Court of Justice, under the Article 177 preliminary ruling procedure, several questions including the compatibility of the United Kingdom measures with Article 30. In Case 244/78 *Union Laitière Normande* v. *French Dairy Farmers Ltd.*,[61] the Court held that, until December 31, 1979, the expiry of the implementation period of Directive 75/106 on the approximation of laws on the making-up by volume of certain pre-packed liquids, including milk, Member States were entitled to maintain their existing rules on permitted sizes. The United Kingdom rules requiring milk to be sold in imperial rather than metric-sized packs were therefore temporarily permissible.

Even after December 31, 1979, however, the United Kingdom continued to maintain controls on UHT milk imports, requiring not only an import licence but also that UHT milk be marketed

---

[57] Council Reg. 804/68 (O.J. Sp.Ed. 1968, p. 176) established the common organisation of the market for milk and milk products. As part of the scheme, Council Reg. 1411/71 (O.J. Sp.Ed. 1971, p. 411), as amended and supplemented by Council Reg. 566/76 (O.J. 1976, L.67/23), provided for the marketing, within a Member State, of milk produced according to a different, accepted formula within another Member State. Council Directive 75/106 (O.J. 1975, L.42/1), adopted under Treaty Art. 100, concerned the approximation of laws of the Member States relating to the making up by volume of certain pre-packed liquids; an annex to the directive made its provisions applicable, *inter alia*, to milk sold by volume.

[58] S.I. 1972, No. 287.

[59] S.I. 1959, No. 277.

[60] S.I. 1977, No. 1033.

[61] [1979] E.C.R. 2663.

only by licensed dealers who had packed the milk in a local dairy. Imported milk had therefore to be opened for re-packing and then re-treated; thus it was uneconomical to market and imports were, in effect, banned. Such imports, according to the Milk Marketing Board and United Kingdom producers, threatened doorstep deliveries, up to 50,000 jobs and possibly £50 million annual income to producers. The Commission brought an action against the United Kingdom under Article 69. In Case 124/81 *Re Ultra Heat-Treated Milk: Commission* v. *United Kingdom,*[62] the European Court held, *inter alia,* that the requirements of an import licence and local processing were prohibited by Article 30. These measures, moreover, could not be justified under the public health exception in Article 36. According to the Court, where a processed product is hermetically sealed immediately after processing and the machinery and methods of processing are broadly similar in all Member States, consumers' health is sufficiently protected if necessary controls are carried out in the country of production, reasonable requirements of the importing country are met, and the imports are certified to that effect and subjected to spot checks. The United Kingdom ban on imports, however, was lifted only in October 1983.[63] While the dispute continued to simmer, new milk regulations were published, requiring a health certificate from the place of origin and place of entry and details of the milk and cream content and the method of heat treatment.[64]

Competition and state aids

The Treaty rules on competition are contained in Articles 85–90 (private and public[65] enterprises), 91 (dumping) and 92–94 (state aids). These rules

---

[62] [1983] E.C.R. 203; noted Wainwright (1983) 20 C.M.L.Rev. 365; see also Case 42/82 *Commission* v. *France* [1983] E.C.R. 1013.

[63] See Jackson, "Imports of Milk and Dairy Products—The Threat from Abroad" (1980–81) 4 *Farm Management* 148; McHardy, "Health Officers Clear French Milk" *The Guardian*, January 4, 1984, at 22.

[64] The Importation of Milk Act 1983 (c. 37) provides enabling powers allowing Agricultural Ministers to make regulations governing the importation of milk and the use of that milk. See now the Food Act 1984.

[65] On public enterprises in EC law, see Evans, "Public Undertakings in EEC Law: Commission Directive on the Transparency of Financial Relations" (1983) 17 J.W.T.L. 445; Page, "Member States, Public Undertakings and Article 90" (1982) 7 E.L.Rev. 19; Mathijsen, "State Aids, State Monopolies, and Public Enterprises in the Common Market" (1972) 37 *Law and Contemporary Problems* 376; Schindler, "Public Enterprises and the EEC Treaty" (1970) 7 C.M.L.Rev. 57; Deringer "The Interpretation of Article 90(2) of the EEC Treaty" (1964–65) 2 C.M.L.Rev. 129.

"shall apply to the production of and trade in agricultural products only to the extent determined by the Council within the framework of Article 43(2) and (3) and in accordance with the procedure laid down therein, account being taken of the objectives set out in Article 39." (Art. 42, para.1)

Prior to Council action, and as long as a national market organisation for a particular product is in existence, a partial shield against competition is given by Article 46, which provides for the imposition of countervailing charges. Rarely invoked,[66] this provision has declined in significance with the establishment of EC common market organisations and the enactment of Regulation 26/62.[67]

Regulation 26/62, Art. 1, provides that, subject to Art. 2 of the regulation, the competition rules shall apply "to all agreements, decisions and practices referred to in Articles 85(1) and 86 of the Treaty which relate to production of or trade in the products listed in Annex II to the Treaty." Article 2 exempts from the operation of Treaty Article 85(1) all such agreements, decisions and practices

"as form an integral part of national market organisations or are necessary for the attainment of the objectives set out in Article 39 of the Treaty. In particular, it shall not apply to agreements, decisions and practices of farmers, farmers' associations, or associations of such associations belonging to a single Member State which concern the production or sale of agricultural products or the use of joint facilities for the storage, treatment or processing of agricultural products, and under which there is no obligation to charge identical prices, unless the Commission finds that competition is thereby excluded or that the objectives of Article 39 of the Treaty are jeopardised."

---

[66] See Décision de la Commission portant fixation d'une taxe compensatoire sur les importations de poudre de lait entier dans la République fédérale d'Allemagne en application de l'article 46 (J.O. 1961, 595); Décision de la Commission portant fixation d'une taxe compensatoire sur les importations du maïs dans la République fédérale d'Allemagne en application de l'article 46 (J.O. 1961, 825); Case IV 42/63H *Re Import of Powered Milk* [1965] C.M.L.R. 270 (Finanzgericht, Hamburg). Art. 46 nevertheless remains applicable: see Case 337/82 *St. Nikolaus Brennerei* v. *Hauptzollant Krefeld*, not yet reported (see (1984) 9 Bull.E.C. at 40). A recent example is Commission Reg. 2541/84 fixing a countervailing charge on imports into the other Member States of ethyl alcohol of agricultural origin produced in France (O.J. 1984, L.238/16).

[67] J.O. 1962, 993.

The Commission has sole power, subject to judicial review, to determine which agreements, decisions and practices fulfill the conditions for exemption.[68]

Regulation 26/62's main purpose is, in principle, to validate existing co-operatives and encourage further collaboration.[69] Yet, it has been interpreted narrowly—as an exception to general Treaty rules—by both the Commission and the Court. The regulation applies only to Annex II products.[70] In order to qualify for exemption from Article 85(1) on the ground that it is necessary for the attainment of Article 39 objectives, an agreement, decision or practice must further all of these objectives, not merely some of them.[71] Plant breeder's rights have been held not to be so distinctive as to require, in relation to competition rules, a different treatment from that given to other commercial or industrial property rights.[72] The Regulation 26/62 exemption, according to the Commission's decision regarding the European sugar industry marathon, applies only when the competition rules jeopardise the implementation of the CAP.[73] The European Court accepted this view in its judgment in the same case, and it also pointed out that the Article 39 objectives do not in any way require recourse to

---

[68] On Commission procedure in competition cases, see Temple Lang, "The Procedure of the Commission in Competition Cases" (1977) 14 C.M.L.Rev. 155; Allen, "Managing the Common Market: The Community's Competition Policy" in H. Wallace, W. Wallace and C. Webb (eds.), *Policy-Making in the European Community* (2nd ed., 1983).

[69] See the Opinion of Advocate General Mayras in Joined Cases 40–48, 50, 54–56, 111, 113–114/73 *Coöperatieve vereniging "Suiker Unie" UA* v. *Commission* [1975] E.C.R. 1663 at 2062. For further discussion, see J. Morley, *British Agricultural Co-operatives* (1975) at 17–18, 130–131, 153–157 and J. G. de Villeneuve (ed.), *Les coopératives agricoles dans le Marché commun* (1969) at 17–26; I am indebted to Mr. J. A. E. Morley MBE for these references. See also Delagneau, "Agricultural Co-operative Marketing within the Context of the EEC Competition Policy" (1976) 27 J.A.E. 53.

[70] See *Re Rennet—An Application by Coöperatieve Stremsel-en Kleuselfabriek before the Commission of the European Communities* (80/234/EEC) [1980] 2 C.M.L.R. 402 (O.J. 1980 L.51/19); Case 61/80 *Coöperatieve Stremsel-en Kleuselfabriek* v. *Commission* [1981] E.C.R. 851.

[71] Case 71/74 *Nederlandse Vereniging voor Fruit en Groentenimporthandel, Nederlandse Bond van Grossiers in Zuidvruchten en ander Geimporteerd Fruit 'Frubo'* v. *Commission and Vereniging de Fruitunie* [1975] E.C.R. 563.

[72] Case 258/78 *L.C. Nungesser KG and Kurt Eisele* v. *Commission* [1982] E.C.R. 2015.

[73] Commission Decision (73/109/EEC), January 2, 1973, relating to a proceeding under Arts. 85 and 86 of the EEC Treaty (IV/26.918—European Sugar Industry), O.J. 1973, L.140/17. See also Commission Decision (78/66/EEC), December 2, 1977, relating to a proceeding under Art. 85 of the EEC Treaty (IV/28.948—Cauliflowers), O.J. 1978, L.21/23.

concerted practices.[74] It implicitly rejected, however, the Commission's view that the exemption applied only to bona fide co-operatives and farmers' organisations, thus accepting, without more, that it also applied to processors. Nevertheless, the exemption concerns only Article 85(1), not Article 86.[75]

Regarding state aids, Regulation 26/62 (Art. 4) provides for the application to Annex II products of Article 93(1) and the first sentence of Article 93(3). All Annex II products are therefore subject to the power of the Commission, in co-operation with Member States, to keep under review all existing state aids and to propose to States any appropriate measures required by the progressive development or functioning of the common market. The Commission is also entitled to be informed, in sufficient time to submit comments, of any plans to grant or alter aid. Regulation 26/62 does not provide for the application to agricultural production and trade of the most important Treaty article on state aids:

> "Save as otherwise provided in this Treaty, any aid granted by a Member State or through State resources in any form whatsoever which distorts or threatens to distort competition by favouring certain undertakings or the production of certain goods shall, in so far as it affects trade between Member States, be incompatible with the common market." (Art. 92(1))

In practice, however, the common market organisations established for most products since the early 1960s provide expressly for the application of the state aids provisions to the sector in question.[76] Nevertheless, with regard to products covered by a common market organisation the application of Articles 92–94 is subordinate to the provisions of the common organisation.[77] The Article 92(2) and (3) exceptions to the Article 92(1) prohibition on state aids do not therefore apply to an aid which is forbidden by

---

[74] Joined Cases 40–48, 50, 54–56, 111, 113–114/73 *Cooperatieve vereniging "Suiker Unie" UA* v. *Commission* [1975] E.C.R. 1663 at 1950; noted Dashwood *et al.* (1975–76) 1 E.L.Rev. 479; see also Gijlstra and Murphy. "Some Observations on the Sugar Cases" (1977) 14 C.M.L.Rev. 45.

[75] It could not therefore have been invoked in Case 27/76 *United Brands Company and United Brands Continental B.V.* v. *Commission* [1978] E.C.R. 207.

[76] E.g. Art. 21 of Council Reg. 2759/75 on the common organisation of the market in pigmeat (O.J. 1975, L.282/1). See generally "State Aids and the Common Agricultural Policy" (1982) 191 *Green Europe* (March).

[77] See Case 177/78 *Pigs and Bacon Commission* v. *McCarren and Company Ltd.* [1979] E.C.R. 2161.

the regulations governing a common market organisation.[78] Accordingly, the state aids provisions of the Treaty are, in principle, fully applicable to the production of and trade in agricultural products governed by a common organisation of the market. In the case of products not covered by a common organisation, the applicability of Articles 92–94 is governed solely by Regulation 26/ 62.[79]

The practical operation of these Treaty articles is directly influenced by the way in which they have been interpreted by the Court. Article 92(1), for example, has been held not to be directly effective.[80] The legality under Article 92 of an existing aid, therefore, is not open to challenge by an enterprise or private individual, and an existing aid remains valid unless and until a decision that the aid must be modified or abolished is taken under Article 93(2). The last sentence of Article 93(3), however, has been held to be directly effective.[81] As a consequence, in principle new aids may not be introduced or existing aids modified once the Article 93(2) procedure for the determination of the compatibility of the aid with the common market has been initiated but not yet taken its course.[82]

The implementation of the state aids provisions rests mainly with the Commission. Although the Treaty provides for judicial remedies under Article 93(2), para. 2, and Article 169, most disputes never reach the Court.[83] Instead, as was the case with the controversial preferential tariff for heating fuel available until

[78] Commission Decision 81/601/EEC (O.J. 1981, L.220/39); see also Case 72/79 *Commission* v. *Italy* [1980] E.C.R. 1411 at 1425.

[79] Conversely, it has been held, by the Oxford County Court, that aids covered by Arts. 92 and 93 are not subject to the Art. 30 prohibition of quantitative restrictions on imports or the Art. 34 prohibition of restrictions on exports: *Potato Marketing Board* v. *Robertsons* [1983] 1 C.M.L.R. 93, following Case 74/76 *Iannelli and Volpi SpA* v. *Ditta Paolo Meroni* [1977] E.C.R. 557.

[80] Case 77/72 *Carmine Capolongo* v. *Azienda Agricola Maya* [1973] E.C.R. 611; Case 74/76 *Ianelli and Volpi SpA* v. *Ditta Paolo Meroni* [1977] E.C.R. 557; Case 78/76 *Steinike* v. *Germany* [1977] E.C.R. 595, noted Dashwood (1977) 2 E.L.Rev. 367.

[81] Case 6/64 *Costa* v. *ENEL* [1964] E.C.R. 585.

[82] Cases 31/77R and 53/77R *Commission* v. *United Kingdom* and *United Kingdom* v. *Commission* [1977] E.C.R. 921.

[83] See Dashwood, "Control of State Aids in EEC Law: Prevention and Cure under Article 93" (1975) 12 C.M.L.Rev. 43; Gilmour, "The Enforcement of Community Law by the Commission in the Context of State Aids: The Relationship between Articles 93 and 169 and the Choice of Remedies" (1981) 18 C.M.L.Rev. 63; Case 40/75 *Société des Produits Bertrand* v. *Commission* [1976] E.C.R. 1. See also Gadbin "Le contrôle communautaire des aides nationales en agriculture" in J. Raux (ed.), *Politique agricole commune et Construction communautaire* (1984).

recently to hot-house horticulturalists in the Netherlands,[84] they are settled, if at all, by negotiation. In addition, the Commission is responsible, under Article 93(1), for proposing "appropriate measures," or guidelines, regarding state aids. In the 1960s it prepared several inventories of aids,[85] and in the mid-1970s it prepared a nine-volume inventory of aids which was not, however, made publicly available.[86] In addition, the Commission has produced guidelines concerning particular types of aids.[87]

Official figures, however, quite apart from the loosely co-ordinated, permitted state aids which constitute the Community's structural policy, represent only the tip of the iceberg. Evidence collected by the House of Lords Select Committee supported "the popularly held view that state aids are an entrenched and extensive feature of European agriculture."[88] The Commission has suggested (though this is contested) that national expenditure on agriculture by the Member States is greater than total EC spending on price support and structural policy together.[89] It includes preferential tax and social security treatment, interest rate subsidies and capital grants, a variety of aids by regional and local governments and other financial aids. Taken individually, these aids may well be admissible under the Treaty, but cumulatively they sometimes amount to a major distortion of previous trading patterns, which may eventually provoke retaliation by affected Member States. A recent example was the French government aids to a turkey processing plant at Guiscriff in Brittany,[90] which led to the British ban on French poultry imports, ostensibly as protection against Newcastle disease. The British restrictions were held to be contrary to

---

[84] The dispute may be followed in scattered issues of *Agra Europe* between early 1981 and late 1983.

[85] "Rapport de la Commission au Conseil sur les mesures d'aides dans l'agriculture" VI/COM (63) 423 final (1963); "Rapport et inventaire sur les aides en agriculture" SEC(66) 920 (1966); "Critères pour l'établissement d'une politique commune d'aides en agriculture" COM (66) 60 final (1966).

[86] See House of Lords Select Committee on the European Communities, *State Aids to Agriculture* (1981) at xv–xvii.

[87] See *ibid.* at 150–153.

[88] *Ibid.* at xxvii.

[89] Commission of the European Communities, *The Agricultural Situation in the Community: 1980 Report* (1981) at 244–245 (Table 60). For criticisms, see House of Lords Select Committee on the European Communities, *State Aids to Agriculture* (1981) at xvii–xviii; S. Harris, A. Swinbank and G. Wilkinson, *The Food and Farm Policies of the European Community* (1983) at 231.

[90] See House of Lords Select Committee on the European Communities, *State Aids to Agriculture* (1981) at 125–126 (Memorandum by the Ministry of Agriculture, Fisheries and Food) and *passim.* See also Case 290/83 *Commission v. France*, not yet reported (O.J. 1984, C.25/3).

Article 30 by the European Court in Case 40/82 *Commission* v. *United Kingdom*.[91] The English High Court (Queen's Bench Division) subsequently held that French producers injured by the restriction may claim damages for breach of statutory duty and, in certain conditions, have a cause of action for misfeasance in public office against the United Kingdom Minister of Agriculture, Fisheries and Food,[92] thus demonstrating the anomalous consequences of current policy on state aids.

General principles of law

The general principles of law recognised by the European Court are derived mainly from two sources: the Rome Treaty, particularly Articles 164, 173 and 215(2); and the legal systems of the Member States, especially Germany and France. They include human rights, equal treatment (non-discrimination), proportionality, and the protection of legitimate expectations; the latter is often considered to be an application of the more general principle of legal certainty, which also embraces non-retroactivity, respect for vested rights and the use of understandable language. All have been applied to agriculture.[93] The extent to which basic human rights, for example, are recognised and protected in EC law has largely been elaborated by the Court in cases concerning the CAP.[94] The principle of equal treatment requires that similar situations shall not be treated differently unless differentiation is

---

[91] [1982] E.C.R. 2793; noted Minor (1983) 8 E.L.Rev. 119; see also Brown, "Britain ordered to end poultry curbs" *The Guardian*, February 1, 1984 at 6; Leith, "Poulet pecking order" *The Guardian*, March 9, 1984, at 11.

[92] *Bourgoin SA* v. *Ministry of Agriculture, Fisheries and Food*, not yet reported (see *The Times*, October 4, 1984 (Law Report); *Financial Times*, October 9, 1984 (F.T. Commercial Law Reports)).

[93] See H. Schermers, *Judicial Protection in the European Communities* (2nd ed., 1979) at 23–64; T. Hartley, *The Foundations of European Community Law* (1981) at 119–140; Usher, "The Influence of National Concepts on Decisions of the European Court" (1976) 1 E.L.Rev. 359; Vajda "Some Aspects of Judicial Review within the Common Agricultural Policy" (1979) 4 E.L.Rev. 244, 341; Wainwright, "Legal Aspects of the Agricultural Policy in the European Community: General Principles of Law—Recent Developments" in St. John Bates *et al.* (eds.), *In Memoriam J.D.B. Mitchell* (1983). The technical complexity and obscurantism of CAP legislation is well-known and regrettable. As part of its 1984 European Parliament election campaign, the U.K. Labour Party established a phone-in service to explain EC terminology; see "Hot line to Eurospeak" *The Guardian*, May 21, 1984 at 1.

[94] *E.g.* Case 29/69 *Stauder* v. *Ulm* [1969] E.C.R. 419 (disposal of surplus butter); Case 11/70 *Internationale Handelsgesellschaft* v. *EVst für Getreide und Futtermittel* [1970] E.C.R. 1125 (deposit system for export licence); Case 44/79 *Hauer* v. *Land Rheinland-Pfalz* [1979] E.C.R. 3727 (prohibition on planting vines).

objectively justified. It is applied to the agricultural sector by Article 40(3).[95] The principle of proportionality states that a public authority may in the public interest impose on citizens only those obligations which are strictly necessary for the purposes to be attained. As part of EC law it was first systematically defined in Case 11/70 *Internationale Handelsgesellschaft* v. *EVst für Getreide und Futtermittel*,[96] which concerned the system of deposits for export licences. The principle of legal certainty forms part of the Community legal order, so that any failure to comply with it is "an infringement of this Treaty or of any rule of law relating to its application" within the meaning of Article 173. This conclusion was reached by the Court in Case 112/77 *August Töpfer and Co.* v. *Commission*,[97] for example, involving the advance fixing of export refunds for sugar.

Assessment

The general principles of law have been used by the Court mainly in reviewing the Commission's and Council's exercise of discretion (see Chap. 3). That they are applied fully to agriculture merely highlights the extent to which, in other respects, agriculture constitutes a special sector under Community law. It is exceptional in enjoying special voting provisions under Article 43(1); particular rules regarding competition and, to some extent, the free movement of goods; and special arrangements for the financing of the agricultural common market, as provided in Article 40(4). Though subject, like industry, to general legal principles and some of the fundamental Treaty rules, it still retains a special legal status.

---

[95] *E.g.* Joined Cases 9 and 11/71 *Compagnie d'Approvisionnement, de Transport et de Crédit SA and Grands Moulins de Paris SA* v. *Commission* [1972] E.C.R. 391 at 420 (*per* Advocate General Mayras); Joined Cases 117/76 and 16/77 *Albert Ruckdeschel and Co. and Hansa-Lagerhaus Ströh and Co.* v. *Hauptzollamt Hamburg-St. Annen; Diamalt AG* v. *Hauptzollamt Itzehoe* [1977] E.C.R. 1753 at 1769; Case 125/77 *Koninklijke Scholten-Honig N.V. and de Verenigde Zetmeelbedrijven "De Bijenkorf" B.V.* v. *Hoofdproduktschap voor Akkerbouwprodukten* [1978] E.C.R. 1991 at 2003. It does not, however, apply to external relations or the internal consequences of external commercial policy: see Case 52/81 *Offene Handelsgesellschaft in Firma Werner Faust* v. *Commission* [1982] E.C.R. 3745; Case 245/81 *Edeka Zentrale AG* v. *Germany* [1982] E.C.R. 2745.

[96] [1970] E.C.R. 1125. The definition used in the text is that given by Advocate General Dutheillet de Lamothe at 1146.

[97] [1978] E.C.R. 1019 at 1033.

Chapter 3

MAKING AND APPLYING CAP LAW

Community Law-Making

Legal bases

The law of the CAP is promulgated primarily by Community institutions, while its implementation rests largely with the Member States. Its legal basis is generally considered to be Article 43(2), which confers on the Council a general power to legislate regarding a common agricultural policy:

> "The Council shall, on a proposal from the Commission and after consulting the Assembly, acting unanimously during the first two stages and by a qualified majority thereafter, make regulations, issue directives, or take decisions, without prejudice to any recommendations it may also make." (Art. 43(2), para. 3)

In addition, however, EC agricultural and food legislation has sometimes been based on Articles 100 and 235. Article 100 empowers the Council, acting unanimously on a Commission proposal and (in specified cases) after consulting the Parliament and the Economic and Social Committee, to issue directives for the approximation of laws directly affecting the establishment or the functioning of the common market. It has been used for the harmonisation of national laws. Article 235 contains a general residual power. It provides that, if action by the Community should be necessary to attain, in the course of the operation of the common market, one of the objectives of the Community and the Treaty has not provided the necessary powers, the Council shall, acting unanimously on a Commission proposal and after consulting the Parliament, take appropriate measures. This article is the legal basis of Community legislation concerning products of

40

secondary processing and other matters, such as forestry, which
though related to agricultural policy lie outside Annex II.[1]

Procedures

The EEC, though still legally distinct, shares with the European
Atomic Energy Community (Euratom) and the European Coal
and Steel Community (ECSC) four institutions: an Assembly (now
called the European Parliament), a Council, a Commission and a
Court of Justice.[2] The latter two have been common to the Communities since the 1957 Convention on Certain Institutions Common to the European Communities, concluded at the same time as
the Rome Treaties; and the former two since the Merger Treaty,[3]
signed on April 8, 1965 and entering into force on July 1, 1967.
The organisation and functions of these four main institutions are
set out in Articles 137–188. Provisions common to several institutions are contained in Articles 188–192.

These formal provisions do not of course necessarily depict the
Community's institutions as they work in practice (see Figure 3.1).
Moreover, CAP law-making involves not only EC institutions but
also interest groups, other social forces and the Member States.
With regard to CAP legislation, two different procedures may be
distinguished: one for Council regulations and directives, and the
other for delegated legislation enacted by the Commission.[4]

For Council legislation, the formulation of proposals and the
preparation and supervision of drafts rests with the Commission.
In practice, however, proposals may stem from many other
sources, such as the Council, a trade association or a Member

[1] Art. 43(2), para. 2, is considered to be the legal cornerstone of the CAP by J.
Megret, J.-V. Louis, D. Vignes and M. Waelbroeck, *Le droit de la Communauté
économique européenne*, Vol. 2: *Agriculture* (1973) at 24, 27. On Art. 100, see
the sources cited in Chap. 2, n. 43. The increasing importance of Art. 235 is discussed in Sasse and Yourow, "The Growth of Legislative Power of the European
Communities" in T. Sandalow and E. Stein (eds.), *Courts and Free Markets*
(1982), Vol. 1.
[2] Only these four are legally designated as Community "institutions" within the
meaning of Art. 4 of the Rome Treaty. On European Community institutions in
the broader sense, see A. Parry and J. Dinnage, *Parry and Hardy's EEC Law*
(2nd ed. 1981) at 13–56.
[3] Treaty Establishing a Single Council and a Single Commission of the European
Communities; T.S. No. 2 (1973)—Part II, Cmnd. 5179, incorporated in T.S.
Nos. 15–17 (1979), Cmnd. 7560–7462.
[4] For a step-by-step description of legislative procedure, see R. Fennell, *The Common Agricultural Policy of the European Community* (1979) at 40–47. See also S.
Harris, A. Swinbank and G. Wilkinson, *The Food and Farm Policies of the
European Community* (1983) at 11–31.

Figure 3.1

The Decision-Making Process

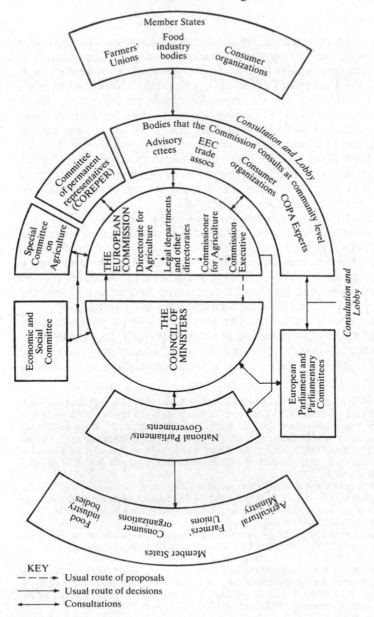

KEY

– – – ▸ Usual route of proposals

────▸ Usual route of decisions

◂────▸ Consultations

Source: J. S. Marsh and P. Swanney, *Agriculture and the European Community* (1980) at 23.

State.[5] Numerous "Special Interest Groups" are represented in Brussels. By far the most important is the Comité des Organisations Professionnelles Agricoles (COPA), which represents the major agricultural organisations in all Member States. Other important organisations are COGECA (Comité Général de la Coopération Agricole), representing agricultural co-operatives, and the Commission des Industries Agro-Alimentaires (CIAA) within the Union des Industries de la Communauté Européenne (UNICE), which represents the agricultural and food manufacturing industries. The Consumer Consultative Committee, established in 1973, includes representatives from the Bureau Européen des Unions de Consommateurs (BEUC), the European Trade Union Confederation (ETUC), the Comité des Organisations Familiales auprès des Communautés Européennees (COFACE) and the European Community of Consumer Co-operatives (EURO–COOP). Different interests are also represented through the EC's advisory Economic and Social Committee (Arts. 193–198) and numerous consultative committees.[6]

In addition to these EC level organisations, the particular configuration of social forces within each Member State may, because of the structure of formal EC decision-making, be expressed as different "national" interests. As Wallace puts it, "[t]he promotion of a so-called 'national interest' in Community bargaining is . . . the consequence of the outcome of a prior battle in each national capital to determine which domestic interest should receive priority."[7] National links with the CAP also include formal and informal relations between the Commission and particular government departments. In the United Kingdom, for example, the Ministry of Agriculture, Fisheries and Food is consulted on proposals and pre-

---

[5] These sources are more important today than was originally envisaged, since the Commission's authority and role in initiating legislation has markedly declined since the 1966 Luxembourg Accords which gave relatively greater power to the Council. On the role of the Commission, see Neunreither, "Transformation of a Political Role: Reconsidering the Case of the Commission of the European Communities" (1972) 10 J.C.M.S. 233; H.J. Michelmann, *Organisational Effectiveness in a Multinational Bureaucracy* (1978).

[6] For further details, see W.F. Averyt, Jr., *Agropolitics in the European Community* (1977); E. Kirchner and K. Schwaiger, *The Role of Interest Groups in the European Community* (1981); Economic and Social Committee of the European Communities, *European Interest Groups and their Relationships with the Economic and Social Committee* (1980); Economic and Social Committee of the European Communities, *Community Advisory Committees for the Representation of Socio-Economic Interests* (1980).

[7] H. Wallace, "Negotiation, Conflict, and Compromise: The Elusive Pursuit of Common Policies" in H. Wallace, W. Wallace and C. Webb (eds.), *Policy Making in the European Community* (2nd ed., 1983) at 69.

pares the brief used by United Kingdom representatives on the Council and its committees. Both the House of Lords Select Committee on the European Communities and the House of Commons Select Committee on European Legislation provide a means for Parliamentary scrutiny of CAP legislation.[8]

Within the Commission, responsibility for agricultural policy lies with the Directorate General for Agriculture (DG VI), one of the largest and most powerful of the fourteen Directorates General. In preparing a proposal, DG VI consults widely with potentially interested bodies and then submits the proposal to the Commission's Legal Service. The Legal Service, which has a monopoly of court appearances on behalf of the Commission and now intervenes on its behalf as a matter of course in all Article 177 cases, includes a CAP team which vets agricultural law proposals for correct legal form. Once subsequently approved by the Commissioner responsible for agricultural matters, a proposal must be approved by a majority of the other Commissioners, either in collegial discussion or by a written procedure. It is then sent by the Commission to the Council.

Within the Council most CAP matters are dealt with by the grouping of the Member States' ministers of agriculture, known as the Agricultural Council. This occurs initially through its subcommittee, the Special Committee on Agriculture (SCA). Originally established under Article 5(4) of the May 12, 1960 acceleration decision,[9] the SCA consists of permanent officials from the Member States. Only in instances also involving other areas of policy is a proposal sent to COREPER (Comité des Représentants Permanents), which is, except in agricultural matters, the Council's most important committee. At every stage Commission officials are closely involved. After a proposal has been considered by the European Parliament and, if necessary, by the Economic and Social Committee, and once it has been agreed by the SCA, it may be put either to the next Council meeting as an "A" point requiring no further discussion or to the Agricultural Council as a "B" point for discussion and decision. Between preliminary and final approval, the proposed legislation is checked by the Council's team of legal-linguistic experts ("jurists-linguists"), including at least one member from each Member State, for its concordance in all EC languages and legal systems. The jurist-linguists also write the legislative preamble.

---

[8] See R. Fennell, *The Common Agricultural Policy of the European Community* (1979) at 49–67. See generally F.E.C. Gregory, *Dilemmas of Government: Britain and the European Community* (1983).
[9] J.O. 1960, 1217.

Most Council legislation, based on Article 43(2), could in theory be decided by a qualified majority, according to the weighting in Article 148(2). In fact, however, no significant use has been made of weighted majority voting since the January 1966 Luxembourg Accords.[10] This compromise, an agreement to disagree, resolved the "empty chair crisis" during which France refused to participate in Council and most other EC activities; it provided that, where very important national interests were at stake, Council decisions would, in effect, be based on unanimity.[11] Perhaps the sole exception to this principle was the enactment, following a deadlock in the negotiations on Britain's disputed budget contribution, of the 1982–1983 farm price proposals, despite abstentions by the United Kingdom, Denmark and Greece. In practice, therefore, voting in the Council is rare. Decisions tend to be made as part of negotiated compromises and package deals, often during the annual agricultural price review.[12]

In acting on legislation, the Council is required by Article 43(2), para. 3, to consult the European Parliament, which now comprises 434 members and since 1979 has been directly elected. The Parliament's work in relation to agriculture is carried out, in the first instance, by an Agricultural Committee, which drafts Parliamentary resolutions and opinions on legislative proposals.[13] The right of the Parliament to be consulted on legislation was recently confirmed by the European Court. In two "isoglucose" cases, Case

[10] Gilsdorf, "La politique agricole commune (Die Gemeinsame Agrarpolitik)" JUR (81) D/00825, typescript (1980) at 5.
[11] (1966) 3 *Bull E.C.* at 5; reprinted in Sweet & Maxwell's *European Community Treaties* (4th ed., 1980) at 249.
[12] See Harris and Swinbank, "Price Fixing under the CAP—Proposition and Decision: The Example of the 1978/79 Price Review" (1978) *Food Policy* 256; Pearce, "The Common Agricultural Policy: An Accumulation of Special Interests" in H. Wallace, W. Wallace and C. Webb (eds.), *Policy-Making in the European Community* (2nd ed., 1983). It remains to be seen, however, whether this form of decision-making, though perhaps inevitable in the circumstances, represents an advance over the unanimity rule, which Paul-Henri Spaak, writing of the Rome Treaties' supranational character, described as "the bane of international organisations, the cause of their substantial ineffectiveness" (P.-H. Spaak, *Combats inachevés* (1969), Vol. 2, at 97; quoted by McAllister, "The EEC Dimension: Intended and Unintended Consequences" in J. Cornford (ed.), *The Failure of the State* (1975) at 182.
[13] The most recent British chairperson of the Agricultural Committee is David M. Curry, M.E.P. North-East Essex (Con), a member of the European Democratic Group, who served as Conservative spokesperson on agriculture before succeeding Sir Henry Plumb, former President of the National Farmers Union, in the committee chair. For a recent exposition of his views, see D.M. Curry, *The Food War: The European Community and the Battle for World Food Markets* (1983).

138/79 *Roquette Frères* v. *Council* and Case 139/79 *Maizena GmbH* v. *Council*,[14] the Court held that consultation of the Parliament is an essential procedural requirement, infringement of which is a ground for the annulment of EC legislation under Article 173. It also confirmed that the Parliament is entitled, as a Community "institution," to intervene, pursuant to Article 37 of the Statute of the Court, in direct actions before the Court without having to establish a specific interest in the outcome. Encouraged by this decision, the Parliament has amended its rules of procedure and taken other steps to strengthen its position in relation to the Commission and the Council.[15] Its influence on CAP legislation is severely constrained, however, by its narrow budgetary powers. The budget is divided into "compulsory" expenditure ("expenditure necessarily resulting from this Treaty or from acts adopted in accordance therewith": Art. 203(4), para. 2) and "non-compulsory" (other) expenditure. To the latter the Parliament can make amendments, but regarding "compulsory expenditure" it is entitled only to propose modifications. Most CAP spending falls under "compulsory expenditure," so that the Council has the final say (see Art. 203(5)).

Council legislation, requiring consultation of the Parliament, is reserved mainly for matters of principle or political importance. Most CAP legislation is enacted instead by the management committee procedure, according to the delegation of power by the Council to the Commission under Article 155. This Article provides that, in order to ensure the proper functioning and development of the common market, the Commission shall, *inter alia*, exercise the powers conferred on it by the Council for the implementation of the rules laid down by the latter. Accordingly, the regulations on the common market organisations for most agricultural products provide for the establishment, for the product in question, of a management committee, headed by a Commission official and composed of representatives from each Member State. Specialist management committees also exist for other matters, such as EAGGF or agricultural structures.[16] Legislative proposals

---

[14] [1980] E.C.R. 333 and [1980] E.C.R. 3393, respectively; noted Leopold (1982) 2 *Oxford Journal of Legal Studies* 454; (1980) 5 E.L.Rev. 431; Jacobs (1981) 18 C.M.L.Rev. 219; Hartley (1981) 6 E.L.Rev. 181.

[15] See Kirchner and Williams, "The Legal, Political and Institutional Implications of the Isoglucose Judgments 1980" (1983) 22 J.C.M.S. 173.

[16] See Bertram, "Decision-Making in the E.E.C.: The Management Committee Procedure" (1967–1968) 5 C.M.L.Rev. 246; Schindler, "The Problems of Decision-Making by Way of the Management Committee Procedure in the European Economic Community" (1971) 8 C.M.L.Rev. 184.

are submitted by the Commission to the appropriate committee, which is entitled to give, by a weighted majority vote (Art. 148(2)), an opinion in favour, an opinion against or an absence of opinion. The opinion of the committee, which in principle is purely consultative and has no decision-making power,[17] does not bind the Commission. In the rare case of a negative opinion,[18] however, the Commission must inform the Council, which then has the power, within one month, to override the Commission's decision either to adopt or to defer the proposed legislation. In Case 25/70 *EVst für Getreide und Futtermittel* v. *Koster*,[19] the legality of this procedure was confirmed by the Court. It held that the Council need not determine all the details of CAP legislation, the requirement of Article 43 being satisfied "so long as the essential elements of the matter to be regulated have been enacted in accordance with the procedure which it lays down." In addition, by the management committee procedure Member States participate continuously in making detailed CAP legislation.[20] A striking instance was Case 57/72 *Westzucker GmbH* v. *EVst für Zucker*,[21] in which a German firm contested the validity of a Commission regulation on the ground that, during the management committee's discussions, the Commission had given in to pressures from Italy and France, each seeking to favour its own particular interests. The Court held that the Commission could legitimately take account of such considerations: one purpose of the procedure was to permit the Commission to intervene rapidly in the economy in close collaboration with national authorities, and conflicts between Member States could be arbitrated by the Commission with reference to a presumed Community interest.

Processes

The making of CAP legislation and the making of EC agricultural policy are generally not identical, even though in the Community law-making, policy-making and politics are almost

---

[17] See ECSC Case 9/56 *Meroni and Co. Industrie Metallurgiche SpA* v. *High Authority* [1957 and 1958] E.C.R. 157.

[18] No negative opinions were given in 1451 votes taken in 1979 (S. Harris, A. Swinbank and G. Wilkinson, *The Food and Farm Policies of the European Community* (1983) at 26).

[19] [1970] E.C.R. 1161.

[20] This aspect of the procedure was expressly recognised by the Court in Case 25/70 *EVst für Getreide und Futtermittel* v. *Koster* [1970] E.C.R. 1161 and Case 31/74 *Galli* [1975] E.C.R. 47.

[21] [1973] E.C.R. 321.

inextricably intertwined.[22] Five ideal types of CAP legislative processes may schematically be discerned. The first two correspond closely to formal procedures: first, for legislation by the Council, acting on a Commission proposal and after consulting the Parliament; and second, for the Commission's exercise of its delegated power by the management committee procedure. The second, unlike the first, takes place largely in committee. Both require careful background preparation, especially by the Commission, but nevertheless are relatively straightforward.

Three other types are highly public and notorious. They may seem to be problematic variations on normal Council legislative procedure but on politically important matters are perhaps the norm. All involve the Commission as broker and the Council (or the European Council) as ultimate decision-maker. One, the third type, is the marathon session. It was a common legislative process in the 1960s, when the basic orientation and the main market organisations of the CAP were established. Agreement on the common organisation for cereals, for example, required lengthy negotiations between December 1961 and January 1962, including almost continuous sessions between January 4–14: "Forty-five separate meetings, 7 of them at night; a total of 137 hours of discussion, with 214 hours in subcommittee; 582,000 pages of documents; 3 heart attacks—the record is staggering."[23] The fourth type is "logrolling." It occurs most often during the annual agricultural price review, the principal EC policy-making session which runs from December through April or May. Issues which are related only indirectly, if at all, to the determination of agricul-

---

[22] For studies of CAP policy-making see: W.F. Averyt, Jr., *Agropolitics in the European Community* (1977); G.G. Rosenthal, *The Men Behind the Decisions* (1975) at 22–26, 79–100; Feld, "Two-Tier Policy Making in the EC: The Common Agricultural Policy" in L. Hurwitz (ed.), *Contemporary Perspectives on European Integration* (1980); Swinbank and Harris, "Price Fixing under the CAP—Proposition and Decision: The Example of the 1978/79 Price Review" (1978) *Food Policy* 256; Pearce, "The Common Agricultural Policy: An Accumulation of Special Interests" in H. Wallace, W. Wallace and C. Webb (eds.), *Policy Making in the European Community* (2nd ed., 1983), Delorme, "L'adoption du prix unique des céréales" in P. Gerbet and D. Pepy (eds.), *La décision dans les Communautes européennes* (1969); D. Pickard, G. Norris and N. Young, "Three Case Histories in Agriculture" unpublished (n.d.). A simulation of CAP policy making is M. Clarke, H. Wallace, C. Webb and J. May, *The European Community: An Exercise in Decision-Making* (n.d.: 1981?)

[23] According to the Commission's first President, W. Hallstein, *United Europe: Challenge and Opportunity* (1962) at 55. Between 1961–1966 agriculture was the main subject of five marathon sessions; see Alting von Gesau, "Les sessions marathon du Conseil des ministres" in P. Gerbet and D. Pepy (eds.) *La décision dans les Communautés européennes* (1969), at 106–107.

tural prices tend to be considered together as parts of a single negotiated package.[24]

A fifth, more protracted, more politically risky and therefore more rare type of legislative process is "stonewalling": the threatened or actual, partial or complete withdrawal of co-operation in Community affairs by a Member State until its demands on a disputed issue are met to its satisfaction. In contrast to "logrolling," "stonewalling" may be initiated unilaterally by a single party. It sometimes involves, at least initially, a single issue. Unlike either "logrolling" or the marathon session, this process may implicate not only the Commission and the Council but also the Court. For example, an Article 169 enforcement action may be brought by the Commission in order to persuade a recalcitrant State back into line. "Stonewalling" usually appears to be oriented primarily towards narrow, national ends, and it may therefore seem at first glance to be simply an obstructive tactic. Viewed in broader perspective, however, it can be recognised as a type of legislative process which in the EC is perhaps inevitable. For in the Community the responsibility for making highly sensitive political decisions lies primarily with the Member States; the ultimate sanction for a State's failure to fulfill its Treaty obligations is not the lawful use of force but diffuse political pressure (see Art. 171); and the survival of the Community depends, ultimately, on Member States' continued participation. In these circumstances, "stonewalling" is, short of withdrawal, the tactic of last resort; precisely because it is rarely used, it remains so important.

Whereas "logrolling" and the marathon session usually lead to legislation, "stonewalling" may result either in legislation or in a political compromise without legal force. In either case the parties' opposing positions may mean that any settlement is provisional and ultimately renegotiable. The political compromise without legal force, which is not however of less practical importance, is exemplified by the Luxembourg Accords, consecrating the settlement of the June 30, 1965, to January 28, 1966 "empty chair crisis." A recent example of "stonewalling" which led to legislation

[24] The 1981 price review, for example, concerned not only the level of agricultural prices but also possible curbs on excess production, notably by extending the principle of producer co-responsibility; implications of the Mediterranean enlargement; U.K. budget contribution; and restructuring of the EC budget; see Pearce, "The Common Agricultural Policy; An Accumulation of Special Interests" in H. Wallace, W. Wallace and C. Webb (eds.), *Policy Making in the European Community* (2nd ed., 1983). On the similar 1978–1979 review, see Harris and Swinbank, "Price Fixing under the CAP—Proposition and Decision: The Example of the 1978/79 Price Review" (1978) *Food Policy* 256.

was the 1978–1980 "lamb war" between Britain and France.[25] In Case 232/78 *Commission* v. *France*,[26] the Court held that France's market support arrangements for sheepmeat prevented imports of British lamb and were therefore incompatible with Articles 12 and 30. "If the Court of Justice finds that a Member State has failed to fulfill an obligation under this Treaty, the State shall be required to take the necessary measures to comply with the judgment of the Court of Justice" (Art. 171). France considered, however, that in order to protect its farmers, the national controls, despite slight alterations, could not be removed before an EC sheepmeat regime was established. For 8 months it refused to comply fully with the Court's decision, even though in January 1980 the Commission applied (unsuccessfully) to the Court for an interim order under Article 186.[27] Eventually the dispute was incorporated into the 1980–1981 annual price review, and in May 1980 agreement on prices was accompanied by compromise on a sheepmeat regime.[28] The legislation included elements of the previous French and British systems: Member States could choose between intervention buying and variable premiums as methods of price and income support.

The "lamb war" shows that "stonewalling" is not only an extreme tactic. If the term "stonewalling" is used to denote an ideal type or analytic device, it represents a process which in some circumstances may be relatively effective in achieving EC legislation. It, like other ideal types, is rarely found alone, and in reality (as in the "lamb war") it is usually combined with other types of legislative process. The "lamb war" also demonstrates that, to a great extent, compliance with the Court's rulings (as with much CAP legislation) is basically a question of interest.[29] But it is overly simplistic to consider the interests at stake merely as "national" interests. Superficially, the "lamb war" may appear to have concerned simply the United Kingdom and France. In fact, however, behind this facade, it involved farmers, exporters, importers, consumers and governments in the two countries; other Member States and non-EC states, such as New Zealand; and a wide range of EC institutions, including the Court, the Council,

---

[25] See Snyder, "The Political Economy of EEC Law: The Sheepmeat Regime," presented at the Annual Conference of the BSA Rural Economy and Society Study Group, Oxford, 1985.

[26] [1979] E.C.R. 2729.

[27] Joined Cases 24 and 97/80R *Commission* v. *France* [1980] E.C.R. 1319.

[28] Council Regulation 1837/80 (O.J. 1980 L.183/1).

[29] See also Editorial Comment, "The Mutton and Lamb Story: Isolated Incident or the Beginning of a New Era?" (1980) 17 C.M.L.Rev. 311.

the SCA, the Commission and the sheepmeat management committee. Nor did the agreement on legislation definitively end the controversy. The sheepmeat regime's provisions on an EC "clawback" of certain variable premiums provoked a further, continuing dispute between the United Kingdom and France.[30] Finally, in the *Kind* case[31] the Court recognised the 1980 sheepmeat regime as essentially temporary.

Legislative measures

Article 189 defines the legislative measures by which the CAP may be given legal force (see also Art. 43(2), para. 3). In order to carry out their tasks the Council and the Commission shall, in accordance with Treaty provisions, make regulations, issue directives, take decisions, make recommendations or deliver opinions. A regulation has general application and is binding in its entirety and directly applicable in all Member States. It is used when uniform legislation throughout the Community is required, as, for example, with most common market organisations.[32] A directive, which can be addressed only to Member States, is binding, as to the result to be achieved, upon the Member State to which it is addressed, but it leaves the choice of form and method to the national authorities. It has therefore been used, for example, in structural policy and the harmonisation of laws.[33] A decision is binding in its entirety upon those to whom it is addressed; these may be one or more Member States, firms or individuals.[34] Recommendations and opinions have no legally binding force.

These legislative acts, though entirely different in principle, are less clearly distinct in practice.[35] The formal designation given to an act by the Council or the Commission is not necessarily determinative. In addition, the distinction between acts as provided in the Treaty has in some instances been eroded. Directives under

---

[30] See Snyder, "The Political Economy of EEC Law: The Sheepmeat Regime," presented to the Annual Conference of the BSA Rural Economy and Society Study Group, Oxford, 1985.

[31] Case 106/81 *Julius Kind K.G.* v. *Council and Commission* [1982] E.C.R. 2885; noted Lenaerts (1983) 20 C.M.L.Rev. 825.

[32] *e.g.* Council Regulation 804/68 on the common organisation of the market in milk and milk products (J.O. 1968, L.148/13).

[33] *e.g.* Council Directive 72/159 on the modernisation of farms (J.O. 1972, L.96/1).

[34] *e.g.* Commission Decision 78/360/EEC (O.J. 1978, L.103/35) authorised certain Member States to sell butter at reduced prices in the form of concentrated butter in an effort to reduce the "butter mountain."

[35] The following paragraph is based on T. C. Hartley, *The Foundations of European Community Law* (1981) at 83–85.

Article 100, for example, are sometimes so detailed as to leave little discretion to Member States.[36] Moreover, the Article 189 list is not exhaustive. For example, during the annual price review the Council or the Commission sometimes uses a declaration—a statement of intent concerning a particular policy—which is simply inserted in the Council minutes.[37] In most instances, the precise legal status or extent of binding force of acts outside the Article 189 list is not in question. Yet, even though Council resolutions are usually considered to be broad political statements with no Treaty basis,[38] it has recently been urged that the Council is legally bound by the Community's Third Action Programme on the Environment.[39]

Law and policy

Though resulting from political processes and policy decisions, CAP law is not simply an expression or a translation of agricultural policy. Instead, three roles of CAP law in relation to policy can be distinguished. First, the relevant Treaty articles and secondary legislation establish a general legal framework and a set of formal procedures according to which, in principle and sometimes in practice, policy is made. Secondly, CAP legislation is a type of legal measure through which the economic instruments of agricultural policy are brought into operation.[40] Thirdly, administrative and judicial decisions on CAP disputes are mainly concerned, in theory, with resolving particular conflicts. On the basis of individual cases, they also, however, delineate, symbolise and thus create more general policy trends. Consequently, CAP law is in some respects discrete, and its distinctive legal form may, to some extent

---

[36] See Dashwood, "Hastening Slowly: The Community's Path Towards Harmonisation" in H. Wallace, W. Wallace and C. Webb (eds.), *Policy Making in the European Community* (2nd ed., 1983) at 181.

[37] S. Harris, A. Swinbank and G. Wilkinson, *The Food and Farm Policies of the European Community* (1983) at 24.

[38] See Case 22/70 *Commission* v. *Council* [1971] E.C.R. 263. See also Case 9/73 *Firma Carl Schlüter* v. *Hauptzollamt Lörrach* [1973] E.C.R. 1135; Case 10/73 *Rewe-Zentral AG* v. *Hauptzollamt Kehl* [1973] E.C.R. 1175.

[39] European Environmental Bureau, "Comments on the Proposed Reform of the Agricultural Structures Directive (COM(83)559 final)" presented at the Seminar on The Impact of Environmental Legislation upon Agriculture, Centre for European Agricultural Studies, Wye College, March 14–16, 1984. For the relevant Council Resolution, see O.J. 1983, C.46/1.

[40] See Daintith, "Legal Analysis of Economic Policy—I" (1982) 2 J.L.S. 191 at 195 on this distinction between economic instruments and legal measures.

independently of particular policy decisions, influence the direction of the CAP.

Constraints on Legislative Action

The Treaty

The enactment of legislation by EC authorities is subject, quite apart from political limitations, to constraints posed by the Treaty. First is the general notion that EC legislative powers are powers of attribution, restricted to matters expressly conferred on the Community by the Treaty. Today this view is open to serious question.[41] Secondly, Article 199, para. 1, requires that annual EC revenue and expenditure shall be in balance, though this does not provide any direct ceiling on CAP expenditure. Thirdly, the Treaty specifies voting requirements: a qualified majority since the end of the second stage under Article 43(2), though unanimous votes or compromise agreements have been the rule since the Luxembourg Accords; Council unanimity for harmonisation directives under Article 100; and the same for the use of the Article 235 residual powers clause. Fourthly, the Treaty requires consultation of the Parliament under Articles 43(2) and 235; such consultation has been held by the Court to be an essential procedural requirement.[42] Under Article 100, if implementation of a harmonisation directive would, in one or more Member States, involve amendment of legislation, the Economic and Social Committee must be consulted. Fifthly, the common market organisations established as part of the CAP are limited to pursuit of the Article 39 objectives[43] and must not discriminate against producers or consumers within the Community (Art. 40(3), subpara. 2: see also Chap. 4).

---

[41] See Arts. 100 and 235; see also T.C. Hartley, *The Foundations of European Community Law* (1981) at 87–96; Sasse and Yourow, "The Growth of Legislative Power of the European Communities" in T. Sandalow and E. Stein (eds.), *Courts and Free Markets* (1982), Vol. 1.

[42] Case 138/79 *Roquette Frères* v. *Council* [1980] E.C.R. 3333; Case 139/79 *Maizena GmbH* v. *Council* [1980] E.C.R. 3393.

[43] "[T]he statement of the objectives contained in Article 39, together with the rules in the second subparagraph of Article 40(3), supplies both positive and negative criteria by which the legality of the measures adopted in this matter may be appraised": Case 114/76 *Bela-Mühle Josef Bergmann KG* v. *Grows-Farm GmbH and Co. KG* [1977] E.C.R. 1211; Case 116/76 *Granaria BV* v. *Hoofdproduktschap voor Akkerbouwprodukten* [1977] E.C.R. 1247 at 1265; Joined Cases 119 and 120/76 *Ölmühle Hamburg AG* v. *Hauptzollamt Hamburg Waltershof* and *Firma Kurt A. Becher* v. *Hauptzollamt Bremen-Nord* [1977] E.C.R. 1269 at 1286.

European Court of Justice

Of equal importance perhaps, especially in a Community in
which the democratic, parliamentary element remains extremely
weak, is the European Court of Justice, composed of 11 judges
assisted by 5 advocates general. The Court plays a crucial role in
determining the practical meaning of CAP legislation and in defining the scope of institutional discretion.[44] The Court's mandate is
to ensure that in the interpretation and application of the Treaty
the law is observed (Art. 164).[45] In addition to its Article 177 preliminary rulings on the interpretation and validity of acts, the
Court has ruled on the legality of numerous CAP measures in
actions to annul (Art. 173), actions for failure to act (Art. 175) and
challenges by a plea of illegality (Art. 184). In actions for annulment and indirect challenges, the grounds of judicial review are
lack of competence, infringement of an essential procedural
requirement, or infringement of the Treaty or of any rule of law
relating to its application and misuse of power (Art. 173). Only the
last two apply in the event of a failure to act.[46]

Judicial decisions to date do not cover all aspects of EC agricul-

---

[44] See generally H. Schermers, *Judicial Protection in the European Communities*
(2nd ed., 1979); G. Bebr, *Development of Judicial Control of the European
Communities* (1981); T.C. Hartley, *The Foundations of European Community
Law* (1981). Concerning agriculture in particular, see G. Druesne, *La politique
agricole commune devant la Cour de justice des Communautés européennes
1958–1978* (1980); Vajda, "Some Aspects of Judicial Review within the Common Agricultural Policy" (1979) 4 E.L.Rev. 244, 341.

[45] See generally L. Neville Brown and F.G. Jacobs, *The Court of Justice of the
European Communities* (2nd ed., 1983); J. Usher, *European Court Practice*
(1983). National courts also interpret and apply Community law: see *e.g.* Bebr,
"How Supreme is Community Law in the National Courts?" (1974) 11
C.M.L.Rev. 3; Bebr, "A Critical Review of Recent Case Law of the National
Courts" (1974) 11 C.M.L.Rev. 408; Forman and Stevens, "The Attitude of
British Courts to Community Law—The First Three Years" (1976) 13
C.M.L.Rev. 388; Maestripieri, "The Application of Community Law in Italy in
1972" (1973) 10 C.M.L.Rev. 340; Maestripieri, "The Application of Community
Law in Italy in 1973" (1975) 12 C.M.L.Rev. 431; Maestripieri, "The Application
of Community Law in Italy in 1974" (1976) 13 C.M.L.Rev. 524; Maestripieri,
"The Application of Community Law in Italy in 1975" (1976) 13 C.M.L.Rev.
530; Mastellone, "The Judicial Application of Community Law in Italy,
1976–1980" (1982) 19 C.M.L.Rev. 153; Simon, "Enforcement by the French
Courts of European Community Law" (1974) 90 L.Q.R. 467; Simon, "Enforcement by French Courts of European Community Law" (1976) 92 L.Q.R. 85.

[46] See T.C. Hartley, *The Foundations of European Community Law* (1981), at
453–456; G. Bebr, *Development of Judicial Control of the European Communities* (1981), at 117.

Constraints on Legislative Action 55

tural policy, and only a small minority of all CAP disputes are ever brought to court. Nevertheless, Articles 38–47 have given rise to more litigation than any other aspect of Community law.[47] The majority of cases have been brought not by farmers but by traders,[48] largely because most CAP policies operate through food manufacturers and distributors rather than through farmers directly.[49] Most cases, therefore, concern imports or exports.[50]

Both on preliminary rulings and on judicial review, the policy of the Court has been to increase the scope and effectiveness of Community law, to strengthen the Community's supranational elements and to enlarge the powers of EC institutions.[51] Its main ideological reference point, the free market principle, has therefore served frequently to legitimate controls on action by the Member States; more occasionally, it has limited the exercise of legislative discretion by the Council or the Commission.[52] The

---

[47] Between 1953 and 1981, 212 of a total 941 direct actions and 368 of a total 949 requests for a preliminary ruling concerned Arts. 38–47 (L. Neville Brown and F.G. Jacobs, *The Court of Justice of the European Communities* (2nd ed., 1983), at 186, 189–190). A similar earlier survey is given in R. Lecourt, *L'Europe des Juges* (1976) at 115–119. See also Commission of the European Communities, "First Annual Report to the European Parliament on Commission Monitoring of the Application of Community Law, 1983," COM(84)181 final (1984). See also Miller, "The Role of the Court of Justice in the Development of Agricultural Policy in the European Communities" (1975) 8 *Vanderbilt Journal of Transnational Law* 745.

[48] Among the important exceptions to this general rule are Case 93/71 *Orsolina Leonesio* v. *Ministry of Agriculture and Forestry of the Italian Republic* [1972] E.C.R. 287; Case 138/78 *Hans-Markus Stölting* v. *Hauptzollamt Hamburg-Jonas* [1979] E.C.R. 713; Case 44/79 *Liselotte Hauer* v. *Land Rheinland-Pfalz* [1979] E.C.R. 3727; Case 152/79 *Kevin Lee* v. *Ministry for Agriculture* [1980] E.C.R. 1495.

[49] S. Harris, A. Swinbank and G. Wilkinson, *The Food and Farm Policies of the European Community* (1983) at 235.

[50] According to a recent classification by subject of cases involving EC law brought before the European Court or national courts between 1953–1983, imports accounted for 148 cases and exports for 111 cases; the next largest category, except for corn (64 cases), concerned prices (41 cases) (calculated from N. March Hunnings, *Gazeteer of European Law* (1983), Vol. 2, at 472–478; note that the subject headings are not mutually exclusive).

[51] T. C. Hartley, *The Foundations of European Community Law* (1981) at 59.

[52] See, respectively: Case 83/78 *Pigs Marketing Board* v. *Raymond Redmond* [1978] E.C.R. 2347; Joined Cases 103 and 145/77 *Royal Scholten Honig (Holdings) Ltd.* v. *Intervention Board for Agricultural Produce*; *Tunnel Refineries Ltd.* v. *Intervention Board for Agricultural Produce* [1978] E.C.R. 2037.

Court has consistently held that, since the implementation of the CAP involves the evaluation of a complex economic situation, the discretion of the Council embraces both the nature and scope of the measures to be taken and, to some extent, the finding of the facts on which to base legislation. Accordingly, the Court, in reviewing the exercise of discretion, must confine itself to examining whether it contains a manifest error, constitutes a misuse of power or clearly exceeds the bounds of discretion.[53] A similarly wide discretion is enjoyed by the Commission and the management committees, and the Court is not entitled to substitute its own evaluation of the facts for that of the competent authority.[54] In addition, an appraisal by the Court of the compatibility of CAP legislation with the Treaty provisions cannot involve, for example, a consideration of the Community's entire policy in a given sector, such as the level of intervention prices for milk.[55]

General principles of law

In reviewing the exercise of Council and Commission discretion, the Court has extensively used as criteria certain "general principles of law." These principles, according to the Court's President,[56] include, first, general interpretative principles with little, if any, binding legal force. They refer to the institutional, economic or social foundations of the Community, such as Member States' solidarity, Community preference and unity of the market. Secondly, the general principles of law include binding though unwritten rules which the EC institutions are in theory bound to observe. They comprise (a) principles often viewed as common to all democratic legal systems, such as respect of fundamental rights and non-discrimination; (b) principles of sound administration, such as the balancing of interests, proportionality and protection

---

[53] See, *e.g.* Case 138/79 *S.A. Roquette Frères* v. *Council* [1980] E.C.R. 3333 at 3358–3359.

[54] See, *e.g.* Case 78/74 *Deuka, Deutsche Kraftfutter GmbH, B.J. Stolp* v. *EVst für Getreide und Futtermittel* [1975] E.C.R. 421 at 432; Case 55/75 *Balkan-Import Export GmbH* v. *Hauptzollamt Berlin-Packhof* [1976] E.C.R. 19.

[55] *Per* Advocate General Capotorti in Case 114/76 *Bela-Mühle Josef Bergmann KG* v. *Grows-Farm GmbH and Co. KG* [1977] E.C.R. 1211 at 1227.

[56] Mertens de Wilmars, "The Case-Law of the Court of Justice in Relation to the Review of the Legality of Economic Policy in Mixed-Economy Systems" (1982) 1 L.I.E.I. 1 at 8–9.

of legitimate expectations; and (c) the notion of legal certainty, including respect of vested rights and the non-retroactivity of legislation.

The principles of non-discrimination (equal treatment) and proportionality have been especially important constraints on EC legislative discretion. They may be defined and distinguished as follows:

> "non-discrimination is concerned with the relationship between various groups of persons and takes the form of equality of treatment by bodies vested with public authority, whereas the principle of proportionality means that the burdens imposed on the persons concerned must not exceed the steps required in order to meet the public interest involved."[57]

Non-discrimination is applied specifically to the CAP by Article 40(3).[58] It was interpreted by Advocate General Capotorti in *Ruckdeschel* as being

> "in addition to contributing to the establishment of healthy conditions of competition, in so far as this is compatible with requirements inherent in the pursuit through the intervention by the authorities on the market of the objectives in Article 39, . . . mainly intended to ensure equality of treatment for individuals affected by the exercise of the Community's power to intervene in the organization of agriculture."[59]

Accordingly, in his view, discrimination consists, first, of the dissimilar treatment of comparable situations. Secondly, EC measures which provoke disturbances in the competitive capacity of undertakings are discriminatory unless otherwise justified. Thirdly, though unjustified difference of treatment constitutes discrimination, differentiation is permissible if based on objective cri-

---

[57] *Per* Advocate General Capotorti in Case 114/76 *Bela-Mühle Josef Bergmann KG v. Grows-Farm GmbH and Co. KG* [1977] E.C.R. 1222 at 1232.
[58] See, *e.g.* Joined Cases 9 and 11/71 *Compagnie d'Approvisionnement, de Transport et de Crédit S.A. and Grands Moulins de Paris S.A. v. Commission* [1972] E.C.R. 391.
[59] Joined Cases 117/76 and 16/77 *Albert Ruckdeschel and Co. and Hansa-Lagerhaus Ströh and Co. v. Hauptzollamt Hamburg-St. Annen; Diamalt A.G. v. Hauptzollamt Itzehoe* [1977] E.C.R. 1753 at 1778.

teria.[60] Derogation from equal treatment may be associated with
the building up of a common market organisation, but aids for this
purpose are, in principle, distinguishable from permanent subsidies to help inefficient producers.[61]

The principle of equal treatment was invoked, for example, in
the "isoglucose" cases. Isoglucose is a high fructose corn syrup
originally developed in the United States. Its production in Europe, mainly from imported maize, resulted from a search for new
products by a starch industry with excess capacity, and, after high
prices followed the 1973–1974 sugar shortage, it first appeared on
EC markets in 1976. Isoglucose cannot yet be crystallised, so com-
petes with sugar only in liquid form.[62] This market is lucrative,
however, and new entrants were strongly resisted by existing processors and producers. In COPA, the latter were led by the Confé-
dération Interprofessionnel des Bettéraviers Européens (CIBE),
the Sugar Beet Producers Trade Association, which is "generally
reckoned to be the most powerful pressure group in European agriculture."[63] Following intense political activity, the Council
enacted regulations, which, *inter alia*, withdrew as from 1977–1978

[60] *Ibid.* This case was one of several concerning the withdrawal of the production
refund on maize used for the manufacture of gritz, a meal used in brewing beer,
and quellmehl, used to keep dough damp during breadmaking. The others
include: Joined Cases 124/76 and 20/77 *S.A. Moulins et Huileries du Pont-à-
Mousson* v. *Office national interprofessionnel des céréales* [1977] E.C.R. 1795;
Joined Cases 241, 242 and 245–250/78 *DGV-Deutsche Getreideverwertung und
Rheinische Kraftfutterwerke GmbH* v. *Council and Commission* [1979] E.C.R.
3017; Joined Cases 64 and 113/76, 167 and 239/78, 27, 28 and 45/79 *P. Dumortier
Frères S.A.* v. *Commission* [1979] E.C.R. 3091; Case 238/78 *Ireks-Arkady* v.
Council and Commission [1979] E.C.R. 2955; Joined Cases 261 and 262/78 *Inter-
quel Stärke-Chemie* v. *Council and Commission* [1979] E.C.R. 3045; Case 256/81
Pauls Agriculture Ltd. v. *Council and Commission* [1983] E.C.R. 1707. For comments, see Wyatt (1978) 3 E.L.Rev. 329; Rudden and Bishop, "Gritz and Quellmehl: Pass it On" (1981) 6 E.L.Rev. 243.
[61] Vajda, "Some Aspects of Judicial Review within the Common Agricultural
Policy—Part II" (1979) 4 E.L.Rev. 341 at 341–344, discussing: Case 153/73
Holtz and Willemsen v. *Council* [1974] E.C.R. 675; Joined Cases 63–69/72 *Werhahn* v. *Council* [1973] E.C.R. 1229; Joined Cases 56–60/74 *Kampffmeyer* v.
Council and Commission [1976] E.C.R. 711.
[62] On the development of isoglucose, see Food and Agriculture Organisation,
Commodity Review and Outlook 1976/1977 (1977). The world's largest purchaser of sugar, Coca-Cola, was recently reported to have authorised the use in
automatic distributors of 75–100 per cent. isoglucose-based sweetener, though
bottled and canned beverages still contain 25 per cent. sugar (see (1984) 28 *La
Lettre de Solagral* at 3). See also Morris "How quotas are saving beet farmers
from ruin" *The Times* (London), June 3, 1982 at 23.
[63] D. Pickard, G. Norris and N. Young, "Three Case Histories in Agriculture"
unpublished (n.d.) at 22. This report (at 8–39) discusses the political and economic context of the isoglucose cases.

the production refund on maize used ultimately for isoglucose, removed the new product from the common market organisation for sugar, and established for isoglucose a separate market regime, including a levy on production.[64] These regulations provoked a rash of judicial proceedings.[65] In Joined Cases 103 and 145/77 *Royal Scholten Honig and Tunnel Refineries* v. *IBAP*,[66] an Article 177 reference, the Court held the production levy to be discriminatory on the ground that, whereas the analogous levy on sugar affected only part of total production, the isoglucose levy applied to the total amount produced. Isoglucose manufacturers did not benefit from a guaranteed marketing scheme similar to that for sugar, and therefore could not reduce the levied proportion by restricting production. Nor, according to the Court, was this difference objectively justified. The mere fact that a new product in a regulated market might cause difficulties, including an increase in surplus production, was not in itself sufficient to justify differential treatment.[67]

The Court has also reviewed CAP legislation by reference to other general principles, such as proportionality, respect for fundamental rights,[68] legitimate expectations[69] and legal cer-

---

[64] Council Reg. 1862/76 (O.J. 1976, L.206/3); Council Reg. 1110/77 (O.J. 1977, L.134/1); Council Reg. 1111/77 (O.J. 1977, L.134/4).

[65] Case 101/76 *Koninklijke Scholten-Honig N.V.* v. *Council and Commission* [1977] E.C.R. 797; Case 125/77 *Koninklijke Scholten-Honig N.V. and de Verenigde Zetmeelbedrijven "De Bijenkorf" B.V.* v. *Hoofdproduktschap voor Akkerbouwprodukten* [1978] E.C.R. 1991; Joined Cases 103 and 145/77 *Royal Scholten-Honig (Holdings) Ltd.* v. *Intervention Board for Agricultural Produce*; *Tunnel Refineries Ltd.* v. *Intervention Board for Agricultural Produce* [1978] E.C.R. 2037, noted Usher [1979] 4 E.L.Rev. 42; Joined Cases 116 and 124/77 *G.R. Amylum N.V. and Tunnel Refineries Ltd.* v. *Council and Commission* [1979] E.C.R. 3497; Case 143/77 *Koninklijke Scholten Honig N.V.* v. *Council and Commission* [1979] E.C.R. 3583.

[66] [1978] E.C.R. 2037.

[67] Reg. 1117/77 was replaced by Reg. 1293/79 imposing on isoglucose a system of production quotas similar to those applicable to sugar. These quotas were challenged, successfully (but on the ground of failure to consult Parliament), in Case 138/79 *Roquette Frères* v. *Council* [1980] E.C.R. 3333 and Case 139/79 *Maizena GmbH* v. *Council* [1980] E.C.R. 3393.

[68] e.g. Case 44/79 *Liselotte Hauer* v. *Land Rheinland-Pfalz* [1979] E.C.R. 3727.

[69] Case 74/74 *Comptoir National Technique Agricole (CNTA) S.A.* v. *Commission* [1975] E.C.R. 533.

tainty.[70] In several leading cases, for example, it held Council legislation which aimed to reduce the "skimmed milk powder mountain" to be incompatible with the principles of non-discrimination and proportionality.[71] The recently introduced milk production quotas are also likely to be challenged on these grounds. Major cases concerning legislation to reduce surplus production are discussed in Chapter 6.

Implementation

General

The implementation of the CAP, even excepting structural policy (see Chap. 7), rests largely with the Member States. EC institutions lay down general principles and basic rules; they cannot delegate responsibility for establishing basic rules, which, though adopted by Member States under Commission delegation, would not be subject to legal control by the Council.[72] Member States are entitled to adopt necessary implementing measures, though in the absence of EC provisions to the contrary they may not reduce the scope or modify the application of Community provisions.[73] If the Council has not yet acted, Member States may in some instances choose appropriate measures, as, for example, in

[70] In Case 4/79 *Societe Coopérative "Providence Agricole de la Champagne"* v. *Office national interprofessionnel des céréales* (*ONIC*) [1980] E.C.R. 2823; Case 109/79 *Sàrl Maïseries de Beauce* v. *Office national interprofessionnel des Céréales* (*ONIC*) [1980] E.C.R. 2883 and Case 145/79 *S.A. Roquette Frères* v. *French State—Customs Administration* [1980] E.C.R. 2917, noted Usher (1981) 6 E.L.Rev. 116, the Court used the device of prospective overruling to uphold the "effects" of a void regulation in the interest of legal certainty; see also Neville Brown, "Agrimonetary Byzantinism and Prospective Overruling" (1981) 18 C.M.L.Rev. 509.
[71] Case 114/76 *Bela-Mühle Josef Bergmann KG* v. *Grows-Farm GmbH and Co. KG* [1977] E.C.R. 1211; Case 116/76 *Granaria BV* v. *Hoofdproduktschap voor Akkerbouwprodukten* [1977] E.C.R. 1247; Joined Cases 119 and 120/76 *Olmühle Hamburg AG* v. *Hauptzollamt Hamburg Waltershof* and *Firma Kurt A. Becher* v. *Hauptzollamt Bremen-Nord* [1977] E.C.R. 1269. See also Neri, "Le principe de proportionalité dans la jurisprudence de la Cour relative au droit communautaire agricole" (1981) 4 R.T.D.E. 652; Schmitthoff, "The Doctrines of Proportionality and Non-Discrimination" (1977) 2 E.L.Rev. 329.
[72] Case 23/75 *Rey Soda* v. *Cassa Conguaglio Zucchero* [1975] E.C.R. 1279.
[73] Case 60/75 *Carmine Antonio Russo* v. *Azienda di Stato per gli Interventi sul Mercato Agricolo* (*AIMA*) [1976] E.C.R. 45; Case 18/72 *N.V. Granaria Graaninkoopmaatschappij* v. *Produktschap voor Veevoeder* [1972] E.C.R. 1163; Case 34/70 *Syndicat national du Commerce extérieur des céréales* v. *Office national interprofessionnel des céréales and Minister for Agriculture* [1970] E.C.R. 1233; Case 94/79 *Criminal Proceedings against Pieter Vriend* [1980] E.C.R. 327.

establishing penalties for violation of EC regulations.[74] In applying CAP rules to particular cases, however, they must in principle avoid jeopardising the aims of the common market. They are therefore required, for example, to select measures appropriate for the purpose,[75] respect the Community character of EC acts[76] and respect any time limits established by the Community.[77]

Nevertheless, with regard to agricultural policy the Member States retain substantial authority. The precise extent to which the Community has legally pre-empted the powers of Member States in this field is not entirely clear.[78] For example, although Member States cannot interfere, by unilateral measures, with the formation of prices at the production and wholesale stages, at least for products covered by a common market organisation, they retain the power to intervene at the retail and consumer price stages, provided that the aims, operation and particularly the price system of the common organisation are not affected.[79] In addition, the Court has held that a temporary national duty intended to be borne by agricultural producers as part of a national incomes policy, but applied in the form of an indirect tax on the value of certain agricultural products subject to a common organisation, was not in principle incompatible with the Treaty: the duty in question applied when the products were delivered for processing, storage or export, and it was payable by the processor, storage undertaking or exporter, which was entitled to recover the amount from the producers.[80] More generally, the Member States have

[74] Case 50/76 *Amsterdam Bulb B.V.* v. *Produktschap voor Siergewassen* [1977] E.C.R. 137.

[75] Case 61/72 *Mij PPW Internationaal N.V.* v. *Hoofproduktschap voor Akkerbouwprodukten* [1973] E.C.R. 301.

[76] Case 34/70 *Syndicat national du Commerce extérieur des céréales* v. *Office national interprofessionnel des céréales and Minister for Agriculture* [1970] E.C.R. 1233.

[77] Case 33/69 *Commission* v. *Italy* [1970] E.C.R. 93.

[78] See Blumental, "Implementing the Common Agricultural Policy: Aspects of the Limitations on the Powers of the Member States" (1984) 35 *N.I.L.Q.* 28. For an earlier view, see Olmi, "The Role of Community and National Institutions in the Implementation of the Common Agricultural Policy" in M. Hodges (ed.), *European Integration* (1972).

[79] See, *e.g.* Joined Cases 16–20/79 *Openbaar Ministerie* v. *Joseph Danis* [1979] E.C.R. 3327; Joined Cases 95–96/79 *Procureur du Roi* v. *Charles Kefer and Louis Delmelle* [1980] E.C.R. 103. See also Berardis, "The Common Organization of Agricultural Markets and National Price Regulations" (1980) 17 C.M.L.Rev. 539.

[80] Joined Cases 36 and 71/80 *Irish Creamery Milk Suppliers Association* v. *Government of Ireland*; *Martin Doyle* v. *An Taoiseach* [1981] E.C.R. 735. See also Case 297/82 *De Samvirkende Danske Landbotoreninger* v. *Ministry of Fiscal Affairs* [1983] E.C.R. 3299.

gained in power relative to EC institutions, particularly the Commission, during the past decade; numerous areas of agricultural policy lie outside EC control. In fact, the CAP has been described, rightly, as being in substance "a co-ordination of national policies."[81]

Market intervention

An especially important aspect of Member States' role is market intervention. Its current legal basis is Council Regulation 729/70,[82] Article 4 of which provides that Member States shall designate the authorities and bodies which they shall empower to effect expenditure on export refunds and intervention purchases. National governments are required to inform the Commission of the name, statutes and administrative and accounting conditions of these authorities and, subsequently, to send the Commission an annual report and summary of accounts. Within this common legal framework, the intervention agencies vary substantially from country to country.[83] Major differences concern previous history and administrative traditions, whether intervention functions are entrusted to a single agency or several different bodies, financial competence, staffing and the extent to which they are interprofessionnel, that is, draw on producers, processors and traders.[84] By the time the CAP was established, the German Einfuhr- und Vorratstellen (EVst; Import and Storage Boards), which were established about 1950 but resembled earlier agencies,

> "already had considerable experience in administering regulations of the type introduced into the EEC after 1962. Indeed, the previous national support arrangements for cereals, livestock and meat resembled more closely the Community sys-

---

[81] J. Pearce, *The Common Agricultural Policy* (1981) at 18. See also Britton, "National Policies within the CAP" (1976) *Food Policy* 405; Harrison, "Land Policies in the Member States of the European Community" (1982) 11 *Agricultural Administration* 159; Feld, "Two-Tier Policy Making in the EC: The Common Agricultural Policy" in L. Hurwitz (ed.), *Attitudes, Nongovernmental Behaviour, and Collective Decision Making* (1980).

[82] J.O. 1970, L.94/13.

[83] See R. Fennell, *The Common Agricultural Policy of the European Community* (1979) at 55–59; on the period up to 1972, see also M. Butterwick and E. Neville-Rolfe, *Agricultural Marketing and the EEC* (1972) at 37–53, *passim*.

[84] M. Butterwick and E. Neville-Rolfe, *Agricultural Marketing and the EEC* (1972) at 49.

tem than those of any other member country, particularly in their use of intervention buying and storage and eventual resale of seasonal surpluses."[85]

French intervention agencies, which handle intervention buying and export refunds, are organised by commodity. The archetype is the agency for cereals, ONIC (Office National Interprofessionnel des Céréales). Its central council is composed of representatives of producers, processors, traders and consumers as well as government-appointed members. Since its foundation in 1936 ONIC has been closely associated with the Association Générale des Producteurs de Blé (AGPB), to the extent that ONIC-licenced buyers deducted from their payment to producers a levy for ONIC's administrative costs and a "voluntary" membership fee for AGPB; one observer discerned "a network of the big grain producers and bureaucrats using a variety of means—interest group, stocking board, EC Consultative Committee, COPA—to obtain the desired end."[86] In Denmark, Ireland and Luxembourg the Ministry of Agriculture handles both intervention measures and export subsidies.

In the United Kingdom, no analogous agency existed at the time of Accession. Accordingly, the European Communities Act 1972, s.6, provided for the establishment of the Intervention Board for Agricultural Produce (IBAP) in charge of a government department. It was to be appointed by and responsible to the Minister of Agriculture, Fisheries and Food and the Secretaries of State concerned with agriculture in Scotland, Wales and Northern Ireland. A body corporate, the Board was to be charged, subject to the discretion and control of the Ministers, with such functions as they may from time to time determine in connection with the carrying out of the obligations of the United Kingdom under the CAP. The Intervention Board for Agricultural Produce Order 1972[87] provided for the members, committees and staff of the Board, its proceedings and the execution and proof of documents. The Common Agricultural Policy (Agricultural Produce) (Protection of Community Arrangements) (No. 2) Order 1973[88] and the Common Agricultural Policy (Protection of Community Arrangements)

[85] *Ibid.* at 42.
[86] W.F. Averyt, Jr., *Agropolitics in the European Community* (1977) at 53.
[87] S.I. 1972 No. 1578.
[88] S.I. 1973 No. 288.

Regulations 1973[89] provided for the keeping of records and other arrangements, including penalties, regarding funds paid out by the Board.

IBAP began operation on February 1, 1973. It is responsible for licensing imports and exports; paying export subsidies and collecting export levies (import levies are collected by HM Customs and Excise); making intervention purchases, paying production refunds and making other payments concerning market support; and mobilising food aid, both under EC obligations and as the agent of the Foreign and Commonwealth Office Overseas Development Administration for United Kingdom obligations. The Intervention Funds (Delegation) Regulations 1972[90] provide for the Home Grown Cereals Authority (HGCA) and the Meat and Livestock Commission (MLC) to act as executive agents on behalf of the Board in their respective spheres, with regard to support buying, storage and selling and providing information about prices under the intervention system. In one case, however, assurances by the MLC concerning monetary compensatory amounts (see Chap. 5) were deemed not to be a sufficient basis for "legitimate expectations"; the MLC was described by the Advocate General as "a national body in the sector (which was not acting on behalf of the Community)" and by the Court as "a private organization."[91] The Intervention Functions (Delegation) (Milk) Regulations 1982[92] empower the Milk Marketing Boards to act for IBAP by carrying out functions which the Board may delegate to them with regard to milk. In 1982 IBAP accounted for a gross expenditure of £1225.9 million, including £298 million borne by the Exchequer and £929.9 million borne by the Community.[93]

IBAP, like other intervention agencies, is legally obliged to pur-

[89] S.I. 1973 No. 424.
[90] S.I. 1972, No. 1679.
[91] Case 146/77 *British Beef Company Ltd.* v. *Intervention Board for Agricultural Produce* [1978] E.C.R. 1347 at 1363, 1355.
[92] S.I. 1982 No. 1502.
[93] Intervention Board for Agricultural Produce, *Report for the Calendar Year 1982* (Cmnd. 8963) (1983) at 19. The Board also received £76.4 million from sale of intervention stocks, which was credited to the Exchequer, and collected levies of £97.4 million, of which £56.6 million was credited to EAGGF and £40.9 million to the Exchequer as part of the U.K. EC "Own Resources" collections (id.). For further information see IBAP's annual reports from 1973 to the present and House of Commons Select Committee on European Legislation, etc., Minutes of Evidence, Thursday, July 3, 1980, "Intervention Board for Agricultural Produce and Minister of Agriculture, Fisheries and Food" (HC 255-iv) (1980). For a complete list of applicable subordinate legislation, see IBAP's annual report for 1982, Annex III at 51. IBAP also publishes a wide variety of information leaflets regarding production subsidies, market support and import and export trade.

chase goods in particular circumstances; such goods are then stored and eventually offered for sale on the internal market or exported outside the Community. Under the common market organisation in cereals, for example "[t]hroughout the marketing year the intervention agencies designated by Member States shall be obliged to buy in cereals . . . which are offered to them and have been harvested in the Community, provided that the offers comply with conditions, in particular in respect of quality and quantity . . . "[94] The European Court has consistently held that access to intervention must be open to all concerned in the functioning of particular product markets. For example, a Member State may not attach supplementary conditions for taking over products which restrict the definition of a "holder" or its entitlement to avail itself of the intervention machinery.[95] Similarly, in interpreting expressions such as "offer" and "when the offer is made," intervention agencies are expected to follow practices which so far as possible are uniform between countries.[96]

The intervention system has been criticised on several grounds (regarding specific products, see Chap. 4). First, the legal obligation to purchase has, in some instances, stimulated firms to produce partly or solely for intervention.[97] Secondly, price support usually operates with respect to partly transformed products. Accordingly, though some offers of products for sale into intervention are received from farmers, most come from traders or first-stage processors. Investment in processing plants has therefore been encouraged, as, for example, in the dairy sector to take advantage of intervention support for skimmed milk powder.[98] Thirdly, despite legal principles specifying uniform practices, it is likely that important differences exist between countries. It is fre-

---

[94] Reg. 2727/75 on the common organisation of the market in cereals, Art. 7(1) (O.J. 1975, L.281/1). A more detailed discussion of the legal aspects of intervention arrangements for cereals may be found in D. Wyatt and A. Dashwood, *The Substantive Law of the EEC* (1980), at 220–238.

[95] Case 34/70 *Syndicat national du Commerce extérieur des céréales* v. *Office national interprofessionnel des céréales and Minister for Agriculture* [1970] E.C.R. 1233.

[96] Case 49/71 *Hagen OHG* v. *EVst für Getreide und Futtermittel* [1972] E.C.R. 23.

[97] van Dijk and Machel, "Future Constraints to the Food Industries Arising from Policy Developments in the Animal Production Sector in Europe" in Organisation for Economic Co-operation and Development, OECD, *Food Industries in the 1980s* (1983) at 179; for the reference to the authors' original symposium paper I am indebted to S. Harris, A. Swinbank and G. Wilkinson, *The Food and Farm Policies of the European Community* (1983) at 238.

[98] S. Harris, A. Swinbank and G. Wilkinson, *The Food and Farm Policies of the European Community* (1983) at 238.

quently alleged, for example, that farmers and processors are treated more favourably in countries with an *interprofessionnel* system than in those in which, like the United Kingdom, the intervention agency is in fact part of a civil service.[99]

The funds for market intervention are by Regulation 729/70 to be made available by the Commission, but any necessary payments are to be made by the Member States.[1] Payments and receipts by an intervention agency on behalf of the Community are governed by the law of the Member State concerned.[2] Member States are required by Regulation 729/70 to take, in accordance with national provisions laid down by law, regulation or administrative action, measures necessary to satisfy themselves that transactions, including intervention buying and export subsidies, financed by the Community through EAGGF are actually carried out and executed correctly; to prevent and deal with irregularities; and to recover sums lost as a result of irregularities or negligence. Any disputes concerning import levies or export subsidies, for example, fall to be resolved by the national courts, following national legal procedures and according to Community law, or, if there is no relevant provision of EC law, according to national law.[3] In the absence of total recovery of sums due, the financial consequences of irregularities or negligence are borne by the Community, with the exception of the consequences of irregularities or negligence attributable to the administrative authorities or other bodies of the Member States. The final arbiter in such cases is the European Court of Justice.[4]

---

[99] See Pearce, "Talking Point" (1982) *Farmers Weekly* (November 5) at 38; House of Lords Select Committee on the European Communities, *State Aids to Agriculture* (1981) at 91–92.

[1] Art. 4 (J.O. 1970, L.94/13).

[2] Council Decision of 21.4.70, Art. 6 (J.O. 1970, L.94/13); Council Reg. 2/71, Art. 1 (J.O. 1971, L.3/1).

[3] See Case 96/71 *R. & V. Haegeman* v. *Commission* [1972] E.C.R. 1005; Case 26/74 *S.A. Roquette Frères* v. *Commission* [1976] E.C.R. 677; Case 265/78 *H. Ferwerda B.V.* v. *Produktschap voor Vee en Vlees* [1980] E.C.R. 617; Case 130/79 *Express Dairy Foods Ltd.* v. *Intervention Board for Agricultural Produce* [1980] E.C.R. 1887.

[4] See Case 11/76 *Netherlands* v. *Commission* [1979] E.C.R. 245; Joined Cases 15 and 16/76 *France* v. *Commission* [1979] E.C.R. 321; and Case 18/76 *Germany* v. *Commission* [1979] E.C.R. 343; noted Usher (1980) 5 E.L.Rev. 152.

Control and liability

The implementation of CAP law by the Member States is subject to control by the Commission, other Member States and individuals.[5] The Commission, in fulfilling its functions under Article 155, may refer matters concerning state aids to the European Court under Article 93(2) or initiate infringement proceedings under Article 169. It may initially obtain information by personal contacts, newspaper accounts, national legislative or judicial reports, Article 177 references or other means. Decisions are then taken according to periodic reviews. Based on reports prepared by Commission services, these reviews cover (a) the implementation of directives, now computerised and numbering about 700; (b) complaints, especially from private traders; (c) likely infringements, on which the Commission may already have a view; and (d) known infringements, concerning which the Commission has already sent the Member State an Article 169 letter asking for observations. However, the Commission, with six lawyers currently dealing with infringements, lacks the staff to verify the laws of all Member States, still less to ensure that enacted legislation is actually applied and enforced. Most cases are settled, if at all, by administrative procedures and compromise rather than by judicial proceedings (see Table 3.1).[6] Such procedures are time-consuming and not necessarily effective. The average time required for a judicial proceeding from the time of filing the complaint to Court judgment is currently seven to eight months. In addition, as the "lamb war" showed, the Court's judgment is not always accepted by the Member States.[7]

---

[5] For material used in this section I am indebted to Commission and Council staff and to G. zur Hausen, "Judicial Control over the Acts of Member States: An Evaluation" presented at the UACES conference on the European Court of Justice Revisited (1984). See generally H.A.H. Audretsch, *Supervision in European Community Law* (1978).

[6] A recent illustration of the relationship between the administrative and judicial phases is the controversy concerning the importation of Italian wine into France; see Case 42/82 *Commission* v. *France* [1983] E.C.R. 1013.

[7] On the Commission's efforts to ensure compliance with the Treaty and the numerous EC regulatory measures, see Commission of the European Communities, "First Annual Report to the European Parliament on Commission Monitoring of the Application of Community Law 1983" COM(84)181 final (1984).

TABLE 3.1

Infringement Proceedings in Agriculture
since 1978
(by stage of proceedings)

	1978	1979	1980	1981	1982	1983
Formal Notice	13	6	29	67	164	76
Reasoned Opinion	6	3	3	31	20	14
Reference to Court	2	3	2	1	8	3

Source: Commission of the European Communities, "First Annual Report to the European Parliament on Commission Monitoring of the Application of Community Law 1983" COM(84)181 final (1984) at 25.

Accordingly, the principal means currently used by the Commission to induce compliance or restrain infringement, in addition to increasingly detailed regulations, is non-payment or non-reimbursement of EAGGF funds. In four 1976 cases, for example,[8] the Commission had refused to recognise that certain expenditure by the Netherlands, France and Germany incurred purportedly in the implementation of the CAP was chargeable to the Fund. Its view was upheld by the Court, which considered that national authorities were not entitled, by means of a broad interpretation of a given EC legislative provision, to favour traders in that State to the detriment of those in other States where a stricter interpretation was applied. Any such distortion of competition could not be financed by EAGGF but instead must be borne by the Member State concerned.

Control of implementation by other Member States under Article 170 is possible but rare, since Member States prefer for obvious reasons to leave enforcement measures to the Commission. In contrast, an individual, in order to seek an annulment of an EC regulation under Article 173(2), must show that the regulation is a disguised decision addressed to itself or that the regulation, though addressed to someone else, concerns it directly and individually. The difficulty of this task means that individual control over the implementation of CAP legislation is more likely to result either from (a) an action in a national court in which the court seeks a preliminary ruling under Article 177 or (b) an action for damages under Articles 178 and 215.

[8] Case 11/76 *Netherlands* v. *Commission*, Joined Cases 15 and 16/76 *France* v. *Commission*; and Case 18/76 *Germany* v. *Commission* [1979] E.C.R. 245; noted Usher (1980) 5 E.L.Rev. 152.

A ruling on an Article 177 reference that a particular EC measure is invalid is generally considered to have no effect beyond the litigation in question.[9] A more efficacious, general means of control may therefore in principle result from individual recourse either to the European Court or to the national court for compensation. For actions against the Community, the relevant Treaty articles are Articles 178, 215(2) and 176. Article 178 provides that the Court of Justice shall have jurisdiction in disputes relating to compensation for damage provided for in the second paragraph of Article 215. Article 215(2) states that, in the case of non-contractual liability, the Community shall, in accordance with the general principles common to the laws of the Member States, make good any damage caused by its institutions or its servants in the performance of their duties. According to Article 176, the institution whose act has been declared void or whose failure to act has been declared contrary to the Treaty shall be required to take the necessary measures to comply with the judgment of the Court of Justice. The European Court, however, has consistently followed what has been called the "Schöppenstedt formula"[10]: "the Community does not incur liability on account of a legislative measure which involves choices of economic policy unless a sufficiently serious breach of a superior rule of law for the protection of the individual has occurred."[11] Consequently, as Hartley concludes,[12] it is extremely difficult to succeed in a tort action against the Community.

A party suffering harm as a result of the implementation of CAP legislation may also potentially claim damages from a national government. In the European Court, however, an action against a Member State may only be brought by the Commission or another Member State (Arts. 169, 170), so that an individual party's right of action must lie in tort, in quasi-contract (restitution) or on the basis of a statutory obligation to pay money brought in a national

---

[9] But see Case 66/80 *International Chemical Corporation SpA* v. *Italian Finance Administration* [1981] E.C.R. 1191, noted Usher (1981) 6 E.L.Rev. 284.
[10] By T.C. Hartley, *The Foundations of European Community Law* (1981) at 512. This book (at 471–546) provides a thorough analysis of Community and concurrent liability. The case is Case 5/71 *Zuckerfabrik Schöppenstedt* v. *Council* [1971] E.C.R. 975.
[11] Joined Cases 83 and 94/76, 4, 15 and 40/77 *Bayerische HNL Vermehrungsbetriebe GmbH and Co. KG* v. *Council and Commission* [1978] E.C.R. 1209 at 1224.
[12] T.C. Hartley, *The Foundations of European Community Law* (1981) at 523. The Court held damages to be payable, however, in Case 256/81 *Pauls Agriculture Ltd.* v. *Council and Commission* [1983] E.C.R. 1707.

court. According to Hartley's analysis,[13] a party whose loss consists in having been unlawfully obliged to make a payment to the national authorities will normally have a quasi-contractual remedy against the national authority, but generally will be unable to proceed in the European Court. In a case in which a national authority has wrongfully refused to make a payment to the applicant, no action may be brought in the European Court, even, it appears, if no remedy is available in the national courts (unless the sole problem is an EC institution's failure to act). Where the party's loss is in tort and not for a specific sum, the action will normally be admissible in the European Court. According to Article 183, an action against the Community may be heard in a national court, but so far no such action has been brought.

---

[13] *Ibid.* at 540–546 and cases cited there; see also Durdan, "Restitution or Damages: National Court or European Court?" (1976) 1 E.L.Rev. 431; Harding "The Choice of Court Problem in Cases of Non-Contractual Liability under E.E.C. Law" (1979) 1 C.M.L.Rev. 389.

Chapter 4

COMMON MARKET ORGANISATIONS

Legal Basis and General Scheme

Rome Treaty

The core of the CAP consists of the common organisation of agricultural markets and the price system and related financial mechanisms. These inter-related yet distinct elements are the main economic instruments of the EC market and price policy, which together with structural policy was initially conceived as the principal means of achieving CAP objectives. Common market organisations are discussed in this chapter, while the price system is considered in Chapter 5.

The market and price policy has its legal basis in Articles 40 and 43. Article 40(2) provides that in order to attain the Article 39 objectives a common organisation of agricultural markets shall be established. Such a common organisation shall, depending on the product concerned, take one of the following forms: (a) common rules on competition; (b) compulsory co-ordination of the various national market organisations; or (c) a European market organisation. In practice, this distinction has been of little importance, since the third form has invariably been adopted. This is partly because national organisations of the market in all products did not previously exist in all Member States.[1] In addition, when the first market organisations were established in the early 1960s, the major political groups, especially in the Netherlands and France, favoured European-level organisations.[2]

Article 40(3) states that the common organisations established in accordance with Article 40(2) may include all measures required

---

[1] See M. Butterwick and E. Neville-Rolfe, *Agricultural Marketing and the EEC* (1972); Barberis, "On Italian Agrarian Policy" in "L'Etat et la politique agraire en Europe: Présentation des politiques agricoles de douze pays de l'Est et de l'Ouest" (1978) 10 *Economies et Sociétés* 1537 at 1547; Organisation for European Economic Co-operation, *Agricultural Policies in Europe and North America: Price and Income Policies* (1957).

[2] See W.F. Averyt, Jr., *Agropolitics in the European Community* (1977) at 43–70; M. Peterson, *International Interest Organizations and the Transmutation of Postwar Society* (1979), *passim*.

to attain the Article 39 objectives. These measures may include but are not limited to the regulation of prices, production and marketing aids, storage and carry-over arrangements, and common machinery for stabilising imports or exports. The common organisation shall be limited, however, to the pursuit of Article 39 objectives. It shall exclude any discrimination between producers or consumers within the Community. Thus, within the framework of a common organisation the Community and its legal agents have very broad powers.

While Article 43(2) confers general legislative powers on the Council, Article 43(3) provides expressly for the replacement of national market organisations by common organisations. The Council may, acting by a qualified majority and in accordance with Article 43(2), replace the national market organisations by the common organisation provided for in Article 40(2) if

"(a) the common organisation offers Member States which are opposed to this measure and which have an organisation of their own for the production in question equivalent safeguards for the employment and standard of living of the producers concerned, account being taken of the adjustments that will be needed with the passage of time;
 (b) such an organisation ensures conditions for trade within the Community similar to those existing in a national market."

These conditions have been the subject of debate.[3]

General scheme

On the basis of its Article 43(2) legislative powers, the Council has enacted regulations establishing common organisations of the market for most temperate zone agricultural commodities. The major exceptions are potatoes and ethyl alcohol of agricultural origin.[4] Each market organisation (often called a "regime") is constituted by a single Council regulation, supplemented as necessary by Council and Commission regulations specific to each product or group of products. In addition, "horizontal" regulations applying to all products have been adopted by the Commission with regard to common questions, such as licenses and export levies.[5]

[3] See J. Megret, J.V. Louis, D. Vignes and M. Waelbroek, *Le droit de la Communauté économique européenne*, Vol. 2: *Agriculture* (1973) at 27–31.
[4] As yet unsuccessful efforts to reach agreement on a potatoes regime are described in D. Pickard, G. Norris and N. Young, "Three Case Histories in Agriculture" unpublished (n.d.) at 62–106.
[5] Commission Regulations 2730/79 (export subsidies) (O.J. 1979, L.317/1); 193/75 (licenses) (O.J. 1975, L.25/10); 645/75 (export levies) (O.J. 1975, L.67/16).

The various common organisations are, in theory, based on the principle that producers' incomes should be determined by the market price.[6] Accordingly, the classic commodity regime, such as that for cereals, employs several instruments. When the price of the commodity falls below a previously agreed minimum, or intervention, price, the Community through its agents intervenes in the market to purchase surplus supplies at the intervention price. To ensure that third country imports cannot be sold into the Community at a price which is lower than an established threshold price, a variable import levy as well as customs duties are applied at EC frontiers. When the world market price of the commodity is lower than the EC price, Community traders are encouraged to export by means of a subsidy (known officially as "export refund"). Conversely, when the world market price is higher than the EC price, exports are inhibited by means of a levy. By domestic price bands (or brackets) and external protection, EC market and price policy aims to maintain at least a minimum domestic price.[7]

Not all of these instruments, however, are used for all products. In fact, EC commodity regimes are extremely diverse. Some diverge radically from the principle that market prices determine producer incomes; others are mutually contradictory. They may with considerable over-simplification be classified, however, into three different groups: common market organisations providing complete price guarantees, those providing partial price guarantees and those without price guarantees.[8] The first group is exemplified by cereals, sugar and dairy products; the second by fruit and

---

[6] This is sometimes called "the market principle" (*e.g.* Melchior, "The Common Agricultural Policy" in Commission of the European Communities (ed.) *Thirty Years of Community Law* (1983) at 439), but such terminology is at best confusing. It implies that CAP prices are determined by supply and demand, whereas in fact they are determined by negotiation and then administered (see Chap. 5). The "market principle," as generally understood, refers to the mechanism of price formation rather than to the source of producer incomes.

[7] The protectionist character of this system has often been criticised; see, *e.g.* Sampson and Snape, "Effects of the EEC's Variable Import Levies" (1980) 88 *Journal of Political Economy* 1026.

[8] Olmi, "Common Organisation of Agricultural Markets at the Stage of the Single Market" (1968–1969) 5 C.M.L.Rev. 359. For further details, see S. Harris, A. Swinbank and G. Wilkinson, *The Food and Farm Policies of the European Community* (1983); M. Butterwick and E. Neville-Rolfe, *Agricultural Marketing and the EEC* (1972); *C.A.P. Monitor,* a continuously updated information service on the CAP published by Agra Europe (London) Ltd.,; European Parliament Secretariat, *Europe Today: State of European Integration*, an annual legislative handbook; and the annual reports by the Commission on *The Agricultural Situation in the Community.*

vegetables, eggs and poultrymeat; and the third by hops. These illustrative examples, the regime for secondary processed products (because of their importance) and some of the general legal issues raised by common market organisations (except regarding surplus production: see Chap. 6) are discussed in the remainder of this chapter.

Some Common Market Organisations

Cereals

Cereals, of which the most important in the EC are wheat, barley and maize, occupy approximately 30 per cent. of total agricultural land in the Community.[9] They also comprise a major proportion by weight of animal feedingstuffs, thereby influencing the market for other major commodities such as poultry and pigmeat. Cereals were therefore, in 1962, among the first agricultural commodities to be regulated by the Community.[10] A unified common price system for cereals, based on the high prices then prevailing in Germany, was established in 1967.[11] The cereals regime[12] includes common and durum wheat, barley, maize, rye, oats, millet, sorghum, buckwheat and first-stage processed cereal products such as starch and glucose.

Generally regarded as the archetypal EC commodity regime, the market organisation in cereals comprises a price and a trading system. Four types of official prices are established. A target price, fixed for Duisberg in the Ruhr, the centre in shortest supply, represents the optimum level for domestic prices. A uniform intervention price for barley, maize, common wheat and durum wheat, which is fixed for Ormes, the area of greatest supply, represents the minimum market price, at which intervention agencies are obliged to purchase. A threshold price is the minimum entry price for third-country imports; the price of imports is raised to the threshold price by a variable levy. These prices are interconnected

---

[9] Commission of the European Communities, *The Agricultural Situation in the Community: 1983 Report* (1984) at 123.
[10] Council Reg. 19/62 (J.O. 1962, p. 933/62).
[11] Council Reg. 120/67 (O.J. Sp.Ed. 1967, 33). See also Delorme, "L'adoption du prix unique des céréales" in P. Gerbet and D. Pepy (eds.), *La décision dans les Communautés européennes* (1969); W.F. Averyt, Jr., *Agropolitics in the European Community* (1977) at 43–58.
[12] Currently governed by Council Reg. 2727/75 (O.J. 1975, L.281/1), as amended by Council Reg. 1451/82 (O.J. 1982, L.164/82).

in a "silo system,"[13] which in 1975 established a common intervention price in feedgrains, thus in principle giving freer rein to market forces, and provided a special reference (floor) price for wheat of breadmaking quality in order to encourage its production. The target, intervention, reference and threshold prices are increased monthly throughout the year to take account of storage costs and to promote orderly marketing.[14] The target, intervention and reference prices, which are wholesale prices expressed in European currency units (ecu: see Chap. 5) for goods of standard quality delivered at warehouse, not unloaded, are fixed by the Council each year for the period from August 1 to July 31 (except that the durum wheat marketing year runs from July 1 to June 30). Threshold prices are fixed by the Commission.[15]

Intervention agencies are required to purchase, at the intervention price, cereals (except for maize) offered to them by any holder, provided that specified minimum quantity and quality standards are met.[16] In addition, Council Regulation 2740/75[17] provides for the possibility of special intervention measures, such as support for private storage, when price levels fall. Special intervention measures are provided for wheat of breadmaking quality. Intervention is restricted, however, by a guarantee threshold. In order to limit expenditure on support for cereals, the common intervention and reference prices are reduced, within limits, in proportion to increases in production in excess of the threshold.[18] Moreover, in order to prevent heavy sales of cereals into intervention near the end of the cereals marketing year just before the price falls to the level of that at the beginning of the year, a carry-over payment may be made to holders of stocks so that the grain

---

[13] Introduced by Reg. 2727/75 and so-called after the shape of the price diagram: see S. Harris, A. Swinbank and G. Wilkinson, *The Food and Farm Policies of the European Community* (1983) at 70–71.

[14] Council Reg. 1453/82 (O.J. 1982, L.164/9).

[15] In fixing agricultural prices, EC institutions enjoy a wide discretion; see Joined Cases 197–200, 243, 245 and 247/80 *Ludwigshafener Walzmühle Erling* v. *Council and Commission* [1981] E.C.R. 3211.

[16] Reg. 2738/75 (O.J. 1975, L.281/49). Member States are excluded from imposing any condition relating to the definition of a holder or its entitlement to avail itself of the intervention machinery: Case 34/70 *Syndicat national du Commerce extérieur des Céréales* v. *Office national interprofessionnel des Céréales and Minister for Agriculture* [1970] E.C.R. 1233. An offer is effective only when received in writing by the intervention agency and on condition that it state where the goods offered are or will be at the time the offer is made: Case 49/71 *Hagen OHG* v. *EVst für Getreide und Futtermittel* [1972] E.C.R. 23; Case 50/71 *Wünsche OHG* v. *EVst für Getreide und Futtermittel* [1972] E.C.R. 53.

[17] O.J. 1975, L.281/54.

[18] Reg. 2727/75 (O.J. 1975, L.281/1).

may be kept in storage at no financial risk until the onset of the new marketing year.[19]

Subsidies based on the area sown and harvested may be granted to producers of durum wheat in Italy, France and Greece.[20] In addition, production refunds are available for certain products, such as maize groats and meal, used in the manufacture of starch and glucose.[21]

Imports from and exports to third countries are subject to an import or export licence, issued as of right to all applicants by the appropriate authority in each Member State. All applications for a licence must be accompanied by a security deposit, either in cash or in the form of a guarantee issued by an institution approved by the authorities of the concerned Member State.[22] Such a deposit system has been held by the Court to be necessary, appropriate and not disproportionate to its object.[23] The issue of an import or export licence establishes the right and creates the obligation to import or export under that licence and during the period of its validity the specified net quantity of the relevant product. Such an obligation may, however, be cancelled or have its period of validity extended in the event of *force majeure,* the precise meaning of which depends on the legal context.[24]

Imports are subject to the payment of a variable levy. Such levies are intended to protect and stabilise the Community market, in particular by preventing fluctuations in world prices from having repercussions within the Community.[25] Consequently, "the levy is

[19] Time limits for applications for such payments are strictly construed: Case 52/72 *Walzenmühle Magstadt Karl-Heinz Kienle* v. *EVst für Getreide und Futtermittel* [1972] E.C.R. 1267.

[20] Council Reg. 3103/76 (O.J. 1976, L.351/1), amended by Reg. 1455/82 (O.J. 1982, L.164/16).

[21] Reg. 2727/75 (O.J. 1975, L.218/1), as amended by Reg. 1877/80 (O.J. 1980, L.184/13). The Court has held that measures providing for quellmehl and pre-gelatinised starch to receive different treatment in respect of production refunds for maize used in their manufacture were incompatible with the principle of equal treatment: see, *e.g.* Joined Cases 117/76 and 16/77 *Albert Ruckdeschel and Co. and Hansa-Lagerhaus Stroh and Co.* v. *Hauptzollamt Hamburg-St.Annen*; *Diamalt AG* v. *Hauptzollamt Itzehoe* [1977] E.C.R. 1753.

[22] Reg. 193/75, Art. 5 (O.J. 1975, L.25/10).

[23] Case 11/70 *Internationale Handelsgesellschaft mbH* v. *EVst für Getreide und Futtermittel* [1970] E.C.R. 1125. But see Case 122/78 *S.A. Buitoni* v. *Fonds d'Orientation et de Régularisation des Marchés Agricoles* [1979] E.C.R. 677.

[24] See Case 158/73 *E. Kampffmeyer* v. *EVst für Getreide und Futtermittel* [1974] E.C.R. 101; Case 186/73 *Norddeutsches Vieh- und Fleischkontor GmbH* v. *EVst für Schlachtvieh, Fleisch und Fleischerzeugnisse* [1974] E.C.R. 533.

[25] See Case 6/77 *N.G.J. Schouten B.V.* v. *Hoofdproduktschap voor Akkerbouwprodukten* [1977] E.C.R. 1291.

fixed on the basis of the day from which the imported goods exercise an influence on the internal market of the Community, that is to say, the date on which they finally reach this market and enter into competition with domestic products."[26] Provision for advance fixing of any applicable levy or export refund may be included in the import or export licence.[27] In fact, levies are fixed in advance on 80 per cent. of cereal import licences, and a market exists among traders for advance-fixed licences.[28]

The Commission has the power to take action in exceptional circumstances to prevent or alleviate disturbance of the internal market by imports or excessive exports.[29] When, for example, world market prices exceed EC prices, an export levy may be imposed; the levy must take account of the quantity of cereals used in the exported product, so that a standard levy is incompatible with EC law.[30]

More frequently, however, EC prices have exceeded world prices. The Community, while importing "strong" North American breadmaking wheat and maize, produces a surplus (and subsidises exports) of common wheat and barley. Although import levies on cereals covered between half and three-quarters of EC budget spending on cereals during the 1970s, imports are declining.[31] But 63.8 per cent. (2590 million ecu: £1452 million) of projected expenditure on cereal market support in the 1984 draft budget was destined for export subsidies.[32] Moreover, high Community prices have encouraged the import, at nil or low variable levies and duties bound in GATT, of "cereal substitutes" such as soya, maize gluten and manioc. Subsequently processed into animal feedingstuffs, these imports displace EC cereals from this par-

---

[26] Case 35/71 *Schleswig-Holsteinische landwirtschaftliche Hauptgenossenschaft eGmbH* v. *Hauptzollamt Itzehoe* [1971] E.C.R. 1083 at 1093–1094; see also Case 113/75 *Frecassetti* v. *Amministrazione delle Finanze dello Stato* [1976] E.C.R. 983.

[27] Reg. 193/75, Art. 2 (O.J. 1975, L.25/10).

[28] S. Harris, A. Swinbank and G. Wilkinson, *The Food and Farm Policies of the European Community* (1983) at 75–76; see also Debatisse, "Hedging and Speculation on the EEC Levy and Restitution Markets" in K.J. Thomson and R.M. Warren (eds.), *Price and Market Policies in European Agriculture* (1984).

[29] Reg. 2727/75, Arts. 19, 20 (O.J. 1975, L.281/1). See also Sack, "The Commission's Powers under the Safeguard Clauses of the Common Organizations of Agricultural Markets" (1982) 20 C.M.L.Rev. 757.

[30] Case 95/75 *Effem GmbH* v. *Hauptzollamt Lüneburg* [1976] E.C.R. 361.

[31] S. Harris, A. Swinbank and G. Wilkinson, *The Food and Farm Policies of the European Community* (1983) at 65; Commission of the European Communities, *The Agricultural Situation in the Community: 1983 Report* (1984) at 126–127.

[32] Commission of the European Communities, *The Agricultural Situation in the Community: 1983 Report* (1984) at 262.

ticular market. Consequently, the Community has sought within GATT and by voluntary restraint agreements (VRAs) to limit imports, for example, of manioc from Thailand.[33]

The protective EC cereals regime, subsidised exports of surplus and imports of "cereals substitutes" for animal feed are not inter-related merely, however, by narrow legal logic. They are also closely connected in the activities of the handful of international trading firms which dominate the world cereals market.[34] Even in 1969, an authority on agricultural marketing observed:

> "In general, the E.E.C. regulations seem to have accentuated the changes in the structure of the grain trade, already taking place in member countries. By increasing the complexity of trading the regulations have given a further filip to concent-ration. The unified market has put a premium on good com-munications, an advantage enjoyed by the international shippers, the few large firms of merchants, and the coopera-tives. . . ."[35]

More recently, it has been suggested that the EC has "in fact created an oligopolistic intra-community market for cereals," since only the largest firms are able to tailor their business accord-ing to its complex regulations.[36] An examination of any links between large trading firms, the food and animal feed industries, American and European states and the Community, which may provide part of the backcloth to the cereals regime, lies outside the scope of this book. Further research should consider the combined socio-economic consequences, however, of the form, content and complexity of this aspect of CAP law.

---

[33] See S. Harris, A. Swinbank and G. Wilkinson, *The Food and Farm Policies of the European Communities* (1983) at 78–81; Norman, "US and Europe head for trade conflict" *The Times* (London), April 27, 1982, at 7; J.-P. Bertrand, C. Laurent and V. Leclercq, *Le monde du soja* (1983) at 60–64; Corbet, "Excesses of the CAP and Thailand's Manioc" (1982) 5 *The World Economy* 208; Siam-walla, "More Aspects of the Manioc Agreement between Brussels and Bang-kok" (1983) 6 *The World Economy* 89; Fievet, "Les accords d'auto-limitation, une nouvelle technique d'accords communautaires" (1982) 262 R.M.C. 597. See also Case 72/69 *Hauptzollamt Bremen-Freihafen* v. *Bremer Handelsgesellschaft* [1970] E.C.R. 427; Case 125/76 *Firma Peter Cremer* v. *Bundesanstalt für land-wirtschaftliche Marktordnung* [1977] E.C.R. 1593.
[34] See D. Morgan, *Merchants of Grain* (1979); see also the Commission documents quoted by S. Harris, A. Swinbank and G. Wilkinson, *The Food and Farm Poli-cies of the European Community* (1983) at 75.
[35] Butterwick, "Grain Marketing in Some Western European Countries" in D.K. Britton (ed.), *Cereals in the United Kingdom* (1969) at 539–540.
[36] Debatisse, "E.E.C. Organisation of the Cereals Market: Principles and Conse-quences" Centre for European Agricultural Studies, Wye College, *Occasional Paper No. 10* (1981) at 32.

Sugar

The common organisation of the market for sugar came into effect in July 1968.[37] It now covers sugar beet, sugar cane, beet and cane sugar, isoglucose, molasses and certain other sugars. The sugar regime differs from the cereals regime in several important respects.[38] (1) It embraces two agricultural crops (sugar beet and sugar cane) and one industrial product (isoglucose). Sugar beet occupies about 1.8 per cent. of land used for agriculture in the Community,[39] whereas sugar cane is grown mainly in tropical, third world countries. (2) Intervention buying applies not to the raw material (sugar beet or sugar cane) but to the processed product (raw or white sugar). (3) Intervention buying is limited by production quotas. (4) Producers, according to the principle of co-responsibility, pay the cost of disposing of surpluses. (5) A specified quantity of third country produce has guaranteed access to the EC market.

The price support system uses five institutional prices: target price, threshold price, intervention price, basic beet price and minimum beet price. The basic beet price represents the price which farmers would receive if producer levies were not charged; in fact, farmers receive a lower price, the minimum beet price, which takes into account the producer levy. The minimum beet price is that which beet factories are obliged at least to pay to growers. In addition, though not an institutionally determined price, the effective support price, composed of the intervention price plus a storage levy, is in effect the minimum market price for sugar.[40]

Production quotas are fixed for each Member State, which then

[37] Council Regulation 1009/67 (J.O. 1967, L.308/1). See also Case 6/68 *Zuckerfabrik Watenstedt GmbH* v. *Council* [1968] E.C.R. 409. It is currently governed by Reg. 1785/81 (O.J. 1981, L.177/4), as amended by Regulation 606/82 (O.J. 1982, L.74/1). On the enactment and development of the sugar regime, see Stevens and Webb, "The Political Economy of Sugar: A Window on the CAP" in H. Wallace, W. Wallace and C. Webb (eds.), *Policy Making in the European Community* (2nd ed., 1983).

[38] S. Harris, A. Swinbank and G. Wilkinson, *The Food and Farm Policies of the European Community* (1983) at 124–126.

[39] Commission of the European Communities, *The Agricultural Situation in the Community: 1983 Report* (1984) at 127.

[40] Accordingly, the sugar regime does not guarantee that producers will obtain the intervention price in all their commercial transactions: Joined Cases 292 and 293/81 *Société Jean Lion et Cie, Société Loiret & Haentjens S.A.* v. *Fonds d'Intervention et de Régularisation du Marché du Sucre (FIRS)* [1982] E.C.R. 3887.

determines quotas for sugar and isoglucose manufacturers.[41] Attempts by the Commission to allocate quotas directly to manufacturers have been resisted by governments, which "tend to regard their country's "A" quota as national property."[42] The manufacturers' quotas consist of a basic "A" quota, which in principle corresponds to domestic market requirements and is eligible for full intervention support, and a "B" quota which as a result of a higher production levy qualifies for support at a reduced rate. Production in excess ("C" sugar) of an undertaking's maximum quota may not be sold within the Community, and the beet from which it is produced does not benefit from a guaranteed price. The allocation of a quota does not give rise to a vested right, hence a reduction in the quota amount does not constitute an infringement of a fundamental right.[43] An individual undertaking's quota may not, however, be reduced by more than 10 per cent. Within this limit, quotas may be transferred within a Member State, though not between beet and isoglucose factories. Special provisions apply to Italy and the French overseas departments, where the 10 per cent. limit does not apply "where the transfer of quotas is made on the basis of restructuring plans in the beet, cane and sugar manufacturing sectors in the region concerned."[44] The whole of the United Kingdom quota is allocated to British Sugar plc, in which the British government was previously a substantial minority shareholder but which since 1981 has been controlled by S. & W. Berisford plc.[45]

Sugar beet is grown under contracts between manufacturers and growers. Terms must conform to statutory outline provisions.[46] In the United Kingdom the detailed terms are agreed between British Sugar and the National Farmers Union. To the extent that rela-

---

[41] Reg. 1781/81, Arts. 25–31 (O.J. 1981, L.177/4).
[42] S. Harris, A. Swinbank and G. Wilkinson, *The Food and Farm Policies of the European Community* (1983) at 128.
[43] See Case 230/78 *S.p.A. Eridania-Zuccherifici nazionali and S.p.A. Società Italiana per l'Industria degli Zuccheri* v. *Minister of Agriculture and Forestry, Minister for Industry, Trade and Craft Trades, and S.p.A. Zuccherifici Meridionali* [1979] E.C.R. 2749; Joined Cases 103–109/78 *Société des Usines de Beauport* v. *Council* [1979] E.C.R. 17.
[44] Reg. 1785/81, Art. 25(2), para. 2 (O.J. 1981, L. 177/4). See also Joined Cases 54–60/76 *Compagnie Industrielle et Agricole du Comté de Lohéac* v. *Commission* [1977] E.C.R. 645; Joined Cases 103–109/78 *Société des Usines de Beauport* v. *Council* [1979] E.C.R. 17.
[45] On relations between BSC and Berisford, see Monopolies and Merger Commission, *S. & W. Berisford Limited and British Sugar Corporation Limited. A Report on the Proposed Merger* (1981) H.C. 241; Commission of the European Communities, *Twelfth Report on Competition Policy* (1982) at 82–83.
[46] Reg. 206/68 (J.O. 1968, L.47/1).

tions between manufacturers and growers are governed by the common market organisation, they fall within the exclusive competence of the Community, so that Member States may no longer adopt unilateral measures concerning sugar production. Nevertheless, in a dispute between a Danish producer/processor co-operative and its supplementary outside suppliers, the European Court interpreted the applicable EC regulation as empowering the Danish government itself to allocate sugar beet delivery rights.[47]

The price and quota systems for sugar have met their initial aims of creating a common sugar market, preserving, within limits, high-cost producers in Italy and Germany and encouraging EC self-sufficiency in sugar beet production.[48] These objectives, perhaps questionable in themselves, have been achieved at the expense of substantial over-production. Although the number of sugar beet factories decreased by 19 from 1972–73 to 1982–83, total EC processing capacity increased by 36 per cent.[49] In order to encourage greater use of sugar by lowering domestic costs to world levels, production refunds are granted on sugar, isoglucose and sugar syrups used in the chemical industries.[50] In addition, storage cost subsidies are paid monthly to beet factories, specialised sugar traders and intervention agencies in order to even out sugar marketing throughout the year.

Intervention purchases, however, are rarely used for sugar. Instead, the principal means of disposing of surpluses is the payment of subsidies to encourage exports to the world market. The cost of subsidies is met by production levies, charged on the white sugar intervention price at a rate of up to 2 per cent. on "A" quota production and of up to 39.5 per cent. on "B" quota production. These levies are charged in the first instance to beet and cane processors, but the latter may pass on to growers 60 per cent. of the cost. For this purpose, surplus which comes to light after the expir-

---

[47] Case 151/78 *Sukkerfabrieken Nykøbing Limiteret* v. *Ministry of Agriculture* [1979] E.C.R. 1. The legislation in question was Art. 1 of Reg. 741/75 (O.J. 1975, L.74/2), laying down special rules for the purchase of sugar beet.

[48] These aims are stated by Stevens and Webb, "The Political Economy of Sugar: A Window on the CAP" in H. Wallace, W. Wallace and C. Webb (eds.), *Policy Making in the European Community* (2nd ed., 1983) at 323. Regarding the second, however, see Case 77/76 *Fratelli Cucchi* v. *Avez S.p.A.* [1977] E.C.R. 987 and Case 105/76 *Interzuccheri S.p.A.* v. *Ditta Rezzano e Cavassa* [1977] E.C.R. 1029 on the incompatibility with the Treaty of the Italian *sovrapprezzo*, a surcharge on home-produced or imported white sugar used to finance the Sugar Equalization Fund for the benefit of domestic growers and processors. See also Case 72/79 *Commission* v. *Italy* [1980] E.C.R. 1411.

[49] Commission of the European Communities, *The Agricultural Situation in the Community: 1983 Report* (1984) at 128.

[50] Reg. 1400/78 (O.J. 1978, L.170/9).

ation of the marketing year in which it was produced must be treated as arising in the marketing year in which it was ascertained.[51] Export subsidies, based on weekly tenders and grant of a licence, cover the difference between EC domestic market prices and world prices. They apply, however, only to "A" and "B" quota sugar. In 1983 such subsidies covered the full cost of exporting surplus "A" and "B" quota sugar; exports of "C" quota sugar, which received no subsidy, amounted to 3.5 million tonnes, 23 per cent. of total EC production.[52]

Consequently, even though in 1981–82 the EC withheld from the world market 1.7 million tonnes of a record production of 15 million tonnes,[53] Community exports have tended to undermine the price objectives of the International Sugar Agreement (ISA). This has led to complaints about EC subsidies under the GATT, and for the first time the current EC sugar regime makes provision for the Community to join the ISA.[54] Nonetheless, the development of EC sugar interests in the context of the Community regime has resulted in a gradual change in EC policy towards third world producers. Since the Sugar Protocol attached to the first Lomé Convention in 1975,[55] a maximum of 1.3 million tonnes of unrefined sugar from the African, Carribean and Pacific (ACP) countries associated with the Community has been imported into the EC free of duties or levies. This preferential agreement replaced the access to the United Kingdom market which Commonwealth producers previously enjoyed under the Commonwealth Sugar Agreement. The EC undertook for an unspecified time to import from ACP countries, at guaranteed prices, specified quantities of unrefined or refined sugar, which ACP countries undertook to supply. Initially the cost of exporting a quantity of sugar equivalent to Lomé Convention imports was passed on to EC processors and producers, but since 1982 it has been chargeable to the Community budget. This change in policy, it has been

---

[51] Case 159/73 *Hannoversche Zucker AG Rethen-Weetzen* v. *Hauptzollamt Hannover* [1974] E.C.R. 121.
[52] Commission of the European Communities, *The Agricultural Situation in the Community: 1983 Report* (1984) at 128–129.
[53] Commission of the European Communities, *The Agricultural Situation in the Community: 1982 Report* (1983) at 139–140.
[54] See Smith, "EEC Sugar Policy in an International Context" (1981) 15 J.W.T.L. 95; Smith, "GATT: EEC Sugar Refunds Dispute" (1981) 15 J.W.T.L. 534; Smith, "Prospects for a New International Sugar Agreement" (1983) 17 J.W.T.L. 308. On EC sugar policy generally, see House of Lords Select Committee on the European Communities, *EEC Sugar Policy* (1980).
[55] O.J. 1975, C.76/35.

suggested, represents a subtle shift in the status of cane sugar from a regular source of supply to a concession.[56]

Dairy products

The common organisation of the market in milk and milk products was agreed in 1964, but a unified price system was not established until 1968.[57] It covers fresh, concentrated and powdered milk and cream; butter, cheese and curds; lactose and lactose syrup; and milk-based compound animal feedingstuffs. Its aim is to "stabilise markets and to ensure a fair standard of living for the agricultural community concerned" (Regulation 804/68, Preamble). A target price for standardised whole milk containing at least 3.7 per cent. fat, delivered to dairy, is fixed each year. It is the price which the Community aims to obtain on producers' milk sales but is not a guaranteed price.

When the dairy regime was established in the Community of the Six, less than 25 per cent. of milk delivered to dairies was eventually consumed as liquid milk or cream; more than 50 per cent. was processed into butter or cheese. Community policy, based on this pattern, aims to support the market price of liquid milk largely by regulating the market for butter, skimmed milk powder and certain kinds of cheese. Intervention prices are fixed for butter, skimmed milk powder, and Grana-Padano and Parmigiano-Reggiano cheese.[58] These intervention prices are related to the target price for liquid milk by a formula known as the Intervention Milk Price Equivalent (IMPE).

Although in principle dairy products are freely traded within the Community, differences in national interest, often reflected in different health and hygiene regulations, have prevented the free circulation of liquid milk (see Chap. 2).

Imports are regulated through the fixing of a threshold price for 12 pilot products, each of which is deemed representative of a group of dairy products.[59] This serves as a basis for calculating

[56] Stevens and Webb, "The Political Economy of Sugar: A Window on the CAP" in H. Wallace, W. Wallace and C. Webb (eds.), *Policy Making in the European Community* (2nd ed., 1983) at 343.

[57] Reg. 13/64 (J.O. 1964, L.34/549); Reg. 804/68 (J.O. 1968, L.148/13), amended by Reg. 1183/82 (O.J. 1982, L.140/1).

[58] Reg. 965/68 (J.O. 1968, L.165/4) and Reg. 685/69 (J.O. 1969, L.90/12) as amended (butter); Reg. 1014/68 (J.O. 1968, L.173/4) and Reg. 625/78 (O.J. 1978, L.84/19) (skimmed milk powder); Reg. 971/68 (J.O. 1968, L.166/8) and Reg. 1107/68 (J.O. 1968, L.184/29) (cheese).

[59] Reg. 823/68 (J.O. 1968, L.151/3), amended by Reg. 561/76 (O.J. 1976, L.67/11).

threshold prices for other dairy products. The wholesale price of imports is raised to the threshold price by a variable levy.[60] Special arrangements provide for the continued import into the United Kingdom of New Zealand butter and cheese; in 1982 the former amounted to 92,000 tonnes, or 7 per cent. of world trade in butter.[61] The Community grants subsidies to encourage the domestic use or export of dairy products or certain processed products based on dairy products. Export certificates are not required for dairy products unless the export subsidy is fixed in advance.[62]

Continuing, large over-production in the dairy sector has long been the most intractable problem in the CAP, accounting, for example, for 42 per cent. of EAGGF Guarantee Section expenditure in 1980 and 30 per cent. in 1981.[63] Attempts by the Community to stem milk production have included a producers' co-responsibility levy, a guarantee threshold for fixing prices and, most recently, milk production quotas (see Chap. 6).

Fruit and vegetables

The common organisation of the market for fruit and vegetables was adopted in 1962.[64] It covers all fruit and vegetables grown in the Community except for peas and beans for fodder, wine grapes and olive oil, for which separate arrangements exist, and potatoes, for which there is no common organisation. Its central tenets are support of registered producers' organisations and the establishment of common quality standards.

Producers' organisations are defined in the basic regulation as any organisation of fruit and vegetable producers which is established on the producers' own initiative for the purpose, in particular, of (1) promoting the concentration of supply and the

---

[60] Preferential treatment concerning the levy does not give rise to vested rights: Case 26/77 *Balkan-Import-Export GmbH* v. *Hauptzollamt Berlin-Packhof* [1977] E.C.R. 2031.

[61] The special provisions are contained in Protocol 18 of the United Kingdom Act of Accession (O.J. 1972, L.73/173) and Council Reg. 1655/76 (O.J. 1976, L.185/1). On New Zealand imports, see Commission of the European Communities, *The Agricultural Situation in the Community: 1983 Report* (1984) at 135.

[62] Commission Reg. 706/77 (O.J. 1977, L.86/13).

[63] Commission of the European Communities, *The Agricultural Situation in the Community: 1982 Report* (1983) at 144. On the EC dairy sector generally, see House of Commons Agricultural Committee, *Economic, Social and Health Implications for the United Kingdom of the Common Agricultural Policy on Milk and Dairy Products*, (1980) 3 vols.

[64] Reg. 23/62 (O.J. Sp.Ed. 1959–62, 97); now governed by Reg. 1035/72 (J.O. 1972, L.118/1), as amended by Reg. 1738/82 (O.J. 1982, L.190/7).

regularisation of prices at the producer stage; (2) making suitable technical means available to producer members for the presentation and marketing of products; (3) marketing virtually the entire output of its members; and (4) adopting and applying rules to improve the quality of the product and controlling the volume of supply. Member States may grant aid to producers' associations during the three years following their establishment. Regulation 1360/78, a horizontal regulation, and Regulation 325/79[65] provide supplementary aid for producers' organisations as part of the Community's Mediterranean policy.

Producers' organisations are entitled to fix withdrawal prices below which they will not put goods supplied by their members on the market, though Member States may fix a maximum withdrawal price. Market prices are supported primarily by compensation for the withdrawal of produce, which is operated by Member States' intervention agencies through registered producers' organisations. Only registered organisations are entitled to withdraw goods from the market. Members are compensated by the organisation's intervention fund, financed by contributions calculated on the quality of goods offered for sale. This fund may be supported by Member States, either directly or through credit institutions, for up to five years from establishment. Support prices are derived from a basic price, which is an indicative price representing generally the price levels in major production areas, and a buying-in price. The latter, despite its designation, is not an intervention price, but instead provides a basis for calculation of the withdrawal price, thereby establishing the amount of compensation paid by intervention agencies to producers' organisations. The basic price and the buying-in price are in fact set at levels far below the normal market price, thus aiming merely to avoid disastrous falls in price rather than to guarantee producers' incomes by intervention purchases. Usually, about 4 per cent.–5 per cent. of produce is withdrawn (see Chap. 6).

Common quality standards apply to a wide range of fruit and vegetables throughout the Community. They include criteria of quality, size, labelling, packaging and presentation. These standards, which usually provide for three different classes, are the basis for withdrawals of produce, export subsidies and reference prices.[66] In implementing these standards, national governments may not, however, make exportation of products conditional on

---

[65] Respectively: O.J. 1978, L.166/1; O.J. 1979, L.45/1.
[66] For criticism of compulsory minimum standards, see Bowbrick "The Case against Compulsory Minimum Standards" (1977) 28 *Journal of Agricultural Economics* 113.

the exporter's being affiliated to a public body or body approved by an official authority.[67]

Community markets are protected from third country competition by a uniform *ad valorem* tariff, which may vary seasonally and from country to country. Certain national restrictions also continue to apply. In addition, under a safeguard clause the Commission is empowered to levy import charges or impose quantitive restrictions or measures having equivalent effect. In adopting such measures the Commission has a broad discretion. The concept of "serious disturbance" or "threat of serious disturbance" is to be considered in light of CAP objectives.[68] The Commission is not required to give an explicit statement of reasons, in relation to Articles 85 and 86, if the "serious disturbances" are capable of endangering Article 39 objectives.[69] Moreover, it is not obliged, under Article 40(3), to limit itself to pursuit of Article 39 objectives and may also seek to achieve the objectives of the common commercial policy.[70]

Export subsidies, which may be fixed in advance, may be granted to EC exports.[71]

The market organisation for fruit and vegetables thus offers only partial price guarantees. Its weak price support is frequently ascribed to the facts that these products are highly perishable, subject to wide fluctuations in annual yield and individual quality, and often traded in fragmented, highly localised markets. A more accurate conclusion, however, may be that the strength of a particular common organisation's income support varies according to the strength of the political interests affected.[72] The characteristics of these products, in any event, are now being modified in conjunction with recent changes in their production, exchange and consumption.[73] Concurrently, under pressure from France and Italy, ostensibly to protect their producers from competition from

---

[67] Case 29/82 *F. van Luipen en Zn BV* [1983] E.C.R. 151. See also Case 94/79 *Criminal Proceedings against Pieter Vriend* [1980] E.C.R. 327.

[68] Case 40/72 *I. Schroeder KG* v. *Germany* [1973] E.C.R. 125 (common market organisation in products processed from fruit and vegetables).

[69] Joined Cases 41–44/70 *NV International Fruit Company* v. *Commission* [1971] E.C.R. 411.

[70] Case 52/81 *Offene Handelsgesellschaft in Firma Werner Faust* v. *Commission* [1982] E.C.R. 3745 (common market organisation in products processed from fruit and vegetables).

[71] Reg. 2518/69 (J.O. 1969, L.318/17).

[72] See A. Zeller, *L'Imbroglio agricole du Marché commun* (1970) at 70–71.

[73] See, e.g. *Report of the Committee of Enquiry on Contract Farming* (Cmnd. 5099) (1972); Mackintosh, "Fruit and Vegetables as an International Commodity: The Relocation of Horticultural Production and Its Implications for the Producers" (1977) *Food Policy* 277.

Greece, Spain and Portugal in an enlarged Community, the EC has adopted stronger support measures as part of its Mediterranean package (see Chap. 7).

Eggs and poultrymeat

The common market organisation for eggs and poultrymeat was introduced in July 1967.[74] Both eggs and poultrymeat are often regarded as "processed cereals," since cereals constitute a major proportion by weight of feedingstuffs; the cereals and the egg and poultrymeat regimes are therefore closely related. There is no internal price support system, partly because of the industrial character of much contemporary production. Measures exist, however, to improve processing and sales and aid production. The most important protective measure is the import levy, which is fixed to take account of the price of feed grain required to produce a given quantity of eggs or poultrymeat. EC producers are also protected by an additional import levy charged on imports below a sluice-gate price.[75] Subsidies, varying according to destination, may be granted to encourage exports.

Hops

The organisation for hops, introduced in 1971,[76] covers hops, hop powder and vegetable saps and extracts of hops. It provides producer subsidies per planted hectare and, as protection against imports, an *ad valorem* duty applied under the EC Common Customs Tariff.

Products of secondary processing

These market regimes contribute to the cost of raw materials for the food processing industry, which produces a high proportion of Europe's food, ranging from below 50 per cent. in France and Italy to about 75 per cent. in Germany and Britain.[77] First-stage processors are often able to recoup costs by intervention sales. Second-stage processors, however, which process already pro-

---

[74] Reg. 122/67 (J.O. 1967, 2293) (eggs); Reg. 123/67 (J.O. 1967, 17) (poultrymeat). The current Regs. are 2771–2776/75 (O.J. 1975, L.282/49), as amended by Reg. 3643/81 (O.J. 1981, L.364/1) for eggs and 2777–2782/75 (O.J. 1975, L.282/77) for poultrymeat.

[75] On the EC poultrymeat regime's effects on trade, see R. Talbot, *The Chicken War* (1978).

[76] Reg. 1696/71 (J.O. 1971, L.175/1).

[77] "Europe's Processed Cuisine" *The Economist*, August 9, 1980, at 88.

cessed products, are sometimes "caught between the rigidities of CAP-supported raw material prices on the one hand, and the pressures from retailers on the other."[78] The trading system for non-Annex II products was established under Article 235 in 1966.[79] It covers goods manufactured from one or more of the following basic products: skimmed milk powder, whole milk powder, butter, various cereals, sugar and molasses. It also covers processed products using other first-stage processed products likened to the basic products, such as potato starch, certain other starches, goods made from fresh milk or cream with a low milk fat content and isoglucose.

Third-country imports are subject to an import duty consisting of an *ad valorem* customs duty and a variable component intended to cover the difference between Community and world prices.[80] Export subsidies, fixable in advance, may be granted for certain products.[81] Exporters may also, under prefinancing arrangements, be paid the export subsidy before the products are manufactured. Prefinancing is designed to put on the same footing EC processors using EC basic products and EC processors using basic products imported from the world market under inward processing arrangements. The latter allow EC processors to import raw materials from third countries duty-free, provided that the processed product incorporating these raw materials is exported within six months. The basic product is imported free of duties, levies and monetary compensatory amounts (see Chap. 5). Subsequently the processed product is exported without an export subsidy being paid on that part of the product accounted for by the imported basic product.[82] Provision is also made for harmonisation of laws and administrative arrangements concerning outward processing traffic.[83]

---

[78] S. Harris, A. Swinbank and G. Wilkinson, *The Food and Farm Policies of the European Community* (1983) at 248. On the U.K. food industry, see J. Burns, J. McInerney and A. Swinbank (eds.), *The Food Industry: Economics and Policies* (1983).

[79] Reg. 160/66 (J.O. 1966, L.195/3361); now based on Reg. 3033/80 (O.J. 1980, L.323/1).

[80] Reg. 3034/80 (O.J. 1980, L.323/7).

[81] See Reg. 565/80 (O.J. 1980, L.62/5); Reg. 3035/80 (O.J. 1980, L.323/27).

[82] Council Directive 95/73 (O.J. 1973, L.120/17), as amended by Commission Directive 681/75 (O.J. 1975, L.301/1). The scope of inward processing as compared to customs warehousing is considered in Case 49/82 *Commission* v. *Netherlands* [1983] E.C.R. 1195.

[83] Council Directive 73/69 (J.O. 1969, L.58/1), as amended by Council Directive 119/76 (O.J. 1976, L.24/58).

General Legal Issues

Introduction

The gradual establishment of these common market organisations since 1962 has raised several general legal issues. Among
the most important, for the ten Member States and potentially also
for Spain and Portugal, are (1) the definition and post-1957 legal
status of national market organisations; (2) the characteristics of a
common market organisation; (3) the relation of common organisations to general Treaty rules; (4) the effects of the existence of a
common organisation on the potential scope of national legislation; and (5) the implications of the absence of a common organisation in a particular product market.[84]

Definition and legal status of national organisations

Following the Rome Treaty's entry into force, the application of
certain general common market rules was provisionally suspended
concerning agricultural products which were then subject to a
national organisation of the market (see Arts. 42, 43(3), 45, 46).
The concept of a national market organisation was not, however,
defined in the Treaty. Accordingly, after discussion in the Commission and the Parliament,[85] it eventually came for consideration
by the Court. In 1963 the Court stated that "a market organisation
is a combination of legal institutions and measures on the basis of
which appropriate authorities seek to control and regulate the market."[86] Subsequently, in the well-known 1974 *Charmasson* case,
the Court defined a national organisation of the market as

> "a totality of legal devices placing the regulation of the mar-
> ket in the products in question under the control of the public
> authority, with a view to ensuring, by means of an increase in
> productivity and of optimum utilization of the factors of pro-

[84] On the European Court's role concerning these issues, see also Druesne, *La politique agricole commune devant la Cour de justice des Communautés euro-péennes 1958-1978* (1980); Neri, "La jurisprudence de la Cour de justice des Communautés européennes relative à l'application de la legislation agricole communautaire" (1982) 5-6 C.D.E. 507.

[85] See J. Megret, J.L. Louis, D. Vignes and M. Waelbroeck, *Le droit de la Commu-nauté économique européenne*, Vol. 2: *Agriculture* (1973) at 29-31.

[86] Joined Cases 90 and 91/63 *Commission* v. *Luxembourg and Belgium* [1964] E.C.R. 625 at 635.

duction, in particular of manpower, a fair standard of living for producers, the stabilization of markets, the assurance of supplies and reasonable prices to consumers."[87]

Thus, a national market organisation comprises a group of inter-related legal measures designed to achieve, on a national level, objectives analogous to those which are under Article 39 to be pursued at EC level by a common organisation. A simple quota system, *in casu* a quota on banana imports into France, could not therefore constitute a national market organisation.

Once the Treaty entered into force, all Member States were subject to the Article 12 standstill provisions. Accordingly, any national market organisations then in existence were, in effect, "frozen."[88] In *Charmasson,* the Court held that, even with respect to a product, namely bananas, for which a common organisation had not yet been established, a national organisation must, during the transitional period, adapt itself to the fullest possible extent to the requirements of the common market with a view to facilitating the establishment of the CAP. Any derogations from general Treaty rules were permitted only provisionally, to the extent necessary to ensure the functioning of the national organisation but without impeding the adaptation involved in the establishment of a common policy. After the end of the transitional period, however, a national organisation could not, even in the absence of a common organisation, derogate unilaterally from general Treaty rules.[89] More recently, in two cases arising from the United Kingdom import ban on main-crop potatoes, the Court held that Article 60(2) of the Act of Accession, which preserved the right of a Member State to delay abolition of quantitative restrictions on imports of an agricultural product if it on accession formed and still forms a necessary part of the national market organisation for that product and no Common Market had yet been introduced, was not a "special provision" under Article 9(2) of the Act and therefore ceased to have effect as of December 31, 1977. Consequently, after the end of the Accession transitional period, any national market organisations are subject to general Treaty rules,

---

[87] Case 48/74 *Charmasson* v. *Minister for Economic Affairs and Finance* [1974] E.C.R. 1383 at 1396. See also Paulin and Forman, "The French Banana Story and Its Implications," (1975) 12 C.M.L.Rev. 399.

[88] Joined Cases 90 and 91/63 *Commission* v. *Luxembourg and Belgium* [1964] E.C.R. 625 at 634.

[89] Case 48/74 *Charmasson* v. *Minister for Economic Affairs and Finance* [1974] E.C.R. 1383 at 1393; see also Case 68/76 *Commission* v. *France* [1977] E.C.R. 515.

regardless of the fact that no common organisation of the market for the product in question has yet been established.[90] According to the Court,[91] Community authorities alone are legally empowered to decide upon the provisional maintenance of any national system of organisation, intervention or supervision regarding an agricultural product once a common market organisation for that product has been definitively established, regardless of whether or not it is yet fully applied.

Characteristics of common market organisations

The Treaty provides for alternative forms of common organisations, some permissible measures and their various functions (see Arts. 40, 43(3)), but it does not define in any detail their basic characteristics.[92] The definition of a common market organisation has therefore been left to the Court. In Case 83/78 *Pigs Marketing Board* v. *Raymond Redmond,* the Court held that "the common organisation of the market in pigmeat, like the other common organisations, is based on the concept of an open market to which every producer has free access and the functioning of which is regulated solely by the instruments provided for by that organisation."[93] In practice, the concept of an open market refers in this context not to the determination of prices by supply and demand; for most Community products the bracket within which prices may fluctuate is fixed in advance and administered. Instead, it refers to the principle that market prices, regardless of how they are determined, constitute the main source of producers' incomes, either by market or intervention sales or by other means.

EC market organisations are administered through a variety of measures. For example, the market organisation in oils and fats, then a weak regime, was described by the Court in 1970 as being

" . . . based on a price policy which is determined in accordance with a number of objectives concerning the level of agricultural income, the putting into effect of a coherent production policy, competitive conditions of trade in the dif-

---

[90] Case 118/78 *C.J. Meijer B.V.* v. *Department of Trade, Minister of Agriculture, Fisheries and Food and Commissioners of Customs and Excise* [1979] E.C.R. 1387; Case 231/78 *Commission* v. *United Kingdom* [1979] E.C.R. 1447, noted Wyatt (1979) 4 E.L.Rev. 359.

[91] Case 82/71 *Pubblico Ministero della Republica Italiana* v. *Società Agricola Industria Latte (SAIL)* [1972] E.C.R. 119.

[92] See also J. Megret, J.L. Louis, D. Vignes and M. Waelbroeck, *Le droit de la Communauté économique européenne,* Vol. 2: *Agriculture* (1973) at 15–19; S. Ventura, *Principes de Droit agraire communautaire* (1967) at 75–84.

[93] [1978] E.C.R. 2347 at 2371.

ferent oils and fats, the stabilization of the markets and the fixing of an appropriate price level to consumers.

"This policy is put into effect by means of a complex system of steps involving purchases, storage and sales by intervention agencies, a set of regulations on imports and exports by means of a system of levies and refunds, as well as measures for restoring the balance and protective measures in case of disturbances affecting the market in question."[94]

Its intervention and protection techniques therefore differed fundamentally from systems based exclusively on the application of customs duties.

All common organisations share, ideally at least, two other features: normative autonomy in relation to the law of the Member States, and uniformity of application of their legal regime throughout the Community.[95] These basic characteristics were clearly affirmed by the Court in Case 31/70.[96] Interpreting Regulation 19/62 on the common organisation of the cereals market as meaning that the same levy must be imposed on imported maize damaged in transit as on imported undamaged maize, the Court stated that such levies derive from the Treaty, not from national law, and are simultaneously applicable in all Member States. They are fixed according to a standard quality, are determined by reference to a price level set according to fluctuating exchange rates and to Common Market objectives, and act as regulators of the market not within a national framework but within that of a common organisation. Similarly, the Court has consistently maintained that uniform interpretation and application of EC rules is necessary to avoid obstacles to the free movement of goods and discrimination contrary to the Treaty.[97]

---

[94] Case 26/69 *Commission* v. *France* [1970] E.C.R. 565 at 577. A different view of the EC regime in question may be found in J.-P. Bertrand, C. Laurent and V. Leclerq, *Le monde du soja* (1983) at 60–61; see also Counter Information Service, *Unilever's World* (n.d.), *passim*.

[95] Neri, "La jurisprudence de la Cour de justice des Communautés européennes relative à l'application de la législation agricole communautaire" (1982) 5–6 C.D.E. 507 at 519.

[96] Case 31/70 *Deutsche Getreide- und Futtermittel Handelsgesellschaft mbH* v. *Hauptzollamt Hamburg-Altona* [1970] E.C.R. 1055.

[97] *e.g.* Case 74/69 *Hauptzollamt Bremen-Freihafen* v. *Waren-Import-Gesellschaft Krohn and Co.* [1970] E.C.R. 451; Case 39/70 *Norddeutsches Vieh- und Fleischkontor GmbH* v. *Hauptzollamt Hamburg-St. Annen* [1971] E.C.R. 429; Case 35/71 *Schleswig-Holsteinische landwirtschaftliche Hauptgenossenschafte eGmbH* v. *Hauptzollamt Itzehoe* [1971] E.C.R. 1083; Case 49/71 *Hagen OHG* v. *EVst für Getreide und Futtermittel* [1972] E.C.R. 23; Case 50/71 *Wünsche OHG* v. *EVst für Getreide und Futtermittel* [1972] E.C.R. 53.

Relation to general Treaty rules

The Common Market organisations established before the late 1960s expressly re-enacted, as part of their legal regime, the Treaty provisions on the free movement of goods, since those provisions had not yet been held to be directly effective. More recent market regulations, however, do not expressly repeat these general rules. Concerning the market organisation in pigmeat, for example, the European Court has stated that the free movement of goods provisions "are to be regarded as an integral part of the common organisation of the market."[98] It has nonetheless recognised that, in exceptional circumstances, common organisations may sometimes derogate from these provisions.[99] In at least one case, however, despite the European Court's decision, a national court has held a national measure compatible with the common organisation but incompatible with the free movement of goods.[1] (See also Chap. 2.)

Common organisations and national legislation

Member States have the authority to determine domestic institutions, such as intervention agencies, for the implementation of CAP law regarding common organisations.[2] The Court has held, however, that, to the extent that they have transferred legislative powers to the Community with the object of ensuring the satisfactory operation of a common market in agriculture, they no longer have the power to adopt legislative measures in this field.[3] More-

---

[98] Case 83/78 *Pigs Marketing Board* v. *Raymond Redmond* [1978] E.C.R. 2347 at 2371, aspects of which have been noted by Leopold (1979) 4 E.L.Rev. 314, McEldowney (1980) 31 N.I.L.Q. 165, Wyatt (1979) 4 E.L.Rev. 115. See also Case 177/78 *Pigs and Bacon Commission* v. *McCarren and Company Ltd.* [1979] E.C.R. 2161, noted Wyatt (1979) 4 E.L.Rev. 472.
[99] Compare Joined Cases 80 and 81/77 *Société Les Commissionnaires Réunis S.à.r.l.* v. *Receveur des Douanes*; *S.à.r.l. Les Fils de Henri Ramel* v. *Receveur des Douanes* [1978] E.C.R. 927, noted Usher (1978) 3 E.L.Rev. 305; and Case 106/81 *Julius Kind KG* v. *Council and Commission* [1982] E.C.R. 2885, commented Lenaerts (1983) 20 C.M.L.Rev. 825.
[1] Joined Cases 36 and 71/80 *Irish Creamery Milk Suppliers Association* v. *Ireland*; *Martin Doyle* v. *An Taoiseach* [1981] E.C.R. 735; *Martin Doyle* v. *An Taoiseach* (judgment of the High Court of Ireland, April 26, 1983 (Barrington J). See also Blumental, "Implementing the Common Agricultural Policy: Aspects of the Limitations on the Powers of the Member States" (1984) 35 N.I.L.Q. 28.
[2] Joined Cases 51–54/71 *International Fruit Company NV* v. *Produktschap voor Groenten en Fruit* [1971] E.C.R. 1107; Case 31/78 *Francesco Bussone* v. *Italian Ministry for Agriculture and Forestry* [1978] E.C.R. 2429.
[3] Case 40/69 *Hauptzollamt Hamburg-Oberelbe* v. *Firma Paul B. Bollman* [1970] E.C.R. 69.

over, once the Community has legislated, pursuant to Article 40, for the establishment of a common market organisation in a given sector, Member States are under an obligation to refrain from taking any measures which might undermine or create exceptions to it, having regard not only to the express provision of the legislation but also to its aims and objects.[4] For example, the action taken by Italy in purchasing durum wheat on the world market and then reselling it in the Community at a price lower than the target price was held to be incompatible with the common organisation of the cereals market.[5] Member States are also precluded from legislating with regard to the formation of producer prices or production controls in so far as such measures interfere with a common market organisation.[6] Yet the establishment of a common organisation does not necessarily exempt producers from the effects of national law designed to achieve objectives, such as the protection of animal health[7] or changes in the tax burden,[8] which differ from those of the common organisation but which nonetheless affect the conditions, cost or volume of production. The precise powers of the Member States in relation to common organisations will continue to be delineated.[9]

The politically delicate nature of this process is exemplified by the United Kingdom's Milk Marketing Boards (MMB).[10] In 1972,

[4] Case 51/74 *P.J. Van der Hulst's Zonen* v. *Produktschap voor Siergewassen* [1975] E.C.R. 79.

[5] Case 60/75 *Carmine Antonio Russo* v. *Azienda di Stato per gli Interventi sur Mercato Agricola (AIMA)* [1976] E.C.R. 45; Case 52/76 *Luigi Benedetti* v. *Munari Filli s.a.s.* [1977] E.C.R. 163.

[6] See, *e.g.* Case 10/79 *Gaetano Toffoli* v. *Regione Veneto* [1979] E.C.R. 3301; Case 166/82 *Commission* v. *Italy*, not yet reported (O.J. 1984, C.79/2). See also J. Usher, *European Community Law and National Law: The Irreversible Transfer?* (1981) at 55; Barents, "New Developments in Measures Having Equivalent Effect" (1981) 18 C.M.L.Rev. 271 at 300–301.

[7] Joined Cases 141 and 143/81 *Gerrit Holdijk* [1982] E.C.R. 1299.

[8] Joined Cases 36 and 71/80 *Irish Creamery Milk Suppliers Association* v. *Ireland*; *Martin Doyle* v. *An Taoiseach* [1981] E.C.R. 735.

[9] See also Blumental, "Implementing the Common Agricultural Policy: Aspects of the Limitations on the Powers of the Member States" (1984) 35 N.I.L.Q. 28.

[10] The subsequent text refers only to the MMB for England and Wales; in the U.K. similar boards exist for Scotland, Aberdeen and District, North of Scotland and Northern Ireland. For further discussion, see P. Self and H.J. Storing, *The State and the Farmer* (1962) at 88–90; M. Butterwick and E. Neville Rolfe, *Food, Farming and the Common Market* (1968) at 110–115, 120–128; M. Butterwick and E. Neville Rolfe, *Agricultural Marketing and the EEC* (1972) at 12–16, 101–122; S. Baker, *Milk to Market* (1973); P. Giddings, *Marketing Boards and Ministers* (1974); Grant "Gotta Lotta Bottle: Corporatism, the Public and the Private and the Milk Marketing System in Britain" *Sussex Working Papers in Corporatism*, No. 3 (1983); Snyder, "The Milk Marketing Board and EEC Law" unpublished paper (1984).

Declarations annexed to the Act of Accession noted provisional agreement by the Community on the MMB's compatibility with the dairy common organisation and the Treaty.[11] Other Member States' criticisms centred, first, on the Board's monopoly control of the purchase and distribution of raw milk; second, on the fact that, for most United Kingdom producers, membership of the MMB was in effect compulsory; and, third, on the MMB's use of returns from liquid milk sales to subsidise the sale at a loss of manufactured milk products, thereby potentially excluding foreign competition. They argued that, in the absence of Council approval under Regulation 26/62, the MMB infringed EC competition rules, particularly Articles 3, 85 and 86. Following numerous proposals, the Council by Regulation 1421/78[12] amended the basic dairy market regulation to provide that a Member State may, at its request and under certain conditions, be authorised to grant a producer organisation the exclusive right to purchase milk in the region concerned and the right to equalise the price paid to producers. The conditions, specified by Regulation 1422/78,[13] included approval by producers' poll, greater separation of processing and manufacturing operations, establishment of prices by negotiation and differentiation of prices according to intended use only in so far as it did not cause distortion of competition in the United Kingdom between United Kingdom and other Member States' products.

In October and November 1978 99.5 per cent. of producers in England and Wales approved the Board.[14] Consequently, Commission Regulation 1565/79[15] provided for the implementation of Regulation 1422/78, and United Kingdom legislation was duly amended.[16] In 1980 the MMB was the largest milk purchaser in England and Wales. Its sales then included only about 5 per cent. of the total retail trade in liquid milk, but after purchasing 16 creameries from Unigate in August 1979 it manufactured approximately 75 per cent. of butter, 79 per cent. of skimmed milk powder and 43 per cent. of all cheese in England and Wales.[17]

---

[11] O.J. Sp.Ed. 1972, L.73/1.
[12] O.J. 1978, L.171/12.
[13] O.J. 1978, L.171/14.
[14] See (1978) 802 *Agra Europe* at P/12.
[15] O.J. 1979, L.188/29.
[16] See Milk Marketing Scheme (Amendment) Regs. 1979 (S.I. 1979 No. 249); Milk Marketing Scheme (Amendment) Regs. 1981 (S.I. 1981 No. 323); Milk Marketing Scheme (Amendment) Regs. 1981 (S.I. 1981 No. 864).
[17] Consumers' Committee for England and Wales, "Report on the Effects of the Milk Marketing Scheme on Consumers" (1981) at 3.

In 1982, however, the MMB's refusal to supply one of its former wholesale customers was challenged, ultimately without success, in the English courts.[18] Moreover, the Irish Dairy Board in August 1981 complained formally to the EC Commission, alleging unfair competition due to cross-subsidisation of manufactured dairy products from liquid sales contrary to Regulation 1422/78.[19] The Commission took action on this issue under Article 169 and also began an investigation of complaints that the MMB operated differential prices for export and domestic products.[20] The United Kingdom Agricultural Minister also asked for an end to dual pricing, following a call by the Commission's financial controller that the United Kingdom repay all EAGGF subsidies to the dairy sector in 1978 and 1979.[21] This claim, which amounted to virtually the same amount as the budget rebate claimed by the British (though officially the similarity was regarded as a coincidence), was subsequently not pursued, ostensibly because it rested on shaky legal grounds.[22] Nevertheless, as of July 1984 the Commission's Article 169 cross-subsidisation action against the United Kingdom was before the European Court,[23] and a reasoned opinion had been issued regarding differential export pricing. Another action by the Irish Dairy Board was before the English courts and likely to reach the European Court on an Article 177 reference.[24]

---

[18] *Garden Cottage Foods Ltd.* v. *Milk Marketing Board*, House of Lords [1984] 1 A.C. 130; [1983] 2 All E.R. 770; [1983] 3 W.L.R. 143; [1983] 3 C.M.L.R. 43, discharging an injunction ordered by the Court of Appeal (Civil Division) in *Garden Cottage Foods Ltd.* v. *Milk Marketing Board* [1982] 3 All E.R. 292; [1982] 3 W.L.R. 514; [1982] 2 C.M.L.R. 542.

[19] (1983) 1020 *Agra Europe* at N/1.

[20] (1983) 1026 *Agra Europe* at P/4.

[21] (1984) 1069 *Agra Europe* at P/3.

[22] (1984) 1067 *Agra Europe* at P/1.

[23] Case 23/84 *Commission* v. *United Kingdom*, filed January 25, 1984; see [1984] O.J. C.51/5.

[24] The MMB's application to strike out certain points of claim on the grounds that the action should have been brought for judicial review and that the action was brought against the wrong defendant was dismissed by the High Court (Queen's Bench Divisional Court) in *An Bord Bainne Co-operative Limited* (*The Irish Dairy Board*) v. *The Milk Marketing Board* [1984] 1 C.M.L.R. 519. The MMB's appeal was dismissed and application for leave to appeal to the House of Lords was refused by the Court of Appeal in *An Bord Bainne Co-operative Limited* (*Irish Dairy Board*) v. *Milk Marketing Board* [1984] 2 C.M.L.R. 584. The Irish Dairy Board's first application to refer certain questions concerning the lawfulness of the MMB's pricing policy to the European Court was refused by the High Court (Commercial Court) in *An Bord Bainne Co-operative Limited* (*The Irish Diary Board*) v. *Milk Marketing Board* [1985] 1 C.M.L.R. 6.

Absence of a common organisation

Potatoes and agricultural alcohol are the only major temperate zone products not subject to a common market organisation. The absence of a common organisation does not, however, "amount to a legal vacuum which the Member States are entitled to fill."[25] National measures regarding products not subject to a common organisation are subject to general Treaty rules, particularly on the free movement of goods. Thus, in *Potato Marketing Board* v. *Robertsons,*[26] the Oxford County Court considered a levy due under the Potato Marketing Scheme from registered potato producers in relation to Articles 34, 37 and 92–94 of the Treaty.

[25] Case 68/76 *Commission* v. *France* [1977] E.C.R. 515 at 531. See also Case 118/78 *C.J. Meijer B.V.* v. *Department of Trade, Minister of Agriculture, Fisheries and Food and Commissioners of Customs and Excise* [1979] E.C.R. 1387; Case 231/78 *Commission* v. *United Kingdom* [1979] E.C.R. 1447, noted Wyatt (1979) 4 E.L.Rev. 359.
[26] [1983] 1 C.M.L.R. 93.

Chapter 5

PRICE AND FINANCIAL MECHANISMS

The Price System

Uniform prices or common policy?

It has sometimes been assumed that the Common Market would eventually lead to uniform prices. The market price of a commodity would thus tend to be the same, after allowing for transport costs, throughout the Community. Today, however, the CAP is based, at best, on a common price policy and, at worst, on uniform methods of calculating prices.

The Rome Treaty (Art. 8) provided that the Common Market was to be progressively established during a transitional period of twelve years. During this period, in so far as progressive abolition of customs duties and quantitative restrictions between Member States might result in prices likely to jeopardise the attainment of Article 39 objectives, each Member State was entitled by Article 44 to apply to particular products a system of non-discriminatory minimum prices. The criteria for establishing these prices were to be determined by the Council, acting on a proposal from the Commission. Similarly, the Commission was to propose, for determination by the Council, a procedure for revising these criteria in order, *inter alia*, to approximate prices progressively within the Common Market (Art. 44(3), para. 3). At the end of the transitional period, a table of minimum prices still in force was to be drawn up. The Council, acting on a Commission proposal and by weighted majority voting, was to determine the system to be applied within the CAP (Art. 44(6)). To be brought into force by the end of the transitional period at the latest (Art. 40(1)), the CAP was to include a common organisation of agricultural markets (Art. 40(2)). The common organisation of the market may include, according to Article 40(3), para. 1, the regulation of prices. Any price policy was to be based on common criteria and uniform methods of calculation (Art. 40(3), para. 3).

The terms of Article 44(3), para. 3, were reflected in the final resolution of the Stresa Conference. Adopted during a period of fixed currencies and stable exchange rates, it drew the attention of the Commission to the importance of a progressive approximation of prices for basic products, particularly cereals.[1] On June 30, 1960, the Commission submitted to the Council its detailed proposals, commonly known as the first Mansholt Plan, for the formulation and implementation of the CAP.[2] During the transitional period the different prices then prevailing in the six Member States were to be harmonised stage by stage. Accordingly, the first cereals regulation, Regulation 19/62, established the principle of common prices for cereals. It provided, in order to smooth the transition, for a system of intra-Community variable levies, which were gradually to be phased out by July 30, 1967. Following the Commission's proposal to the Council that a single, Community-wide target price for cereals be adopted for the 1964–65 marketing year, it was agreed to accelerate price harmonisation. In fact, however, agreement on the cereals target price was not reached until December 15, 1964, and its entry into force was postponed until July 15, 1967.

Regulation 120/67[3] brought into force a single price system for cereals. Its preamble recited, *inter alia*, that the creation of a single market in cereals depended, in part, on the adoption of a single price system, that is,

> "a system comprising, as provided for in Article 13 of Regulation No. 19, a target price valid for the whole Community, a single threshold price, a single method of fixing intervention prices and finally a single frontier crossing point for the Community to be used for determining c.i.f. prices for products from third countries."

---

[1] Commission de la Communauté économique européenne, *Recueil des Documents de la Conférence agricole des Etats membres de la Communauté économique européenne à Stresa du 3 au 12 juillet 1958* (1958) at 224.

[2] Commission de la Communauté économique européenne, "Proposition concernant l'élaboration et la mise en oeuvre de la politique agricole commune en vertu de l'article 43 du traité instituant la CEE" COM(60)105 (1960). See also Riesenfeld, "Common Market for Agricultural Products and Common Agricultural Policy in the European Economic Community" (1965) *University of Illinois Law Forum* 658 at 661–662. The importance placed by the Commission on the approximation of prices was emphasised in one Commission member's statement that, of the 1960 proposals, "[t]he most important objective was undoubtedly that of achieving a single price for a given product over the European market as a whole" (J.F. Deniau, *The Common Market, Its Structure and Purpose* (1962) at 3, quoted in Heathcote, "Agricultural Politics in the European Community" Department of Political Science, Research School of Social Sciences, Australian National University, *Occasional Paper No. 7* (1971) at 8).

[3] O.J. Sp.Ed. 1967, 33.

Such a price structure presumed that the product was one in which the EC was largely self-sufficient, that further production should be encouraged, that imports were to be admitted as exceptions subject to conditions and also that world prices were generally lower than EC prices.[4] Despite the continuity of these presumptions as the basis of EC price policy, the system of uniform, Community-wide prices achieved for several commodities in 1967 was in fact very short-lived. On August 10, 1969, the French franc was devalued by 11.1 per cent. and on October 26 of the same year the German mark was revalued by 9.3 per cent. These changes marked the beginning of a period of instability and crisis in the international monetary system. They brought the brief period of real common prices within the CAP effectively to an end.

The assumption that the Common Market necessarily entailed uniform agricultural commodity prices was therefore not borne out by political events. Nor, at least with the benefit of hindsight, is it supported without reservation by the Rome Treaty or by economic theory. The Rome Treaty does not legally require a system of uniform agricultural commodity prices at either the wholesale or the retail stage. Article 40(3), para. 3, provides that any common price policy shall be based on common criteria and uniform methods of calculation. Given this condition, however, prices for a given agricultural commodity need not be the same throughout the Community.[5] The assumption that the CAP requires uniform prices has also been criticised, again using hindsight, from the standpoint of neoclassical economic theory. The criticism rests on the ground that the basic assumptions underlying the theoretical argument in favour of uniform prices do not hold in the Community. These assumptions are, first, that the main purpose of price policy is to allocate resources. Second, the pattern of resource allocation which is in some sense best for society as a whole reflects the cost structure of the lowest-cost producers. Third, the optimally efficient allocation of resources, reflecting comparative advantage, results from competitively determined market prices. CAP prices are not, however, designed to play this allocative role. Instead, market prices for most agricultural com-

---

[4] Usher, "Agricultural Markets: Their Price Systems and Financial Mechanisms" (1979) 4 E.L.Rev. 147 at 150. On EC price policy, see *id., passim,* and Tarditti, "Price Policies and European Economic Integration" in K.J. Thomson and R.M. Warren (ed.), *Price and Market Policies in European Agriculture* (1984).

[5] See also J. Megret, J.V. Louis, D. Vignes and M. Waelbroeck, *Le droit de la Communauté économique européenne,* Vol. 2: *Agriculture* (1973) at 17. On the extent to which agriculture is nonetheless subject to general Treaty rules, such as the provisions on the free movement of goods, see Chap. 2.

modities covered by common market organisations are subject to
supply and demand only within a pre-determined, administered
price bracket. Their main objective is to support farmers'
incomes.[6]

Structure and aims

The archetypal CAP price structure is that established for cereals by Regulation 120/67.[7] It provided for the fixing, simultaneously and before August 1 of each year, of a target price for
common wheat, durum wheat, barley, maize and rye; a basic intervention price for common wheat, durum wheat, barley, rye and, in
particular circumstances, maize; and a guaranteed minimum price
for durum wheat. Other, derived intervention prices were fixed for
common wheat, durum wheat, barley, maize and rye. The
threshold price was to be set with reference to Rotterdam, the largest grain importing port. Only later were regionalised intervention prices abandoned; the "silo system" was introduced in 1975
(see Chap. 4).

The legality of this price structure and its analogues for other
products has been upheld by the European Court. For example, in
Case 30/67 *Industrie Molitoria Imolese*[8] the Court held that the
scheme of regionalised or derived intervention prices for cereals
was an integral part of a price system considered indispensable to
the establishment of a common organisation of the market. Similarly, the Court subsequently rejected a claim by German millers
and others for damages resulting from the replacement of the multiple intervention price system by a single derived intervention
price. It held that if, in adopting a single derived intervention price
system, the Council omitted to correct the disadvantages to which
German cereal meal producers were indirectly subject as compared to their French competitors, nevertheless such an omission
was not capable of rendering the provision illegal. The Council
was not obliged, therefore, to ascertain whether circumstances of a
special kind could militate against the application of provisions
which would normally have been satisfactory.[9]

The Commission has described the CAP as "a system of support

[6] T. Heidhues, T.E. Josling, C. Ritson and S. Tangermann, "Common Prices and
Europe's Farm Policy," Trade Policy Research Centre, *Thames Essay No. 14*
(1978); see also S. Harris, A. Swinbank and G. Wilkinson, *The Food and Farm
Policies of the European Community* (1983) at 39–40.
[7] O.J. Sp.Ed. 1967, 33.
[8] Case 30/67 *Industrie Molitoria Imolese* v. *Council* [1968] E.C.R. 115.
[9] Joined Cases 63–69/72 *Wilhelm Werhahn Hansamühle* v. *Council* [1973] E.C.R.
1229.

of farmers' incomes mainly through the support of market prices."[10] That the price structure is directed primarily at the income of producers rather than of others in the food chain has been confirmed by the Court. In Case 2/75 *Mackprang*,[11] German cereal millers challenged a Commission decision authorising the Federal Republic to limit intervention purchases to cereals harvested in Germany. The applicants, following a fall in the forward rate of the French franc, had purchased in France cereals which they planned to offer for intervention in Germany. At the time of the Commission decision the cereals were in transit, and an offer in proper form had not yet been made to the intervention agency. Upholding the Commission decision, the Court stated (at 616) that the intervention system was set up with a view to guaranteeing to producers, having regard to the regionalisation of prices, a market for their cereals at reasonable prices when there were no markets available providing normal profit margins. In Joined Cases 67–85/75 *Lesieur Cotelle* the Court rejected a claim by French oil millers for damages allegedly resulting from the Commission's exercise of its powers relating to subsidies and monetary compensatory amounts on colza and rape seed. It stated that "in so far as Regulation No. 136/66 is intended to give guarantees, the latter relate to colza seed farmers and not processors. . . ."[12]

Price fixing

The basic regulations for common market organisations establish dates for the fixing of prices. These dates, however, have rarely if ever been followed since the late 1960s. Instead, all agricultural prices are considered together with other outstanding policy items during the annual price review, beginning in December and ending in the spring.[13]

---

[10] Commission of the European Communities, "Reflections on the Common Agricultural Policy" COM(80)800 final (1980) at 3.

[11] Case 2/75 *EVst für Getreide und Futtermittel* v. *Firma C. Mackprang* [1975] E.C.R. 607.

[12] Joined Cases 67–85/75 *Lesieur Cotelle et Associés* S.A. v. *Commission* [1976] E.C.R. 391 at 410.

[13] On the 1978–1979 and 1980–1981 reviews, respectively, see Harris and Swinbank, "Price Fixing under the Cap—Proposition and Decision: The Example of the 1978/79 Price Review" (1978) *Food Policy* 256; Pearce, "The Common Agricultural Policy: The Accumulation of Special Interests" in H. Wallace, W. Wallace and C. Webb (eds.), *Policy Making in the European Community* (2nd ed. 1983). A party wishing to challenge the failure of EC institutions to fix prices according to the dates provided in the relevant regulations would, however, find it virtually impossible to show that it was directly and individually concerned by the provision.

Prices are expressed in the form of a Council regulation. Consequently, the procedure is formally governed by Article 43(2), para. 3, which provides that regulations implementing the CAP shall be made by the Council, acting on a proposal from the Commission and after consulting the Assembly, acting unanimously during the first two stages and by a qualified majority thereafter. The Commission, in making proposals, consults a wide variety of groups, particularly COPA. Proposals are based on the so-called "objective method," which in principle takes account of price trends, production costs, agricultural incomes and the financial consequences for the EC budget.[14] The Parliament has, in practice, little voice in fixing prices, because CAP expenditure constitutes "expenditure necessarily resulting from this Treaty" under Article 203(4), para. 2. Since the Luxembourg compromise the Council has tended to fix agricultural prices by means of a package deal; the major recent exception was in 1982–83 (see Chap. 3).

In fixing agricultural prices EC institutions are bound by the Treaty but nonetheless enjoy broad discretion. In 1980 the threshold price for durum wheat was challenged by a group of German wheat millers and a pasta producer. The applicants claimed that the gap between the threshold prices of common and durum wheat was excessive, leading to the substitution of common for durum wheat in manufacturing pasta. The result was a weakening of their market position to the advantage of Italian manufacturers whose location near the growing areas of durum wheat in the Community enabled them to obtain supplies at prices near the intervention price, whereas the German manufacturers obtained durum wheat meal imported from the United States at the threshold price. Dismissing the application, the Court held that, in determining policy with respect to the fixing of agricultural prices, the relevant EC institutions enjoy wide discretionary powers, regarding not only the establishment of the factual basis of their action but also the definition of the objectives to be pursued, within the framework of the Treaty provisions, and the choice of the appropriate means of action.[15]

Article 40(3), para. 2, provides that the common organisation of agricultural markets shall be limited to pursuit of the Article 39

[14] See de Veer, "The Objective Method" (1979) 6 *European Review of Agricultural Economics* 279; Swinbank, "The Objective Method, A Critique" (1979) 6 *European Review of Agricultural Economics* 303.
[15] Joined Cases 197–200, 243, 245 and 247/80 *Ludwigshafener Walzmühle Erling* v. *Council and Commission* [1981] E.C.R. 3211.

objectives and shall exclude any discrimination between producers or consumers within the Community. The objective set forth in Article 39(1)(*e*) of ensuring that supplies reach consumers at reasonable prices must, however, according to the Court, "be considered in the light of the agricultural policy as a whole as laid down by the Treaty and cannot be taken to mean the lowest possible prices."[16] This objective is not infringed unless the measures in question "give rise to prices which would appear obviously unreasonable on selling to consumers."[17] Moreover, the fact that EC institutions adopt a policy on agricultural price levels for a long period does not confer on traders any entitlement to the preservation of such advantages as the established policy may have allowed them. Nor does it impose any limitation on the freedom of the Commission and the Council to adjust their policy in step with data reflecting the evolution of the market and with changes in the objectives to be pursued.[18] (See also Chap. 2.)

In sectors covered by a common organisation, especially one based on a common price system, Member States are no longer competent to take unilateral national action affecting the machinery of price formation established by the EC regime.[19] They may, however, intervene in price formation at the wholesale and retail stages, provided that the intervention does not jeopardise the aims or operation of the common organisation (see Chaps. 3 and 4). Nevertheless, the Court has held that national rules imposing a price freeze at the distribution stage for milk-feed products for calves were contrary to the requirements of the basic regulation on the common organisation of the market for milk and milk products.[20]

Price and market

A basic postulate of the CAP is that farmers' incomes are to be derived mainly from consumer prices. Hence EC-fixed prices, which are ultimately translated into consumer prices, are to be sufficiently high as to provide a fair standard of living for the agricultural community. In practice, the postulate means that farmers'

[16] Case 34/62 *Germany* v. *Commission* [1963] E.C.R. 131.
[17] Case 5/73 *Balkan-Import-Export GmbH* v. *Hauptzollamt Berlin-Packhof* [1973] E.C.R. 1091 at 1112.
[18] Joined Cases 197–200, 243, 245 and 247/80 *Ludwigshafener Walzmühle Erling* v. *Council and Commission* [1981] E.C.R. 3211.
[19] See, *e.g.* Case 31/74 *Filippo Galli* [1975] E.C.R. 47.
[20] Case 5/79 *Procureur Général* v. *Hans Buys, Hans Pesch, Yves Dullieux and Denkavit France S.à.r.l.* [1979] E.C.R. 3203.

incomes stem primarily from market sales, as compared, for example, to deficiency payments financed through the tax system. It does not, however, necessarily imply that CAP prices, and hence farmers' incomes, are determined solely by the intersection of supply and demand. Most EC agricultural product markets are managed (or administered) rather than "free" markets, and prices for the major temperate zone commodities fluctuate only within an agreed price bracket. In addition, although in principle the CAP may not completely eliminate the operation of the market,[21] it also incorporates numerous mechanisms which derogate fundamentally from its basic postulate; these include production aids, production refunds, various structural aids and restrictions on production.[22] In these respects at least, while EC price policy has contributed to the internationalisation of the production and exchange of agricultural commodities,[23] the CAP price system may seem to be an exception to the capitalist market ideology which is often considered to be embodied in the Rome Treaty.[24] In fact, it forms part of a regulatory system which represents one pole of the policy spectrum in the Community's mixed economy.

Translation of EC into National Prices

Units of account

Common agricultural prices in the EC today refer to the prices of particular commodities as expressed in European Currency Units (ecu). The ecu is not a fictitious currency but an accounting

---

[21] See Joined Cases 80 and 81/77 *Société Les Commissionnaires Réunies S.à.r.l.* v. *Receveur des Douanes*; *S.à.r.l. Les Fils de Henri Ramel* v. *Receveur des Douanes* [1978] E.C.R. 927; see also the Opinion of Mr Advocate General Verloren Van Themaat in Joined Cases 197–200, 243, 245 and 247/80 *Ludwigshafener Walzmühle Erling KG* v. *Council and Commission* [1981] E.C.R. 3211 at 3265.

[22] See Melchior, "The Common Agricultural Policy," in Commission of the European Communities (ed.) *Thirty Years of Community Law* (1983) at 439–440, 450–452.

[23] Lacroix and Mollard, "Firmes multinationales et politiques étatiques: deux éléments-clé de l'internationalisation agro-alimentaire en Europe occidentale" in "L'internationalisation du secteur agro-alimentaire en Europe. Recherche comparative sur douze pays de l'Est et de l'Ouest" (1982) 16 *Economies et Sociétés* 1195 at 1206.

[24] For two similar assessments, from different political standpoints, of the Treaty's economic assumptions, see M. Newman, *Socialism and European Unity* (1983), Appendix II at 284; and Hodges, "The Legacy of the Treaty of Rome: A Community of Equals?" (1979) 35 *The World Today* 232 at 234. See also McAllister, "The EEC Dimension: Intended and Unintended Consequences" in J. Cornford (ed.), *The Failure of the State* (1975) at 176–182.

device. Any economic integration scheme which has some common financial arrangements, but whose members have different currencies, requires an accounting device (*numéraire*) by which to express common financial obligations. In the Community, the ecu serves, as did its predecessors, as this common denominator. In the terminology of private international law, it is a currency of account, while the different currencies of the Member States are currencies of payment.[25]

Article 40(3), para. 3, provides that any common price policy shall be based not only on common criteria but also on common methods of calculation. Article 207, para. 1, provides further that the Community budget shall be drawn up in the unit of account determined by subsequent regulations. Regulation 129/62[26] originally defined the unit of account as the value of 0.88867088 grammes of fine gold, which was then the official value of the United States dollar. Its Article 2 provided that, when sums given in one currency were required to be expressed in another currency, the exchange rate to be applied was that corresponding to the par value communicated to and recognised by the International Monetary Fund. With agreement on common price levels in the mid-1960s, EC agricultural prices were to be fixed in terms of the unit of account, and then converted into the national currencies of the Member States at the official declared exchange rate of each national currency as against the dollar. Thus, the agricultural prices fixed in units of account were translated into the different national currencies at a common support level.

In 1969, however, this apparently stable system was fundamentally shaken. The devaluation of the French franc and the revaluation of the German mark brought the period of real common prices, that is, as evaluated in stable currencies of payment as well as in the currency of account, effectively to an end.[27] These events, greatly over-simplifying, had several other implications:

---

[25] A currency of account is that currency in which an obligation, such as that created by a judgment, is measured or expressed, whereas a currency of payment is that currency in which the obligation is to be discharged: *per* Lord Denning in *Woodhouse A.C. Israel Cocoa Ltd.* v. *Nigerian Produce Marketing Co. Ltd.* [1971] 2 Q.B. 23 at 54; see also F.A. Mann, *The Legal Aspect of Money* (4th ed., 1982) at 199.

[26] O.J. Sp.Ed. 1959–62, 274.; J.O. 30.10.62, p. 6.

[27] For further discussion, see R.W. Irving and H.A. Fearn, "Green Money and the Common Agricultural Policy" Centre for European Agricultural Studies, Wye College, *Occasional Paper No. 2* (1975); S. Harris, A. Swinbank and G. Wilkinson, *The Food and Farm Policies of the European Community* (1983) at 187–214; Usher, "Agricultural Markets: Their Price Systems and Financial Mechanisms" (1979) 4 E.L.Rev. 147 at 155–15.

first, the introduction of a new accounting unit; second, special exchange rates ("green money") for the agricultural sector; and, third, a system of border taxes and subsidies (monetary compensatory amounts; m.c.a.s) in intra-Community agricultural commodity trade.

After early 1971 the link between the dollar and gold was broken, the dollar was devalued, fixed parities were abandoned and European currencies were allowed to float. Regulation 129/62, which had been amended in 1968,[28] was amended again in September 1973 to facilitate derogations.[29] From mid-1973 to March 1979, the unit of account for agricultural purposes was assumed to have the same value as the European Monetary Unit of Account, the basis of the so-called "joint float."[30]

On March 13, 1979, the European Monetary System (EMS) came into force,[31] replacing the former unit of account with the ecu. The ecu was introduced into the CAP on April 9, 1979. Although in principle the ecu was to be neutral with regard to the CAP, in practice it proved necessary to express the unit of account formerly used in agriculture in terms of the ecu. Regulation 652/79 provided for conversion at the rate of 1 ua = 1.208953 ecu.[32] The ecu is a "basket" currency unit, equal to the sums of specified amounts of the Member States' currencies. The Greek drachma is not included in the calculation of the ecu. Although the United Kingdom is not a member of the EMS, sterling is an element in the ecu "basket" and has a national central rate. At the end of 1982 the United Kingdom central rate was 1 ecu = £0.5605.[33]

"Green money"

In addition to the modification of the CAP (and EC) unit of account, a second major change in Community financial mechanisms resulting from the events of the late 1960s and early 1970s was the introduction of "green money." "Green money" is not in fact a currency. It is a set of rates of exchange between the CAP unit of account, now the ecu, in which agricultural prices are fixed, and the Member States' national currencies, in which transactions

---

[28] Reg. 653/68 (O.J. 1968, L.123/4).
[29] Reg. 2543/73 (O.J. 1973, L.263/1).
[30] Gilsdorf, "The System of Monetary Compensation from a Legal Standpoint: Part I—The System and its Effects." (1980) 5 E.L.Rev. 341 at 352–353.
[31] Regs. 3180/78 (O.J. 1978, L.379/1); 3181/78 (O.J. 1978), L.379/1).
[32] Reg. 652/79 (O.J. 1979, L.84/1).
[33] Commission of the European Communities, *The Agricultural Situation in the Community: 1983 Report* (1984) at 181.

involving CAP expenditure and receipts actually take place. As such, it is used only in the agricultural sector.

Between 1962 and 1969 the exchange rates used for CAP purposes were the exchange rates for national currencies as against the United States dollar declared to the IMF.[34] In 1969, however, after the devaluation of the franc and the revaluation of the mark, the French and German governments were unwilling to accept the implications of the change in their currencies' market values for domestic farm and food prices. They refused to alter immediately the rates at which the EC unit of account was converted into their respective national currencies for CAP purposes. Although they were authorised to maintain existing price levels and gradually to phase in the agricultural exchange rates, this adjustment was overtaken by events in the early 1970s. Accordingly, by the 1971 Smithsonian Agreement the set of exchange rates used for agricultural purposes differed from market rates. Subsequently, on the accession of the United Kingdom and Ireland to the Community, a special "representative rate" of exchange for the pound for agricultural purposes was also established.[35] Later measures recognised conversion rates other than official parities[36] and facilitated derogations from Regulation 129/62 for Member States which wished to establish separate exchange rates for agriculture.[37] In 1975 Regulation 475/75[38] provided for special exchange rates to be used in agriculture. These separate rates, re-enacted each year, are legally designated as representative rates, sometimes known as official conversion rates for agricultural purposes and referred to more generally as "green" rates. They apply only to the agricultural sector and not, for example, to short-term economic policy and commercial policy measures.[39]

The legality of "green" rates which differed from market rates was challenged in Case 138/78 *Hans-Markus Stölting* v. *Hauptzollamt Hamburg-Jonas*.[40] A German milk producer objected to the co-responsibility levy on the ground, *inter alia*, that it infringed the Article 40(3) prohibition of discrimination. He argued that, since the levy was established in units of account, its conversion into national currencies at different green rates led to unequal bur-

---

[34] Reg. 129/62, Art. 2(1) (O.J. Sp.Ed. 1959–62, 274; J.O. 30.10.62, p. 6).
[35] Reg. 222/73 (O.J. 1973, L.27/4).
[36] Reg. 509/73 (O.J. 1973, L.50/1).
[37] Reg. 2543/73 (O.J. 1973, L.263/1).
[38] O.J. 1975, L.52/28.
[39] Case 78/77 *Firma Johann Lührs* v. *Hauptzollamt Hamburg-Jonas* [1978] E.C.R 169.
[40] [1979] E.C.R. 713.

dens among Member States in relation to their actual monetary situation. The European Court, on an Article 177 request for a preliminary ruling, stated that:

> "those exchange rates apply whenever it is necessary to convert into national currencies the amounts expressed in units of account laid down in the provisions on guide prices, intervention prices and other prices provided for in a common organisation of the market . . . . Although in certain transactions the application of these exchange rates may possibly involve advantages or disadvantages which may appear as discrimination, it none the less remains true that in general such application serves to remedy monetary situations which in the absence of a measure such as Regulation No. 878/77 [reenacting Regulation 475/75] would result in much more serious, obvious and general discrimination. Although it is not without serious drawbacks, the adoption of the system of so-called green exchange rates is therefore justified by the prohibition on discrimination and the requirements of the common agricultural policy."[41]

Similarly, in Case 49/79 *Richard Pool* v. *Council*,[42] the Court upheld the validity of the "green pound" system. Rejecting an application for damages under Article 215, it considered that the aims of prices fixed within the common organisation for beef and veal were to determine the application of intervention measures and to adjust the level of levies and refunds applicable in trade with non-Member States. The price system did not guarantee to individual traders that their produce would be disposed of at the precise price level determined by EC rules. Consequently, that level, expressed in units of account, could not be used as a basis for comparison with market prices in order to establish that damage had been caused.

The "green rate" for each national currency is the means by which CAP prices fixed in ecu are actually translated into the different currencies of the Member States. Regardless of the existence of common CAP prices expressed in the ecu unit of account, "green rates" may result in substantial differences in real agricultural prices. During much of the 1970s, for example, the "green pound" was greatly overvalued, and the "green mark" greatly undervalued, as compared to the two currencies' respective mar-

---

[41] [1979] E.C.R. 713 at 723.
[42] [1980] E.C.R. 569 at 581.

ket rates. The difference in real CAP support prices in the United Kingdom and Germany, which had the lowest and the highest such prices, respectively, in the EC, was 60 per cent. at one time in 1976.[43] For 1981–1982 the United Kingdom "green rate" was 1 ecu = £0.6187, as compared to a market rate at the end of 1982 of 1 ecu = £0.5605.[44]

"Green rates" are in principle fixed by the Council following a proposal by the Commission. Generally, however, it has been left to the individual Member States to indicate to the Council whether and to what extent they wish to amend their "green rate." Changes in the "green rate" often influence domestic farm prices and food prices much more directly than do changes in ecu CAP prices. For example, when during the 1970s the "green pound" was overvalued as compared to the market rate for sterling, each ecu of CAP prices translated into fewer pounds sterling (because of the overvalued "green pound,"*i.e.* higher exchange rate for agricultural purposes) than would have been the case if the "green pound" had been aligned with the sterling market rate. Accordingly, farm support prices and farm incomes were lower, food prices were lower and United Kingdom m.c.a. payments (see next section) to the EC budget were higher than would otherwise have been the case. A devaluation of the "green pound" would, conversely, have meant higher guaranteed farm prices, higher food prices and lower export charges.

The intricate politics of "green money" were illustrated by the controversy concerning the attempt by the United Kingdom Minister of Agriculture in 1978 to obtain a "green pound" devaluation. This was opposed by Germany and Benelux

> "who could not get anything extra for their own farmers through a green currency devaluation and were annoyed that Mr. Silkin could get an increase for his own farmers while pressing for low price increases for Community farmers as a whole."[45]

It is not surprising, therefore, that, according to the 1978 Parliamentary Report to the Labour Party conference, "[t]he key instrument in the administration of agricultural policy [was] the representative rate (the Green Pound) for the application of EEC

---

[43] S. Harris, A. Swinbank and G. Wilkinson, *The Food and Farm Policies of the European Community* (1983) at 194.

[44] Commission of the European Communities, *The Agricultural Situation in the Community: 1983 Report* (1984) at 181.

[45] Grant, "The Politics of the Green Pound, 1974–79" (1981) 19 J.C.M.S. 313 at 326.

agricultural support prices in the United Kingdom."[46] Consequently, Member States through the Council have sometimes fixed "green rates" product by product or so as to coincide with the marketing year of different products.[47] For example, in March 1976 the practice was introduced of delaying the application of a new "green rate" until the start of the marketing year for each product.

The fixing of "green rates" and their potential alignment with central market rates are subject only to a limited extent to judicial review. A member of the Commission's Legal Service, writing in a personal capacity, considered that:

> "Judicial review in this field will have to be confined to examining whether the maintenance of a given price level following the fixing of a green rate is arbitrary. An arbitrary manner of fixing rates would be one which dictated *exclusively* by national interests that are contrary to the objectives of the common agricultural policy."[48]

The fixing of "green rates" is also limited by the convention that changes can only move "green rates" towards, and not away from, the central rate for the particular currency. It has been suggested that departure from this convention would constitute "a serious infringement of the law."[49]

For much of the life of the Community, therefore, uniform agricultural prices have been replaced by a common unit of account (now the ecu) which is converted into the various national currencies at different, artificial rates of exchange ("green rates"). These rates of exchange are used only for agricultural purposes, are not necessarily equal to market rates and remain largely subject to control by the individual Member States.

Monetary Compensatory Amounts

Introduction

The changes in the international monetary system during the early 1970s had a third effect on the CAP: the introduction of

---

[46] Quoted in Grant, "The Politics of the Green Pound, 1974–79" (1981) 19 J.C.M.S. 313 at 313. The author of this case study considers the overvaluation of the green pound in relation to sterling to be the central issue in British agricultural policy between 1974–79.

[47] Reg. 878/77 (O.J. 1977, L.106/27).

[48] Gilsdorf, "The System of Monetary Compensation from a Legal Standpoint: Part II—Legal Basis of and Limits to the System" (1980) 5 E.L.Rev. 433 at 437; see *also Case 112/77 August Töpfer & Co. GmbH* v. *Commission* [1978] E.C.R. 1019

[49] *Ibid.* (1980) 5 E.L.Rev. 433 at 440.

monetary compensatory amounts (m.c.a.s). M.c.a.s are border taxes and subsidies designed, in principle, to compensate for the different price levels resulting from the differences in the rates at which CAP prices are translated into national currencies. Together with the unit of account and "green money," m.c.a.s compose the EC's agri-monetary system.[50]

M.c.a.s were introduced by Council Regulation 974/71[51] following the floating upward of the German and Dutch currencies in 1971. Their purpose was to maintain the value of prices in national currency by preventing distortions in trade, in other words, to compensate for the fact that, in countries in which "green rates" were below market rates, imports had in real terms become cheaper and exports more expensive. Subsequently, m.c.a.s were introduced in trade with Italy, because the value of the lira had increased in terms of the dollar, the currency in relation to which the value of European currencies were then measured.[52] Council Regulation 2746/72[53] brought m.c.a.s within the CAP and made them compulsory where applicable. In 1973 m.c.a.s were extended to currency which was depreciating.[54] Today, for countries whose "green rates" are above market rates (and whose agricultural prices are therefore theoretically below the prices set in ecu), m.c.a.s are granted as a subsidy on imports but due as a levy on exports (negative m.c.a.s). Conversely, for countries whose "green rates" are below market rates, m.c.a.s are due as a levy on imports but granted as a subsidy on exports (positive m.c.a.s). Thus, the m.c.a. system, in principle, evens out the differences in

[50] The literature on the EC's agri-monetary system is vast, but especially useful introductions include: Mackel, "Green Money and the Common Agricultural Policy" (1978) *National Westminster Bank Quarterly Review* 33; R. Fennell, *The Common Agricultural Policy of the European Community* (1979) at 89–102; S. Harris, A. Swinbank and G. Wilkinson, *The Food and Farm Policies of the European Community* (1983) at 187–214; Strauss, "Economic Effects of Monetary Compensatory Amounts" (1983) 21 J.C.M.S. 261; Tangerman, "What is Different about European Agricultural Protectionism?" (1983) 6 *The World Economy* 39. On the legal aspects in particular, see Gilsdorf, "The System of Monetary Compensation from a Legal Standpoint: Part I—The System and its Effects" (1980) 5 E.L.Rev. 341, "Part II—Legal Basis of and Limits to the System" (1980) 5 E.L.Rev. 433; Usher, "Agricultural Markets: Their Price Systems and Financial Mechanisms" (1979) 4 E.L.Rev. 147.

[51] O.J. 1971, L.106/1.

[52] See Case 94/77 *Fratelli Zerbone Snc.* v. *Administrazione delle Finanze delle Stato* [1978] E.C.R. 99.

[53] O.J. Sp.Ed. 1972, 64.

[54] Reg. 509/73 (O.J. 1973, L.50/15).

national agricultural prices which are due to differences in "green rates."

Legality

The legality of m.c.a.s was first challenged following the introduction of such charges by France and Germany, respectively, after the devaluation of the franc and the revaluation of the mark. In two cases the Court affirmed the validity of temporary m.c.a.s as based on short-term economic policy measures under Article 103 or protective measures under the transitional period safeguard clause in Article 226.[55]

Regulation 974/71 established the system which, as amended, is currently in force, according to which m.c.a.s, when applicable, are compulsory and financed from EC funds. In 1973 this system was challenged in several cases. For example, Case 5/73 *Balkan-Import-Export*, a request for a preliminary ruling, concerned the imposition of m.c.a.s on the importation into Germany of sheep's milk cheese from Bulgaria. The Court, while recognising that m.c.a.s constituted a partitioning of the market, considered that:

" . . . here they have a corrective influence on the variations in fluctuating exchange rates which, in a system of market organisation for agricultural products based on uniform prices, might cause disturbances in trade in these products.

Diversion of trade caused solely by the monetary situation can be considered more damaging to the common interest, bearing in mind the aims of the common agricultural policy, than the disadvantages of the measures in question.

Consequently these compensatory amounts are conducive to the maintenance of a normal flow of trade in the exceptional circumstances created temporarily by the monetary situation.

They are also intended to prevent the disruption in the Member State concerned of the intervention system set up under Community Regulations.

Furthermore, these are not levies introduced by some Member State unilaterally, but Community measures which, bearing in mind the exceptional circumstances of the time, are

---

[55] Case 37/70 *Rewe-Zentral des Lebensmittel-Grosshandels GmbH* v. *Hauptzollamt Emmerich* [1971] E.C.R. 23; Joined Cases 9 and 11/71 *Compagnie d'Approvisionnement, de Transport et de Crédit S.A. and Grands Moulins de Paris S.A.* v. *Commission* [1972] E.C.R. 391.

permissible within the framework of the common agricultural policy."[56]

Accordingly, it upheld the validity of Regulation 974/71, based on Article 103 of the Treaty. In its decision, however, the Court made it clear that such measures, if intended to be other than temporary, needed to be based on Articles 40 and 43.[57] Regulation 2746/72 gave the m.c.a. system this legal basis.[58] (The more recent reticence of the Court concerning m.c.a.s is discussed later.)

Application

M.c.a.s are to be applied when, in specified conditions, the difference between a country's representative ("green") rate and its currency's spot market rate "would lead to disturbances in trade in agricultural products" (Reg. 974/71, Art. 1(3)). In authorising or refusing to authorise the application of m.c.a.s according to this criterion, EC institutions have wide discretionary powers. For example, the Court has held that the Commission may find that there is a risk of disturbance in trade in agricultural products merely on the basis of an appreciable fall in a currency's rate of exchange and may state its reasons for that finding in a reference to the conditions set out in Regulation 974/71, Art. 1(1). Moreover, when deciding whether there is a risk of such disturbance, the Commission may make evaluations of a general nature, taking into consideration groups of products, either of basic products or of both basic and derived products, as well as the state of the market and monetary factors resulting from the value of the currencies of the Member States. Judicial review is limited to examining whether the exercise of discretion contained a manifest error or constituted an abuse of power or whether the authority did not clearly exceed the bounds of its discretion.[59]

M.c.a.s are charged on products which are subject to interven-

---

[56] Case 5/73 *Balkan-Import-Export-GmbH* v. *Hauptzollamt Berlin-Packhof* [1973] E.C.R. 1091 at 1113. See also Case 9/73 *Carl Schlüter* v. *Hauptzollamt Lörrach* [1973] E.C.R. 1135; Case 10/73 *Rewe-Zentral AG* v. *Hauptzollamt Kehl* [1973] E.C.R. 1175; Case 136/77 *Firma A. Racke* v. *Hauptzollamt Mainz* [1978] E.C.R. 1245.

[57] [1973] E.C.R. 1091 at 1108–1109.

[58] O.J. 1972, 64. See also Olmi, "Agriculture" JUR(79) D/01575, typescript (1979) at 36.

[59] Case 29/77 *S.A. Roquette Frères* v. *French State—Administration des Douanes* [1977] E.C.R. 1835. See also Case 43/72 *Merkur-Aussenhandels-GmbH* v. *Commission* [1973] E.C.R. 1055; Case 55/75 *Balkan-Import Export GmbH* v. *Hauptzollamt Berlin-Packhof* [1976] E.C.R. 19.

tion arrangements and also on products whose prices are dependent on the price of products subject to intervention.[60] One test of the latter is whether the price of the allegedly price-dependent product fluctuates appreciably according to variations in the price of the intervention product; for example, the price of powdered whey has been held not to depend on the price of skimmed milk powder.[61] Alternatively, it is sufficient if the m.c.a.s applicable to a basic product have a considerable incidence or effect on the price of the processed product.[62] In addition, m.c.a.s may validly be fixed for products derived from the processing of agricultural products and not coming under Annex II if they are the subject of a specific arrangements under Article 235, always provided that the m.c.a.s applicable to the basic products have a considerable incidence on the price of the processed products.[63]

Each Member State is assigned an m.c.a. percentage, based on the percentage difference between its "green rate" and its central market rate. For most countries which are members of the EMS (Germany, Benelux countries, Denmark, Ireland, France), the m.c.a. percentage is calculated from the difference between its "green rate" and its ecu central rate. The result is a "fixed m.c.a.," so-called because it changes only with a change in either the "green rate" or the central rate, which is infrequent. The United Kingdom and Greece, which are not members of EMS, and Italy have "variable m.c.a.s," which are calculated from the percentage difference between the "green rate" and the market rate of exchange against the ecu over a specified reference period. The m.c.a. for basic products is calculated by applying the m.c.a. percentage to the intervention price (or equivalent), converted from ecus to national currencies at the "green rate" for each country. For other products it is obtained by multiplying the m.c.a. for the basic product by a specified coefficient, representing the incidence of the price of the basic product on that of the price of the processed product.

---

[60] Reg. 974/71, Art. 1(2) (O.J. 1971, L.106/1).
[61] Case 131/77 *Firma Milac, Gross-und Aussenhandel Arnold Nöll* v. *Hauptzollamt Saarbrücken* [1978] E.C.R. 1041.
[62] Joined Cases 12 and 84/78 *Re Monetary Compensatory Amounts for Durum Wheat: Italy* v. *Commission*; *Tomadini SNC* v. *Amministrazione delle Finanze dello Stato* [1979] E.C.R. 1731.
[63] See, *e.g.* Case 151/77 *Peiser and Co. KG* v. *Hauptzollamt Hamburg-Ericus* [1979] E.C.R. 1469; Case 11/78 *Italy* v. *Commission* [1979] E.C.R. 1527; Case 95/78 *Dulciora S.p.A.* v. *Amministrazione delle Finanze dello Stato* [1979] E.C.R. 1549.

In calculating the incidence (or extent of price dependence) for purposes of m.c.a.s, the Commission has a wide margin of discretion, which may extend even to general assessments. Thus the Court has held that, while EC institutions must ensure, in exercising their powers, that the amounts which traders are charged is no greater than is required to achieve the aim which the authorities wish to accomplish, it does not necessarily follow that that obligation must be measured in relation to the individual situation of any one particular group of operators.[64] The whole system of m.c.a.s is founded on the principle that these amounts are based not on the price actually paid for the goods but on basic amounts fixed by the Commission from week to week. Some disadvantages are therefore unavoidable, in the Court's view, because of the necessity of uniform application and speedy administration.[65] Nevertheless, EC discretion concerning m.c.a.s has been restricted by the Court in some respects. For example, the m.c.a. on a processed product may not exceed the total m.c.a.s on the different basic products of which the processed product is composed.[66] In addition, the Commission may not adopt a system of calculating m.c.a.s which results in applying to processed products m.c.a.s the burden or the benefit of which continually exceeds the amount necessary to take account of the incidence of the m.c.a. applicable to the basic product.[67]

This brief account of the operation of the m.c.a. system is, necessarily, greatly over-simplified, but nevertheless it is clear that for individual traders the aims and complexity of m.c.a.s may entail a great detail of uncertainty. This may result, for example, from the use by the Commission of a flat rate basis of calculation. The Court has held, however, that traders cannot object that a particular m.c.a. was unnecessary in a specific case, since m.c.a.s are generally calculated by a flat-rate method, both in being calculated on the basis of leading products and in being calculated only

[64] Case 5/73 *Balkan-Import-Export GmbH* v. *Hauptzollamt Berlin-Packhof* [1973] E.C.R. 1091.
[65] Case 7/76 *IRCA* (*Industria Romana Carni e.Affini S.p.A.*) v. *Amministrazione delle Finanze dello Stato* [1976] E.C.R. 1213.
[66] See Case 95/78 *Dulciora S.p.A.* v. *Amministrazione delle finanze dello Stato* [1979] E.C.R. 1549.
[67] Case 4/79 *Société Coopérative "Providence Agricole de la Champagne"* v. *Office national interprofessionnel des céréales* (*ONIC*) [1980] E.C.R. 2823; Case 109/79 *S.à.r.l. Maiseries de Beauce* v. *Office national interprofessionnel des céréales* [1980] E.C.R. 2883; Case 145/79 *S.A. Roquette Frères* v. *French State—Customs Administration* [1980] E.C.R. 2917, noted Usher (1981) 6 E.L.Rev. 147; see also Neville Brown, "Agrimonetary Byzantinism and Prospective Overruling" (1981) 18 C.M.L.Rev. 509.

on a weekly basis and with a delay in taking effect.[68] Nor can the
system be expected to eliminate the differences in situation of
importers or exporters in the Member States or to shelter them
from the consequences of variations in national exchange rates.[69]
Moreover, prior to the enactment of Regulation 243/78[70] providing for advance fixing of m.c.a.s, an individual trader had no legal
entitlement to the maintenance of a particular situation. In Case
97/76 *Merkur*,[71] for example, the Court stated that the liability of
the Community for injury suffered by traders as a result of the
adoption of legislative measures governing the m.c.a. system could
only be incurred if, in the absence of any overriding public interest, the Commission were to abolish or modify the m.c.a.s applicable in a specific sector with immediate effect, without warning,
in the absence of any appropriate transitional measures, and if
such abolition or modification was not foreseeable by a prudent
trader. The principle of legitimate expectations may be invoked
when, for example, the trader has, subject to a deposit, obtained
export licences fixing a subsidy in advance.[72] In the absence of that
or a similar arrangement, no special transitional arrangements are
required beyond the gap between the promulgation of the regulation and its entry into force.[73]

Under the so-called "equity regulation,"[74] however, Member

---

[68] See Case 5/73 *Balkan-Import-Export GmbG* v. *Hauptzollamt Berlin-Packhof*
[1973] E.C.R. 1091; Case 29/77 *S.A. Roquette Frerès* v. *French State—Administration des Douanes* [1977] E.C.R. 1835.
[69] Case 7/76 *IRCA (Industria Romana Carni e Affini S.p.A.)* v. *Amministrazione
delle Finanze dello Stato* [1976] E.C.R. 1213.
[70] O.J. 1978, L.35/5, as amended; today governed by Reg. 1160/82. (O.J. 1982,
L.134/22). Usually the m.c.a. is that in force on the day that imported goods are
entered with customs or placed into customs control for export. In the case of
advance-fixed m.c.a.s, however, the percentage is usually that in force on the
day on which the application for a certificate is lodged or, in the case of tenders,
that in force on the last day for the submission of tenders. Advance-fixed m.c.a.s
are possible only on trade with third countries.
[71] Case 97/76 *Merkur Aussenhandel GmbH and Co. KG* v. *Commission* [1977]
E.C.R. at 1078. See also Case 84/78 *Angelo Tomadini S.n.c.* v. *Amministrazione
delle Finanze dello Stato* [1979] E.C.R. 1801; Case 96/77 *S.A. Ancienne Maison
Marcel Bauche and S.à.r.l. François Delquignies* v. *Administration Française des
Douanes* [1978] E.C.R. 383.
[72] See Case 74/74 *Comptoir National Technique Agricole (CNTA)* v. *Commission*
[1975] E.C.R. 533.
[73] See, *e.g.* Case 84/78 *Tomadini S.n.c.* v. *Amministrazione delle Finanze dello
Stato* [1979] E.C.R. 1801; Case 146/77 *British Beef Company Ltd.* v. *Intervention
Board for Agricultural Produce* [1976] E.C.R. 1347.
[74] Reg. 926/80 (O.J. 1980, L.99/15).

States could waive the application of a newly introduced m.c.a. or
an increase in an existing m.c.a. arising from a change in an EMS
central rate or from a decision to abandon a central rate and allow
a currency to float. This applied only to contracts concluded prior
to the monetary decision but executed after it, though it did not
usually apply to contracts in respect of which the relevant m.c.a.s
could have been fixed in advance. With respect to the forerunner[75]
of this regulation, the Court held that it gave Member States a
margin of discretion, which permitted them to judge the application of the discretionary measure to each individual case, including circumstances such as to justify the grant of or exemption from
m.c.a.s.[76] The "equity regulation" was repealed in April 1984.[77]

Payment and collection

Since 1973 each Member State has in principle been responsible
for collecting or disbursing its own m.c.a.s, though the sums form
part of the Community budget.[78] The main exception is the
"exporter pays" system, according to which amounts payable on
imports into a Member State with negative m.c.a.s from elsewhere
in the Community may, by agreement, be paid in the exporting
Member State.[79] This principle applied to exports to the United
Kingdom from other Member States from May 1976 to April 1980,
when the United Kingdom acquired a positive m.c.a.
National authorities are required to ensure on behalf of the
Community and in accordance with Community law that m.c.a.s
are paid and collected. In the absence of EC provisions it is for the
national authorities to decide as to the recovery of m.c.a.s unduly
charged on the basis of EC regulations subsequently declared
invalid and also to settle according to the applicable national law
all ancillary questions, such as whether the fact that it may have

[75] Reg. 1608/74 (O.J. 1974, L.170/38).
[76] Joined Cases 12, 18 and 21/77 *Debayser S.A.* v. *Commission* [1978] E.C.R. 553.
[77] Reg. 1084/84 (O.J. 1984, L.106/26).
[78] Reg. 1112/73 (O.J. 1973, L.114/4).
[79] Reg. 974/71, Art. 2(*a*), as amended by Reg. 1112/73 (O.J. 1973, L.114/4). The
"exporter pays" system was initially proposed by the Commission as a "cosme-
tic" move to minimise EAGGF expenditure, according to S. Harris, A. Swinbank and G. Wilkinson, *The Food and Farm Policies of the European
Community* (1983) at 318. Within the context of the m.c.a. system, the tariff
classification made by the exporting Member State is not binding, in the absence
of EC legal provisions on the subject, on the authorities of the importing Member State: Case 5/78 *Milchfutter GmbH and Co. KG* v. *Hauptzollamt Gronau*
[1979] E.C.R. 1597.

been possible for the improperly imposed charge to be passed on to other traders or to consumers should be taken into account.[80]

Proposed abolition

The introduction of separate "green rates" was initially designed to maintain the fiction of common CAP prices, whereas the m.c.a. system was intended to sustain the notion that the EC constituted an agricultural common market. With the passage of time, however, these "temporary" expedients have been seen to have other implications. The agri-monetary system, as a Commission study pointed out, has substantially shielded the agricultural sector from the effects of monetary changes.[81] "Green money" is employed by the Member States mainly to translate ecu prices into national currencies according to national economic policies.[82] The m.c.a. system splits the Community into national trading zones separated by border taxes and subsidies, thereby distorting trade and encouraging fraud.[83] In addition, it contributes to substantial, hidden financial transfers between countries and between different social groups. Germany, for example, has benefitted from the agri-monetary system, first by higher farm prices, second by positive m.c.a.s as export subsidies financed from the EC budget, and third by lower prices, relative to its farmers' incomes as compared to those in other countries, for agricultural raw materials.[84] More generally, producers in countries with an appreciated currency and consumers in countries with a depreciated currency have been favoured by m.c.a.s; so have food-exporting countries as compared to food-importing countries.[85] As reflected in case law, the m.c.a. system has created

---

[80] Case 130/79 *Express Dairy Foods Ltd.* v. *Intervention Board for Agricultural Produce* [1980] E.C.R. 1887.

[81] Commission of the European Communities, "Report on the Economic Effects of the Agrimonetary System" COM(78)20 Final (1978); updated by Commission des Communautés Européennes, "Communication de la Commission au Conseil sur les Effets économiques du Système agri-monétaire" COM(84)95 Final (1984).

[82] See Ritson and Tangermann, "The Economics and Politics of Monetary Compensatory Amounts" (1979) 6 *European Review of Agricultural Economics* 119 at 143.

[83] See, *e.g.* D.A.G. Norton, "Ireland, the CAP, Trade Distortion and Induced Smuggling Activity 1974–1981" (1982).

[84] See Hu, "German Agricultural Power: The Impact on France and Britain" (1979) 35 *The World Today* 453 at 456–457.

[85] See Gilsdorf, "The System of Monetary Compensation from a Legal Standpoint: Part II—Legal Basis of and Limits to the System" (1980) 5 E.L.Rev. 433 at 436–437.

great uncertainty for traders, and hence indirectly for producers and consumers. By virtue of its technical complexity, it discriminates against consumers and small firms and in favour of large, especially multinational companies.[86] The abolition of m.c.a.s has been proposed by the Commission on several occasions since at least 1976.[87] Even the Court has been critical of the m.c.a. system and hesitant to extend it. In two cases arising from 1975 Franco-Italian wine war, for example, it stated that m.c.a.s were justified in trade between Member States only by the necessity of correcting the effects of fluctuating exchange rates, and it suggested that the failure of Member States to co-ordinate their monetary policies was contrary to Article 105.[88] The main stumbling block to the abolition of m.c.a.s has been Germany's reluctance to allow a fall in domestic farm prices as expressed in marks. In March 1984, however, the Council of Ministers during the annual price review approved a programme for the dismantling of existing m.c.a.s, which was encapsulated in Regulation 855/84.[89] This regulation created, in effect, a "green ecu" worth 3 per cent. more than the real ecu, thus removing about a third of Germany's positive m.c.a. without lowering domestic farm prices expressed in marks. Subsequently, Germany was to reduce its m.c.a.s further by revaluing the "green mark," and other countries' increased negative m.c.a.s were to be removed by devaluations. Any remaining positive m.c.a.s for Germany and the Netherlands were to be abolished by the beginning of the 1987–1988 marketing year. Special aids, including a degressive

[86] See, *e.g.* Swinbank, "The British Interest and the Green Pound" Centre for Agricultural Strategy, University of Reading, *Paper No. 6* (1978) at 31; Debatisse, "E.E.C. Organisation of the Cereals Market: Principles and Consequences" Centre for European Agricultural Studies, Wye College, *Occasional Paper No. 10* (1981) at 32.

[87] See Commission of the European Communities, "Communication on Longer-Term Measures in the Field of Monetary Compensatory Amounts" COM(76)600 Final (1976); Commission of the European Communities, "Proposal for a Council Regulation relating to the Fixing of Representative Rates in Agriculture" COM(77)482 Final (1977): Commission of the European Communities, "Adjustment of the Common Agricultural Policy" (1983) 4 *Bulletin of the European Communites* (Supplement) at 18–19.

[88] Joined Cases 80 and 81/77 *Société Les Commissionnaires Réunis S.à.r.l.* v. *Receveur des Douanes*; *S.à.r.l. Les Fils de Henri Ramel* v. *Receveur des Douanes* [1978] E.C.R. 927 at 947. For further discussion, see Neri, "La jurisprudence de la Cour de justice des Communautés européennes relative à l'application de la législation agricole communautaire" (1982) 5–6 C.D.E. 507 at 533–537.

[89] O.J. 1984, L.90/1. See also Agra Europe, "The Common Agricultural Policy and the Prospects for Reform" (1984) *Agra Briefing No. 2* at 8–9. On the context, see Avery, "Reforming the Common Agricultural Policy" (1984) 40 *The World Today* 173.

contribution by the Community for 1985 and 1986, were agreed for German agricultural producers. Initially set at 3 per cent. of the ex-VAT price, this aid was increased to 5 per cent. at the 1984 Fontainebleau Summit. Article 3 of the regulation provided that this special aid was to be deemed compatible with the Common Market.

Chapter 6

CONTROLS ON SURPLUS PRODUCTION

Surplus Production

EC definition

The most controversial aspect of the CAP, apart from its cost, is surplus production. The CAP, as many people see it, stimulates European farmers to produce an ever-increasing quantity of agricultural commodities. At high guaranteed prices these products cannot all be sold, and the excess is therefore stored, dumped on the world market or ploughed into the ground. While the policy benefits farmers, its inevitably high cost falls mainly on consumers, especially the poor. By distorting patterns of production and distribution in the world food economy, it imposes special burdens on third world countries. This conception of waste and unnecessary expense captures the essence of structural surplus, the EC term for overproduction. It is not wholly accurate, however, since political responsibility for the use of high market prices as an instrument of farm income support lies as much with national governments as with the Community.

EC agricultural and food policy is oriented towards self-sufficiency, at least in the major temperate zone crops.[1] It aims *inter alia* "to assure the availability of supplies" (Art. 39(1)(*d*)) by means of a market and price policy, which at the same time is the main instrument for supporting farm incomes. In principle, imports enter the common market only for products in which the Community is not self-sufficient; as a result of the variable levy, potential imports of other products are displaced by domestic pro-

---

[1] See Carey, "European Food Policy: Rules of the Game" in D.N. Balaam and M.J. Carey (eds.), *Food Politics: The Regional Conflict* (1981). A member of the Commission's Legal Service, while recognising that EC policy was oriented too much towards self-sufficiency, nevertheless suggested that a food policy based on low consumer prices and reliance on imports would be contrary to the Treaty: see Gilsdorf, "La politique agricole commune (Die Gemeinsame Agrarpolitik)" JUR(81)D/00825 (n.d.) at 34–35.

duction. Production in excess of self-sufficiency is defined as surplus production. In the context of the CAP's structure, including administered prices and a variable levy,[2] structural surplus refers to that part of total production in respect of which administered prices can be maintained only by intervention buying or export subsidies.[3]

Structural surplus thus differs from cyclical surpluses, due, for example, to fluctuations in the harvest because of weather conditions. The former is defined principally in relation to a given administrative, political and legal framework; the latter simply reflects the extent to which many aspects of agriculture, as compared to industry, remain dependent on nature. Moreover, structural surplus differs from surplus production as usually understood in neoclassical economics. If, for example, supply exceeds demand in a free or competitive market, the price should in principle fall so as to result in either an increase in demand or a drop in supply. In the EC, however, agricultural prices do not, in theory, perform this allocative function, and the existence of structural surplus does not necessarily lead to changes in demand or supply. Similarly, structural surplus differs also from the idea in Marxist economic theory of a social surplus product, which refers to a permanent surplus of the means of subsistence.[4]

The EC concept of structural surplus resembles the neoclassical definition in describing the existence, at a particular price (though determined differently in each instance), of oversupply in relation to demand. It is not concerned directly, however, with the various factors which influence the structure of demand, such as, for example, relations between classes, the distribution of income, employment opportunities or the age structure of the population. It does not refer, therefore, to production of food in excess of basic needs, however determined. Instead structural surplus denotes overproduction which is systematic and systemic: it results from the operation of particular socio-economic forces within a given set of policy decisions, institutional structure and legal framework. In other words, within the general logic of a capitalist economy, it stems from the adoption of a food policy of self-sufficiency and the guaranteed purchase of agricultural products at unnecessarily high prices.

[2] The great variety of common market organisations should be borne in mind; see Chap. 4.
[3] See J. Marsh and C. Ritson, *Agricultural Policy and the Common Market* (1971) at 35.
[4] See E. Mandel, *Marxist Economic Theory* (1968) at 42–45, 95–98.

124 *Controls on Surplus Production*

Self-sufficiency and surplus

Excess agricultural production as compared to demand in European countries is not a new phenomenon. Although World War II and the immediate postwar period were marked by food shortages, agricultural production in the OEEC (later OECD) countries surpassed pre-war levels by 1949–50. By the 1950s it had become a cause of concern.[5] The disposal of supplies of pigmeat, milk and eggs in the United Kingdom, for example, was not possible at the time without heavy subsidies.[6] In the fledgling European Community, the EEC Commission in its first general report noted:

> "In the past, attempts to increase agricultural incomes have been based on the too one-sided principle of increasing production. True, this has led to a marked increase in productivity per worker, especially as there was a simultaneous decrease in the number of persons employed in agriculture. However, the increase in production has led to new difficulties on the markets. In view of the fact that production of the major products is increasing more vigorously than consumption, surpluses are appearing on the various markets and their disposal is causing serious difficulties and worries."[7]

Between the end of the war and the late 1950s, the population of the OEEC countries increased by about only 20 per cent. Agricultural production, however, increased by approximately 50 per cent., largely as a result of the technological revolution in agriculture involving increased use of industrially produced inputs and new production methods.[8]

This trend has continued, and especially since the mid-1970s the Community has been at least self-sufficient in most temperate zone products (see Table 6.1: 100 represents self-sufficiency). Surpluses exist in sugar and cereals, but the largest overproduction is in the dairy sector.

Surplus production relative to domestic requirements comes

[5] Organisation for European Economic Co-operation, *Agricultural Policies in Europe and North America: Price and Income Policies* (1957) at 420–423.
[6] See P. Self and H.J. Storing, *The State and the Farmer* (1962) at 71–73.
[7] Commission of the European Economic Community, *First General Report on the Activities of the Community* (1958) at 70.
[8] M. Tracy, *Agriculture in Western Europe* (2nd ed. 1982) at 232. On the gradual industrialisation of agriculture from the 1950s, see L. Malassis, *Economie agro-alimentaire, I: Economie de la consommation et de la production agro-alimentaire* (1973) at 236–255.

TABLE 6.1

Classification of the Main Agricultural Products in the Community
according to degree of self-sufficiency (^{1})

Exceeding 100%		Around 100%		Below 100%	
Sugar	124	Oats	98	Grain maize	62
Poultrymeat	108	Potatoes	101	Rice	83
Concentrated		Eggs	102(^{2})	Fresh fruit	
milk	154	Fresh milk		(other than	
Butter	118	products	101	citrus)	83
Whole-milk		Beef/veal	102	Citrus fruit	44
powder	337	Pigmeat	101	Sheepmeat and	
Skimmed-milk		Fresh vege-		goatmeat	73
powder	126	tables	98	Vegetable oils	
Barley	112	Wine	103	and fats	—
Wheat	118				
Rye	107				
Cheese	106				

(^{1}) Crop products: average for 1979/80, 1980/81 and 1981/82. Livestock products: average for 1979, 1980 and 1981.
(^{2}) 1982/83 marketing year.

Source: Commission of the European Communities, *The Agricultural Situation in the Community: 1983 Report* (1984) at 110.

mainly from Ireland, the smaller northern European countries and France. Table 6.2 shows the degree of self-supply in certain agricultural products in 1973–1974 and 1980–1981 for EC 10, EC 9 and the individual Member States. It indicates the patterns of surplus production in various countries and the contribution made by the individual Member States to EC structural surplus in different commodities. The greatest surpluses of whole-milk powder, for example, are produced in Ireland (4300), France (1941) and Denmark (1793). Ireland also produces the largest surplus of skimmed milk powder (1270). Surplus concentrated milk comes primarily from Denmark (433) and the Netherlands (372). Excess butter derives mainly from the Netherlands (313), Ireland (299) and Denmark (219). Sugar surpluses are produced particularly in the Benelux countries (260) and France (219), but almost every Member State produces sugar in excess of its domestic requirements. The EC wheat surplus is due largely to French production (205). The United Kingdom produces particular surpluses in whole-milk

TABLE 6.2

Degree of Self-Supply in Certain Agricultural Products (in %)

		EUR 10	Greece	EUR 9	Germany
1	2	3	4	5	6
Cereals					
Total wheat	1973/74	104	98	104	90
	1980/81	119	135	118	105
Rye	1973/74	98	100	98	98
	1980/81	101	100	101	100
Barley	1973/74	105	93	106	88
	1980/81	113	96	114	90
Sugar	1973/74	:	:	91	98
	1980/81	:	:	136	133
Wine	1973/74	:	:	99	59
	1980/81	:	:	102	44
Milk products					
Fats	1973	:	:	102	106
	1981	:	:	:	120
Proteins	1973	:	:	113	113
	1981	:	:	:	128(*)
Whole-milk powder(¹)	1973	231	0	208	89
	1981	377(*)	0(*)	393(*)	144
Skimmed-milk powder	1973	143	0	137	183
	1981	126(*)	0(*)	126(*)	238
Concentrated milk	1973	130	5	140	98
	1981	154(*)	25(*)	177(*)	142
Cheese	1973	103	100	102	87
	1981	106(*)	92(*)	107(*)	95
Butter(²)	1973	98	83	101	114
	1981	118(*)	70(*)	119(*)	128
Poultrymeat	1973	102	98	103	50
	1981	110	101	110	63

(*) »1980«
(¹) Includes whole-milk powder for Italy.
(²) Including butteroil.

Source: Commission of the European Communities, *The Agricultural Situation in the Community: 1983 Report* (1984) at 239–240.

France	Italy	Nether-lands	Benelux	United Kingdom	Ireland	Denmark
7	8	9	10	11	12	13
191	88	46	61	60	54	123
205	82	58	71	90	45	127
124	81	83	94	30	50	104
114	93	44	91	74	0	124
175	28	75	60	98	99	105
176	39	37	81	131	111	108
140	63	118	183	30	105	138
219	108	160	260	48	111	196
100	118	0	10,1	0	0	0
103	130	0	3,4	0	0	0
116	81	246	101	58	171	229
121(*)	75(*)	247(*)	99	:	230(*)	220
124	75	130	114	96	162	140
118(*)	66(*)	142(*)	124	:	176(*)	177
308	0	427	259	74	2100	763
1941	13(*)	587(*)	265	429	4300(*)	1793
157	1	60	195	186	753	172
121	0(*)	68(*)	275	258	1270(*)	120
201	90	311	18	99	0	660
199	53(*)	372(*)	27	128	0(*)	433
115	82	243	47	61	600	258
115	80(*)	229(*)	41	71	555(*)	443
117	65	548	106	19	203	325
122	67(*)	313(*)	103	57	299(*)	219
108	98	366	115	99	108	278
137	99	282	88	99	95	230

128   Controls on Surplus Production

powder (429), skimmed milk powder (258) and concentrated milk
(128).

Production per unit or per unit cost is not equal throughout the
Community, however, and large farms contribute proportionately
more milk per head (or more cereals per hectare) to Community
surpluses. To take the dairy sector as an example, the average
herd in the Community of Ten in 1981 was 14.2 cows, while the
average yield per cow was 4172 kg (see Table 6.3). The three
Member States with the largest average herds were the United
Kingdom (56.1 cows), the Netherlands (36.2 cows) and Denmark
(25.8 cows). These countries' herds also had the highest average
annual yields: 4831 kg/cow in the United Kingdom, 5156 kg/cow in
the Netherlands and 4725 kg/cow in Denmark. Since then yields
have increased, and in 1984 highly mechanised, capital intensive
United Kingdom dairy farms with computerised compound feed-
ing systems could produce between 7,000 and 8,000 litres per
head.[9]

TABLE 6.3

Size and Yield of EC Dairy Farms by Member State (1981)

Member State	Average Headage	% Holders with more than 50 Head	Average Yield
United Kingdom	56.1	44.8	4831
Netherlands	36.2	27.7	5156
Denmark	25.8	11.6	5115
Luxembourg	24.1	6.9	3893
Belgium	18.3	4.4	3880
France	15.4	2.5	3756
Germany	12.7	1.5	4545
Ireland	15.8	6.2	3314
Italy	6.4	1.6	3394
Greece	2.6	0.1	3089

Source: Commission of the European Communities, *The Agricultural Situation in the Community: 1983 Report* (1984) at 291, 365.

The cost of disposing of this surplus production accounts for a
very high proportion of the EC budget. Total agricultural expendi-

[9] See the supplement on dairy farming in *Farmers Weekly*, March 16, 1984.

ture constituted between 63.1 per cent. and 75.5 per cent. of the annual Community budget between 1979 and 1984. The Guarantee Section, devoted to price and market support, absorbed most agricultural expenditure; during the same period it accounted for between 59.9 per cent. and 72.7 per cent. of the total EC budget.[10] Most Guarantee Section expenditure, in turn, concerned surplus production. Of total agricultural expenditure in 1982, for example, price subsidies accounted for 39.2 per cent. (4745.2 million ecu: £2659.6 million), export subsidies 39.4 per cent. (4764.2 million ecu: £2670.3 million), storage costs 15 per cent. (1818m ecu: £1019.0 million) and withdrawals from the market and similar operations 5 per cent. (602.8 million ecu: £337.9 million).[11] Milk products and cereals represented 29.6 per cent. and 15.5 per cent., respectively, of total Guarantee Section expenditure in 1983. More than 10 per cent. of total Guarantee spending concerned export subsidies on dairy products, and a slightly smaller proportion went for export subsidies on cereals.[12]

In assessing the implications of this financial burden, it should be borne in mind that agriculture is the Community's only commonly financed policy. Moreover, surplus production to some extent is inevitable within the framework of an agricultural policy which aims at security of supply through self-sufficiency, instead of obtaining food supplies primarily from world market trade. The "butter mountains" of 260,000 tonnes at the end of 1976 and 128,000 tonnes in early 1984, measured against Community food requirements based on then current levels of consumption, amounted respectively to only 61 days' and three weeks' supplies. Dairy products as a whole, however, are by any standards clearly in surplus: the 1,100,000 tonnes of skimmed milk powder in Community stores at the end of 1976 would have required over five years to clear at unsubsidised prices. A more serious problem, however, is that of distribution. CAP price and market policies, including those which encourage overproduction, are of benefit mainly to larger farmers, suppliers and processors rather than small farmers and consumers.[13]

---

[10] Commission of the European Communities, *The Agricultural Situation in the Community: 1983 Report* (1984) at 155.
[11] *Ibid.* at 264.
[12] *Ibid.* at 262–263.
[13] See Consumers Association, "The Common Agricultural Policy" *Money Which?* (1977) 334 at 334–335; Annand, "It's the rich who get CAP's pleasures" *The Guardian*, February 22, 1984, at 21.

Policies, Instruments and Measures

Introduction

With regard to commodities in surplus, the Community has attempted both to control supply and to manage demand. Each of these policies embraces a variety of instruments, each of which in turn may entail numerous legal measures. A supply-oriented policy, for example, may include limits on production; storage; withdrawal from the market; destruction of surplus produce; and import controls.[14] A demand-oriented policy may employ subsidised intra-Community sales; diversion to alternative uses; exports; and the creation of new markets. Supply and demand policies are usually combined in relation to a particular product, and different instruments are frequently employed in conjunction. A particular instrument may also serve several aims; exports, for example, may dispose of excess supply and stimulate demand by creating new markets, while at the same time being less expensive than subsidising intra-Community consumption.

Supply controls

Production Limits—Restrictions on production range from indirect limitation by graduated levy through direct restriction by production quota to an absolute prohibition of production.

A common form of indirect restriction on production in the Community is the graduated producer levy. The levy increases as production increases above an established threshold, so in principle the price mechanism is used to limit production. For example, Regulation 2727/75,[15] as amended, on the common organisation of the market in cereals provides for a guarantee threshold to be set annually for all cereals except durum wheat and rice. When the average production for the last three marketing years exceeds the guarantee threshold for the particular product, the common intervention and the reference prices for the following year are automatically reduced by 1 per cent. for every one million tonnes in excess of the threshold, up to a maximum of 5 per cent. The threshold is adjusted, however, according to the level of imports of cereal substitutes into the Community. Similar guaran-

---

[14] See generally Organisation for Economic Co-operation and Development *Supply Control in Agriculture* (1973); House of Lords Select Committee on the European Communities, *Supply Controls* (1983).
[15] O.J. 1975, L. 281/1.

tee thresholds apply to other products, such as processed tomatoes, currants and sultanas.

A more direct restriction on producers is the production quota.[16] In the Community's mixed economy, such quotas generally do not set an absolute limit on production. Instead, they establish a ceiling which producers may exceed, but above which either (a) regular support mechanisms, such as price guarantees, no longer apply or (b) production is subject to a levy. The latter is exemplified by the milk production quotas and super-levy introduced in 1984 (discussed later), while an example of a combined system is the Community arrangement for sugar.

Under the common organisation of the market for sugar (including isoglucose; see Chap. 4), each Member State is allocated an "A" quota and a "B" quota to which a minimum price applies. No minimum price is set for sugar ("C" quota) above the basic quota. Quotas may be transferred between beet factories or between isoglucose factories but not between beet and isoglucose factories. The legality of this system was implicitly assumed by the Court in Case 230/78 *Eridania*,[17] an Article 177 reference for a preliminary ruling on the validity and interpretation of Article 2(2) of Regulation 3331/74 on the allocation and alteration of basic quotas. The Court stated, however, that the exercise by Italy of its power under the article to alter basic quotas was subject to the existence and requirements of a restructuring plan. In addition, such a power was to be exercised only to the extent necessary for implementation of the plan. Moreover, it was limited, first, by the objectives and principles of the CAP as stated in Article 39; secondly, by the objectives of the common market organisation, in particular the aim of protecting the interests of beet and cane producers; and, thirdly, by the general principles of Community law, in particular the principle of proportionality.

---

[16] Aspects of quotas are discussed in Harvey, "Saleable Quotas, Compensation Policy and Reform of the CAP"; Hubbard, "The Use of Marketing Quotas in the EC Dairy Sector"; and Sturgess, "The Common Agricultural Policy for Sugar: Possible Improvements and Lessons" in K.J. Thomson and R.M. Warren (eds.), *Price and Market Policies in European Agriculture* (1984).

[17] Case 230/78 *S.p.A. Eridania-Zuccherifici nazionali and S.p.A. Società Italiana per l'Industria degli Zuccheri* v. *Minister of Agriculture and Forestry, Minister for Industry, Trade and Craft Trades, and S.p.A. Zuccherifici Meridionali* [1979] E.C.R. 2749. Practical recognition of the legality of the sugar levy was given by its incorporation in the sources of the Community's own resources by Council Decision of April 21, 1970, Art. 2 (J.O. 1970, L.94/1); see also Olmi, "Agriculture" JUR(79)D/01575 (1979) at 25.

According to the scheme, processors of sugar within the "A" and "B" quotas must pay a minimum levy of 2 per cent. of the white sugar intervention price. If the resulting sum is insufficient to pay the export subsidies for "A" and "B" quota sugar, however, an additional levy up to a maximum of 30 per cent. of the intervention price may be charged on "B" quota sugar. A further 7.5 per cent. levy on "B" quota sugar may also be charged if necessary to meet the cost of export subsidies. The Court has held that excesses which come to light after the expiration of the marketing year in which they were produced are to be treated for the purpose of the production levy as arising in the marketing year in which they were ascertained.[18] In addition, quantities of white sugar produced from sugar sweepings from a previous sugar year (and therefore already included in the calculation) are to be excluded when the quantity of sugar for purposes of the levy is being calculated.[19] The required levy does not include the cost of financing exports up to the amount imported under the Lomé Convention; this sum is charged directly to the budget. Accordingly, the minimum price for "A" quota sugar is 98 per cent. of the basic beet price, whereas that for "B" quota sugar is 60.5 per cent. of the basic beet price. The levy is paid by processors, which may pass on to producers 60 per cent. of the cost. "C" quota sugar must be sold without subsidy on the world market or a fine paid.

Such producer levies, like that for milk (see below), are based on the principle of co-responsibility. The Commission has argued that co-responsibility should be recognised as the Community's fourth basic principle, in the sense that

> "any production above a certain volume to be fixed, taking into account the internal consumption of the Community and its external trade, must be charged fully or partially to the producers."[20]

Thus defined, the principle has applied to sugar since the first EC sugar regime was introduced in 1968. In the dairy sector, it was initially introduced in 1977 and was recently extended by the impo-

---

[18] Case 159/73 *Hannoversche Zucker AG Rethen-Weetzen* v. *Hauptzollamt Hannover* [1974] E.C.R. 121.
[19] Case 94/75 *Süddeutsche Zucker-Aktiengesellschaft* v. *Hauptzollamt Mannheim* [1976] E.C.R. 153.
[20] Commission of the European Communities, "Reflections on the Common Agricultural Policy" COM(80)800 (1980) at 18. On the context, see Pearce, "The Common Agricultural Policy: The Accumulation of Special Interests" in H. Wallace, W. Wallace and C. Webb (eds.), *Policy Making in the European Community* (2nd ed., 1983) at 161–170.

sition of a supplementary levy on milk production in excess of a quota. Since 1982 it has formed part of the regimes for cereals and other products. Such a policy instrument has the effect of reducing the price paid to producers, thereby perhaps curtailing supplies. It does not, however, have any direct effect on prices paid by consumers. From the consumers' standpoint, it is therefore less effective, though also less politically risky, than a straightforward price cut.[21] The co-responsibility principle has also been criticised for being oriented towards minimising EC expenditure instead of promoting structural change. It has also been charged that the co-responsibility levy in the dairy sector has been used mainly to promote the expansion of markets by exporters and agribusiness firms.[22] Nevertheless, at least one economist has compared price cuts, the original dairy co-responsibility levy and a supplementary levy and concluded that a supplementary levy was potentially the most effective in controlling surplus production.[23]

The most direct form of production limit used in the Community is a temporary ban on production. Concerning the wine sector, for example, Regulation 1162/76, Article 2(1),[24] imposed a prohibition on the planting of all new vines for a period of three years. This ban was challenged by means of an Article 177 reference in Case 44/79 *Hauer*.[25] The approach taken by the Court was as follows:

> "Even if it is not possible to dispute in principle the Community's ability to restrict the exercise of the right to property in the context of a common organization of the market and for purposes of a structural policy, it is still necessary to examine whether the restrictions introduced by the provisions in dispute in fact correspond to the objectives of general interest pursued by the Community or whether, with regard to the aim pursued, they constitute a disproportionate and intolerable interference with the rights of the owner, impinging upon the very substance of the right of property."[26]

---

[21] See the Memorandum submitted by the Consumers in the European Community Group (U.K.), in House of Commons Agriculture Committee, *Economic, Social and Health Implications for the United Kingdom of the Common Agricultural Policy on Milk and Milk Products* (1980), Vol. 2: *Minutes of Evidence*, at 141.

[22] See "The Infernal Food Machine" (1981) 85 *Agenor* at 33–35.

[23] Parton, "Levy Policies and EEC Agricultural Surpluses" Report to the Social Science Research Council (U.K.), HR. 6844 (n.d.).

[24] O.J. 1976, L.135/32.

[25] Case 44/79 *Liselotte Hauer* v. *Land Rheinland-Pfalz* [1979] E.C.R. 3727; noted Usher (1980) 5 E.L.Rev. 209.

[26] *Ibid.* at 3747.

The Court placed special emphasis on the fact that, despite its wide scope, the ban was temporary in nature and designed to deal immediately with overproduction, while at the same time forming part of a more general structural reform. It held that the ban did not entail any undue limitation upon the exercise of the right of property. Accordingly, the Court interpreted the measure as applying to applications for authorisation of new planting of vines submitted before the entry into force of the regulation. In addition, the prohibition was in the Court's view unaffected by the question of the suitability or otherwise of the land for wine-growing, as determined by provisions of national law.

The common organisation of the market for wine which is currently in force provides for even more stringent controls on production. Regulation 337/79, Article 30, as amended,[27] prohibits all planting of new vines until August 31, 1990. Exemptions are allowed only in two sets of cases. The first comprises those quality wines for which demand exceeds supply; even then exemptions may be authorised by the Commission only at the request of individual Member States and if particular controls are applied. The second group of exemptions includes areas intended after September 1, 1984, for the cultivation of parent vines from root stock; areas intended for new planting by government or private sector reallocation measures; development plan areas in Member States whose quality wine production during specified years was less than 60 per cent. of total wine production; and areas intended for wine growing experiments.

Storage Aids—In order to adjust seasonal supplies to demand, the Community undertakes public storage and grants financial aid for private storage for various products, including beef, pigmeat, sugar and wine. For example, Regulations 989/68[28] and 1091/80[29] provide general and specific rules concerning storage aids for beef, while Regulations 2763/75[30] and 1092/80[31] make similar provision for pigmeat. As of September 1983, public intervention stocks of beef stood at 350,000 tonnes.[32] Financial aid is given for short-term and long-term storage of wine. Payments made by national

---

[27] O.J. 1979, L.54/1; amended by Reg. 454/80 (O.J. 1980, L.57/7).
[28] J.O. 1968, L.169/10.
[29] O.J. 1980, L.114/18.
[30] O.J. 1975, L.282/19.
[31] O.J. 1980, L.114/32.
[32] Commission of the European Communities, *The Agricultural Situation in the Community: 1983 Report* (1984) at 136.

governments for storage are reimbursed by the Community for contracts which are concluded, even allowing for administrative delays, before a statutory cut-off date.[33]

Withdrawal—Withdrawal from the market is the principal means of price support for fruit and vegetables. This system is based on that previously used in the Netherlands. In the Community withdrawal is carried out for intervention agencies by producers' associations, whose members are subsequently compensated for withdrawn produce at rates substantially below normal market prices. Usually only about 4–5 per cent. of total production is withdrawn. In 1982–1983, for example, withdrawn products included 3.2 per cent. of total EC production of pears, 11.1 per cent. of apples and 1.6 per cent. of cauliflowers.[34] By the terms of Regulation 1035/72 on the common market organisation for fruit and vegetables,[35] such produce must be disposed of outside normal commercial channels. It may, for example, be distributed free to charitable organisations or for welfare purposes, be used when fresh or after processing as animal feed, be distributed free as processed products for welfare purposes or be distributed free to children in schools. Member States are responsible for organising this distribution. Withdrawn produce may also be destroyed.

Destruction—Regulation 1035/72 provides that, when it is apparent that products liable to be withdrawn or bought in cannot be disposed of in time in one of these ways, Member States may decide to compensate, at a standard rate, fruit and vegetable producers who undertake not to dispose of a certain quantity of their produce, in particular in order to use such products on their own holdings (Art. 21(2)). Member States are required to take all appropriate measures to prevent and punish any abuse of the arrangements which they decide to apply under this provision (Art. 21(4)). According to EC authorities, "[i]t is only where none of these [other] uses is possible that the product is considered a total loss."[36] This statement, though perhaps true, is misleading to the extent that it implies that only a small proportion of withdrawn produce is destroyed. Although the blaze of adverse publicity

[33] See Case 1251/79 *Re Wine Storage Contracts*: *Italy* v. *Commission* [1981] E.C.R. 205.
[34] Commission of the European Communities, *The Agricultural Situation in the Community: 1983 Report* (1984) at 130. Figures for each country and for the entire Community for 1980–81, 1981–82 and 1982–83 are given in *id.* at 356–357.
[35] J.O. 1972, L.118/1.
[36] "Withdrawal of Fruit and Vegetables from the Market" (1979) *Green Europe* (November) at 2.

136   *Controls on Surplus Production*

which followed the large-scale destruction of surplus apples in
1967–1968 led to the tightening-up of the legislative provisions
regarding withdrawal,[37] these changes in the regulations do not
appear to have changed the pattern of disposal of withdrawn produce in any major way. It is even more misleading, however, to
suggest that the CAP support system leads to the destruction of
fruit and vegetables in vast quantities.[38] In fact, as Table 6.3 shows
for 1978–1979, a high proportion of withdrawn fruit and vegetables
are destroyed, but only a small proportion of total EC production
is actually withdrawn.

Destruction is also used in relation to other products. A cow
slaughter premium to reduce the dairy surplus has been in operation since 1969; it was claimed in one of the few European Court
cases involving a farmer.[39] Regulation 1200/82[40] now provides for
the payment of a premium for the slaughter of cattle other than
cows. The premium may be paid when the average market price
falls below a set target price. This cattle slaughter premium,
though in force since 1974, is in fact used only in the United Kingdom. Some forms of transformation of products also amount to
destruction. For example, Regulation 2144/82[41] provides for the
preventive distillation, special distillation and compulsory distillation of wine; the last applies when before January 20, the year's
output exceeds normal consumption by five months. (See also
denaturing, below.)

Import Controls—Import controls are a supply-oriented
measure in that they affect the supply of a particular commodity
on the EC market. The most important instrument is the variable
levy. Import licences are also required for various products, and
the EC Common Customs Tariff also limits imports (see Chap. 4).
Proposals have also been made since 1964 to introduce a tax on
imported vegetable oils and fats, which are used in the manufacture of margarine and therefore compete with butter. Oilseed
crushers and margarine manufacturers have consistently opposed
such a tax, and thus far no such proposal has been adopted.

[37] See M. Butterwick and E. Neville-Rolfe, *Agricultural Marketing and the EEC*
(1972) at 191. The regulation then in force was Reg. 159/66 (J.O. 1966, 3282;
unofficial translation by the Foreign Office (1967)).
[38] See, for example, Brown, "EEC makes a hash of its salad days" *The Guardian*,
May 14, 1984, at 1; Kenworthy, "Farmers dump 2 million 'caulis' " *The Sunday
Express*, July 22, 1984, at 5.
[39] Case 93/71 *Orsolina Leonesio* v. *Ministry for Agriculture and Forestry of the Italian Republic* [1972] E.C.R. 287; see also Case 39/72 *Commission* v. *Italy* [1973]
E.C.R. 101.
[40] O.J. 1982, L.140/32.
[41] O.J. 1982, L.227/1.

Table 6.4
EC Withdrawal and Disposal of Fruit and Vegetables:
1978–79 Marketing Year

Description	EC Withdrawals					UK Withdrawals				Withdrawals of Marketable Production	
	Tonnes	Human Consumption %	Animal Food %	Destroyed %	Processed %	Tonnes	Human Consumption %	Animal Feed %	Destroyed %	EC %	UK %
Cauliflowers	43,459	9.9	18.3	71.8	—	6,237	—	3.5	96.5	2.79	2.5
Tomatoes	19,634	10.9	42.5	46.6	—	—	—	—	—	0.38	—
Peaches	38,262	13.6	0.4	15.2	70.8	—	—	—	—	2.46	—
Pears	26,569	5.4	32.6	0.7	61.3	—	—	—	—	1.23	—
Apples	378,974	3.2	56.8	7.0	33.0	5,478	0.1	30.2	69.7	5.50	1.8
Grapes	19	100.0	—	—	—	—	—	—	—	—	—
Mandarins	53,122	14.7	7.7	77.6	—	—	—	—	—	14.55	—
Oranges	104,614	3.3	30.3	63.2	3.2	—	—	—	—	6.45	—
Lemons	24,581	9.5	—	90.5	—	—	—	—	—	3.31	—
Total	689,234					11,715					

Source: House of Lords Select Committee on the European Communities, *Fruit and Vegetables*, HL 147 (1981) at 99.

Demand management

   Subsidised Sales—The most well-known of EC schemes to subsidise domestic sales of surplus commodities are perhaps the sale
of skimmed milk powder at reduced prices and the consumer butter subsidy. Surplus skimmed milk powder was purchased by
several large companies, such as Nestlé, and then used to create an
artificial market for bottled baby milk, especially in the third
world.[42] The consumer butter subsidy[43] was paid in the United
Kingdom in 1982 on 175,666 tonnes of butter at a net cost, borne
by EAGGF, of £48,722,744.[44] Other similar measures for dairy
products include Regulation 1598/77[45] providing for school milk
subsidies; Regulation 649/78[46] on reduced-price sales of concentrated butter; and Regulation 262/79[47] providing for the sale of
intervention butter at greatly reduced prices for the manufacture
of pastry products, ice cream and other foodstuffs. With regard to
the last, the Court has held that even where the successful tenderer
does not itself carry out processing, it is necessary to establish that
the processing complies with statutory conditions and have been
produced within the prescribed period before the deposit can be
released; the forfeiture of such a deposit is not in the nature of a
penalty or disproportionate to its object.[48]
   Alternative Uses—Instruments to encourage alternative use of
surplus produce previously included denaturing premiums. Under
Regulations 1403/69 and 2739/75 concerning cereals and sugar,

---

[42] See A. Chetley, *Baby Foods* (1983); (1982) 108 *The New Internationalist* (February); War on Want, "Breast or Bottle?" (1982); and materials available from the
Baby Milk Action Coalition. I am grateful to Jill Cottrell for bringing some of
this and related material to my attention.
[43] Reg. 1269/79 (O.J. 1979, L.161/8).
[44] Intervention Board for Agricultural Produce, *Report for the Calendar Year 1982*
(1983) at 12. The Commission has recommended the abolition in two-stages of
the consumer butter subsidy, and a 75 per cent. reduction of the subsidy was
agreed by the Council in March 1984; see Gardner, "Commission Proposals on
CAP Reform" (1983) 1042 *Agra Europe* E/1 at E/3; Agra Europe, "Changes in
the EEC Dairy Policy" *Agra Briefing No. 1* (1984) at 10. Some effects of food
subsidies are discussed in Ritson, "Who gets a subsidy?" *New Society*, January
23, 1975 at 194.
[45] O.J. 1977, L.177/17.
[46] O.J. 1978, L.86/33; see also Joined Cases 66 and 99/81 *Pommerehnke* v. *Bundesanstalt für Landwirtschaftliche Marktordnung* [1982] E.C.R. 1363.
[47] O.J. 1979, L.41/1.
[48] Joined Cases 99 and 100/76 *N.V. Roomboterfabriek "De Beste Boter" and Firma
Josef Hoche, Butterschmelzwerk* v. *Bundesanstalt für landwirtschaftliche Marktordnung* [1977] E.C.R. 861.

respectively,[49] premiums were granted to encourage the conversion of excess stocks into animal feedingstuffs. Coloured grains, fish oil or fish-liver oil was mixed with the product in order to make it unfit for human consumption. It is not surprising, therefore, that recourse to denaturing was described by Advocate General Mayras as "justified only as 'ultima ratio,' as an expedient calculated to reduce surpluses which could not otherwise be used,"[50] or by Advocate General Warner as being only "seen as preferable to that [practice] at one time used in certain parts of the world of dumping great quantities of wheat in the sea."[51] With regard to the grant and the amount of denaturing premiums, the wide scope of the Commission's discretion was consistently recognised by the Court.[52] Nevertheless, Member States retained considerable authority to act according to national law. Since EC legislation did not regulate in detail the procedure for supervising the denaturing of cereals, for example, Member States had the power to specify detailed arrangements, including subjecting plants to a system of special approval and requiring that managers possess personal qualities ensuring reliability.[53] They could also define methods of denaturing other than colouration so long as the same guarantees were provided.[54] If, however, the denatured product was eventually used for a purpose other than animal feed, the recipient of the premium could be required to reimburse it, even if the contrary use was by a third party.[55] The practice of denaturing aroused considerable opposition and was eventually suspended.[56]

Production refunds and processing aids are currently granted by the Community for various products. Regulation 1400/78[57] provides for production refunds on sugar, isoglucose and sugar syrups

---

[49] J.O. 1969, L.180/3; O.J. 1975, L.281/5.
[50] Case 57/72 *Westzucker GmbH* v. *EVst für Zucker* [1973] E.C.R. 321 at 347.
[51] Case 3/73 *Hessische Mehlindustrie Karl Schöttler KG* v. *EVst für Getreide und Futtermittel* [1973] E.C.R. 745 at 756.
[52] See *ibid.* and Case 78/74 *Deuka, Deutsche Kraftfutter GmbH B.J. Stolp* v. *EVst für Getreide und Futtermittel* [1975] E.C.R. 421.
[53] Case 3/73 *Hessische Mehlindustrie Karl Schöttler KG* v. *EVst für Getreide und Futtermittel* [1973] E.C.R. 745.
[54] Joined Cases 146, 192, and 193/81 *Baywa* v. *Office fédéral de régulation des marchés agricoles* [1982] E.C.R. 1503.
[55] Case 77/81 *Zuckerfabrik Franken* v. *Germany* [1982] E.C.R. 681.
[56] Concerning cereals, for example, denaturing was at first suspended when the premium was fixed at zero and subsequently ended in 1976 when the present intervention price system came into force (Reg. 1143/76, O.J. 1976, L.130/1, deleting Art. 7(3) of Reg. 2727/75, O.J. 1975, L.281/1).
[57] O.J. 1978, L.170/9.

used in the chemical industry. Regulation 1152/78[58] provides for aids to processors of tomato concentrate, tinned peeled tomatoes, other tomato products and some fruit products; these aids are conditional on processors entering into contracts with producers to buy specified quantities at established minimum prices. This controversial measure[59] has encouraged the spread of contract production.

Export—The use of export subsidies, designed to encourage the export of EC surplus and other production to the world market, is specified by the basic regulations on common market organisations. Subsidies accounted for 39.4 per cent. and 36.7 per cent. of EAGGF spending in 1982 and 1983, respectively.[60] For milk products alone, expenditure on export subsidies for 1984 was estimated to account for 2,213 million ecu (£1240.4 million), 13.4 per cent. of the total agricultural budget.[61] The most controversial scheme has been the sale of fresh butter to the Soviet Union, which quite apart from any diplomatic reasons has been used as a means of surplus disposal because it is less expensive than subsidising domestic sales and, unlike the latter, uses up surplus stocks.[62] In 1980 the previously loose controls on such exports were replaced by a tendering scheme,[63] and today general export refunds apply and an export licence is required.[64] Export refunds may vary according to the product or the destination; with regard to the latter, the Court has held that a Member State entrusted with paying the refund may lawfully require proof that the goods have been given customs clearance and put into free circulation at

---

[58] O.J. 1978, L.144/1.
[59] See de Zulueta, "Mafia harvest riches from EEC's £150m tomatoes" *The Guardian*, October 26, 1980, at 9; S. Harris, A. Swinbank and G. Wilkinson, *The Food and Farm Policies of the European Community* (1983) at 160–161.
[60] Commission of the European Communities, *The Agricultural Situation in the Community: 1983 Report* (1984) at 264.
[61] *Ibid.* at 262.
[62] See "Butter Exports: One Useful Measure to Reduce Community Stocks" (1979) *Green Europe* (November). According to the Commission, disposal of surplus by export costs about half as much as disposal on the domestic market; see Commission of the European Communities, *The Agricultural Situation in the Community: 1983 Report* (1984) at 139. In addition, export sales, unlike domestic sales, clear the market: "only 15 per cent. of each tonne of butter on which just as large (*i.e.* as the export subsidy) a subsidy is paid is actually increased consumption and therefore removed from the surplus" (Agra Europe, "The Common Agricultural Policy and the Prospects for Reform" *Agra Briefing No. 2* (1984) at 7.
[63] Reg. 400/80 (O.J. 1980, L.46/14).
[64] Reg. 583/83 (O.J. 1983, L.70/26).

the destination.[65] World markets for butter, skimmed milk powder and whole-milk powder, for example, have declined since 1981. Nevertheless, sales of surplus and intervention stocks have provided a new market for some importers and exporters. One firm in the meat sector trades in the United Kingdom and on the continent and with eastern European countries and the Middle East; its sales in 1983, though still mainly from other sources, were reported at £21 million.[66]

In addition to commercial sales, food aid has been used by the Community partly to dispose of surpluses since the 1967 Food Aid Convention, which came into effect in 1968.[67] EC food aid is based mainly on cereals, skimmed milk powder and butteroil. The current basic regulation is Regulation 3331/82,[68] while the implementing Regulation 1278/84 specifies the quantities, products, countries and conditions of aid for 1984.[69] Regulations 1974/80[70] and 1354/84,[71] respectively, provide general rules concerning food aid in cereals and dairy products. During the 1970s, the EC provided an estimated 19 per cent. of total world food aid, surpassed only by the United States with 58 per cent.[72] Under the 1980 Food Aid Convention, the Community is to provide annually 1,650,000 tonnes of cereals, 150,000 tonnes of skimmed milk powder and 45,000 tonnes of butteroil; this represents approximately 22 per cent. of rich country commitment of food aid in cereals and about two-thirds of world milk food aid. In 1979–1980 a major review of EC food aid was undertaken by the Court of Auditors, which criticised the complexity, fragmentation and delay in EC procedures.[73]

[65] Case 125/75 *Milch, Fett- und Eier-Kontor GmbH* v. *Hauptzollamt Hamburg-Jonas* [1976] E.C.R. 771.

[66] May, "Placing for Global" *The Guardian*, May 11, 1984, at 17.

[67] See Talbot, "The European Community's Food Aid Programme: An Integration of Ideology, Strategy, Technology and Surpluses" (1979) *Food Policy* 269; Wainright, "The Execution of Community Food Aid to Developing Countries" (1976) 13 C.M.L.Rev. 367; Snyder, "Food Policy and the International Law of Development," presented at the Anglo-French Symposium on Aspects of the International Law of Development, London, 1985. See generally Maxwell and Singer, "Food Aid to Developing Countries: A Survey" in P. Streeten and R. Jolly (eds.), *Recent Issues in World Development* (1981).

[68] O.J. 1982, L.352/1.

[69] O.J. 1984, L.124/1.

[70] O.J. 1980, L.192/11.

[71] O.J. 1984, L.142/1.

[72] Pronk, "Food Aid" in M. Tracy and I. Hodac (eds.), *Prospects for Agriculture in the European Economic Community* (1979) at 297.

[73] See Huddleston, Merry, Raikes and Stevens, "The EEC and Third World Food and Agriculture" in C. Stevens (ed.), *EEC and the Third World: A Survey 2— Hunger in the World* (1982) at 28–32.

The effects of food aid, from other countries as well as from the Community, on third world countries have also been criticised; regardless of whether food aid acts as a disincentive to local producers, "there is little doubt that food aid has in many cases been associated with many food imports."[74] In order to integrate food aid more fully into the EC's development policy and formally break the link between food aid and surplus disposal, the Commission has proposed that the legal basis of food aid be changed from Article 43 to Article 235.[75] The current basic regulation, however, is based on both Articles.

Creation of Markets—A final instrument of demand management is the creation of new markets. In addition to the extent to which food aid may develop markets,[76] Regulations 723/78, 270/82, 272/82, 1993/78 and 507/82[77] provide for sales promotion, publicity and market research in order to increase the use of EC milk products outside the Community. The Community finances up to 75 per cent. of expenditure on technical assistance to improve marketing conditions, consumer information and publicity in third countries regarding dairy products.

Legal Issues: The Dairy Sector

Introduction

The determination of EC policies concerning surplus production is first and foremost a question of political economy. It involves relations of power and influence among different classes, interest groupings and governments in the Member States, their relation-

---

[74] Raikes, "Flowing with Milk and Money: Situating EEC Policies in Relation to Agriculture and Food Production in Africa", presented at the Second Conference of the Review of African Political Economy, University of Keele, Staffordshire, 1984, at 19.

[75] See Olmi, "Agriculture" JUR(79) D/01575 (1979) at 72, n. 20; Gilsdorf, "La politique agricole commune (Die Gemeinsame Agrarpolitik)" JUR(81) D/00825 (n.d.) at 24–25; see also S. Harris, A. Swinbank and G. Wilkinson, *The Food and Farm Policy of the European Community* (1983) at 273. Consistently with this view, the Commission in 1972 decided that food aid was not eligible for export subsidies; the Court disagreed: see Case 13/72 *Netherlands* v. *Commission* [1973] E.C.R. 27.

[76] On market development as an effect of U.S. food aid, see, *e.g.* F.M. Lappé and J. Collins, *Food First* (1980 ed.) at 286–288; R. Burbach and P. Flynn, *Agribusiness in the Americas* (1980) at 66–68; see also S. George, *How the Other Half Dies* (1977) at 192–213.

[77] Respectively: O.J. 1978, L.98/5; O.J. 1982, L.28/10; O.J. 1982, L.28/17; O.J. 1978, L.230/8; O.J. 1982, L.61/15.

ships with EC authorities and their manifold ties with multi-national companies and third countries. In addition, however, EC policies towards surplus production raise complex legal issues. To what extent does Community law limit the choice of policy instruments? Are there any legal constraints on the exercise of discretion by EC authorities in implementing policies designed to stem surplus production? May a party harmed by Community surplus control policies or by the lack of an effective policy obtain compensation for damage? An answer to the third question has already been sketched (see Chap. 3) so far as is possible within the scope of this book. The remainder of this chapter briefly considers the first two questions, using examples from the dairy sector.

The dairy sector

The Community's dairy sector has long been marked by structural surplus.[78] The extent of overproduction in the individual Member States and in the EC as a whole is shown in Table 6.2 (above). Between 1973–81 the number of dairy farms in the Community (EC 9) declined by 4.8 per cent. and headage declined by 0.2 per cent.,[79] but total production increased as a result of improvements in the quality and age structure of herds and increased efficiency in production, especially by the use of concentrated feedingstuffs. From 1981 to 1982, for example, average yield per cow rose by 3.8 per cent. to 4,382 kg, and total milk production increased by 3.5 per cent. Most of the resulting 3.4 million extra tonnes of milk was converted into the two intervention products, butter and skimmed milk powder. Intervention stocks at the end of 1982 stood at 112,000 tonnes of butter and 574,000 tonnes of skimmed milk powder.[80] Yet EC consumption is declining, and since 1981 world consumption has also decreased, leading to a fall in the Community's share of world markets for butter, skimmed milk powder and butteroil.[81] The dairy sector accounted for 30.3 per cent. (5,006 million ecu: £2,805.9 million) of total estimated CAP expenditure for 1984. Intervention buying accounted for 2,793 million ecu (£1565.5 million), or 16.9 per cent. of total CAP spending; 2213 million ecu (£1204.4 million), or 13.4 per cent. of total CAP spending, was designated for dairy export subsidies.[82]

[78] For a recent review, see Agra Europe, "Changes in the EEC Dairy Policy" *Agra Briefing No. 1* (Revised) (1984).
[79] Commission of the European Communities, *The Agricultural Situation in the Community: 1983 Report* (1984) at 292.
[80] *Ibid.* at 132.
[81] *Ibid.* at 134.
[82] *Ibid.* at 263.

Potential solutions to the complex problems of the dairy sector are difficult to agree and put into practice. That such is likely to be the case is clearly suggested by the lack of coincidence in the configurations of four different variables. These variables are (1) production of dairy products in the Member States as compared to their varying national requirements; (2) the shares of the different Member States in total EC production; (3) the importance of dairying in the various Member States' national economies; and (4) the size, extent of concentration and average yield of dairy farms in the various countries. The first and fourth are shown in Tables 6.2 and 6.3, respectively; the others are shown in Table 6.5.[83]

TABLE 6.5

Importance of Dairying in EC Member States (1982)

Member State	% of value of dairy production in EC	% of value of agricultural production in each Member State	Yield (kg/head)
United Kingdom	15.6	22.3	5057
Netherlands	12.1	27.8	5278
Denmark	5.0	24.2	5115
Luxembourg	0.2	37.1	4116
Belgium	2.8	17.3	3942
France	23.0	17.1	3949
Germany	23.3	24.2	4683
Ireland	3.8	33.5	3436
Italy	11.9	11.7	3469
Greece	2.4	8.9	3089*

*1981 figure

Source: Commission of the European Communities, *The Agricultural Situation in the Community: 1983 Report* (1984) at 190–193, 291.

Table 6.5 omits productivity according to size of farm, but in 1980 the 30 per cent. of EC dairy farms which had five or fewer cows accounted for only 15 per cent. of total output.[84]

---

[83] This Table is based on Table 5.1, referring to 1980, in S. Harris, A. Swinbank and G. Wilkinson, *The Food and Farm Policies of the European Community* (1983) at 93. Average yields shown in Table 6.5 refer to 1982; those shown in Table 6.3 refer to 1981.

[84] Memorandum submitted by the Consumers in the European Community Group (U.K.), in House of Commons Agriculture Committee, *Economic, Social and Health Implications for the United Kingdom of the Common Agricultural Policy on Milk and Dairy Products*, Vol. 2: *Minutes of Evidence* (1980) at 141.

Accordingly, in relation to any particular proposal the different interests in the dairy sector overlap and cut across each other. They do not coalesce clearly in favour of any surplus control policy except perhaps the status quo.

Legal issues

The principal legal issues with respect to Community policies on surplus production concern the exercise of discretion by EC authorities, first, in the choice of policy instruments and, secondly, in the implementation of legal measures. These issues have been raised in challenges by private parties to the Community's attempts to control overproduction. It deserves to be emphasised that no cases have been brought against the Community by parties seeking to stem overproduction or to contest the EC's failure to adopt particular policies, such as price reduction. Such challenges, however, would be extremely difficult, if not impossible, to mount successfully, as the preceding chapters have shown.

Case 138/78 *Stölting*[85] concerned a challenge to the Community's choice of the co-responsibility levy as a policy instrument. The co-responsibility levy was introduced under Article 43 by Regulation 1079/77.[86] The preamble of this regulation recited that "the Community market in milk products is marked by structural surpluses arising from an imbalance between supply and demand," so that

"a more direct link should be established between production and outlets for milk products in order gradually to restore equilibrium between production and market requirements and to reduce the heavy cost incurred by the Community as a result of the present situation and in particular of the large surpluses which exist. . . . "

Accordingly, the regulation provided that a levy shall be due from all milk producers on milk supplied to an undertaking treating or processing milk and, in certain cases, on milk sold by the producer in the form of other milk products. Producers in designated mountain and hill areas were exempt from the levy. In the case of deliveries to an undertaking treating or processing milk, the levy was to be deducted by the buyer from the payment made to the producer, and transferred monthly to the designated agency (IBAP in the U.K.). The levy and associated measures to expand dairy pro-

[85] Case 138/78 *Hans-Markus Stölting* v. *Hauptzollamt Hamburg-Jonas* [1979] E.C.R. 713.
[86] O.J. 1977, L.131/6.

duct markets were to be considered as forming part of the
measures to stabilise agricultural markets (Art. 5). The levy proceeds are considered by the Commission as falling outside general
revenue which constitutes part of the Community's "own
resources" and are therefore shown in the budget as negative
expenditure. Regulation 1822/77[87] provided detailed rules for collection of the levy. The levy was initially set at 1.5 per cent. of the
milk target price; the basic rate is 3 per cent. for 1984–1985.

Stölting came to the Court as a reference for a preliminary ruling
under Article 177. The plaintiff in the main action was a German
milk producer, who had objected when the co-responsibility levy
was deducted from the sum due for 4,204 kg of full cream milk
which he delivered to a dairy in September 1977. The action was a
test case, since only 37.32 DM was at stake: the imposition of the
levy was questioned by the majority of some 500,000 members of
the Deutsche Bauernverband.[88] Stölting argued that the co-
responsibility levy had no legal basis. It was a fiscal charge which
could be imposed only under Article 201, providing, in relation to
the establishment of the Community's own resources, for the exercise of the treaty-making power by the Member States; the procedures required by the article had not been followed in this case.
The character of the levy, in his view, was suggested by the fact
that none of its proceeds had necessarily to be allocated to the milk
sector; all could be expended in any area,[89] as was typically the
case with a general fiscal levy.

Advocate General Mayras, considering this argument, emphasised the wide discretion of EC authorities. In addition to the usual
Article 40(3) intervention measures, they could also take exceptional measures, such as introducing charges on producers in a surplus sector without imposing a financial burden on other
producers. The co-responsibility levy thus was distinguishable
from the ill-fated protein deposit scheme (see below). A more
specific, but equally difficult question concerned the choice of
instrument. Both the Commission and the Council viewed the levy
as a negative price, and therefore equivalent (in its effects on producers) to a price reduction. When confronted with the question as
to whether a straightforward price reduction might not have been
preferable, the Council did not expressly answer; the Commission's answer, though ambiguous, was that the levy would

[87] O.J. 1977, L.203/1.
[88] According to Advocate General Mayras, [1979] E.C.R. 713 at 725.
[89] This was not prohibited by the Reg., as the Commission had agreed in a written
answer to a Parliamentary question (Reply to W.Q. 752/77 of Mr Klinker; O.J.
1979, C.52/18).

reduce producers' incomes but, unlike a price reduction, would not benefit the consumer. Concerning this point, the Advocate General remarked:

> "This answer confirms a choice of economic policy which seems to me to be in certain respects regrettable. However, my comments only concern expediency, and it does not appear to me that the legal validity of the contested regulation can be affected by this."[90]

He considered the levy, regardless of any shortcomings, to be "in the nature of a marketing mechanism."[91] Since producers themselves were to bear the burden, the levy could be based on Article 43. Article 201, in the Advocate General's opinion, did not deprive the Council of the power, within the framework of specific rules, in particular regarding the CAP, to generate revenue "which by its direct link with measures affecting expenditure in the sector at issue reduces the impact thereof."[92]

This view was largely followed by the Court. The contested regulation, according to the Court, was intended to contribute to the stabilisation of markets. It therefore remained within the limits of Articles 39 and 40, so that the Council was entitled to adopt it on the basis of Article 43. Concerning the choice of the levy as a policy instrument, the Court remarked:

> "This difference of opinion concerns in particular the expediency and effectiveness of the measure adopted in the regulations in question. If a measure is patently unsuited to the objective which the competent institution seeks to pursue this may affect its legality, but on the other hand the Council must be recognized as having a discretionary power in this area which corresponds to the political responsibilities which Articles 40 and 43 impose upon it. As it is directed towards restraining production in the face of the surpluses observed, the co-responsibility levy contributes to the objective of stabilizing markets. Nor does the level of the rate of the levy appear to be disproportionate in relation to the facts referred to by the Council."[93]

Accordingly, the Court held that the questions raised in the case disclosed no factor which affected the validity of the regulations providing for the co-responsibility levy.

[90] [1979] E.C.R. 713 at 728.
[91] *Ibid.* at 729.
[92] *Id.*
[93] *Id.* at 722.

EC authorities therefore have a wide discretion in the choice of policy instruments, so long as the instrument chosen is designed to contribute to the stabilisation of the particular product market and is not patently unsuited to the purpose. In such a case, the choice of instruments would appear to be limited only by general legal principles, such as respect for fundamental legal rights and proportionality. In Case 44/79 *Hauer*,[94] the Court held that the Community's discretion extended to the prohibition, at least temporarily and in specific conditions, of the use of land for the purpose of producing a commodity already in surplus. In other circumstances, the choice of policy instruments may be effectively limited, however, by the requirements of the Community's policy making and legislative process. For example, as part of the late 1960s Mansholt Plan the Commission apparently proposed a directive limiting the area of land used for agricultural purposes, but this proposal was not accepted by the Council.[95]

The implementation by EC authorities of measures designed to curb surplus production is limited particularly by fundamental rights, essential procedural requirements under Article 173, and the principles of non-discrimination and proportionality. Perhaps the most well-known challenge to EC legislation on the last two grounds, apart from the "isoglucose cases" (see Chap. 3), was the "skimmed milk powder cases."[96] Regulation 573/76[97] was enacted to reduce surplus stocks of skimmed milk powder. It established an obligation to purchase skimmed milk powder held by intervention agencies for use in feedingstuffs for animals other than young calves. The granting of aids for certain vegetable protein products or the free circulation in the Community of certain imported animal feed protein products was subject to the provision of a security or the submission of a standard Community document. The security, if deposited, would be released on production of the docu-

---

[94] Case 44/79 *Liselotte Hauer* v. *Land Rheinland-Pfalz* [1979] E.C.R. 3727.
[95] Gilsdorf, "La politique agricole commune (Die Gemeinsame Agrarpolitik)" JUR(81)D/00825 (n.d.) at 34.
[96] Case 114/76 *Bela-Mühle Josef Bergmann KG* v. *Grows-Farm GmbH and C. KG* [1977] E.C.R. 1211; Case 116/76 *Granaria BV* v. *Hoofdproduktschap voor Akkerbouwprodukten* [1977] E.C.R. 1247; Joined Cases 119 and 120/76 *Ölmühle Hamburg AG* v. *Hauptzollamt Hamburg Waltershof* and *Firma Kurt A. Becher* v. *Hauptzollamt Bremen-Nord* [1977] E.C.R. 1269; Joined Cases 83 and 94/76, 4, 15 and 40/77 *Bayerische HNL Vermehrungsbetriebe GmbH and Co. KG* v. *Council and Commission* [1978] E.C.R. 1209 (liability); Case 101/78 *Granaria BV* v. *Hoofdproduktschap voor Akkerbouwprodukten* [1979] E.C.R. 623 (liability).
[97] O.J. 1976, L.67/18.

ment, which constituted proof of the purchase and denaturation of a certain quantity of skimmed milk powder. This protein deposit scheme replaced an initial Commission proposal, which was not adopted, for the compulsory incorporation of skimmed milk powder in compound animal feedingstuffs at the 2 per cent. level.[98] The regulation entered into force on March 15, 1976, and applied under October 31, 1976.

The question of the validity of this regulation came before the Court on Article 177 references from courts in Germany and the Netherlands.[99] In Case 114/76 *Bela-Mühle*, for example, the defendant in the main action, who operated a battery-hen unit, refused to pay the cost of the securities for the issue of protein certificates, which had been passed on to it by the applicant, who ran a concentrated feedingstuffs factory and had been charged the amount by its own suppliers. The defendant argued that Regulation 563/76 was incompatible with the principles of non-discrimination and proportionality. The Court held that the measure was discriminatory in distributing the costs of the scheme between the various agricultural sectors. As the Advocate General pointed out,[1] the burden of costs of disposing of skimmed milk powder resulting from surplus milk production was in fact borne not by milk producers but primarily by poultry farmers and pig breeders. In addition, the Court held that the measure contravened the principle of proportionality, since the purchase price of the skimmed milk powder was three times higher, for equivalent protein value, than that of the substances which it replaced. The obligation to purchase skimmed milk powder at such a disproportionate price, in the Court's view, was not necessary to attain the objective of disposing of surplus stocks; less onerous means could have been used.[2] Accordingly, Regulation 563/76 was held to be null and void.[3]

---

[98] See Pickard, Norris and Young, "Three Case Histories in Agriculture," unpublished (n.d.) at 40–61.

[99] Case 114/76, Case 116/76, Joined Cases 119 and 120/76: see n. 96 above.

[1] [1977] E.C.R. 1211 at 1231.

[2] For further discussion, see Vajda, "Some Aspects of Judicial Review within the Common Agricultural Policy" (1979) 4 E.L.Rev. 244, 341; Neri, "Le principe de proportionnalité dans la jurisprudence de la Cour relative au droit communautaire agricole" (1981) 4 R.T.D.E. 652; Schmitthoff, "The Doctrines of Proportionality and Non-Discrimination" (1977) 2 E.L.Rev. 329.

[3] Nevertheless, the Court later dismissed applications under Art. 215 for damages allegedly resulting from an increase in the price of feedingstuffs as a result of Reg. 563/76: see Joined Cases 83 and 94/76, 4, 15 and 40/77 *Bayerische HNL Vermehrungsbetriebe GmbH and Co. KG* v. *Council and Commission* [1978] E.C.R. 1209.

In March 1984 the Community introduced a system of milk production quotas and a 'super levy.' Regulations 856/84[4] and 857/84[5]
provide for national quotas based on 1981 deliveries plus 1 per
cent. In addition, a Community reserve is established to supplement the guaranteed quantities of Member States in which the
implementation of the levy system raises particular difficulties concerning supply or production structures. Member States may
choose to implement the quota and supplementary levy system at
the level of either the producer or the dairy. If the system is implemented at the level of the farmer, the "super levy" is 75 per cent.
of the target price for milk in excess of the quota; the same applies
in the case of direct sales to consumption. If the system is implemented at the level of the dairy, the applicable levy on production
above the quota amount is 100 per cent. of the milk target price.
Regulation 856/84 recites explicitly that the introduction of such a
levy system, initially for a period of five years, is "the most effective method, and the one having the least drastic effect on the
incomes of producers" and that the purpose of the levy is "to regulate and stabilize the market in milk and milk products" (Preamble). It provides that the levies "shall be regarded as intervention
measures designed to regulate agricultural markets and shall be
allocated to the financing of expenditure in the milk and milk products sector" (Art. 5). Additional provisions for the scheme are
established by Regulation 1371/84[6] and Regulation 1557/84.[7] The
former provides that the Community reserve for April 2, 1984, to
March 31, 1985, is to be distributed between Ireland (245,000
tonnes), Luxembourg (25,000 tonnes) and United Kingdom for
the region of Northern Ireland (65,000 tonnes).

This arrangement is extremely complex, leaves considerable discretion within fixed limits to the Member States and inevitably
constitutes a highly differentiated system. Many farmers in the
United Kingdom greeted it with dismay; others were reported to
be organising a legal challenge, mainly on the grounds that the
quota and super levy system was incompatible with the principles
of non-discrimination and proportionality.[8] At the time of writing
(August 1984), it remains to be seen whether such challenges will

[4] O.J. 1984, L.90/10.
[5] O.J. 1984, L.90/13.
[6] O.J. 1984, L.132/11.
[7] O.J. 1984, L.150/6.
[8] See, *e.g.* the supplement on dairying in *Farmers Weekly*, March 16 1984; Collins,
"Mary in the dairy with the giveaway milk" *The Guardian*, May 5, 1984 at 23;
Black, "Farmer's quota challenge" *The Sunday Times* (London), June 24, 1984,
at 3.

be successful. It is likely, however, that in any case with regard to the quotas the European Court will give special emphasis to the severe problem of overproduction in the EC dairy sector and the inherent difficulties of attempting to resolve such economic and political issues by the use of legal rules.[9]

---

[9] On the implementation of the scheme, see House of Commons Agriculture Committee, *The Implementation of Dairy Quotas*, HC 14 (1984).

Chapter 7

STRUCTURAL POLICY

Prelude to a Common Policy

Foundations

Agricultural structure includes "the whole body of production and living conditions of a given region."[1] The legal basis of EC structural policy lies in the Rome Treaty, while its political foundations are reflected in the resolutions of the 1958 Stresa Conference.

Article 39(1) of the Treaty firmly links structural and market policies by providing that the CAP's objectives shall include

> "(a) to increase agricultural productivity by promoting technical progress and by ensuring the rational development of agricultural production and the optimum utilisation of the factors of production, in particular labour;
> (b) thus to ensure a fair standard of living for the agricultural community, in particular by increasing the individual earnings of persons engaged in agriculture."

In working out the CAP and the special methods for its application, account is to be taken of agricultural structure, particularly according to Article 39(2) of

> "(a) the particular nature of agricultural activity, which results from the social structure of agriculture and from structural and natural disparities between the various agricultural regions;
> (b) the need to effect the appropriate adjustments by degrees;
> (c) the fact that in the Member States agriculture constitutes a sector closely linked with the economy as a whole."

---

[1] "Decision concerning the Co-ordination of Policies on Agricultural Structure" (1962) 3 *Bulletin of the EEC Commission* (Supplement) at 1.

In addition, Article 42 provides, with regard to the applicability to agriculture of the rules on competition, that the Council may, in particular, authorise the granting of aid for the protection of enterprises handicapped by structural or natural conditions or within the framework of economic development programmes. Finally, Article 43 provides for the eventual submission by the Commission of proposals for implementing the measures specified in Title II, Agriculture.

In proposing such measures, the Commission was to take into account the work of an agricultural conference of the Member States (Art. 43(2)). The Stresa Conference of July 1958 resulted in a resolution[2] that gave special attention to structural policy. The delegates resolved that agriculture should be considered as an integral part of the economy and society; close links should therefore be established between market and price policies and structural policy. The improvement of agricultural structures should aim to make possible incomes and a return on capital in agriculture equal to those in other economic sectors. A basic feature of European agriculture was the family farm. Consequently, its economic and competitive position should be improved; aids should be given to less favoured areas if necessary to facilitate reconversion; and suitable retraining schemes and a more active rural industrialisation policy should be adopted so as gradually to resolve the difficulties of marginal areas.

Initial structural policy

Submitted according to Article 43(2), the Commission's first major proposals on the common agricultural policy included both market and structural instruments.[3] The latter, however, consisted not of a common policy but instead of EC co-ordination of national structural policies. Accordingly, in November 1960 the Council issued a statement that:

> "Action must be taken to co-ordinate and improve the measures by which the Member States seek to improve the structure of agriculture; the necessity of such action stems in part from the way in which structural and market policies affect each other, in part from the need to seize every oppor-

---

[2] J.O., ler août 1958, 281/58.
[3] Commission de la Communauté économique européenne, "Proposition concernant l'élaboration et la mise en oeuvre de la politique agricole commune en vertu de l'article 43 du traité instituant la CEE" COM(60)105 (1960).

tunity to increase the economic strength and competitiveness of agriculture."[4]

Council Decision of December 4, 1962[5] established a Standing Committee on Agricultural Structures, composed of representatives of the Member States and chaired by a representative of the Commission. It was to examine national structural policies and their relationship to regional development and market and price policy. It was also entrusted with the task of helping the Commission to prepare an annual report of national policies, their effectiveness and possible means of co-ordination. On the basis of this report, the Council was to adopt necessary co-ordinating measures. The basic Regulation 25/62 on the financing of the CAP provided that up to one third of EAGGF funds could be allocated to structural expenditure.[6]

Regulation 17/64,[7] the principal measure during the period which concerned structural policy, established the conditions for granting aid from EAGGF. It provided that Guidance Section aid shall relate to (a) the adaptation and improvement of conditions of production in agriculture; (b) the adaptation and guidance of agricultural production; (c) the adaptation and improvement of the marketing of agricultural products; and (d) the development of outlets for agricultural products (Art. 11(1)). Projects to be grant-aided had to "contribute to the improvement of the social and economic conditions of persons engaged in agriculture" (Art. 14(2)(c)). Priority was to be given to projects "which are part of a comprehensive system of measures aimed at encouraging the harmonious development of the overall economy of the region where such projects will be carried out" (Art. 15(1)). Aid was to consist of capital subsidies in a lump sum or instalments. For a given project, the EAGGF grant was limited to not more than 25 per cent. of the total cost; the benefitting party was required to contribute not less than 30 per cent. and except in particular circumstances a contribution was to be made by the Member State. Applications were submitted to the Commission through the Member State concerned and had to be approved by the Member State.

---

[4] "Decision concerning the Co-ordination of Policies on Agricultural Structure" (1962) 3 *Bulletin of the EEC Commission* (Supplement) at 2.

[5] J.O. 17.12.62, 2892.

[6] Art. 5(2); J.O. 1962, 991/1. In March 1963 the Commission proposed a European Fund for Structural Improvements in Agriculture, but this proposal was not adopted; see "Proposal for a Council Regulation on the European Fund for Structural Improvements in Agriculture" (1963) 4 *Bulletin of the EEC Commission* (Supplement) at 4.

[7] O.J. 1964, 586/103.

Approximately half of the total funds allocated under this measure concerned agricultural infrastructure, such as land reparcelling and irrigation; the remainder financed improvements in processing and marketing structures.[8] Commission decisions granting Guidance Fund aid for the enlargement and/or development of certain sugar refineries in Italy were challenged in Joined Cases 10 and 18/68 *Eridania*.[9] The applicants argued that the aid distorted the conditions of competition in the sugar industry. The Italian sugar quota was to be divided among those granted aid and other undertakings, including the applicants; aid would therefore lead to a decrease in the applicants' production quota or, in any event, to greater difficulty in disposing of sugar in excess of the quota. In dismissing the application, the Court held that the applicants were not entitled to bring proceedings under Article 173. The mere fact that a measure may influence competitive relationships on a particular market could not, in the Court's view, suffice to allow any trader in any competitive relationship whatsoever with the addressees of the measure to be regarded as directly and individually concerned.

The Mansholt Plan

It is likely that few, if any, small farmers benefitted directly from this regulation.[10] In any event, the co-ordination of national policies did little to alter the basic structure of European agriculture.[11] Accordingly, in 1968 Sicco Mansholt, then Commissioner responsible for agriculture, proposed a programme of far-reaching reforms in the structure of Community agriculture over a ten-year period.[12] "Agriculture 1980" included proposals for reorganising

---

[8] S. Harris, A. Swinbank and G. Wilkinson, *The Food and Farm Policies of the European Community* (1983) at 220.

[9] Joined Cases 10 and 18/68 *Società "Eridania" Zuccherifici Nazionali and Others v. Commission* [1969] E.C.R. 459.

[10] See also S. Harris, A. Swinbank and G. Wilkinson, *The Food and Farm Policies of the European Community* (1983) at 220.

[11] National policies during the period are described in Organisation for Economic Co-operation and Development, *Structural Measures in Agriculture* (1972).

[12] Commission des Communautés européennes, "Memorandum sur la réforme de l'agriculture dans la Communauté économique européenne" COM(68)1000 (1968). Part A, the general memorandum, and Part B, statistical appendices, were published separately as: "Memorandum on the Reform of Agriculture in the European Economic Community and Annexes" (1969) 1 *Bull. E.C.* (supplement) at 1. For analysis of the Mansholt Plan and its implications, see J. Marsh and C. Ritson, *Agricultural Policy and the Common Market* (1971) at 142–161; A. Zeller, *L'Imbroglio agricole du Marché commun* (1970) at 217–284.

agricultural markets in order to eliminate surpluses, particularly through a price policy designed to create a new price structure based on demand, production costs and specified patterns of production. It also comprised structural measures to reduce the number of people actively employed in agriculture from 10 million in 1970 to 5 million in 1980. The land area used for agricultural purposes was to be reduced during the same period by at least 5 million hectares, of which approximately 4 million hectares would be turned into woodland. The plan also envisaged the creation of production units of "adequate" economic dimensions. Minimum size specifications were to vary not only according to product but also from one region to another. Nevertheless, the new units, though not large by United States standards, would "definitely be a good deal [larger] than . . . the majority of farms" then found in the Community.[13] Producers' associations and groupings of producers' councils were to be encouraged. A reduction in the EC dairy herd was intended to make way for greater emphasis on beef production.

These proposals aroused great opposition, both among the governments of the Member States and among farmers. France considered that the Commission had no mandate to propose a common structural policy and could only offer recommendations for co-ordinating national programmes. Germany was reluctant to embrace any project which might imply any collectivisation of the means of production. The Dutch, with national structural measures underway, did not wish particularly to subsidise Community policies. In March 1971, approximately 80,000 farmers demonstrated in the streets of Brussels. The main national proponent of the plan was Italy, which, in a spring 1971 compromise on farm prices, was able "to force upon the reluctant Council the principle of joint responsibility for common projects of structural reform."[14]

---

[13] (1969) 1 *Bull. E.C.* (Supplement) at 37: "For staple crops like grains or root crops, for example, production units would have to have at least 80 to 120 hectars, in dairy farming they would keep 40 to 60 cows and in meat production 150 to 200 head of cattle, in poultry farming they would have to turn out 100,000 birds a year or, if they go in for eggs, keep 10,000 laying hens, and in pig farming they would fatten 450 to 600 animals at a time."

[14] Heathcote, "Agricultural Politics in the European Community" Department of Political Science, Research School of Social Sciences, Australian National University, *Occasional Paper No. 7* (1971) at 27. See also the case study of structural policy making in G.G. Rosenthal, *The Men Behind the Decisions* (1975) at 22–26, 79–100.

Towards a Common Structural Policy

Context

The two decades from 1950 to 1970 marked a minor watershed in the history of European agriculture. The agricultural labour force in most major European countries (U.K. excepted) declined by more than half, and the number of holdings decreased by approximately one-third. The number of tractors, however, increased tenfold; farms tended more often to specialise; labour productivity augmented more than five times; the value of agricultural production more than doubled; and consumers increasingly favoured animal products and sugar rather than potatoes and grain. Multinational firms, long important in trade, were predominant by the late 1950s in the agricultural machinery and agrochemical sectors. The centralisation and concentration of capital were by 1970 central features of the food processing and distribution industries. Accordingly, agricultural producers came increasingly under the sway of large companies operating upstream or downstream. Yet, though the world of the peasant farmer was thus irrevocably transformed, most agricultural units are still relatively small in size. Despite substantial variations in the size and composition of holdings from country to country and within countries, the basic production unit remains the family farm, albeit profoundly transformed by and dependent on capital and the state.[15]

---

[15] See Priebe, "The Changing Role of Agriculture 1920–1970" in C.M. Cipolla (ed.), *The Fontana Economic History of Europe*: *The Twentieth Century, Part 2* (1976) at 416–421; S.H. Franklin, *The European Peasantry*: *The Final Phase* (1969) at 6–15; Kouloussi, "L'emploi dans l'agriculture des 9 pays de la CEE" (1983) 263 *Revue du Marché Commun* 12; "L'internationalisation du secteur agro-alimentaire du Europe: Recherche comparative sur douze pays de l'Est et de l'Ouest" (1982) 16 *Economies et Sociétés* 1117; J. Bombal and P. Chalmin, *L'Agro-alimentaire* (1980) at 27–45; L. Malassis, *Economie agro-alimentaire, I*: *Economie de la consommation et de la production agro-alimentaire* (1973) at 227–403; Mackintosh, "Fruit and Vegetables as an International Commodity: The Relocation of Horticultural Production and Its Implications for the Producers" (1977) *Food Policy* 277; *Re Floral* (O.J. 1980, L.39/51), noted Faull (1981) 6 E.L.Rev. 199; *Re Nodet-Gougis/Lamazou*, in Commission of the European Communities, *Tenth Report on Competition Policy* (1980) at 88–89; Case 258/78 *L.C. Nungesser K.G. and Kurt Eisele* v. *Commission* [1982] E.C.R. 2015; Burns, "A Synoptic View of the Food Industry" in J. Burns, J. McInerney and A. Swinbank (eds.) *The Food Industry: Economics and Policies* (1983) at 11–14; Bergmann, "Background Thoughts and Elements for a Discussion on Agricultural Structures in Europe 1980–1990" (1974–75) 2 *European Review of Agricultural Economics* 459; Nallet and Servolin, "Le statut juridique du paysan. Du Code civil à la tutelle réglementaire" (1981) 23 *Sociologie du Travail* 14.

The altered and ambiguous economic status of the typical European farmer is reflected, perhaps, in the fact that CAP law lacks a judicial definition of "agricultural holding." In Case 85/77 *Santa Anna Azienda Avicola*[16] the plaintiff in the main action had a holding in Italy producing eggs and raising poultry. Using purchased feedingstuffs, it marketed eggs, day-old chicks and fattened poultry. After the enterprise was "modernised," the Italian social security office claimed contributions at a higher rate, arguing that the plaintiff's business now constituted an industrial undertaking. According to Italian law, agricultural holdings paid lower social security contributions than did industrial undertakings; the former were also eligible for more favourable treatment regarding taxation, subsidies, credit, fuel and electricity and the regulation of environmental pollution.[17] The Court held, however, that it was impossible to find in the Treaty provisions or rules of EC secondary legislation any general uniform Community definition of "agricultural holding," universally applicable in all the provisions laid down by law and regulations relating to agricultural production.

Similarly, in Case 139/77 *Denkavit*[18] the Court interpreted Articles 39 and 40(3) and Regulation 2464/79, which permitted Germany to counter the internal effects of currency revaluation by granting aid to "agricultural producers." The plaintiff company produced feedingstuffs and, on the basis of contracts with farmers, fattened calves for sale on its own substitute milk-based fodder. It had no agricultural land, however, and under German law was therefore an industrial undertaking. German legislation excluded "industrial farming undertakings" from eligibility for the grants. The Court held that the concept of "agricultural producer" was not precisely defined in the Treaty; it was therefore to be defined *ad hoc* in relation to each particular agricultural rule or set of rules derived from the Treaty. Any national legislative definition was permissible and not discriminatory so long as it was based on objective distinctions and compatible with the purposes of any applicable EC regulations and the Treaty. Consequently, the Court stated in a further case[19] that, for the purposes of the grants

---

[16] Case 85/77 *Società Santa Anna Azienda Avicola* v. *Istituto Nazionale della Previdenza Sociale (INPS) and Servizio Contributi Agricola Unificati (SCAU)* [1978] E.C.R. 527.

[17] According to the plaintiff's argument, as summarised by Advocate General Reischl: [1978] E.C.R. 527 at 543.

[18] Case 139/77 *Denkavit Futtermittel GmbH* v. *Finanzamt Warendorf* [1978] E.C.R. 1317.

[19] Case 36/79 *Denkavit Futtermittel GmbH* v. *Finanzamt Warendorf* [1979] E.C.R. 3439.

concerned, the particular nature of agricultural activity, which resulted from the social structure of agriculture, justified the Federal Republic in giving priority to the sectors of the agricultural economy which had suffered the most direct loss of income from the revaluation, namely those concerned with working the soil. Such a distinction at least was not arbitrary; it could not be regarded as discrimination between producers as prohibited by Article 40(3).

These judicial decisions thus generally leave the definition of "agricultural holding" to the Member States. National policies therefore determine the economic, political and symbolic importance (or otherwise) of the family farm. CAP law, as interpreted by the Court, places relatively few, if any, direct restrictions on the industrialisation of agriculture.

The 1972 directives

Based on a Council Resolution of May 25, 1971, concerning the new orientation of the CAP,[20] three 1972 directives enacted some of the less controversial parts of the Mansholt Plan into legislation. Their purpose was described by Finn Olav Gundlach, then Commissioner for agriculture, as being to "make it more tolerable from the social and regional point of view to conduct the type of price policy which the market situation demands."[21] They were, in other words, to serve as a counterbalance to the increasing industrialisation of agriculture under the aegis of agro-industrial firms and national governments.[22] The Mansholt controversy made it clear that Member States were unprepared to relinquish the formulation of structural policy entirely to the Community, including other Member States. As stated in the preamble to Directive 72/159, the causes, nature and gravity of structural problems in agriculture varied enormously from region to region. It followed, therefore, that

"the best results can be achieved if, acting on the basis of Community concepts and criteria, Member States implement

---

[20] O.J. 1971, C.52/7.
[21] Gundlach, "Prospects for the Common Agricultural Policy in the World Context" in M. Tracy and I. Hodac (eds.), *Prospects for Agriculture in the European Community* (1981) at 431.
[22] See Balogh, Durand–Drouhin, Mollard, Quaden and Hunek, "La politique agraire à l'Est et à l'Ouest de l'Europe" in "L'Etat et la politique agraire en Europe: Présentation des politiques agricoles de douze pays de l'Est et de l'Ouest" (1976) 10 *Economies et Sociétés* 1344.

the common measures individually through their own legislative and administrative procedures, and if, in addition, they themselves determine, on the basis of conditions laid down by the Community, the extent to which such measures should be intensified in or concentrated on certain regions."

Consequently, whereas the initial, limited EC structural policy had been effected by regulation, the 1972 measures were in the legal form of directives.

Directive 72/159 on the modernisation of farms[23] provided for the introduction by Member States of a system of selective incentives to farmers whose farms were considered suitable for development. According to the directive, a farm was considered suitable for development if the farmer practised farming as the main occupation, possessed adequate occupational skill and competence, undertook to keep accounts and drew up a development plan which would lead after six years to income comparable to the average for non-agricultural workers in the region in question. Incentives for persons submitting a development plan were to include priority allocation of land released under Directive 72/160, interest rate subsidies except for the purchase of land or of pigs, poultry or calves intended for slaughter, and loan guarantees. Farmers whose income was comparable to that of non-agricultural workers, but whose farm structure was such as to jeopardise the maintenance of that income, were eligible for partial interest rate subsidies. The Guidance Section of EAGGF was to reimburse Member States 25 per cent. of eligible expenditure under the directive.

Article 3 of the directive provided that Member States were to define what was meant, for purposes of the directive, by the expression "a farmer practising farming as his main occupation." Such definitions were required, however, in the case of a natural person, to include the conditions that the proportion of income from farming be not less than 50 per cent. of total income and that working time devoted to non-farming activities be less than half of total working time. Italy's application of this article was questioned in Case 121/78 *Bardi*.[24] The plaintiff in the main action, a feedingstuffs producer, had agreed to supply maize to a limited partnership engaged in fattening animals. The contract was to be deemed cancelled, however, if the partnership proved unable to obtain a licence to import calves from non-EC countries. The defendant was informed by the Italian regional authority that it could not receive a licence because it was a company, and there-

[23] J.O. 1972, L.96/1.
[24] Case 121/78 *Guiseppe Bardi* v. *Azienda Agricola Paradiso* [1979] E.C.R. 221.

fore did not fulfil the conditions for such licences as specified by a Foreign Trade Ministry circular. The circular stipulated that the expression "agricultural producers" within the meaning of Commission Regulation 2902/77 concerning the licences was to be deemed to apply only to those who satisfied the requirements of the Italian law implementing Council Directives 72/159, 72/160 and 72/161. This law, in turn, provided that except for co-operatives only those persons qualified whose principal income was farming, in that they devoted to farming at least two-thirds of their working time and derived therefrom at least two-thirds of their earned income. Consequently, the defendant did not even apply for a licence and cancelled the contract, whereupon the plaintiff sued for specific performance.

On an Article 177 reference, the Court pointed out that "the presumed effect of the reference in the circular to that legislative provision is to reserve the benefit of the import quota in question to individual farmers who personally devoted most of their time to farming. . . . "[25] It held, first, that Italy was entitled, under the regulation in question, to specify the categories of agricultural producers who might benefit from the import quotas of animals under partial or total suspension of the levy within the framework of a policy intended to help improve cattle rearing and beef and veal production structures. Second, it considered that the obligation on Member States arising from Directive 72/159 was satisfied by the Italian restriction of the benefit to farmers practising farming as their main occupation.

Whether structural expenditure must concern solely agricultural purposes was in question in Case 152/79 *Kevin Lee*.[26] The plaintiff, an office clerk and part-time farmer, acquired two holdings, one of eleven acres and one of four acres, in County Sligo in 1972. In November 1974 he applied for planning permission to erect three separate dwellings on the four-acre portion. He obtained planning permission in February 1975 and subsequently sold two of the built-up sites. In February 1975 he also applied to join, and was accepted into, the Irish Farm Modernisation Scheme, which implemented Directive 72/159. Since under the Scheme he was classified as a farmer to whom Article 14(2) of the Scheme applied, he was eligible for a grant under Part IV of the Scheme, which provided for granting of certain aids to farmers who were not eligible for the incentives available under the Directive's mandatory provisions. The plaintiff then applied for a grant for part of the cost of

[25] *Ibid.* at 232.
[26] Case 152/79 *Kevin Lee* v. *Minister for Agriculture* [1980] E.C.R. 1495.

installing a pump and an underground pipe to a drinking trough for cattle; in the pipe he inserted a T-junction leading to a tank which was to act as a reservoir for the three private dwellings. In August 1977, the grant was approved for a proportion of the cost of extending the pipeline and installing a drinking trough but not for boring the original water supply and installing the pump. The Irish Minister of Agriculture refused to grant the entire sum on the ground, *inter alia*, that the works carried out did not relate exclusively to farm development or modernisation as provided by the scheme.

The case came before the European Court on an Article 177 reference for a preliminary ruling. Advocate General Warner, in his Opinion (at 1513), considered that, while Directive 72/159 applied only to farm development for agricultural purposes, it did not preclude the apportionment of expenditure incurred partly for this purpose and partly for another. The Court stated simply that the directive was concerned only with the development of land for agricultural purposes within the framework of a reform of agricultural structures, and it may not apply to the provision of a water supply carried out with a view to the construction of dwelling-houses. It left to the national court the decision as to whether the provision of a water supply "was carried out principally in order to service dwelling-houses or whether a part of that work related to the modernization of a farm."[27]

The Court also considered the plaintiff's challenge to the provision in the Irish scheme that the Agricultural Minister's decision would be final. It held that Directive 72/159 must be understood as obliging or, as the case may be, authorising the Member States to establish or maintain schemes which satisfy, generally, the criteria laid down by the Community in regard to the reform of agricultural structures, but which, for the rest, are constituted in accordance with the national law of the Member States. Accordingly, in its view, Directive 72/159 contained no specific obligations regarding the provision of judicial remedies in respect of administrative decisions taken in the framework of the national provisions implementing it; this matter remained subject to the national law of each Member State.

Directive 72/160[28] concerned measures to encourage the cessation of farming and the reallocation of agricultural land for the purposes of structural improvement, either by increasing the size of farms or for uses related to afforestation, recreation or public

[27] *Ibid.* at 1506.
[28] J.O. 1972, L.96/9.

health. It provided for the introduction by Member States of the grant of an annuity to encourage the cessation of farming by farmers and their employees aged between 55 and 65 years and a premium, to be paid entirely by the Member State, calculated by reference to the agricultural area released. Grants were subject to the conditions that, where the recipient was a farmer, at least 85 per cent. of the agricultural area released be either removed permanently from agricultural use or leased for a minimum of 12 years or, in some cases, to other farmers. EAGGF was to refund 25 per cent. of Member States' expenditure, except that 65 per cent. was reimbursed in agricultural regions where the proportion of the working population engaged in agriculture was higher than the EC average, the gross domestic product per capita at factor cost was lower than the EC average, and measures to encourage the cessation of farming were not yet in operation.

Directive 72/161[29] provided for socio-economic guidance and training for farmers in order to raise the level of general, technical and economic knowledge. Provision was made for the creation of guidance schemes or their development within already existing schemes, training advisors and the award of grants or allowance for attendance at training courses. Generally, and within limits, EAGGF was to reimburse 25 per cent. of expenditure. This directive was amended by Directive 81/529,[30] which provided for the introduction by Member States of special training programmes for leaders and managers of co-operatives in order to promote, through producers' groups, new activities regarding agricultural processing and marketing.

These three directives shared a common legal form, a common legal basis (Art. 43), a common method of Community financing and procedures by which the EC was to oversee their implementation by the Member States.[31] Regulation 729/70[32] on the financing of the CAP provided that the Guidance Section was to finance "common measures" adopted in order to achieve the Article 39(1) structural objectives. In contrast to Guarantee Section spending, which as "necessary" or "obligatory" expenditure is in principle unlimited, Guarantee Section expenditure is subject to periodically agreed ceilings. The credits allocated to the Guidance Section from September 1, 1972, were 285 million units of account per

---

[29] J.O. 1972, L.96/15.
[30] O.J. 1982, L.197/44.
[31] See Olmi and Bourgeois, "Les directives sur la réforme de l'agriculture dans la Communauté" (1973) 5 C.D.E. 511 at 527–544.
[32] O.J. 1970, L.94/13; amended by Reg. 3509/80 (O.J. 1980, L.367/87).

year. After the first enlargement, this was increased to 325 million units of account a year.[33] For the period from 1979–1984 the total appropriation was 3,600 million ecu, or 720 million ecu per year. Although the Guidance Section was initially intended to receive 25 per cent. of total CAP funds, today the proportion allocated for structural policy amounts to approximately 5 per cent.[34] Contrary to the sentiments expressed in the Stresa Conference resolution, there is little if any obvious link between expenditure under the two EAGGF sections.[35]

These directives leave to Member States the responsibility not only of specifying the details for implementation but also of deciding whether particular provisions will in fact be adopted. Accordingly, the application of the three socio-structural directives has varied widely among the Member States. In the United Kingdom, Directive 72/159 has been implemented by the Agriculture and Horticulture Development Scheme,[36] Directive 72/160 by the Farm Structure (Payment to Outgoers) Scheme[37] and Directive 72/161 by existing institutions, especially the Agricultural Training Board and the Agricultural Development and Advisory Service (ADAS).[38] As of May 1982, however, Directive 72/159 had still not been effectively implemented in Italy; neither Italy nor Denmark had implemented Directive 72/160; and Directive 72/161 had not been promoted vigorously except in France.[39]

---

[33] Reg. 2788/72 (J.O. 1972, L.295/1; O.J. Eng.Sp.Ed. 1972, 28–30.12.72, p. 91).

[34] Commission of the European Communities, *The Agricultural Situation in the Community: 1983 Report* (1984) at 161.

[35] See House of Lords Select Committee on the European Communities, *Socio-Structural Policy* (1982) at xv, 14–15.

[36] The Agriculture and Horticulture Development Regs. 1980 (S.I. 1980 No. 1298), as amended by The Agriculture and Horticulture Development (Amendment) Regs. 1981 (S.I. 1981 No. 1708), The Agriculture and Horticulture Development (Amendment) Regs. 1983 (S.I. 1983 No. 508), The Agriculture and Horticulture Development (Amendment) (No. 2) Regs. 1983 (S.I. 1983 No. 924), and The Agriculture and Horticulture Development (Amendment) (No. 3) Regs. 1983 (S.I. 1983 No. 1763).

[37] See The Farm Structure (Payments to Outgoers) Scheme 1973 (S.I. 1973 No. 1403); The Farm Structure (Payments to Outgoers) Scheme 1976 (S.I. 1976 No. 2126); The Farm Structure (Payments to Outgoers) (Variation) Scheme 1981 (S.I. 1981 No. 1709); The Farm Structure (Payments to Outgoers) (Extension of Duration) Scheme 1983 (S.I. 1983 No. 1882).

[38] The current legal framework of the Board is provided by the Agricultural Training Board Act 1982 (c. 9). On ADAS, see Woods, "Rapid Evaluation of a Policy and a Service: Socio-Economic Advice in England and Wales" (1980) 31 *Journal of Agricultural Economics* 55.

[39] See the Memorandum from the Ministry of Agriculture, Fisheries and Food, in House of Lords Select Committee on the European Communities, *Socio-Structural Policy* (1982) at 2–6.

Among the numerous obstacles to application of the directives were the differing political and economic structures of the Member States, pre-existing national laws and constitutional arrangements, and the inherent delicacy and complexity of the exercise given the Community's relative lack of legitimacy, shortage of staff and necessary dependence on national authorities. As the Commission complained in 1983:

"Very often, . . . the national legislation has weakened or antagonized the effects of the common measures. Thus, in some Member States the existing tenancy legislation, which gives the tenant, and subsequently his heir, an almost absolute security of tenure while at the same time effectively controlling rental charges, has a decidedly adverse effect on land mobility via tenancy. Furthermore, in the majority of Member States the cessation of farming is not obligatory on the receipt of the old-age pension. In such cases, the pension is regarded as a supplement to farm income, and is thus likely to lead to a reduction in the rate of land mobility."[40]

In addition to thus proving ill-adapted to European economic conditions since the mid-1970s, the directives have also been frustrated by national constitutional arrangements. In Italy, following a controversy over the respective powers of the central and regional governments, special legislation was enacted to enable the Italian Council of Ministers, in particular conditions, to take necessary measures to implement the directives in substitution of regional authorities.[41] In addition, however, the application of the directives has sometimes had deleterious effects on already impoverished regions, such as the Italian Mezzogiorno.[42] In the United Kingdom, the House of Lords Select Committee on the European Communities concluded in 1982 that Directive 72/159 had had some effect but brought about no major changes, Directive 72/160 had had little effect and Directive 72/161 "has been, and may well

---

[40] Commission of the European Communities, *The Agricultural Situation in the Community: 1983 Report* (1984) at 72–73. A useful summary of French policy is Naylor, "Retirement Policy in French Agriculture" (1982) 33 *Journal of Agricultural Economics* 25.

[41] See Mastellone, "The Judicial Application of Community Law in Italy, 1976–1980" (1982) 19 C.M.L.Rev. 153 at 164–166.

[42] See Podbielski, "The Common Agricultural Policy and the Mezzogiorno" (1981) 19 J.C.M.S. 331; De Benedictis, "Agricultural Development in Italy: National Problems in a Community Framework" (1981) 32 *Journal of Agricultural Economics* 275.

continue to be, beneficial."[43] In principle, Member States are required to inform EC authorities of progress in the implementation of directives. Despite the computerisation of the Community's 700 directives and an improved monitoring system, however, the Commission has relatively few means of ensuring the application of directives on structural reform.[44]

Processing and marketing

Applications for aid to individual projects under Regulation 17/64 were accepted only until 1979, since this Regulation was replaced in 1977 by Regulation 355/77[45] on common measures to improve the conditions under which agricultural products were processed and marketed. Aid was to be granted by the Commission for common measures by financing projects included in specific programmes and meeting particular conditions. The programmes were to be drawn up by the Member States. Projects included any project involving public, semi-public or private material investment relating wholly or partly to buildings and/or equipment for

(a) rationalising or developing storage, market preparation, preservation, treatment or processing of agricultural products;
(b) improving marketing channels;
(c) better knowledge of the facts relating to prices and to their formation on the markets for agricultural products.

The regulation did not apply to investments at retail level. Projects were required to relate to the marketing of Annex II products or the production of the processed products set out in that Annex. In addition, by Council decision acting by a qualified majority on a Commission proposal, they could include the processing of agricultural products listed in Annex II into goods not covered by the Annex or the marketing of such goods, if and in so far as the product or marketing of the goods constituted a major outlet for the agricultural products involved. Projects must contribute "to

---

[43] House of Lords Select Committee on the European Communities, *Socio-Structural Policy* (1982) at xvi.
[44] See generally Commission of the European Communities, "First Annual Report to the European Parliament on Commission Monitoring of the Application of Community Law, 1983" COM(84)181 final (1984). Evaluations of EC structural measures may be found in Commission of the European Communities, *The Agricultural Situation in the Community: 1983 Report* (1984) at 71–82; House of Lords Select Committee on the European Communities, *Socio-Structural Policy* (1982); M. Tracy, *Agriculture in Western Europe* (2nd ed. 1982) at 346–350.
[45] O.J. 1977, L.51/1.

improving the situation of the basic agricultural production sector in question, in particular they must guarantee the producers of the basic agricultural product an adequate and lasting share in the resulting economic benefits" (Art. 9(1)).

Applications for aid were to be submitted through and approved by the relevant Member State. In relation to each project, the applicant was expected to contribute at least 50 per cent. and the Member State not less than 5 per cent. of the cost. The EC grant was to constitute not more than 25 per cent., with the exception that the Commission could increase this maximum to 30 per cent. in particular cases; this limit has since been increased (see below). Grant aid from EAGGF was not, however, to affect the conditions of competition in such a way as to be incompatible with the Treaty. The regulation was initially valid for five years but was later extended to January 1, 1985.[46]

Article 15(2) of the regulation excluded from possible grant any project which was eligible for EC aid under other "common measures" within the meaning of Regulation 729/70, Article 6(1). This Article of Regulation 355/77 was interpreted by the Court in Case 107/80 *Adorno*,[47] which concerned the respective spheres of application of Directive 72/159 and Regulation 355/77. The plaintiff ran two holdings composing 176 hectares in the Piedmont area of Italy, producing mainly wine. In April 1979 he applied for financial aid under Regulation 355/77 for the creation of a new wine-making centre, designed to improve the processing into wine of grapes produced on the farm, to rationalise the storage and preservation of the wine, to improve transport between the various terrains and to shorten the marketing channels for the wine. The Commission rejected his application on the ground that it fell within the scope of Directive 72/159. The plaintiff was not eligible for structural aid under the directive, however, because his income was higher than comparable non-agricultural incomes in the region. Consequently, he brought an action under Article 173 for annulment of the Commission's decision.

The Commission argued that Regulation 355/77 and Directive 72/159 were alternatives, having different aims, concerning different types of farms, having different impacts on production and serving different socio-economic purposes.[48] Advocate General Capotorti considered, however, that the two measures could over-

---

[46] Reg. 3073/82 (O.J. 1982, L.325/1).
[47] Case 107/80 *Giacomo Cattaneo Adorno* v. *Commission* [1981] E.C.R. 1469.
[48] See the Opinion by Advocate General Capotorti: [1981] E.C.R. 1469 at 1490–1491.

lap. The regulation had been drafted on the assumption that agricultural producers and processors were legally distinct, but that was "not sufficient to justify the assumption that should the two functions . . . be assimilated the regulation is rendered inapplicable."[49] In fact, in his view, assuming this to be the case,

> "the larger the extent of the producing and processing undertaking, the greater the improvement will be in the situation in the relevant agricultural production sector. In other words, where a farm occupies a significant place in an agricultural production sector . . . and itself processes the basic product, the benefits for production . . . will be a natural consequence of rationalizing processing methods."[50]

Largely accepting this position, the European Court declared the Commission's decision void. It stated that

> "projects for improving the processing and marketing of agricultural products from the same farm as that in which the investment is to be made are in no way excluded from the scope of the regulation if they are capable of making an effective contribution towards rationalizing processing and marketing structures."[51]

Article 9 of the regulation provided that projects must contribute to improving the situation of the agricultural production sector in question, and in particular guarantee producers an adequate and lasting share of the resulting benefits. This provision, in the Court's view, did not restrict the scope of the regulation to that case alone. The applicant's project, however, was designed not to raise the farm's profitability by improving production conditions but rather to improve processing and marketing; it did not therefore fall within the scope of Directive 72/159.

Aid under the regulation has generally gone to projects close to the farm gate, as the Commission has given a narrow interpretation to Article 7. Funds are in effect apportioned among the Member States; the United Kingdom's share of the original allocation was just under 15 per cent. This aspect of the regulation has drawn particular criticism, and so has the cumbersome administra-

---

[49] *Ibid*. at 1492.
[50] *Ibid*. at 1493.
[51] *Ibid*. at 1485.

tion of the grant system and delays, up to two years, in taking decisions.[52]

Producers' organisations

Since the Stresa Conference the Commission has urged support for producers' organisations,[53] partly in order to redress an imbalance of power in agricultural marketing and partly as a means of centralising supply and adapting production to market requirements. Regulation 1360/78,[54] a horizontal regulation, is designed to encourage the formation of producer groups and associations of such groups regarding specified products in Italy, Belgium, southern France and the French overseas departments and Greece. In these regions Member States are to recognise such groups and associations, including existing ones, which apply for recognition and fulfill certain conditions. The groups are to consist either of individual producers or of individual producers and organisations, consisting solely of individual producers, for producing or increasing the returns from agricultural products. Such groups or associations are required to fulfil certain conditions; to contribute, through the activities in respect of which they request recognition, to the achievement of Article 39 objectives; to decide on and apply common rules for production and marketing; to provide for the whole production of their members to be marketed according to specified conditions; to allow, under certain conditions, for the withdrawal of members from the group; to give proof of adequate economic activity; to exclude any discrimination running counter to the operation of the common market and the achievement of general Treaty objectives; to have legal personality or sufficient legal capacity; to keep proper accounts; and not to hold a domi-

---

[52] See House of Lords Select Committee on the European Communities, *Socio-Structural Policy* (1982), *passim*.

[53] See S. Ventura, *Principes de Droit agraire communautaire* (1967) at 97. A convenient summary of provisions up to 1979 is given by R. Fennell, *The Common Agricultural Policy of the European Community* (1979) at 206–211; see also Melchior and others, "The Common Agricultural Policy" in Commission of the European Communities (ed.), *Thirty Years of Community Law* (1983) at 444, 461. See also Boisson and Maurel, "Les groupements de producteurs et la Politique agricole commune: Le cas de la viticulture languedocienne"; Lamoureux, "L'extension des disciplines édictées par les organisations de producteurs"; Megret, "Le rôle des groupements de producteurs dans la politique commune des marchés agricoles"; in J. Raux (ed.), *Politique agricole commune et Construction communautaire* (1984).

[54] O.J. 1978, L.166/1; amended by Reg. 3086/81 (O.J. 1981, L.310/3) consequent to Greek accession.

nant position in the common market unless necessary for the pursuit of Article 39 objectives. The minimum volume of production, turnover or land under cultivation and the minimum number of members of producer groups and their associations are established by Commission Regulation 2083/80.[55]

Member States must grant officially recognised groups gradually decreasing aid during the three years following recognition to encourage formation and facilitate operations. Aid may include interest rebates, loan guarantees and flat rate grants for setting up producer groups. Allowable formation and operating expenditures are provided by Commission Regulation 2084/80.[56] EAGGF refunds amount to between 25–50 per cent. of chargeable expenditure. Specific rules provide for producers' associations regarding particular products. For example, Regulation 1413/82[57] amended Regulation 136/66 on the establishment of the common market organisation for oils and fats to provide aid for groups of olive oil producers.

Reorientation

Regions

The 1972 socio-structural directives and related measures were based on the assumptions that western European economies would continue to expand, that people leaving agriculture would continue to find employment in urban industry and that increasing agricultural and food production would continue to be matched by consumer demand. These assumptions were undermined, however, by the 1973 oil crisis and the world recession, which had an especially severe impact on rural, generally poorer areas and labour intensive industries. These events encouraged a gradual reorientation of EC structural policy, which in addition to numerous sectoral measures[58] has included a greater emphasis on regionally specific policies.

---

[55] O.J. 1980, L.203/5; as amended by Commission Reg. 1612/82 (O.J. 1982, L.180/21).
[56] O.J. 1980, L.203/9.
[57] O.J. 1982, L.162/6.
[58] A convenient summary to 1982 is European Parliament Secretariat, *Europe Today: State of European Integration 1982–83* (1983), s.3.737. For a general survey of recent structural policy, see Commission of the European Communities, *The Agricultural Situation in the Community: 1983 Report* (1984) at 82–89.

Apart from the establishment of the Regional Development Fund,[59] Council Directive 75/268[60] on mountain and hill farming and farming in certain less-favoured areas was perhaps the first EC measure concerned expressly with particular regions. Its stated aims were to ensure the continuation of farming, maintain a certain minimum population level and conserve the countryside in certain less-favoured areas. The directive authorised Member States to grant compensatory allowances to farmers in specified areas with at least three hectares (two hectares in the Mezzogiorno) of "utilised agricultural area" who undertook to pursue a farming activity in accordance with the aims of the directive for at least five years. It also provided for the grant of aids to farms suitable for development, including aids for tourist or craft industry purposes, aids to joint investment schemes for fodder production and improvement and equipment schemes for pasture and hill grazing land, and aids for farms not capable of meeting a specified level of earned income. The less-favoured areas, the boundaries of which Member States were required to communicate to the Commission,[61] included mountain areas in which farming is necessary to protect the countryside and characterised by a short growing season, steep slopes or a combination of the two. They also include farming areas with infertile land, low productivity and rural depopulation. The Guidance Section of EAGGF was initially to reimburse Member States 25 per cent. of eligible expenditure under the scheme, except that in Ireland and Italy the rate was 50 per cent.[62] This directive constituted a major departure from the earlier socio-structural directives in differentiating expressly

[59] Reg. 724/75 (O.J. 1975, L.73/1), as amended by Reg. 214/79 (O.J. 1979, L.35/1). See also Council Resolution of February 6, 1979, concerning the guidelines for Community regional policy (O.J. 1979, C.36/10). The Communication of the Commission on Regional Aid Schemes (O.J. 1979, C.31/9) set forth the principles which the Commission intended to apply to existing or future regional aid schemes; these principles, in EC jargon, are differentiated ceilings of aid intensity, transparency, regional specificity, sectoral repercussion of regional aid, and supervision.

[60] O.J. 1975, L.128/1; amended by Directive 80/666 (O.J. 1980, L.180/34).

[61] The less-favoured areas in the U.K., following communication by the U.K. Government to the Commission, were listed in Council Directive 75/276 (O.J. 1975, L.128/231).

[62] The directive was implemented in Britain by the Hill Livestock (Compensatory Allowances) Regs. 1975: see *Re Slaughter of Hill Cattle in Scotland* (Case 3B/659/78) before the Parliamentary Commissioner for Administration (The British Ombudsman) [1979] 2 C.M.L.R. 505.

between regions and between producers and in providing for direct income payments.[63]

A broader regional approach was adopted by the Commission in 1977. To meet longstanding French and Italian demands and offset the likely impact of the Second Enlargement, it proposed a series of measures known as the Mediterranean Package.[64] Among the proposals adopted were an increase to 50 per cent. of EAGGF aid under Regulation 355/77; Regulation 1362/78[65] on a programme for the acceleration and guidance of collective irrigation works in the Mezzogiorno; Regulation 1760/78[66] on a common measure to improve public amenities, including electricity, water supply and roads; Council Directive 78/627[67] on a programme to accelerate the restructuring and conversion of vineyards in certain Mediterranean areas of France; Regulation 269/79[68] establishing a common measure for forestry in certain Mediterranean parts of France and Italy; Regulation 270/79[69] on the development of agricultural advisory services in Italy; and Regulation 1944/81[70] establishing a common measure for the adaptation and modernisation of the structure of production of beef, veal, sheepmeat and goatmeat in Italy.

In 1979 proposals by the Commission[71] led to two further developments: specific programmes for regions other than Mediterranean areas, and the introduction of integrated development programmes. An example of the former is the various measures

---

[63] S. Harris, A. Swinbank and G. Wilkinson, *The Food and Farm Policies of the European Community* (1983) at 224. On the implementation of the directive in different Member States, see House of Lords Select Committee on the European Communities, *Socio-Structural Policy* (1982), *passim.*

[64] See Commission of the European Communities, "Mediterranean Agricultural Problems" COM(77)140 (1977); Commission of the European Communities, "Guidelines concerning the Development of the Mediterranean Regions of the Community, together with Certain Measures relating to Agriculture" COM(77)526, (1977) 2 Vols.; Commission of the European Communities, "Financial Consequences of the Proposals for Measures to Assist Mediterranean Agriculture" COM(77)674 (1974). A good discussion of the economic aspects is S. Harris, A. Swinbank and G. Wilkinson, *The Food and Farm Policies of the European Community* (1983) at 147–186.

[65] O.J. 1978, L.166/11.

[66] O.J. 1978, L.204/1.

[67] O.J. 1978, L.206/1.

[68] O.J. 1979, L.38/1.

[69] O.J. 1979, L.38/6.

[70] O.J. 1981, L.197/77.

[71] Commission of the European Communities, "Proposals on Policy with Regard to Agricultural Structures" COM(79)122 (1979).

concerning Ireland. They include programmes for drainage in the West of Ireland[72] and in border areas[73]; a programme comprising the subdivision of common land, fencing, infrastructure, establishment of production guidelines, marketing and processing, afforestation and training of counsellors in the West of Ireland[74]; and measures to promote the production of cattle for slaughter in Ireland and Northern Ireland.[75] Other measures concern general agricultural structures in Northern Ireland[76] and processing and marketing conditions in the cattlefeed sector in Northern Ireland.[77]

Integrated development programmes have been enacted for the Western Isles of Scotland,[78] the Department of Lozère in France[79] and certain less-favoured areas of Belgium,[80] among other areas. The programme for the Outer Hebrides, for example, comprises measures concerning the afforestation of marginal land, improvement of the processing and marketing of agricultural products, development of fisheries and development of tourism, crafts and other activities. EAGGF reimburses 40 per cent. of eligible expenditure on agricultural measures, with specified exceptions, forming part of a programme forwarded by the United Kingdom and approved by the Commission and concerning structural improvements. Such programmes have been promulgated by regulations.[81]

The environment

These structural measures have generally paid little attention to the potentially disastrous effects of agricultural production on the environment. An exception, though only in principle, is the less-favoured areas directive, which aims "to ensure the continuation of farming, thereby maintaining a minimum population level and conserving the countryside."[82] The main orientation of EC structural policy has been toward rationalising state aids, maintaining

[72] Directive 78/628 (O.J. 1978, L.206/5).
[73] Directive 79/197 (O.J. 1979, L.43/23); Reg. 2195/81 (O.J. 1981, L.214/5).
[74] Reg. 1820/80 (O.J. 1980, L.180/1) amended by Reg. 1932/84 (O.J. 1984, L.180/1).
[75] Reg. 1054/81 (O.J. 1981, L.111/1).
[76] Reg. 1942/81 (O.J. 1981, L.197/17).
[77] Reg. 1943/81 (O.J. 1981, L.197/23).
[78] Reg. 1939/81 (O.J. 1981, L.197/6).
[79] Reg. 1940/81 (O.J. 1981, L.197/9).
[80] Reg. 1941/81 (O.J. 1981, L.197/13).
[81] See generally House of Lords Select Committee on the European Communities, *Socio-Structural Policy* (1982), *passim*.
[82] Directive 75/268, Art. 1.

farmers' incomes and encouraging intensive production, most often without regard to the environmental consequences of farm amalgamation, overgrazing or the clearance of woodland. Since 1973, for example, nearly £2 million has been spent to increase agricultural production by draining the Fens.[83] Similarly, in order to stimulate agricultural "development" in the less-favoured areas of the West of Ireland, Regulation 1820/80[84] provides for the reimbursement by EAGGF of 50 per cent. of the cost of specified land "improvements," including the subdivision and fencing of common land, fencing and pasture measures on individually owned mountain and hill pasture, and the removal of superfluous fences, ditches and walls. According to the evidence presented to the House of Lords Select Committee by the Exmoor Society, the combined effect of Community and United Kingdom policies

> "is to produce a range of policies which are contradictory in operation. Subsidies are paid to farmers to leave farming altogether, but others are grant aided to increase output. Grants are paid for ploughing, draining and fencing but compensation is paid NOT to carry out these operations. These grants and the annual subsidies have been destructive of the moorland as the acute shrinkage of Exmoor—and other areas—has shown.[85]

It is not surprising, therefore, that since the mid-1970s these and other aspects of the CAP have increasingly been criticised for "subsidising the degradation of the environment."[86]

The 1957 Rome Treaty which laid the legal basis of the CAP predated the rise of the environmental movement as an important political force. The Community's first Action Programme on the Environment[87] was not adopted until 1973. Its implementation has been hindered by political opposition, by the fragmentation of responsibility for environmental legislation within the Community and by the lack of a solid legal basis. The Treaty contains no explicit reference to the protection of the environment, which therefore

---

[83] Waterman, "How the Agricultural Fund is Helping to Drain the Fens" (1984) 1–2 *Europe 84* 16.

[84] O.J. 1980, L.180/1.

[85] Memorandum by the Exmoor Society, in House of Lords Select Committee on the European Communities, *Socio-Structural Policy* (1982) at 145.

[86] J.K. Bowers and P. Cheshire, *Agriculture, the Countryside and Land Use* (1983) at 102. See also M. Shoard, *The Theft of the Countryside* (1980); R. Body, *The Triumph and the Shame* (1982); R. Norton-Taylor, *Whose Land Is It Anyway?* (1982). See generally House of Lords Select Committee on the European Communities, *Agriculture and the Environment* (1984).

[87] O.J. 1973, C.112/1.

falls uneasily within regional policy or rests legally on Article 235 (requiring Council unanimity). In the absence of major agricultural consequences, however, it cannot be legally based on Article 43.

Such concerns have come strongly to the fore during the recent debates on the revision of the 1972 socio-structural directives and Regulation 355/77.[88] The former have now been extended,[89] while an amended version of the second was finally adopted in June 1984.[90] In the interim, the Community's Third Action Programme on the Environment was approved by the Council in February 1983.[91] Not all of its provisions are likely to be implemented by the Member States, but nevertheless it is possible that more effective measures for the protection and conservation of the rural environment may form part of structural policy. In this respect, as in others, real reforms will only take place through knowledge of CAP law and the subtleties of practical politics.

---

[88] See especially House of Lords Select Committee on the European Communities, *Agriculture and the Environment* (1984); B. Duesenberg and B. Girling (eds.), *The Impact of Environmental Legislation upon Agriculture*, Centre for European Agricultural Studies, Wye College, *Seminar Papers No. 16* (1984).

[89] They were first extended to June 30, 1984, by Directive 84/140 (O.J. 1984, L.72/24). The Commission proposed to replace the three directives by a regulation (O.J. 1983, C.347/1), but in the absence of Council agreement it requested a second extension, which was apparently granted without a specific proposed text to October 31, 1984.

[90] See the Commission proposals (O.J. 1983, C.347/1; O.J. 1983, C.347/15) and Council Reg. 1932/84 (O.J. 1984, L.180/1).

[91] O.J. 1983, C.46/1.

INDEX

'The authors succeed in providing the essential links between different levels of communication and building a holistic picture of human communication activities. The tasks set for students are inventive and stimulate critical thinking and creativity. A wide range of knowledge is presented in the light of learning and acquiring the skills necessary to pass examinations.'

Dr Elena Macevičiūtė, Swedish School of Information and Library Science

'The best single textbook currently available.'

Frank Robinson, Newcastle College

'Well written, organised and inventive, it sets standards by which future textbooks will be judged.'

Times Educational Supplement

'Students and teachers alike will warmly welcome this book. It addresses the needs of AS students in a lively, pragmatic, intelligent and, above all, accessible way, and is written by authors who understand fully the needs of their audience. A must for any AS student.'

Patrick Russell, George Abbott School, Guildford

Other books for Media and Communication Studies

Media Studies: The Essential Resource
Philip Rayner, Peter Wall and Stephen Kruger

AS Media Studies: The Essential Introduction
Philip Rayner, Peter Wall and Stephen Kruger

Communication Studies: The Essential Resource
Andrew Beck, Peter Bennett and Peter Wall

▼ AS COMMUNICATION STUDIES:
THE ESSENTIAL INTRODUCTION

fully-updated, easy-to-use second edition of the popular AS *Communication Studies: Essential Introduction* is designed to support students of Communication Studies at level. The authors, who are experienced Communication Studies teachers and examiners, introduce students step by step to the main forms of communication – verbal, non-verbal, intrapersonal and group; they provide guidance on developing effective communication skills and advise on how these can be used to prepare for and pass examinations. This second edition features updated case studies and colour illustrations, as well as providing more guidance on coursework and exam preparation. Individual parts address:

- communication studies
- effective communication practice
- texts and meanings in communication
- themes in personal communication
- using communication skills to pass examinations.

AS *Communication Studies: The Essential Introduction* will give students the confidence to tackle every part of an introductory course in Communication Studies. Its key features include:

- activities
- worked exam questions
- suggestions for further reading
- glossary of key terms
- case studies of how theoretical concepts can be applied in everyday situations.

Andrew Beck is Principal Lecturer in Applied Communication at Coventry University, editor of *Cultural Work* (2003) and the author of *Get Set for Communication Studies* (2005) and *Communication Skills and Social Work* (2005). **Peter Bennett** is Head of Communications at the Rowley Regis Centre of Dudley College, Chief Examiner for Communication Studies at A Level, co-editor of *Communication Studies: the Essential Resource* (2003), and co-author of *Framework Media: Channels* (2003). **Peter Wall** is Chair of Examiners for Media and Communication Studies at A Level, co-editor of *Communication Studies: The Essential Resource* (2003), author of *Media Studies for* GCSE (2002) and co-author of *Framework Media: Channels* (2003).

AS COMMUNICATION STUDIES

THE ESSENTIAL INTRODUCTION

Second edition

Andrew Beck, Peter Bennett, Peter Wall

Routledge
Taylor & Francis Group

LONDON AND NEW YORK

First published 2001
by Routledge
2 Park Square, Milton Park, Abingdon, Oxon OX14 4RN

Simultaneously published in the USA and Canada
by Routledge
270 Madison Ave, New York, NY 10016

Reprinted 2002, 2003

Second edition published 2005

Routledge is an imprint of the Taylor & Francis Group

© 2001, 2005 Andrew Beck, Peter Bennett, Peter Wall

Typeset in Novarese and Bell Gothic by Keystroke, Jacaranda Lodge, Wolverhampton
Printed and bound in Italy by Printer Trento

British Library Cataloguing in Publication Data
A catalogue record for this book is available from the British Library

Library of Congress Cataloging in Publication Data
Beck, Andrew, 1952–
  AS communication studies: the essential introduction / by Andrew Beck,
Peter Bennett and Peter Wall. – 2nd ed.
  p. cm.
Rev. ed. of: Communication studies. 2002.
Includes bibliographical references and index.
1. Communication. I. Bennett, Peter, 1961– II. Wall, Peter. III. Beck, Andrew,
1952– Communication studies. IV. Title.
  P90.B34 2004
  302.2–dc22   2004020066

ISBN 0–415–33118–8 (hbk)
ISBN 0–415–33117–x (pbk)

▼ CONTENTS

▼ FIGURES

▼ DIAGRAMS

▼ INTRODUCTION TO THE SECOND EDITION

'He promised a new start.
I made no comment.
What should I resent?'

T. S. Eliot: *The Waste Land*

Research has suggested that 'new' is the word used most frequently in advertising. What you are reading, then, is almost certainly an advertisement of sorts, an extended version of the book's new blurb which talks about how this version of what was once considered 'essential' is newer and presumably better. It is also then a series of 'plays', of strategies for convincing you at least that what you have is a cut above what went before (and which you probably don't have).

In fact, in essence, nothing very much has changed. Communication is still 'at the heart of our everyday lives' as the first edition claimed and this is still an all-purpose introduction to the study of communication. If you find it more tightly focused (from its title onwards) on the new AQA AS specification, it is simply because this is now the 'introductory' Communication Studies qualification, the lowest level at which Communication Studies is formally examined. Moreover we were all involved, with others, in the creation of that specification as a means to deliver the key strands of Communication Studies as a discipline. As the specification has bedded in, so our work here has become more focused and streamlined.

What we have attempted to do, encouraged by the often gratifyingly positive and thoughtful feedback we have received from readers, is to try to listen and learn lessons. We have tried to make the good stuff more useful and tried to iron out the inconsistencies of structure which for some were interfering with a clear sight of what is essential. The proof of the pudding will, as always, be in the eating.

HOW THIS BOOK IS ORGANISED

This book aims to give you a start in your study of communication. It opens up a path into an often complex discipline. It looks at the principal theories that have been developed about, while at the same time exploring the character of, communication in a modern technological age. It is designed to help you explore and understand communication from both theoretical and practical perspectives. We offer you advice on how to enhance your own communication skills. We look at key perspectives in communication by considering approaches to textual analysis. We explore key aspects of the communication process between individuals and within groups.

You might be working with the book by yourself or with a group of fellow students led by a teacher. Whichever way you're using the book, here are a few hints on how to make best use of it.

You can work with the book in any order you wish. If you start at the beginning and proceed right the way through to the end, then you should appreciate that there's a structure here. Part 1 sets the scene for your studying Communication. Part 2 looks at ways and means by which you can become more effective communicators, and examines the forms and functions of communication in a number of contexts – including working through a coursework portfolio. Parts 3 and 4 will be of special interest to students preparing for AQA's AS Communication Studies, as they reflect the three units of study. Part 3 introduces you to the tools you can use to analyse communication texts; it also introduces you to a wide range of (sometimes complementary, sometimes conflicting) theories about communication. Part 4 looks at themes in personal communication; it introduces you to key concepts relating to verbal and non-verbal communication, intrapersonal communication and group communication. Finally, Part 5 offers advice on and assistance in preparing for and sitting public examinations in Communication Studies.

On the other hand, you might want simply to dip into the book without working through it in sequence. If you do this, then look to the titles of each part, and to the titles of the sections into which the parts are divided. And, in all parts, look to the headings that break up the text and which tell you what's coming.

Whenever a key term is introduced you will find that we offer a definition of that term. Whenever we want you to explore a concept, theory or perspective we offer activities (in shaded boxes). It's often the case that we want you to engage in that activity before you go any further – because what you'll discover doing that activity will inform how you read the next part of the text. It's sometimes the case that we will explain something to you, then ask you to undertake an activity to reinforce your learning, or to test the truth or reliability of what we've said. Shorter definitions of key terms in the text are offered in the Glossary at the end of the book.

We hope this book offers you a readable introduction to Communication Studies. We hope it helps you in your explorations of Communication Studies and that it stimulates you to take your studies further. If that's what you want, then the Further Reading sections and Bibliography will help you to find out more about the world of Communication Studies.

Andrew Beck, Peter Bennett and Pete Wall
Leamington Spa, Stourbridge, Wakefield
Autumn 2003

PART 1: STUDYING COMMUNICATION

▼ 1 WHAT DO YOU MEAN BY 'COMMUNICATION'?

In the first part of this book we will be looking to briefly map out the Communication Studies 'territory'.

- We will ask 'What is "communication"?' and looking at a wide range of answers.
- We will start to explore some of the issues of Communication Studies and present a couple of broadly theoretical approaches to these issues.

Communication is at the heart of our everyday lives. From the moment we wake in the morning, thinking about the challenges of the day ahead, to the moment we drift off to sleep last thing at night, we are constantly in the process of communicating. We do so either as senders of messages or receivers of messages. In some cases, such as our early morning thoughts, the communication is within and to our self.

Just think how important the process of communication is in so many everyday situations.

- We speak to, listen to and interact with other people. We do this face to face or on the telephone. We communicate in formal situations (such as sitting in class listening to a teacher) as well as in informal situations (chatting with friends or family).
- We use written language to communicate. We read and write letters, notes, reports, essays, instructions and shopping lists. Many of us use electronic technology to send and receive e-mails or to surf the Net.
- Wherever we go we are the receivers of messages. Newspaper headlines, billboards, street signs, shop windows, public announcements and traffic lights all send us messages. In a media-saturated society they compete for and demand our attention to the point where it is impossible to ignore them.
- We use the mass media as a source of messages that offers us both information and entertainment. We listen to the radio, to CDs or minidiscs; we watch television and DVDs, and we read newspapers and magazines.

- We communicate with ourselves when we think, consider, plan or have a sudden moment of anxiety.
- Even when we think we are not communicating, we usually are. Facial expressions, bodily posture, even the way in which we occupy the space about us, are all methods of communicating our attitudes, ideas and feelings to the world at large. Indeed, it has been argued that it is impossible *not* to communicate.

As communication is such an important part of our everyday lives, it is hardly surprising that people have chosen to study it. By doing so, it is possible to understand more fully how communication works. Some people believe that such study can help to make us more efficient and effective communicators.

Some commentators have tried to represent Communication Studies as a new arrival on the scene. This is easy to disprove. Key theorists such as Ferdinand de Saussure and Charles Peirce, whose work forms a foundation for Communication Studies, were born and worked in the nineteenth century. Fundamental models of the communication process (such as Claude E. Shannon and Warren Weaver's) were devised and published in the late 1940s. Since the 1970s, Communication Studies has been an established discipline in British secondary, further and higher education. What sometimes confuses people about Communication Studies is that it draws on, and its work is informed by, work in other related disciplines. Thus, as a student of Communication Studies, you will encounter elements of Psychology, Sociology, Philosophy and Linguistics, as well as Cultural Studies. But you'll still be studying communication, and you'll be studying the world from the perspective of Communication Studies.

'Studying the world' is an expansive phrase but hardly an exaggeration since it is much more difficult to say what is excluded from our study than what is included. Paul Watzlawick's much-quoted formulation sums up the problem and potential of the discipline: 'One cannot not communicate,' he claimed (1967). Put simply, this particular game is always 'on'. Communication is what we do, when the 'we' concerned is 'humans', that species the philosopher Aristotle dubbed 'social animals'. As if to confirm this, Communication theorist Colin Cherry has suggested that 'communication makes social life possible' and the triangle is complete, for the moment.

Communication is in a pure and poignant way the proof of our existence ('a souvenir just to prove that we were here' as the song has it) and, at the same time, a place where we have that debate. It is about identity and culture and context because it is about us and in us and through us. We are its theme; we are its channels. Communication represents or constitutes our desire to have meaning, to replace silence with sound and inaction with action.

What we are essentially doing in Communication Studies is considering the significance of everyday life: the importance of appearance and performance and context. Context recurs because it is, as Margaret Atwood has suggested, 'all'. We more often ask 'where?' than 'what?', and 'where?' usually brings us both quicker and closer to the hardest question, 'why?' Of course the particular will always override the general, what is *there* will always overtake 'what *is* there?' Take this crisp ten pound note and consider its status, it existence, its meaning. Why is it, for example, that one of the conditions of getting permission to reproduce this 'text' in colour was a guarantee that it would be impossible to create forged banknotes from its reproduction.

Figure 1.1 A ten pound note

ACTIVITY . . .

- What is this (precisely)?
- Who is it for?
- What does it mean?
- Why is it valuable?

When Raymond Williams made his formal definition of Communication as an area of study in 1962, he began with the question 'What do we mean by communication?' This part addresses this question but it will do it practically rather than theoretically, examining where communication is to be found rather than redefining what it is. Williams provided some significant clues in his initial survey arguing for a new 'emphasis': 'that society is a form of communication, through which experience is described, shared, modified and preserved' (Williams 1962: 10).

Williams' book *Communications* makes powerful appeals for a new set of ways of looking at reality which are still relevant today. Here is his invitation to students of communication:

> We need to say what many of us know in experience: that the struggle to learn, to describe, to understand, to educate is a central and necessary part of our humanity. This struggle is not begun, at second hand, after reality has occurred. It is in itself a major way in which reality is formed and changed . . . Communication begins in the struggle to learn and describe.
>
> (Williams 1962: 11)

Figure 1.2 *Crowds leaving Old Trafford. Courtesy of Dale Smith*

ACTIVITY

Look at the image of Old Trafford. Try to identify those elements that communicate to you. Where are we? What is the event likely to be? Who are these people (age, gender, class)? How do we know all of this?

Stepping into the above photograph is an act of engagement with the world of communication and of communication texts. What is principally represented here is a piece of the built environment in the south of Manchester entitled 'Old Trafford'. What this structure represents – that is, what is communicated by it – is a matter for debate, possibly heated debate. If, as a reader of this communication you are a member of what zoologist Desmond Morris called 'the football tribe', you are likely to have a strongly positive or negative attitude towards it. On the other hand, if you are ignorant of or uninterested in 'ball-based Saturday afternoon rituals', your response is likely to be neutral or even aggressive. In fact it might be said that instead of communicating, the image is in fact operating as a barrier to communication, causing communication to deteriorate.

COMMUNICATION TEXT Discrete unit of communication, that is anything that can be identified as communicating in its own right; a signifying structure composed of signs.

COMMUNICATION BARRIER Anything that impedes the communication process or causes it to deteriorate. There are four types of identifiable barrier to communication:

1 **Mechanical**: physical impediments.
2 **Psychological**: internal pressures on sender/receiver.
3 **Semantic**: lack of or partial understanding.
4 **Organisational**: structural dysfunctions in groups.

For merchandising purposes, 'Old Trafford' has been labelled 'the theatre of dreams'; in other words this meaning has been assigned to it. You can buy miniature representations of the football ground with this legend engraved on the base, where the significance of the word 'theatre' can easily be seen as a reference to the concentrated atmosphere of 'the cauldron'. This is an interesting representation in the sense that when you stand outside Old Trafford, or in fact inside it, you are struck by the awesome size of it and are tempted by its resemblance to a Gothic cathedral rather than to a theatre. We use the word 'tempted' because clearly making connections between places like a football stadium and a cathedral is making links between the activities that take place in them. This is to confuse form (that is, shape and structure) with function (that is, use and purpose).

ACTIVITY . . .

Look at some specific buildings in your area where you either live or study. Look for buildings under the following categories:

■ cathedral, church, mosque, temple
■ civic building (e.g. town hall)
■ house
■ hospital
■ library.

Then consider the degree to which your description of them, or your thoughts about them, or the vocabulary you use about them derives from either their form (that is, what you see) and/or their function (that is, what you know about them).

What you are doing in the above activity is clarifying your perception of the world around you and recognising the extent to which even that perception is shaped by your experiences of language, culture and society. You are being asked to consider the extent to which even seeing is an 'interested' activity – that is it isn't 'objective'. When we see 'Old Trafford', we are looking at a coded message which we must and will decode according to our experiences and experience. The essence of Communication Studies is in the recognition that our experience of the world as human beings is essentially the experience of communication texts – which must be understood.

COMMUNICATION AND MASS MEDIA TEXTS

Clearly, no understanding of our perception of 'Old Trafford' would be complete without a consideration of the role of the mass media in our perception and interpretation of human activities. It was Bill Shankly who claimed, for example, that 'Football's not a matter of life and death; it's more important than that', but it was newspapers and television that broadcast his words and repeated them until they stuck.

ACTIVITY . . .

A Communication Studies A Level question (from AEB in 1999) asked candidates to 'consider the media coverage of a sport of your choice'. Looking at a sport other than football, consider what meanings the press and television give to sport – that is:

- What words do they use?
- How do they treat the participants?
- What values do they attach to the sport concerned? Compare these to the reasons why you play sport or why you believe sport should be played.

Whatever your findings, it is very difficult not to conclude that much of sport's social meaning is constructed by mass media for a range of purposes: from ensuring that there are eight pages or three minutes of sport on any day to reopening old wounds and restating matters of national identity. When, in advance of a European football championship semi-final between England and Germany, the *Daily Star* used the headline 'HERR WE GO: Bring On The Krauts' there was widespread criticism. The *Star* described Germany as 'the old enemy' and ended its front page with the slogan 'LET BATTLE COMMENCE'. Interestingly the coverage was very like that reserved for explicit campaigns of war such as the Falklands and the Gulf conflicts, with a call to fans to support 'the England boys' and including a pastiche of the Kitchener 'Your Country Needs You' First World War propaganda poster.

It is not our job here to analyse this text in depth but rather to reflect the degree to which our society is represented by and in such texts. If we as individuals are sometimes betrayed or revealed by what we consciously and unconsciously say, this may be equally true of the deliberate and accidental pronouncements of our society in its forms of mass communication.

ACTIVITY . . .

Take a single copy of a national newspaper.

- Analyse its values solely from its headlines.
- Try to describe the newspaper's 'personality'.
- List its preoccupations (themes), its 'heroes' and its 'villains'.

THE ILLUSTRATED MAN: THE HUMAN FIGURE AS TEXT

In the stadium illustration that appears on page 6, some people are represented moving in front of the camera. These people would probably have opinions as to the meanings of 'Old Trafford' and sport. They themselves are communicating at a number of levels. In other words, they constitute 'text' in a number of ways: as a crowd/group held together by a common context and purpose; as a group sharing certain demographic variables like gender, ethnicity and age, uniformed to some extent; as a series of individuals expressing their own identities through subtle modifications of clothing, of hairstyle, of attitude. This photograph is merely a still frame from a real movie which is their lives and in which the theme is communication.

ACTIVITY . . .

How specifically do you express your own individual personality? List the most significant TEN ways (e.g. 1. My hairstyle, plus comment – 'it's been this long since . . .'). PROMPT: your clothes, appearance, props, locations, roles.

In exploring what makes up your expressed identity, you are in fact rehearsing the content of much of your communication course. This will include a consideration of such matters as domestic architecture, interior design, industrial and commercial design, clothing, hairstyle, body adornment and modification as well as the various sorts of language we use. Communication Studies begins with reading the self and then extends to other people.

Figure 1.3 *Still from* Once Were Warriors *(New Zealand Film Commission, 1994). Courtesy of the Kobal Collection*

Consider the significant elements of the appearance of the man in the illustration and the ways in which he can be read – that is, what are the factors that will likely affect the way he is read? Make two lists: features of the man as text which might affect reading; and features/characteristics of reader which might affect reading.

This is an extreme version of the confrontations that we have every day with 'other people' and we all have our own ways of dealing with this world of 'otherness' – that is, with those people who are not us. It is relatively easy to classify those people whom we encounter on a day-to-day basis in terms of the relative depth of our relationship with each of them: from family and intimates through workmates and fellow students to relatively infrequent 'total strangers'. As we meet (to us) new people, we like to think that we judge them according to their behaviour and react to them accordingly. On reflection, however, it is probably truer to say that we judge them according to our behaviour, our experience, our norms and our prejudices.

Who are your friends? How long have you known them? Where did you meet? To what extent are they 'similar' to you in looks, interests, gender, ethnicity or class? To what extent is this 'sameness' extended the closer you get to 'home' (i.e. how far are your best friends especially like you)?

Friendship is a loaded activity, it depends heavily on social experience and therefore is bound to be value-laden. What we communicate to others subconsciously may in fact operate as an informal and unconscious 'invitation to treat', a beacon for potential relationships. In other words, who we are, superficially, might be a significant factor in the relationships we form. After all, what are relationships but exchanges of communication, structures within which codes are employed and messages are delivered? What are relationships, after all, but communication texts?

When Umberto Eco (an Italian author and critic) proclaimed in 1973, 'I speak through my clothes', he was just identifying one element of a considerable paradigm, a set in which every gesture and intonation, every affectation and attitude is potentially significant. This set constitutes the human figure as communicator, the variety of codes through which this significant text has significance. The tension remains between those elements that are intentional and those that are not: those that are given to be read and those that simply 'leak'.

PARADIGM   A sign set from which one might be chosen to contribute to a syntagm. Paradigms define their individual members with reference to all others in the set. To select from a paradigm is at that moment to reject all other signs in that set, just as by selecting something (or nothing) to cover your feet today you have rejected all other possibilities. This choice from a paradigm of 'foot coverings' has contributed to the syntagm which constitutes the things you are wearing today. When Peugeot's 'lion' went 'from strength to strength', it got its strength partly from the paradigm of 'elite animals' from which it was chosen and partly because that paradigm does not include 'weasel', 'frog' and 'sloth'.

KEY TERM

NON-VERBAL LEAKAGE   The tendency of non-verbal codes wholly or partly to contradict or to undermine intentional and verbal communication, e.g. lack of eye contact may betray the telling of an untruth.

KEY TERM

Take one example of a youth subculture (e.g. punk, headbanger) and classify its intentional non-verbal communication or iconography, i.e. its visual sign-system. Compare this with a similar list for an adult 'genre', e.g. teachers, business people, lawyers, doctors.

As in almost all cases in Communication Studies, context is a primary determinant. Teachers and doctors, for example, in a social context may display their identity in less obvious ways or not at all. Context will affect the reading but will rarely invalidate texts altogether. Mepham (1974) has claimed that: 'social life is structured like a language'. As such it is of primary interest to us as students of its particular vocabulary, grammar and syntax.

Since Communication Studies was first mapped out as an area of study, there have been many advances in Communication and Information Technology. Mobile phones, personal computers, digital and interactive technology have all had a profound impact on how, what, where and why we communicate. If anything, the pace of technological change is increasing, and these advances in Communication and Information Technology may well be set to have an even greater influence on our lives in the future. It is against this background that this book has been written.

▼ 2 APPROACHES TO STUDYING COMMUNICATION

In this section we will briefly outline two contrasting approaches to the study of communication.

- We will look at the *process* approaches to studying communication.
- We will look at the *semiotic* approaches to the study of communication.

It is probably this capacity to communicate with ourselves and with others which, more than any other single factor, distinguishes the human animal from other animals. More than the capacity to communicate in many different forms, the capacity to think and to organise those thoughts into systems distinguishes the human animal from other animal societies. We can act, we can reflect upon our actions, and we can draw conclusions about the actions of others. As Cherry (1978) has observed, 'Self-awareness and the sense of social responsibility have arisen as a result of organised thoughts. Systems of ethics and law have been built up. Man has become self-conscious, responsible, a changeable creature.'

CODES

One of the first things we discover when studying communication is that all communication is coded. Although we all use codes in our communication behaviour right from our earliest days, we are not always aware of this. Awareness of the existence of codes often first arises when we encounter groups of people using what we term 'jargon'. Indeed, our awareness often first reveals itself as frustration. 'If that's what they meant, why didn't they say so?' It's a common complaint of students and people in the working world that other people 'wrap up' what they're trying to say in fancy words, in jargon, in long words that sound impressive but which don't seem to mean very much when closely analysed. Of course, these complaints are all too often justified. People do tend to wrap up or dress up what they're saying in a way they think will impress other people. Developing the ability to see through people who do this is what Neil Postman has termed 'acquiring a crap detector'.

On the other hand, we must be careful not to reject completely those expressions that puzzle us. Certain groups of people express themselves in certain ways because that is the agreed and commonly used method. In other words, they use codes. Codes are sets of signs and symbols which have meaning for people who are members of specific social or working groups (even families often have their own coded ways of speaking which prevents outsiders gaining access to those families and engaging in constructive communication with them). You can often tell what a person's job is by paying close attention to the words they use and the ways in which they express themselves. All signs and symbols work as a shorthand method of communication.

For example, if you were driving a car or riding a bike and came across this road sign, you'd know what it meant.

Figure 1.4 *Hump-back bridge hazard sign*

It would be silly – and dangerous – if you were presented with a sign that said:

> If you continue driving or riding on the road that you are now driving or riding on, you will encounter a hump bridge. Take care to reduce speed to ensure you don't damage your vehicle, and use your eyes and ears because vehicles approaching from the other side of the bridge may be obscured by the hump of the bridge and may not be as careful as you are.

It would be silly because we know what the road sign means, and when we come across it we consciously or subconsciously remind ourselves of the advice that was presented in the second written sign. Thus we can see that there exist codes to which we already have the key. We know how to unlock the door of specific coded communications and extract their meanings. It's for this reason that we don't have mayhem on our roads. If we all stick to the conventions and guidance in the coded system of road signs, then all road users get along with one another.

Although we will look at theories that have been devised to explain and to study the communication process in greater detail in Part 3, it is appropriate to take a brief look at them here. It's also appropriate to state quite clearly that there is more than one approach to the study of communication. In one way it is quite easy to explain why this should be so – different types of communication require different types of study, analysis, explanation and evaluation. In other ways it is less easy – different theories seem to compete to explain the same or similar kinds of communication.

You would imagine that a book about communication would easily be able to define the word. But it's not that easy. As John Fiske admits in the first sentence of his *Introduction to Communication Studies* (1990), 'Communication is one of those human activities that everyone recognises but few can define satisfactorily.' Colin Cherry, an early commentator on communication working in the 1950s, offered this definition which is a good starting point: 'Broadly: the establishment of a social unit from individuals, by the shared use of language or signs. The sharing of common sets of rules, for various goal-seeking activities. (There are many shades of opinion)' (Cherry 1978). A number of conclusions can be drawn from this: (a) Cherry conceives of communication as a social act; and (b) he conceives of communication as sharing (this isn't surprising given that we derive the word 'communication' from the Latin verb *communicare*, which means 'to share').

In the study of communication two main schools of thought exist.

> **SCHOOL OF THOUGHT** Where groups of academics come together because they feel the same way about particular issues.

KEY TERM

The first school of thought, usually known as the process school, characterises communication as the transmission and reception of messages. The second school of thought, usually known as the semiotic school, conceives of communication as the generation and sharing of meanings.

THE PROCESS SCHOOL OF COMMUNICATION

This approach to the study of communication originated in the study of tele-communications. Claude E. Shannon was employed by the Bell telephone corporation in the United States of America in the 1940s. To begin to solve problems occurring in telecommunications, he devised what he called a mathematical model of communication (see Diagram 3.1, page 119). He was concerned to eliminate or lessen the effect of disruptions to the communication process. He called this 'noise'. He believed that if you could place a mathematical value on 'noise', then you could work out by how much the signal being transmitted would have to be boosted to overcome the 'noise'. As this model originated in telecommunications, it is concerned with the transmission of signal and the effectiveness of transmission. So the process school of thought came into being, a school of thought which interpreted communication as being about the process of transmission and reception of signals.

A simple model of the process approach to communication can be represented by this diagram:

Source	⇨	Transmitter	⇨	Channel	⇨	Receiver	⇨	Destination

Diagram 1.1 *Simple process model of communication*

The source is the idea in someone's mind. The transmitter is the physical device used to communicate with. The channel is the medium used to communicate through. The receiver is the physical means of receiving a transmitted signal. And the destination is the original idea now in the mind of the person communicated with.

ACTIVITY . . .

Take the road sign for a hump-back bridge on page 14 and explain how it functions in terms of the process approach to communication.

THE SEMIOTIC SCHOOL OF COMMUNICATION

This approach to the study of communication takes its name from the Greek word for sign: *semeion*. Independently of each other, the Swiss linguist Ferdinand de Saussure and the American philosopher Charles Peirce (pronounced 'purse') took *semeion* and devised the words 'semiology' and 'semiotics' (de Saussure 1983; Peirce 1966). In many ways semiotics is more concerned with how communication works than about why communication exists or what communication is. It assumes that all codes are arbitrary, that there isn't any logical reason why we use one particular sign. It assumes that the meaning we get from signs comes in part from the creator of the sign, in part from our experience of the sign, and in part from the sign itself. In other words, communication is an active dynamic process.

KEY TERM

SIGN The basic unit of communication, the building block from which all communication is constructed.

Our thinking about semiotics can be helped by Diagram 1.2 (where 'producer' is the origin of the message, 'consumer' is the destination of the message, and 'text' is the message itself). What we call 'meaning' is what is generated as a result of an inter-action between all three elements.

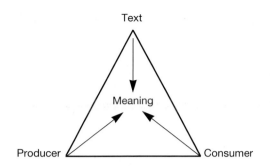

Diagram 1.2 *General model of semiotics*

ACTIVITY . . .

State the basic differences between the process and semiotic schools of thought.

FURTHER READING

Cherry, C. (1978) *On Human Communication: A Review, a Survey and a Criticism*, 3rd edn, Cambridge, Mass/London: MIT Press.

Fiske, J. (1990) *Introduction to Communication Studies*, 2nd edn, London: Routledge.

Williams, R. (1962) *Communications*, Harmondworth: Penguin.

PART 2: EFFECTIVE COMMUNICATION

In this part of the book we look at how you can develop the skill of effective communication. We consider the development of this skill in the contexts of written communication, verbal communication and the use of new technology.

- We look at the study skills required by students of Communication Studies.
- We give advice on projects and course work.

We are all born with the capacity to communicate. We are all capable of making utterances and gestures that enable us to send messages to other people. Being able to communicate well is, however, a skill. It is a skill that we need to learn if we are to do it effectively.

So what makes a person an effective communicator? Unfortunately, contrary to the claims of countless self-help guides, there is no simple answer to this question. Effective communication is a result of a combination of factors. It relies on the capacity of the communicator to utilise a range of different skills, some of which we are probably born with, some of which we have to learn.

To help you to become a more effective communicator you should bear in mind that you will need to communicate in a range of different situations. Some of these will require you to use skills in communicating formally. Making a speech and writing a report are examples of formal communication. Others will require you to communicate informally, for example sending a note to a friend, or chatting to a stranger on the bus. Whatever the situation, there are some useful guidelines that you should bear in mind when you start to compose your message.

Sales Office Administrator

wanted for busy electronic component distributor based in glorious countryside near Balsall Common. Excellent computer, **communication and interpersonal skills are a pre-requisite**. Excellent career prospects for someone wanting to move into a fast-moving sales environment. Salary £12,000 p.a. plus bonus plus benefits.

**A.P.B. GROUP LIMITED
CONSTRUCTION OR ENGINEERING
GRADUATE**

An opportunity exists to join our management team in a busy civil engineering environment. Practical experience of sites and a good knowledge of Health & Safety Law an advantage. **Must have good communication skills**, be computer literate & have a full clean driving licence.
Applications in writing to:
Mr A Graham, Managing Director
A.P.B. Group Limited

Grade G Community Nurse (RNMH)

£20,830 – £24,090 per annum

Full-Time, 37½ hours per week

We are constantly seeking to expand and improve our Learning Disability Service, and we have your future very much in mind too, with a clear career structure and a whole range of personal development opportunities, including individual performance reviews, clinical supervision, good in-house training opportunities and excellent support and mentoring.

This role offers considerable autonomy in decision making and scope to see your own progressive ideas implemented. You will manage a caseload and a team of community staff, assessing client need, implementing and evaluating care programmes and setting standards of care, as well as being involved in teaching staff and students.

A good communicator and teamworker, with the ability to lead and develop people, you must be innovative, highly motivated and able to work on your own initiative. RNMH, diploma/degree in Community Health Studies and ENB 807 or equivalent are essential.

Car driver essential, lease car scheme in operation.

This post offers the chance to live and work in one of England's most attractive areas, close to the Cotswolds, yet within easy reach of the UK motorway network and the major cities of Coventry and Birmingham.

Please quote job reference number: 41/1934

Lecturer/Senior Lecturer in Management Sciences
(Temporary for one year)
£14,902 – £30,636 pa

You will contribute to the teaching of Management Science and/or Applied Statistics at both undergraduate and postgraduate levels, as well as play an important role in research and course-related activities.

With a good first or higher degree in the Management Sciences area, you will have at least two years' lecturing or professional experience. Evidence of research/professional collaboration and an interest in one or more of the following: multivariate analysis, survey analysis, data warehousing and data mining would be an advantage.

You will be a team-player with **good communication and presentation skills** and the ability to work under pressure to meet deadlines.

Suitably experienced candidates may be appointed at senior lecturer level.

Please quote reference 535/00 Interview data 13 December 2000

Figure 2.1 Job advertisements – the importance of communication skills – with the need for communication skills highlighted

The first point relates to the concept of empathy. Empathy is the act of putting yourself in someone else's shoes in order to see issues and ideas from their perspective rather than your own. Another way of saying this is that you should be sensitive to the needs of your audience. One way to do this is to consider how you would respond to the message if you were one of them. We have all sat through a long boring class in which the teacher has paid little heed to the feelings and needs of the audience. Similarly, each of us has been trapped in a conversation with a boring and uninteresting person who seems completely insensitive to the response, or perhaps more accurately the lack of response, they are getting from their victim. In both cases the communicator is showing a lack of sensitivity to the audience. The more sensitive you are to the needs of your audience, the more likely you are to communicate effectively with them.

The second point you should consider is how best to organise the information you want to communicate to make it comprehensible to the receiver. This is especially true of a formal communication situation, such as making a speech or writing a report. The need to plan and organise information into a logical and user-friendly structure is vital. Taking time to plan and organise your message is also a useful tool in less formal contexts. Take, for example, a situation where you need to telephone someone in order to obtain information. Planning what you are going to say in advance will almost certainly produce a more positive result than dialling the number and finding yourself tongue-tied when the caller answers. Often a simple checklist will remind you of the points you want to make.

The third point to remember is not to underestimate the importance of feedback. Feedback is a key aspect of the communication process. Feedback is the way people let us know how they are responding to the information we are giving them. A room full of people all with puzzled looks on their faces should indicate to a presenter that there is a lack of clarity about the information that is being transmitted. Similarly, people falling asleep while you are talking to them does not always mean that they need a good night's rest. Learning to recognise feedback and responding to it is an important factor in communicating effectively.

ACTIVITY . . .

Observe other people communicating in a range of different situations: your teacher in class, your family at meal times, or your friends or classmates during breaks.

- How effective are they at communicating?
- Is there any evidence that they have planned what they are going to say?
- How sensitive are they to the needs of their audience?
- What do you think makes some people better at communicating than others?

▼ 1 WRITTEN COMMUNICATION

In this section we consider the following.

■ Some important elements of written communication.
■ How to structure your writing for purpose.
■ Writing a letter.

Let us start by looking at written communication. Writing has been a highly prized skill throughout history. With a largely illiterate population until the middle of the Victorian era, being able to write conferred great powers on those who possessed it. Today, although most of the population has at least a functional level of literacy, people who are able to write effectively and confidently are often seen as an intellectual and cultural elite, a privileged minority. Our education system, and more specifically the examination system, privileges skills in written communication above most of the skills taught in school.

When it comes to writing, very few people get it right first time. Writing is invariably a process of drafting, editing and redrafting to arrive at an acceptable finished product. This calls on the writer to be prepared on occasion not only to revise many times over, but also to listen to and, where necessary, act on the advice and criticisms of other people. A book like this one, written by three people, has undergone not only a heavy editing process, but also substantial redrafting and revision before it was considered fit for students.

Effective writing is about clarity, precision and concision. Good writing is also appropriate to the purpose, context and audience for which it is intended. An effective writer is one who creates a message with these points in mind.

So how are clarity, precision and concision achieved in written communication? As you will see from the resources section at the end of the book, there are a number of books that offer advice on how to write effectively. Some of these, such *The New Fowler's Modern English Usage* (1998), are most useful for checking grammatical accuracy. Perhaps the best way to improve your own style of writing is to consider the work of people who have perfected the art of writing with purpose and efficiency. George Orwell is a good example of a writer whose work bears these hallmarks of clarity and precision. In fact Orwell wrote a particularly helpful essay entitled 'Politics and the English Language' (Orwell 2000) in which he outlines the principles of good writing. The essay is well worth reading, but the following summary of Orwell's key points should help you to start thinking about how you can improve your own style of writing.

1   Never use a metaphor, simile or other figure of speech which you are used to seeing in print. The first person to write the phrase 'raining cats and dogs' used a witty figure of speech to describe stormy weather. To use the phrase now is simply to repeat a cliché or worn-out method of saying something. It is best therefore to avoid using a cliché. Instead try to find a fresh way of expressing yourself that will have an impact on your reader.

2   Never use a long word when a short one will do. In other words, try to keep it simple. There may be occasions when you need to use a long word because it is technically correct and there is not a simple word you can use instead. Look out, though, for occasions when you lapse into long 'formal' words which can sound pompous. 'Endeavours to engage her in caresses' is a line from a poem by T. S. Eliot in which he pokes fun at young clerk. 'Tries to kiss her' would be a more simple and direct way of expressing the idea.

3   If it is possible to cut out a word, cut it out. A helpful exercise when you are revising what you have written is to read through and delete any words that are unnecessary.

4   Never use the passive where you can use the active. This refers to sentence construction. A simple active construction has a subject doing something to an object, for example: 'The child [subject] kicked [verb] the ball [object].' A passive construction puts this object at the beginning of the sentence – for example, 'The ball was kicked by the child.' You can see that, if you use the active, your sentence will be more direct and more dynamic. Often people will use a passive construction when they wish to evade responsibility. In this way we have people saying things like 'The train was delayed by my actions' rather than 'I delayed the train'.

5   Never use a word or phrase from another language, a scientific word or a jargon word if you can think of an everyday English equivalent.

6   Break any of these rules rather than say anything plain silly. In the end common sense should always prevail over rules. Provided you are writing with clarity and precision, you shouldn't become obsessed by rules. The acid test must always be to consider how the receiver will react to your words.

You may wish to consider an additional point to Orwell's advice – that is, the importance of writing short sentences. Never strain a sentence by trying to include more information than it is capable of holding. Too many ideas in one sentence can make it indigestible. If you find yourself writing a long sentence, try to break it down into two or more shorter sentences. In this way your meaning should become clearer.

A useful source of information and ideas on writing clearly is the website of the Plain English Campaign (www.plainenglish.co.uk).

As we have suggested, it is important to bear in mind your purpose and the context in which you are writing. Just as you need the right tools to change a wheel on a car, so you need the right tools for the job of writing. A note for the milkman, an academic essay and a love letter are all examples of different types of message. However, their context and purpose are so different that each requires an individual approach if it is to be effective. Each of these messages demands the use of a different set of conventions. If you ignore these conventions, you will produce a message that loses its impact because of its inappropriateness. Most written communication is intended to inform. It is a method of passing information from one person to another, or to a group of people. However, there are often additional reasons for writing beyond the simple act of informing. For example, you may wish to persuade someone to do something. On the other hand, you may wish to entertain. You may wish to do both at the same time.

ACTIVITY . . .

What do you think are the main differences between a note for the milkman, an academic essay and a love letter? Try writing the opening of an essay in the style of a love letter and vice versa.

The message that you compose and the intention you have in composing it may not necessarily be the same as the message and intention that the recipient receives. What you thought to be an entertaining and persuasive message may be read as tedious and threatening.

The risk of misunderstanding can be reduced if you remember to place yourself in the position of the recipient. You need to take into account a number of factors when you consider your audience. The most important of these is the level of knowledge or expertise it has of the topic about which you are communicating. This should determine the register you will adopt. For example, if you are explaining some aspect of an academic subject to another student, you can assume that they will have a basic vocabulary to describe key aspects of the subject. In Communication Studies, for example, that student would probably have some understanding of terms used in semiotics, such as 'denotation' and 'connotation'. If, on the other hand, you were writing for a person with no knowledge of semiotics, it would be inappropriate to use subject-specific jargon.

KEY TERM

JARGON The specialised vocabulary which people who have knowledge and understanding of a particular subject use when communicating with one another. The legal profession and the computing industry are places where you can expect to find professional jargon. Similarly, someone who repairs your car will use jargon to describe a fault or problems with the engine. Some people hide behind jargon. They use a vocabulary that is baffling to others who do not share their expertise in the subject.

Despite the fact that many people feel uncomfortable around jargon, its use is frequently essential to make yourself understood in a precise way. For example, when you are analysing a text for Communication Studies, you will need to employ some of the terms you have learned for semiotic analysis. If it is a print text, you would also need to use the vocabulary for describing the presentation of information through typographical devices, such as italics or 72 point type. Taking account of the level of expertise that your audience possesses is an important matter if you are to make yourself understood.

Similarly, it is important to estimate the level of linguistic sophistication your reader possesses. It is easy to get this wrong. If you employ too high a register, you are likely to confuse your reader. On the other hand, too low a register may appear patronising and insensitive and, although the reader may understand what you have written, they may be so antagonised that communication isn't achieved.

REGISTER   Describes the level of language being used. The appropriateness of a register is determined by the audience being addressed, the context in which it is being addressed and the subject matter being communicated.

KEY TERM

STRUCTURE

Structure is an essential ingredient in creating an effective written message. Structure means planning and arranging your ideas in such a way that they have a logical organisation. This will enable the person receiving the message to decode it. Structure is a means of organising the flow of your ideas into a form that can be readily assimilated by your audience.

If you are to achieve a logical structure to your written communication, you must be prepared to think ahead about what you want to say. This means working out a plan of what you intend to say before you put pen to paper. One way of doing this is simply to take a piece of paper and write down everything that comes into your head about the message you are going to create. Once you have done this, try to number the points in a sequence that will take you from the start of what you want to say to the end. This numbered sequence will then form your plan. You may well find that each numbered idea represents an individual paragraph for what you want to say.

The paragraph is an important tool in writing. Paragraphs are used to put together connected ideas. A paragraph is a group of sentences each covering the same theme. A new paragraph should represent for the reader the next stage in the development of an idea or argument.

Look at how a news story is constructed in a newspaper. It does not matter whether it is tabloid or broadsheet. You will notice newspaper paragraphs are generally much shorter than, say, in an academic essay. This strategy helps the reader digest the information in manageable portions.

Now look at the structure of a newspaper story. Consider the sequence in which the information is given. What do you notice about the ordering of the paragraphs? Why do you think typographical devices are used to make the first paragraph stand out from the others?

KEY TERM

TYPOGRAPHY   The use of different types and styles of lettering in printed texts.

WRITING A LETTER

In an age of fast-developing electronic communications technology, the importance of the letter has begun to diminish. It still remains, however, an important method of communicating information. Choosing the most appropriate channel of communication is an important element in the success of a message. Often you will be called upon to decide whether a letter or a telephone call is the more appropriate channel. You may consider a fax or an e-mail or a mobile phone text message as an alternative.

A letter does offer certain advantages to both the sender and the receiver of a message. It is a good idea to take these into account when deciding how to send your message. Unlike a telephone call, a letter is a permanent form of communication. It also carries with it some degree of formality. In business, a letter often signifies the transmission of a formal message between two people or organisations, as opposed to the relative informality of a telephone call. Perhaps most importantly, a letter gives the receiver time to consider a response. A telephone call can often put the receiver 'on the spot' with the demand for an immediate answer. A letter allows time for the receiver to think about the contents and respond in a more assured and comfortable way. Of course, the danger is that no response at all will be forthcoming.

Imagine you need to get some information for a project from a large organisation, such as a television company or a national charity. Why do you think a letter would be an effective way of doing this? What points would you need to bear in mind when writing your letter?

Your response to this activity should have included the importance of addressing your letter to an appropriate recipient. Ideally this should be a named person in the organisation. You can usually find the names of people with specific roles, such as public or customer relations, by doing some research on the Internet or in a library. Failing that, you can either phone and ask reception for the name of such a person, or you can write to the person using either a job title or the departmental name. (The formal term for someone's job title is their designation.) For example, you might direct your letter to the Head of Customer Relations.

You should also have considered the content of your letter. Every week large organisations receive letters from students asking for help and information. Many respond by sending out an all-purpose information pack, which they hope will cover the needs of most students. This is due in part to the fact that most commercial organisations are too busy to answer individual queries. It is also due to the fact that many students don't state precisely what they want in their letters. An effective letter will make clear exactly what it is you require. It must also meet those important guidelines of clarity, precision and concision. Indeed, it can be argued that a good letter will not exceed one side of A4 paper.

▼ 2 VERBAL COMMUNICATION

In this section we compare verbal and written communication, and look specifically at the following.

■ Where to find information.
■ How to make an effective telephone call.
■ The elements of contributing verbally in a meeting.

Verbal communication is generally much less formal than written communication. Many of the verbal messages that we produce are quite casual exchanges with other people. As a consequence many people tend to speak without thinking.

In Part 3 we will look at verbal communication in the wider context of themes in human communication in general and the more specific context of language. What follows here has a more practical orientation and is intended to help you become a more effective communicator.

Clearly, it would be ridiculous to suggest that every utterance should be carefully prepared in advance. Spontaneity is an important characteristic of verbal exchanges. However, you will find there are a number of occasions when planning in advance what you are going to say is important. These situations include the following.

■ Asking for and giving information.
■ Making a telephone call.
■ Making a presentation.
■ Contributing to a meeting.

Our general principles of effective communication are important here. Remember to:

■ think about the needs of your audience
■ organise what you have to say into a logical structure
■ respond to feedback

Similarly, the importance of speaking with clarity, precision and concision cannot be over-emphasised.

SEEKING INFORMATION

ACTIVITY . . .

Imagine you are walking through a town or city that you know well. Someone asks you the way to the town hall. What factors would you bear in mind about your audience before composing your reply?

Your response to the above activity should tell you a lot about the principles of effective verbal communication. First, you would need to make some assessment of the person asking for the information. You may need to consider such points as these.

1   How do they intend to get to the town hall – on foot, by car? If it is not immediately apparent, you may need to ask.
2   An elderly person or a person with a disability may not be able to follow the route you were going to describe. If, for example, that route involved climbing steps, then you might need to think of an alternative route.

This is a good example of empathy – where you are looking at the message from the viewpoint of the recipient, imagining yourself in their position.

Second, before you compose your reply, it is important that you plan what you are going to say. It may be that there is a map of the town nearby and you can show the person the route using that. Otherwise you need to construct the journey mentally and organise it in such a way that it is clear to recipient. You need also to cut out unnecessary detail that might confuse.

ACTIVITY . . .

Think of those occasions when you have asked for directions and received a bewildering response. What aspect of the message you received was it that made it difficult for you to understand? When you are looking for directions in a crowded street, what criteria do you use in choosing someone to ask?

If you are to compose an effective message offering directions, you will need to do the following.

1   Assess the needs of the recipient, identifying any possible barriers to effective communication.
2   Think through the most efficient way of explaining the route to be taken.
3   Organise your directions into a simple, easy-to-follow form. This probably means giving the information in sequence, reinforced by offering such handholds as key landmarks.
4   Look for feedback signals from the receiver. Head nods or confused facial expressions should help you assess the effectiveness of your communication.

5   Be prepared to repeat or reinforce all or some of your message in the light of this feedback.

MAKING A TELEPHONE CALL

Making a telephone call to give or obtain information requires a very similar approach. However, because the telephone is a channel of communication that relies exclusively on sound, it requires other factors to be taken into account.

Just as we suggest the need to plan your message for face-to-face communication, so it is important to do so with a telephone call. A checklist of points that you wish to make can be a useful guideline for handling the call. Indeed, it is always a good idea to have pen and paper nearby, not only to note down what you want to say, but also to note down points from the person at the other end. Breaking off a conversation to find a pen will make you seem amateur and disorganised, as well as disrupting the communication process.

When you initiate a telephone call start by making it clear who you are. It is always a good idea to give your name, even if you are not known to the person you are calling. Next explain clearly and concisely what it is you want. If it is a large organisation, this is a good point to ensure you are speaking to the person best able to help you.

Suppose when you make a call you are greeted by an answering system. Many people at this point hang up and try to call later. This can be frustrating for the person you are calling, especially as Caller ID and Ringback systems allow the source of the call to be traced. It is a good idea to ensure that you have a message ready to leave on the answering system. This should include your name, telephone number and brief details of what you want. Some people also leave the time and date of the call, although increasingly this information is stored automatically by answering machines.

Responding to feedback remains an important part of telephone communication, even though visual signals such as facial expression are not available to us. On the telephone, as well as listening to the words that people say in response, you need to be aware of paralanguage. (Paralanguage is discussed in detail on pages 171–172, 182–184.) Be prepared to pick up on and respond to such non-verbal clues in the voice as intonation, volume and hesitation. Silence can often say more than speech at the other end of the telephone.

CONTRIBUTING TO A MEETING

Another situation in which good verbal communication skills are required is taking part in meetings. As you will see from the sections on group communication, meetings are formalised situations in which a group gets together for a specific purpose. There are many different types of meeting. Some, such as annual general meetings (AGMs), form part of an ongoing procedure that plays a key role in the functioning of a group or organisation. Other meetings, such as a group of students getting together to plan a coursework project, may be less formal or only take place to achieve one immediate purpose. Whatever type of meeting you are involved in, you will need your communication skills if you are to play an effective role in the meeting.

Most meetings have someone who takes charge. This person is usually called the chair. The chair's functions are many and will vary from meeting to meeting. However, it is this person's responsibility to ensure that correct procedures are followed in the meeting. The chair also determines the order in which issues are discussed. This is set down in the form of an agenda, usually written, published and circulated prior to the start of the meeting.

Agenda for meeting

The next Communication meeting will take place at 1500 hours on Friday, 3 September 2004 in Room 203.

Agenda

1   Apologies for absence
2   Minutes of previous meeting
3   Matters arising
4   Financial matters
5   Main restaurant
6   Any other business
7   Date of next meeting

As we have suggested, meetings vary in their degree of formality. As you can see from the example, a typical meeting will start with a welcome from the chair and introductions if new people are present.

ACTIVITY . . .

It is common in meetings for people to introduce themselves by saying a few words about what they do or what their interests are. Imagine you are attending a meeting for the first time. Jot down some notes with which to introduce yourself. Remember that the type of meeting and the sort of people attending are likely to determine how you do this.

Other typical formalities at a meeting are opportunities for people who are absent to have their apologies read out and also a check on the accuracy of the minutes of the previous meeting.

Minutes of a meeting

Minutes of Communication Meeting held at 1500 hours on Friday, 3 September 2004 in Room 203 for Front Office Cashiers, Restaurant Cashiers and Night Auditors

Present: J. Ellroy
             D. Hammett
             E. Leonard (Chair)
             S. Paretsky
             R. B. Parker (Secretary)
             I. Rankin

1   *Apologies for absence*: R. MacDonald.

2   *Minutes* of 3 August 2004 meeting were confirmed.

3   *Matters arising* from 3 August 2004 meeting minutes:
— Incorrectly completed registration cards are to be passed back to Reception.
— Present difficulties for charging for room service will be removed when revised charges are introduced at the end of this month.

4   *Financial matters*
— Mr Leonard thanked front office cashiers for helping restaurant cashiers during the busy holiday period.
— Ms Parker informed the meeting that from October all assistant front office cashiers will be given additional training to work with new financial procedures.

5   *Main restaurant*
— Ms Parker reported that prices for the carvery have now been clarified.
— The question of breakfast price for children was raised. It was felt that half adult price was insufficient discount for children.

6   *Any other business*
— Mr Rankin, who will be leaving next month, was thanked and wished well for the future.
— Mr Ellroy was congratulated on his promotion to front office cashier.

7   *Date of next meeting* was set for Friday, 1 October 2004.

8   *The meeting closed* at 1540 hours.

These minutes are likely to be important to the current meeting because the first agenda item usually requires the group to work through them, discussing matters that have arisen out of the previous meeting.

If you have a contribution you wish to make to the discussion of any item, you should always do this through the chair. It is important that you do not address your remarks to individual members of the group, but rather you should make your point to the group as a whole by addressing your comments through the chair. Of course, getting the attention of the chair in order to be able to contribute is in itself a skill. An effective chair, however, will be conscious of the need to encourage everyone to contribute, so quietly waiting your turn rather than butting in is probably the better strategy.

Once you have the opportunity to make your contribution, there are a number of points to bear in mind. First, make sure that what you are saying is relevant to the point being discussed. Don't, for example, raise an issue that is better covered under another agenda item. Second, remember our advice about clarity, concision and precision. Try to plan what you want to say, then say it clearly and succinctly. If you can link in your ideas to build on the contribution of a previous speaker, then do so. Finally, do not take issues personally. Remember that meetings are about debates and issues, not personalities, even though it may seem like it at times. Your contribution will be much more highly valued if you stick to the issues under consideration, rather than making personal attacks on other members of the group.

▼ 3 COMMUNICATION AND INFORMATION TECHNOLOGY

In this section we look at the following developments and their use in communications.

- Computers.
- Document creation.
- The Internet.
- E-mail and attachments.

We have just spent time looking at types of written and verbal communication that can be described as traditional. This is because in many respects they have changed little over a long period of time. Although we have mentioned the use of computers and software programmes such as PowerPoint, the impact of technology has not been central to our discussion of the principles of effective communication. The world of communication is constantly changing. Some people feel that it is doing so at an alarming rate. Chief among these changes is the way in which communication technology is becoming central to our lives. Indeed, some people argue that one of the chief social divisions is between those who have access to communications technology and those who do not. These groups have become known as the information rich and the information poor.

The communications revolution is having a profound impact on the way each of us lives our life. The number of people who work from home using communication technology to connect to the office has increased rapidly in recent years. E-mail, mobile phones and tele-conferencing have all affected people's working patterns to the point where the workplace itself is a far less significant feature of their lives. Traditional information sources such as newspapers and books are confronted by competition from electronic media such as the Internet. In our homes, technology is beginning to converge to the point where mass communications technology such as the television and personal communication technology such as the telephone are joining forces. Not only does our television set offer a vast choice of digital programming, but also it allows us to receive personal text messages sent from someone's mobile phone, to edit our own programmes, to choose the news we want to see and to take a virtual tour of our favourite supermarket. We now have portable communications technology that will allow us to do many of these things on the move.

USING A PC

It is difficult for anyone who has grown up using a personal computer to appreciate how the Information and Communication Technology revolution has influenced the way in which we communicate. Writing and creating documents is now much easier thanks to the features that a personal computer offers. We will now look at how to get the best from your PC when you are writing and creating documents.

Perhaps the singular most telling advantage that a PC brings to writing is the capacity to store what you have written. A computer's hard disk together with CDs and floppy disks enable us to store documents we have created and to retrieve them whenever necessary. These facilities are all available to writers even on the most basic of word processing packages.

What this means for most users of the technology is that it is now much easier to get down ideas, shape them, save them, revise them and edit them. In addition the computer allows a final version to be produced and printed with layout and design to a high degree of sophistication.

So how can you get the best from using a PC? Well, every user of a computer will have developed a method for getting the best from it, but it is useful to consider here some of the ways in which you can use this tool to help you become more effective in your own communication. Assuming that you have the basic skill to open a word processing package and to use the keyboard, however slowly, then you are on the road to getting the best from your PC as a communication tool. Listed below are some ideas to help you become a more effective communicator using a PC.

Use the PC to get your ideas down quickly. Once you have opened a document do not worry about simply getting your ideas down in note form. Sometimes just a set of headings is enough to act as a reminder of your ideas. The flexibility of a word processing programme will then allow you to move from section to section filling in the detail as appropriate. The drag and drop facility will later allow you to shift round blocks of text or even single words to re-order the material as you require. You may find it useful to use some method of formatting your document, such as using headings in bold or uppercase letters as a way of getting down main headings and then filling in the text below them.

The typeface that you use to create a document does not have to be the same typeface you will use for the final version. It makes sense, therefore, to experiment with different typefaces when you are inputting words. Some typefaces on the screen are more friendly on the eye than others.

Another advantage of using PC as a writing tool is that it can help you to organise your ideas as you go along. In addition to organising your material under headings, PCs allow you to create bullet points and to number paragraphs. It is certainly worth spending some time familiarising yourself with these features to see how you can get them to work for you. Intelligent use of bullet points or numbering can help bring clarity to your writing by separating out and structuring your ideas into a logical order.

Do not forget to save your work at regular intervals. This is especially important if you are using a PC that is accessible by other people. Do not wander off and leave a document open. Other people may not respect your privacy or may even shut down your work to get on with their own. Even if you have exclusive use of a computer, back up your work at intervals using a floppy disk or CD. Unexpected crashes or power cuts should not then wreck your hard work.

It is a good idea to devise a system of file names for your documents. This is especially true when you have different versions of the same material. Numbering different versions should help. If you do get mixed up between versions of a document, look at the 'properties' menu. This will tell you when the document was first created and when it was last revised.

PCs have allowed people a lot more flexibility about the way in which they write. The fact that it is easy to save a document and then revise it at a later date has given people a lot more freedom to try out ideas, then go back and develop and revise them at a later date. Many people use a PC to get down their ideas quickly without too much concern at this stage for style or the observation of grammatical conventions. Once the ideas are in place, these can be attended to later. Most word processing packages have grammar and spellchecks to help you with these aspects of writing.

Spend some time familiarising yourself with the grammar and spellcheck functions of your software. It is possible to have them running as you write so that errors are indicated as you input material. Some people find this irritating and prefer to disable the function and run the checks at the end of a session or even when they have completed the whole document. One function you may like to keep running is auto-correct which automatically corrects common errors such as transposed letters or literals. Look in the auto-correct menu at some of the options for setting this up.

Remember, too, that software packages are designed to work in many different countries. Do make sure that you have yours set to the appropriate version of English (English [United Kingdom] will avoid US spellings).

The cut-and-paste facility on your PC saves you a lot of time. This allows you to copy material from another document and to paste it into the one you are working on. It means that if you have previously worked on an idea, it is a simple matter to lift any appropriate material into what you are currently working on.

Be aware, though, that if the material is not your own you must attribute it to its source. Lifting other people's ideas without giving them credit is called plagiarism and is heavily frowned upon, especially in academic circles.

Once you have finished putting all the material you feel is appropriate into a document, then it is time to do a final edit. You may find it useful to look back at the section on writing style on pages 22–27. One job you can very easily do on a PC is to run through a document and look for all the redundant words that can be deleted. If you have been set a word limit, then use the word-count menu to check you are inside this.

Many word processing packages have a useful readability index included. This tool calculates how accessible your document is to the reader by checking on sentence and paragraph lengths. A number of indices may be used. For example, the Flesch Reading Ease Score uses word length and sentence length to calculate readability on a 100 point scale. You should aim to score between 60 and 70 to make your writing accessible. Another handy statistic that is usually available tells you the number of passive sentences you have written. Remember Orwell's advice on style and try to keep the number of such sentences to a minimum.

Many people find editing a document on screen difficult. Reading through a long document on screen can cause eyestrain. You may find it useful to print out your document and make any amendments or corrections on this hard copy. This also has the advantage that you can work anywhere and at anytime. Of course, the downside is that you will have to spend time making the changes on the computer later.

Editing may also involve some reorganising of your material. Assuming you have created appropriate headings and, where necessary, subheadings, you should have a logical structure in place. Make sure that the material itself is organised logically under these appropriate headings.

Do not forget to choose the most appropriate typeface or font for your document. It is an easy matter to change the font to see which looks best. Many people feel that Times New Roman, for example, gives your document a sense of authority. A typeface such as Courier, on the other hand, has more of a typewritten quality that may suggest that the document is an initial draft or suggestion, rather than a definitive statement.

Remember that a properly edited document will be friendly to the reader. From the title at the head through to the last paragraph, there should be a consistency of style and format that makes it easy for a reader to find their way through the document.

CREATING DOCUMENTS IN SPECIFIC FORMATS

There are likely to be a number of occasions when the document you need to produce will fit into an existing format. These formats include letters, reports and memoranda. Similarly, you may wish to create a document such a curriculum vitae (CV) that you can update at later intervals. Templates and Wizards are particularly helpful tools if this is what you want to do.

A template is a pre-existing format that you can select which will wrap up your own document. Often a package will offer several different styles of template, each appropriate to a particular context. For example, if you are preparing a letter, you will be offered a choice of template according to the type of letter you want to produce, from a formal business letter to an informal letter to a friend or relative. If none of the templates is appropriate for your needs, you may wish to create your own, for example a letterhead. Indeed, it is possible to create and file a range of stationery templates in a corporate style for yourself.

GETTING TO GRIPS WITH E-MAIL

Electronic mail, or e-mail, has become one of the most popular methods of communication, especially in the business world. It has fundamentally changed the way in which many people and organisations communicate. At the same time it has created a raft of issues relating to confidentiality and security.

E-mail is a system that uses the Internet to send messages between people and organisations. Perhaps its most important feature is that it enables almost instantaneous communication anywhere in the world. In this way it has many of the qualities of the telephone or fax as a method of getting information quickly from one source to another. However, unlike a telephone call, e-mail is in the form of a permanent written communication. Maybe more importantly, unlike the telephone call it does not demand an instant response, despite the speed at which it travels. Experienced and practised e-mailers, however, often expect almost instantaneous replies to their e-mails.

GETTING CONNECTED

In order to send or receive e-mail you will need access to a PC with a modem connected to a telephone line. You will also need to have an account with an Internet Service Provider (ISP), many of which provide free access and connection. You will most likely have to pay for a local telephone call to this provider. Once connected, you may be asked to register with the ISP's e-mail service. However, many people prefer to register with an e-mail service that is not tied to a specific ISP. This means that if you change providers at a later date you can keep the same e-mail address.

Your e-mail address is very like your postal address or telephone number. Changing it means you have to tell everyone the new one. So it is a good idea to get yourself an address and hang on to it. This is especially true if you have obtained a distinctive and memorable address. As the Internet gets busier, the demand for e-mail addresses gets greater and people with common family names will find it more difficult simply to use their name as the first part of their address.

It is also worth bearing in mind that when you set up your e-mail account it is possible to have several different accounts. This could be for different members of a family. Some people choose to have more than one identity for different groups of contacts.

Before you choose an e-mail service it is worth checking to see if you will be able to access your e-mail from any computer with an Internet facility. Usually you will be given a password that allows you to pick up and send messages from anywhere in the world. This is a very useful facility if you move around a lot.

If you are going to send a lot of e-mails, it is a good idea to get a programme that will allow you to compose your messages offline. This means writing them when you are not connected to your ISP and running up a telephone bill for yourself or someone else. A package such as Outlook Express will enable you to write your messages and store them until you are ready to send several in one batch. At the same time as you connect to send out these messages, you will also receive any incoming messages. This method will allow you to send and receive your mail once or twice a day using fairly short connection times.

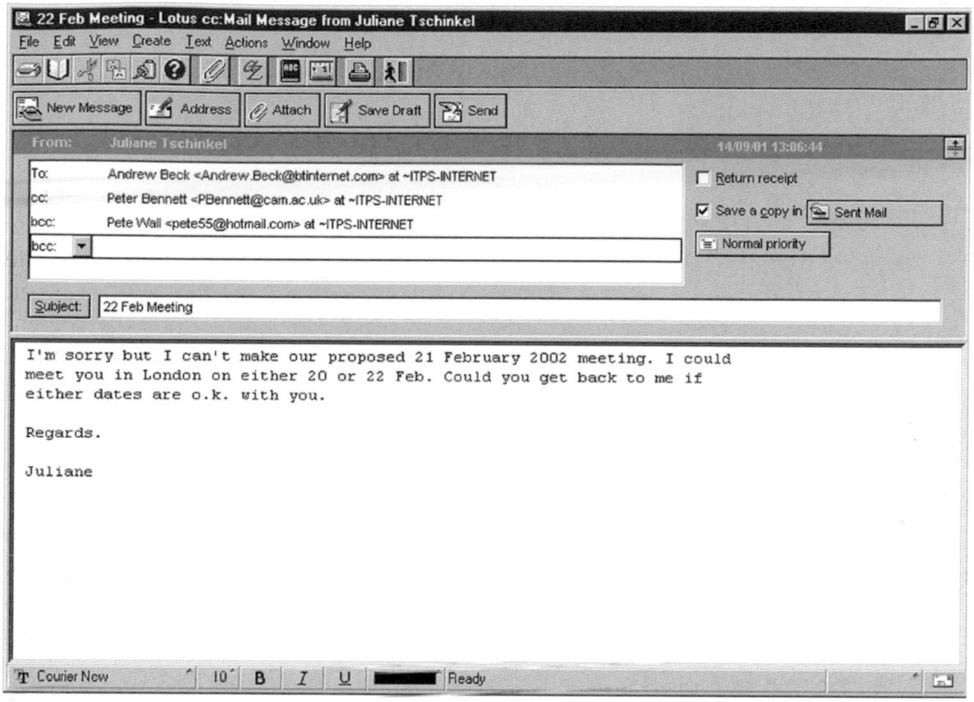

Figure 2.2 *E-mail set-up*

Whatever package you use for sending e-mails, you will be provided with an onscreen form to use.

The spaces, or 'fields', at the top obviously require you to fill in details, in much the same way as a memorandum. Getting the address completely accurate, down to the last dot, is vital, otherwise your message will not be delivered. As you use e-mail more and more you will build up an address book of contacts. Simply clicking on the address book icon will enable you to call up your list and select the person you wish to write to.

The abbreviation cc stands for carbon copy. This allows you to send a copy of your e-mail to other people. Generally this is done when you need to keep someone else informed of your message to someone else. It can also be used as a lever to get the receiver to take action because another person, perhaps their boss, has been made aware of the contents of the message.

The abbreviation bcc stands for blind carbon copy. In essence this means that the receiver of the e-mail will not be aware that you have sent a copy to someone else. Obviously this could be seen as a little underhand. However, there may be situations when you may need to use this function.

With regard to the subject of your e-mail, ideally every e-mail you send should be about just one topic. If you need to discuss more topics, then it is recommended that you use a separate e-mail for each. The reason for this is that it will help the receiver to retrieve the information in your e-mail more easily at a later date, if this proves necessary. Always try to indicate the content accurately in the subject field. It is tempting to be witty in choosing a subject but this can be frustrating for the receiver if they are later searching for one of your messages on a particular topic.

Keeping your message to a single topic also makes it easier for the receiver to reply. An important facility in e-mail software is the reply button. This enables you to send a reply to the message by automatically reproducing the appropriate details on the e-mail form and also printing the original message to which you are composing your reply. This has the advantage that the receiver does not have to search out the original message in order to make sense of the reply.

E-mail is a relative newcomer as a method of communication. As such it does not carry with it a lot of the heritage of the letter, for example. Doubtless one day famous people will have their collected e-mails published, probably on a website. For the moment there is not a great deal of case history that determines the rules of composing e-mails.

The codes that do exist are determined by efficiency and courtesy. Writing each individual e-mail on one topic is an example of both. Such an e-mail, as we have suggested, is easier for the receiver to deal with and therefore more efficient. Equally, it is courteous not to overburden the receiver with information by sending e-mails that run to several 'pages' and cover a whole range of topics. Such courtesies are an example of 'netiquette'.

KEY TERM

NETIQUETTE Describes the conventions for using e-mail as this channel of communication is used more widely. This new word is derived from a contraction of the two words 'network' and 'etiquette'. There are a number of sites, such as those of university computer service departments, which spell out their own rules for using e-mail. You may find it helpful to visit one of these to see what advice they offer.

One especially useful rule to bear in mind is to think about the receiver of your communication at all times. On page 29 we talk about the importance of empathy with the receiver of a message. This is especially true of e-mail. Many people are new to the medium. They may not be skilled in using the keyboard. Extending to them courtesy and tolerance is essential. Similarly, when you are sending messages you should bear these points in mind.

- Be as brief as possible. Do not fill the screen with unnecessary words. It is hard on the eyes.
- If you pass on other people's messages, do not change or edit them. Do not forget to acknowledge the original sender.
- Do not impersonate other people. Do not use the potential anonymity of e-mail to harass or intimidate other people.

- Reply promptly to messages you receive. If you are away for a period of time set up the auto reply function in your programme to let people know.
- Remember that the legal constraints that apply to print documents are equally applicable to e-mail. Be careful, for example, not to make defamatory comments about people and publish these to a third party. You risk a libel action if you do.

You should also remember the importance of organisation when dealing with messages. Most of you will deal with your snail mail (i.e. ordinary postal mail) by filtering incoming messages, saving important ones and throwing away junk mail. Similarly with e-mail, file the important messages and delete those you do not need to keep. With outgoing e-mail keep a copy of everything. You may wish to save hard disk space by saving only those messages you need to.

Finally, remember that, unless you go to the trouble of encrypting a message, e-mail is potentially an insecure medium. Examination boards, for example, do not allow examiners to send draft examination papers by e-mail. If you have confidential material you wish to send, snail mail may be the better option.

ATTACHMENTS

If you have a long and complex document or even an illustration to send, then you can use a file attachment to your e-mail message. All you have do is click on the attachment icon, usually a paperclip, and either type in the name of the file you wish to send or click on browse and select it from the list. Remember that to open the file the receiver must have compatible software. They may not be able to open a word-processed document if they are using e-mail through their television set.

This attachment function allows a large amount of material to be transmitted to, from and between computers. It is an invaluable resource for example for writers who work collaboratively or where documents need to be previewed, edited and revised by a group of people who are geographically remote. It allows amendments and suggestions to be communicated quickly between people without postal delays and the need for extensive re-typing.

▼ 4 STUDY SKILLS FOR COMMUNICATION

In this section we will look at the skills required to study Communication.

- We will offer guidance to help you prepare yourself for effective study, such as motivating yourself and acquiring study techniques.
- We will describe techniques and strategies you can use to study effectively and efficiently, such as note-taking, effective reading and critical thinking.

The most important study skill you need to develop is how to be an active student. Many students are passive. They believe that if they arrive on time for classes, read the right books and take notes, then all they will have to do is turn up at the examination and regurgitate what they have 'learned'. Such students might be likened to empty containers passing along a conveyor belt, believing that knowledge and information can simply be poured into them. At the end of the conveyor belt all they have to do is spit out this knowledge and information, before joining the next conveyor belt that will take them on to the next stage of their study.

Such a model may once have had some use. However, modern assessment methods, especially in a discipline such as Communication Studies, are concerned with something other than testing your skills to absorb and regurgitate facts. Nowadays, students are expected to apply what they have learned. It is this competence in applying what you have learned that is tested in both coursework and examinations.

Research has shown that active learning is a far more effective method than passive learning. In the 1970s researchers at the California Institute of Technology investigated different methods of obtaining and retaining information. We can summarise what they found in the form of Diagram 2.1 (opposite).

The diagram shows the percentage of information retained by participants 48 hours after obtaining it by the methods shown. As you can see, the active processes at the bottom of the pyramid are far more effective than the passive ones at the top. It's also worth noting that those methods that seem to be most time-effective (one-hour lecture or one-hour textbook-reading session) are least effective in terms of the information retained. On the other hand, those methods that are less time-effective, such as a

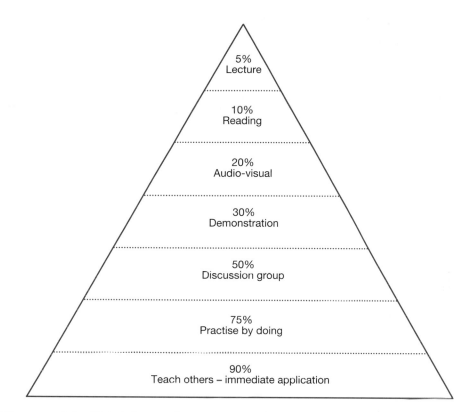

Diagram 2.1 *Obtaining and retaining information*

discussion group, where you will have to take turns, listen to other opinions as well as stating your own position, are more effective in terms of retaining information. Clearly, those learning methods that will be most time-consuming will also be the most effective in the acquisition of knowledge and the development of skills.

If you are to engage actively in the learning process, you will need to be prepared to set time aside to do this. For example, you will find it useful to get together with other groups of Communication Studies students to discuss some of the key issues you are trying to get to grips with. Similarly, the shared viewing (and subsequent discussion) of a live television programme or video tape or a DVD may well prove helpful in formulating ideas around an important topic. Whatever device is employed, it is clear that it is far better to do than to be done to. Active participation in the learning process will always achieve much more than passive consumption of other people's work.

Making your learning active rather than passive clearly goes far beyond the immediate demands of succeeding in your Communication Studies course. Ultimately, it is a life skill that will not only have applications in study at a higher level, but will also influence your effectiveness in your chosen career. But let us get back to some of the basics of studying communication.

Here are some key questions that can help you focus your studies. Each question relates to a key aspect of study.

Question	Aspect
Why am I studying?	Motivation
How do I keep myself studying?	Gratification
How do I maintain my attention when studying?	Climate
Where should I study?	Location
What techniques or strategies should I use when studying?	Study techniques

Let us consider each of these aspects in turn.

MOTIVATION

A good question to ask yourself is 'Why am I studying?' Sadly, many students drift into a course of study without considering what they hope to get from it. So it is a good idea to ask yourself why you are studying communication. The answer may well be a negative one, such as 'Because I could not get on to the biology course'.

It might be that you have identified the course as a means to an end – 'If I pass the examination, I will get the job I want or a place on the degree course.'

Fortunately, most students have much more positive reasons for joining the course. Whatever the case, it is essential that you recognise the value that the course and subsequent examination have for you. If you cannot see these, then ask someone, perhaps your teacher, for help. What you must avoid doing is coming up with the answer 'I don't know'. If you can't see why you're studying, you could experience difficulty staying with that course of study.

Assuming that you can find positive answers to your goals in taking the course, it is probably a good idea to put these down in writing. You might also consider putting this 'statement' in a prominent position. In this way, if your attention starts to wander, or if you feel aimless and demotivated or unsure about what you should be doing, you will be reminded of these goals and should get yourself back on the right track of engaging in productive activity to realise these goals.

You may also like to consider telling close friends, family and colleagues about your goals. These people may be a valuable source of support through their concern to ensure you achieve the goals you have set yourself.

GRATIFICATION

Gratification is about the often difficult job of how to keep yourself going with your studies. Here are three strategies that can help you keep up your levels of motivation.

State your goals

You should see immediately that this relates closely to the point made above. However, let's consider two sorts of goal. Long-term goals are generally a fair distance in the future. They are likely to include such issues as completing a piece of assessed coursework or passing a particular unit in the examination. Short-term goals are much closer; 'By the end of the week' is a short-term goal. Setting yourself these short-term goals is an important method of keeping yourself on the right track. So, for example, you may have decided that by the end of the week you will be able to apply the process model of communication. You will probably find it helpful to use a diary or the calendar on your PC to note down these short-term objectives. Alternatively, prepare a list at the beginning of each week setting out what you want to achieve. Crossing them off one at a time can be very therapeutic, and you will feel suitably gratified by your achievement.

Give yourself rewards

What should immediately follow the achievement of a short-term goal is rewarding yourself. Although achieving the goal is a gratification in itself, you can add to this feeling by indulging in an activity that you enjoy in order to reinforce your achievement. Earning leisure time by achieving short-term goals can be a most effective motivating factor throughout your course of study, if not your life. If you have put in an appropriate amount of hard work, then the reward of leisure time can gratify you, refresh you, and provide you with the energy and impetus to maintain yourself in your studies.

Surface your satisfaction

Surfacing your satisfaction can help keep you studying. Don't be afraid to share your successes and achievements with your family and friends. Their pats on the back can be a source of great encouragement. Keep an eye out for television and radio programmes that have relevance to your study. Demonstrate your knowledge and skills to yourself and others by critically discussing these programmes. Similarly, keep a look-out for magazines and books that may be relevant to Communication Studies. Be prepared to talk about what you have learned whenever the conversation permits. In other words, do not make your new-found knowledge a secret – surface it. In this way you will derive satisfaction from being able to talk about topics in a constructive, detailed and animated fashion. Not only should your achievement not be a secret, but also your satisfaction in your achievement should be shared.

CLIMATE

Effective time management is another important aspect of making yourself effective in your studies. Preparing yourself a weekly timetable is the first step to ensure this effective personal time management. For study purposes build every aspect of your life in any given week into this timetable. You need to include such items as work, travel, eating, sleeping as well as the recreational time you have earned.

Of course, all the time management in the world cannot take account of unforeseen and pressing matters. The secret of dealing with these is to timetable them away. This does not mean ignoring them. What it means is that you should find an appropriate time and place to deal with them rather than letting them intrude on your studies. At first sight this may seem harsh, but it is far better to deal with them in this way than to commit time and energy to a problem that may even resolve itself without any action on your part.

Finally, remove any people who might intrude on your study time. Inform people in your family and social circle that you have studies to complete and tell them politely but firmly that you do not wish to be disturbed.

If you organise your time in the above fashion, you should create an effective climate in which to devote your complete attention to your studies.

LOCATION

As human beings, we tend to associate specific locations with specific activities. Therefore it is a good idea to find a specific location that you can associate with study. If you are fortunate enough to be able to designate a space in your home exclusively for study, so much the better. If not, you may have to consider opting for a space at your school or college or, if that is inconvenient, perhaps a local library. Alternatively, you may have to compromise around such a deal as using the kitchen for a study space when it is not being used for other purposes. What is important is that other people recognise and acknowledge your space and respect your right to peace and tranquillity when you occupy it.

Once you have established your space, it is a good idea to customise it to your needs. A clear space in which to work that is well lit and comfortable is a good starting point. Increasingly important is access to a computer. If you are sharing the use of a computer, you should check the advice on page 36.

Ideally your workspace needs to have all the materials that you are likely to need close at hand. This means not only obvious things like paper and pens but also textbooks, dictionaries and other appropriate reference works. There will be occasions when you will also need audio-visual equipment for playing video and audio-tapes. The fewer excuses you have for leaving your workstation to search for resources, the more likely you are to stay focused on your studies.

Getting your workstation right for your needs will inevitably be a matter of trial and error. Be prepared to make changes if there are aspects that do not suit your style of working. On the other hand, be prepared to hang on to those aspects that you feel make you more effective in your studies.

STUDY TECHNIQUES

If you are going to be an active student, there are a number of techniques that you need to learn. Let us look at three key skills that you will need before considering how these might fit into formulas that will help you remember how to be an active student.

Reviewing

Before you begin any study session, such as reading a textbook, locate where the topic falls into your study programme. You can do this by making a review, either mentally or on paper, of all you have studied so far. In this way what you are about to study can be seen as a key jigsaw piece in the larger picture of your study. The reason why you are studying it should also emerge. If you do not engage in this review, it is likely that the study you are undertaking will be aimless and you will simply be going through the motions without perceiving how it fits into the pattern as a whole.

Previewing

Make sure you know what you are about and that it is appropriate for your needs. Later in this section, when we look at using textbooks, we consider some of the key points you need to check before proceeding to use a book. Carefully previewing a source of information (whether it's a book, programme or lecture) should ensure that you do not waste time considering material that is inappropriate to your needs. It also makes sense to preview the shape of the study session. Knowing when a session will start and when it will end should indicate to you just how long your active study session is going to take.

Questioning

The activity of questioning both yourself and others can make your study more active. Raise your awareness levels at the start of a study session by asking yourself questions about what you need to know and what the writer or speaker is going to say. If you have asked yourself these questions before the session begins, you will find yourself more alert and able to maintain this questioning frame of mind throughout the session.

Make a note of those points you find questionable or mysterious. When the session is over follow up these issues, either by asking people who may know or by seeking clarification from other sources. When you start engaging in this questioning activity it is a good idea to write down your questions. As you become more experienced you are likely to find that it will become something you can do without consciously thinking about it.

A USEFUL FORMULA

Here is a useful formula that should help you become skilled in active study when you are using a textbook or other written source of information. It should help you to apply some of the techniques described above. The formula is SQ3R. This stands for:

Diagram 2.2 *The SQ3R model*

1   **Survey** is the activity of reviewing and previewing what you know, what you need to know, and how this fits into the larger plan of your study.
2   **Question** is about using this technique to ensure purposeful engagement with the study materials.
3   **Reading** should be active. It is recommended that you read through any material twice: the first time to give you the main ideas; the second to make notes.
4   **Recall** is about digesting what you have read. Once you have read through the material, stop and tell yourself the main points. This will help you to test how effective your reading has been. If you have taken notes, ideally these will be an accurate account of the original material.
5   **Review** is the final stage of the process. This involves looking back at the four previous stages and checking the effectiveness of the process of study. You need to carry out the following.

- Check that the questions you wanted answered have been answered. You should also see if any new questions have emerged and think about how you might answer them.
- Re-read the material to ensure you have grasped all the important points.
- Check to see if there are any gaps in your notes. If so, you should fill them in. This is also a good point at which to check for connections between the material you have just studied and those topics you have previously studied.

LISTENING

It is useful to make a distinction between hearing and listening. Most people can hear, in that they can receive and distinguish sounds within a specific frequency range. Hearing, however, is a passive activity. It is something that happens *to* us, rather than something that we do. On the other hand, listening is active. You may have come across the common notion that people 'hear but do not listen'. In a class or lecture it is very likely you will hear the words being spoken. You may not necessarily listen to them. There may be a number of reasons why you do not listen.

- You are not interested in what is being said.
- You are preoccupied with a personal problem.
- Something is taking place nearby that you find more interesting.

In *Interpersonal Communication* (1999) Peter Hartley identifies another problem that can occur when we listen. He suggests that there are people who appear to be listening but who are not doing so. He categorises them into three groups.

1   **Pretend listeners**: These are people who seem to be listening and responding to what is being said but whose minds are in fact elsewhere.
2   **Limiting listeners**: They listen in a limited way by tending to focus on specific comments or topics and distorting or misinterpreting other things that are said to them.
3   **Self-centred listeners**: Such people are concerned only with their own views and are looking only for your agreement.

Consider occasions when you have been talking to someone and they have exhibited one of the above listening patterns. What do you think was their reason for doing so? Do you think you could ever be accused of listening in any of these ways?

Most people are born with the capacity to hear; listening is a skill they have to develop. The best sort of listener is one who is active. Active listening implies helping the transmitter to get their message over as effectively as possible. An effective listener demonstrates a willingness to participate in the communication process. This can be achieved in a number of different ways, including:

- paying attention to and showing interest in the message
- indicating if we are understanding the message or not
- showing how we are reacting to the message.

A good listener will also be aware that some signals will indicate that they are bored or growing impatient. Clearly, it is best to avoid these and identify positive strategies to support a speaker in getting the message across.

As you will see on pages 171–186, where we look at non-verbal communication (NVC), eye contact is one important method for signalling your response to what someone is saying. Similarly, head nods can be used to encourage a speaker to expand, develop or simply continue with a particular train of thought. Smiling or laughing at a humorous comment can demonstrate that you have picked up the subtle implications of what they are saying. Equally, laughing in the wrong place can be quite discouraging to a speaker, so make sure that a witty comment was intended as such.

You should listen in order to comprehend and make sense of another person's utterances. To achieve this not only must you listen carefully and avoid getting distracted but also you should avoid being selective in what you hear. For example, you are likely to fail to grasp a message if you insist on jumping in before a person has finished speaking. This way you will only understand a half-formulated communication. In order to make sure you have understood a message, you need to finish listening to it and to evaluate it. As Hartley (1999) points out, 'Delay evaluation of what you have heard until you fully understand it.' This means you need to check at various points in the communication process that you are understanding what is being communicated. For example, you might use a quizzical look or even a direct verbal intervention to encourage a speaker to reformulate a message to overcome some barrier to your understanding. This may simply be an unfamiliar word that needs defining.

Evaluation is an important process. We need to grasp all of the message and not just part of it. This can be difficult if a message is complex or technical, or if it uses terminology unfamiliar to you. In order to become effective at listening we need to practise it.

We can think faster than we can speak. When you are listening to someone else speaking, what are your thought processes? How do you exploit the difference in speed between what you think and what they say?

NOTE-TAKING

The skill of making notes from a range of sources (such as lectures, class discussion or reference books) is vital for every student. Similarly, making sense of your notes from these sources over a period of time can mean the difference between success and failure.

The key to effective note-taking is to be conscientious and to stick to an organisational method that works. For many students this will mean not only taking an initial set of notes but also revisiting these notes while they are fresh and expanding or developing them in such a way that they will make sense later. Many students find the most efficient method of doing this is to transfer hand-written notes on to a computer at the earliest opportunity. If no computer is available, then writing them up in long hand into a logical and clear format is the next-best thing.

Choose a topic you have covered recently, either in Communication Studies or another subject. Now look through your notes and see how easy it is to retrieve information on the topic. What has the result told you about your level of organisation?

ORGANISATION

Organisation is a skill closely linked to note-taking. The most accurate and detailed set of notes imaginable will be quite worthless if you cannot retrieve them for use when you want them.

Whatever system of storage you have, be it a computer or simple A4 binder, you need to develop a method of filing and organising your notes in such a way that you can confidently gain access to them whenever you need to refer to them. If you are able to store information on a computer hard disk, don't forget to make a back-up copy on a floppy disk – especially if you are not the only person using the computer.

However, the need for organisation goes far beyond simply filing your notes for easy retrieval. Probably the single most effective way to improve your skill in studying lies in organising your time. This is frequently termed 'time management'. The simple act of drawing up a timetable or action plan of how you can utilise the hours in your day can help you to optimise the use of your time. This can be especially important to a Communication Studies student; time spent on recreational activities and time spent on study can sometimes become blurred. A visit to the cinema, for example, might well be considered a pleasurable social activity as well as an aspect of your study of communication. It is up to you to try to make sure you get the best of both worlds.

INFORMATION RETRIEVAL

We live in an information-rich society. Indeed, many people see a new division within society between those who have access to information and those who don't. In general students belong to the former category, especially where they have access to the Internet and the skills and knowledge necessary to retrieve information from it. However, the privilege of such access has its downside. So much information is now available through the average student's PC that it is very easy to suffer from an overload. It is important to learn how to be selective in gaining access to and retrieving information. Equally important is how to make the most effective use of what you have obtained.

Despite some potential drawbacks, the Internet has become a real boon to students, allowing instant access to information 24 hours a day. For the student who has taken the trouble to learn how to use it effectively, it is a valuable shortcut to rich sources of information which just a few years ago might well have involved waiting several weeks for a library to obtain a book from elsewhere in the country.

SOURCES OF INFORMATION

Even though we live in an age of electronic information, books are still an important source for the Communication Studies student. Indeed, many publishers believe that books are set to grow in both importance and popularity as society is keen to have access to more and more information encouraged by such innovations as the Internet.

Using a textbook is an important skill that needs to be developed. The first challenge is to find the right book. You will need to consider both the content of the book and the level at which it is pitched.

A lot of Communication Studies books are aimed at students who are well ahead of A Level and are used to a much more sophisticated level of language and concepts than people at your stage of study. Unless you are prepared to spend hours wrestling with complex language and concepts (and spending lots of time looking up unfamiliar words), these books will not be very helpful. Equally there is a wide range of Communication Studies books covering a variety of different topics. Finding the best one for your needs is bound to be tricky. Here are some tips to help you select the right book at the right level.

- **Check cover copy**. If you are browsing in a library or bookshop, read the copy (the words) that appear on the book's cover to see if the book covers the topics you are looking for.

- **Check the contents page** to assess further if it covers the right ground. You may also find information about the level at which the book is aimed. Ideally you want a book that is geared to the needs of a reader looking for an introduction to the topic. You can check this further by reading half a page of the text inside the book to see how easy or difficult you find it to grasp.
- **Check the name of the writer(s)**. It may also be a good pointer to the usefulness of the book. Is this a writer whose name you have heard mentioned in other books or in class perhaps? Throughout this book you will find suggestions for further reading. You'll need to decide which authors you find talk to you at a level and in a way that you can understand and feel happy with.

Once you have found the right book, the next step is to learn how to get the best from it. It is always a good idea to read the introduction to any textbook. This should tell you about the approach the writer is going to take and what they intend to cover.

It is unlikely that you will have the time to read a whole book, so you need to learn how to select the sections that are especially relevant for what you are doing. One device that may help here is the index. This will outline for you all the references to a particular topic. Where these are fairly detailed you will find they run across several pages (e.g. 68–73), so that is always a good place to start looking. Note also that most textbooks give a chapter summary at the beginning of every chapter. This gives an outline of what is covered in the chapter. It is a good idea, therefore, to check each chapter in turn to see if it is likely to contain any relevant material. To help you with this, look at the section headings within each chapter as a way of navigating your way to the information you are looking for.

The next stage is to make some notes. Some students like to photocopy useful sections of books. If you do this, you need to check with your school or college that you are not breaking copyright laws. While photocopying can be a useful tool, it is often much better to make some notes from the book you are using. There are a couple of reasons why this is so. First, the process of transferring information in this way helps to reinforce your learning – not least because you have to read and understand the original before you can write down your own version. Second, it is important to acquire and practise the skill of summarising other people's ideas in your own words. Taking notes will help you to perfect this skill. On a very few occasions you will want to lift direct quotations from a book. When you do so, remind yourself they are direct quotations by putting them in inverted commas. This way you will not forget to attribute the ideas to their original source when you come to write up your essay or report.

EFFECTIVE READING

Most people can read. However, many people have just one method of reading; this is to look at every word. This means that they are slow readers. Reading for the efficient taking in of information is a skill that has to be learned. If you only read at one speed, it is likely that you are reading inefficiently and spending a lot more time than is necessary. The faster you read something, the less time it takes. This means you are less likely to get bored by the process. In the same way that a car has different gears for different situations, so too should you have different speeds for different types of material. Here are some of the different speeds at which you should be able to read, together with suggestions for the uses to which these reading speeds should be put.

1   **Scanning**: It is possible to scan information at between 1,000 and 2,000 words per minute (wpm). Scanning is useful when you are seeking a specific item of information such as a name, a statistic or a key phrase from a document. It takes practice to be able to look at printed information at this speed, but it will save you a lot of time and trouble.

2   **Skimming**: Skimming at 800 to 1,000 wpm is about moving your eyes left to right and from top to bottom of a page in order to locate information you are looking for. You will not read every word or phrase. However, skimming should enable you to grasp the gist of a document. It is particularly useful when you are standing in a library or bookshop trying to decide whether a book is going to be worth taking home with you.

3   **Rapid reading**: For most general reading you want to aim at a speed within this range. If your reading speed is below 300 wpm, it is likely you are wasting your time. If you think that by reading slowly you are taking in everything, bear in mind that you do not need to exceed a level of between 70 and 80 per cent comprehension and retention of information. This is due in part to the fact that up to 30 per cent of what you're reading will be redundant. (Redundancy is defined and explored in more detail on pages 119–122, but basically if a communication is low on new information and highly predictable, then it is said to be redundant – it's easy to understand and you don't have to examine every single word closely in a written communication.)

4   **Slow reading**: A speed of 150–300 wpm is the sort of speed at which you might need to read if you are dealing with difficult material containing ideas or language that you are unfamiliar with. If you need to have complete understanding of a document, you will need to read at this speed if you are to comprehend the material.

5   **Studying**: 10 to 200 wpm. At this speed you will be doing some very close reading of a text. You may well find yourself going back over material to consider its meaning. You may also be taking notes as you read. You are not reading slowly because you can't help it, rather you are doing it to ensure you completely grasp the material you are tackling.

Don't forget to write down all the details of a book you use. Later in this section we look at the important practice of referencing and describe a procedure for referencing books. Every time you use a book make a note of:

Author
Title
Publisher
Date of publication
ISBN (International Standard Book Number)

It is also a good idea to make a note of the page numbers from which your notes have been taken. If you are using a reader or collection of essays by different people, don't forget that you also need a note of the name of the individual contributor whose work you are using.

An important reason that you need to make a note of the source of your information is that when you come to use it in an essay or a piece of coursework you have to attribute it. This means you should not try to claim it is an original idea of your own and you should acknowledge the source from which it comes. If you don't, you can be accused of plagiarism, which means taking and using other people's ideas without properly acknowledging them.

ACTIVITY . . .

At what speed are you reading this part of the book? Is the speed you are reading appropriate to:

■ the content of the book
■ your purpose in reading it?

THE INTERNET

The Internet is a great boon to all students but for the Communication Studies student it also offers some unique advantages as well as disadvantages. The chief advantage is the way it provides swift access to contemporary information. A problem with much of the information in a textbook is that it may become out of date.

If you are using a computer that doesn't belong to you, make sure you have a plentiful supply of disks on which to store things you find. It is a good idea to reserve one disk for keeping a list of bookmarked sites that you have found especially useful. If you download something to a disk for future reference, keep a detailed note of the contents of that disk on the label so you can find it again without having to search through each of your disks in turn.

Most of the sites relevant to Communication Studies are pitched at a sophisticated level of understanding. This is because a lot of research into the discipline takes place in higher education, especially in the USA. Just as you will have found it necessary to dip into a textbook to see if it is useful or not, so it is with a website.

However, before you do this, it is a good idea to learn how to use a search engine to the best effect. Search engines such as Yahoo!, Lycos or Google are the means by which you can enter keywords to identify what you are looking for. They will list all of the sites on the Internet that seem relevant to your search. This often amounts to several thousand, so it will pay you to do some initial research into how to get the best from the search engine you have chosen to use. Click on the help icon on the home page of the search engine and it will tell you how you can use such devices as inverted commas and plus and minus signs to limit your search. It is really worthwhile familiarising yourself with these devices if you are going to make searches that produce a manageable amount of information for you to follow up.

Figure 2.3 *Computer screen with search results for key word enquiry*

BIBLIOGRAPHY AND REFERENCES

It is important that you acknowledge other people's ideas when you produce work for Communication Studies. To lift material from published sources without acknowledging where it came from is called plagiarism (see page 54). Widespread access to the Internet has made plagiarism more prevalent in some academic disciplines. Of course, in a complex area such as Communication Studies there is a huge amount of published material that you may wish to refer to across a range of different disciplines. The fact that material is available from such diverse sources makes it more important that you properly acknowledge what you have used. Referencing and acknowledging source material is important whatever level of academic study you are engaged in. Proper referencing enables the reader to check the source you have quoted. By doing so they are able to ensure that you have accurately represented what that person has said. It may be that you have interpreted material in a specific way. A reader checking back may feel that the material you have quoted is open to other interpretations and that you have chosen one that particularly suits your own argument.

A bibliography is a list of sources, usually books, that you have cited (or used) in an essay. Whenever you produce a written piece of work, it is essential that you give such a list at the end. You will find a bibliography at the end of most textbooks. Communication Studies students will need to make references to a wide range of publications: books by a single author; contributions made by an author to a collection or anthology; a journal article; a publication from an organisation or corporation; a newspaper article; a television programme; a film; a website; or a song or a piece of music.

The Harvard system of referencing is the most frequently used in Communication Studies. Below you'll find examples of how you should refer to the various sources listed above using this system.

You will have noticed that within the main text, the name(s) of the author(s) appear as well as the year of publication. See for example a reference to Hartley (1999) on page 49. If the name of the author has not been mentioned explicitly, it should also appear within brackets. For example, (Hartley, 1999). this should follow the actual quoted or referred to source.

When you make your own bibliographies or references, make sure that you stick to the punctuation and type style given – right down to the use of the comma, the colon and the full stop.

Book:
Strinati, D. (2000) *An Introduction to Studying Popular Culture*, London: Routledge.

Contribution made by an author to a collection or an anthology:
de Saussure, F. (1996) 'The object of linguistics', in P. Cobley (ed.) *The Communication Theory Reader*, London: Routledge.

Journal article:
Brophy, P. (1986) 'Horrality – the textuality of contemporary Horror films', *Screen*, 27 (1): 2–13.

Publication by an organisation or corporation:
Independent Television Commission (1991) *The ITC Code of Advertising Standards and Practice*, London: ITC.

A newspaper article:
Brown, M. (2001) 'Bubbling Over', *The Guardian*, February 12.

Television programme:
Coronation Street (2001) ITV, December 16.

Film:
Soderbergh, S. (1999) *The Limey*, Artisan Pictures Inc.

Website:
Taylor & Francis,
http://www.mediastudiesarena.com/mediastudiesarena/books/textbooks.html (2001, February 12)

Song or piece of popular music:
Scanner vs. D. J. Spooky (1999) 'Synchronism', *The Quick and the Dead*. Sulphur Records, MELCDDDI.

WRITING AN EVALUATION

It is common in much academic study to ask students to produce their own evaluation of work they have done. In the Assessment and Qualifications Alliance (AQA) GCE Communication Studies coursework units students are required to produce an evaluation or review of the work they have done. This takes the form of a self-assessment in which you are asked to identify and consider what you have achieved. You will sometimes hear the process described as self-reflexivity. This means that you are being asked to look in on yourself and reflect on what you have achieved. Implicit in this process is the notion of how you might improve on what you have done, if you were given the chance to do it again. In both AQA coursework units, marks that count towards your final grade are awarded for this process.

The process of evaluation does not invite you to seize the opportunity to praise the work you have produced in the hope that an examiner will agree with you about its value. Evaluation should be more concerned with the process of learning than of fishing for marks. In Communication Studies the evaluation presents you with the opportunity to link the theory that you have learned to the process of communication that has been part of your practical work. For example, if you have given an oral presentation, your evaluation of it should to some extent focus on theories of interpersonal communication. You might like to address such issues as your use of register and language more generally. You may also like to consider how you dealt with feedback from your audience but linking in some of the theoretical work you have done on the role of feedback.

CRITICAL THINKING

Critical thinking is a key term in the evaluation process. 'Critical' does not carry with it the negative connotation of finding things that are wrong. 'Critical' in this sense means the skill to stand back from the work you have produced and to make an assessment of it. This assessment should be objective, avoiding any sense of bias because it is your own work. Indeed, the best type of evaluation looks at what has been produced as though it were done by someone else.

'Critical' carries with it the sense of analysing in order to understand how something functions This should be an important signal that you are expected to do more than simply describe the process of preparing a presentation or making a project. Critical thinking requires you to go deeper and show you understand why you worked in the way that you did.

Similarly, your evaluation needs to concern itself with the issue of how effective was your communication in terms of its purpose and the audience at which it was aimed. You may wish to consider how it might be improved. Equally important is to think about what you have learned from the process not only in terms of communication theory but also in terms of your own skills as a communicator (including what you need to do to develop and improve these skills).

Now that we have looked at ways of studying effectively, we will move on to see how those skills can be used to study communication itself.

▼ 5 COMMUNICATION PRACTICE: PROJECTS AND COURSEWORK

In this section we will examine the practical aspects of your studies. We will also look at how your study skills from the previous section will help.

■ We will work through a sample AS-style project.
■ We will look at the skills of research, planning, writing and reviewing in the context of a coherent practical investigation.
■ We will look at some examples of AS coursework.

Here we're going to look at how you can prepare to take part in, to observe and to analyse 'live' communication. You will be able to bring these skills of participation, observation and analysis to the preparation and development of your own communications – verbal, written, presentational and representational.

For example, in AQA's AS Communication Studies specification, students are required to conduct an investigation into an aspect of communication skills. The unit has four elements of assessment.

1   A 500 word research 'essay' (for 'essay' you should read 'report').
2   The preparation materials and visual support materials for a ten-minute oral presentation to interested other people (fellow students).
3   The oral presentation itself.
4   A 500 word review.

GENERAL ADVICE

In a sense the first piece of advice has been given implicitly: look first at what you have to do, clearly identifying what's required of you, what the tasks demand of you. These task demands will define the scope, character and substance of your research. Five hundred words at AS Level is a significant challenge, if only because there will not be the room to write at such length that you might arrive at the required standard. Five hundred words should act as a cue, a prompt. It may be saying the following.

- Be modest in the choice and scope of your investigation; what you find out cannot use more than 500 words to explain.
- Carefully draft and redraft your essay: economy and concision are valued; so carefully choose your words.
- Remember the standard is AS; it is based on what a 17-year-old student can be expected to achieve after one year (or less) of study.

These are important messages, and understanding them can make a significant difference to your achievement. As students of communication, you are always being asked to communicate about communication. We live in a world of communication texts and coursework assignments are classic, formal examples of decidable texts. Questions, tasks and assignment titles are written to allow candidates to demonstrate their knowledge and understanding of communication principles but they are not always entirely transparent. They do not set out to trip up candidates but with wit and experience you can learn to read them for the support they often give. By looking for the implications of what is said and the particular words used, you can often get a feeling for a task.

GETTING STARTED

It is useful to appreciate the spirit of a piece of assessment, for in this you might find clues as to how the assessment should be approached. For example, if the audience for the task is young, then an implication might be that the approach you require is a lively and adventurous one. To see the emphasis of a piece of assessment, we need to know its context. In the case of AS Communication Studies unit 1, the context is the module's content, which might usefully be summarised as:

- knowledge and understanding of communication skills
- perspectives and techniques
- skills of investigation and research
- note-making and oral presentation skills
- exploration of conventions of communication and communications
- importance of non-verbal communication
- skills of evaluation.

This part focuses on skills, methods and techniques. The Communication Practice module prioritises skills, and the unit test (a coursework 'portfolio') rewards both practical work and theoretical perspectives. Fifty per cent of the unit marks are given directly to practical work, to the preparation for and delivery of an oral presentation. In spite of the fact that investigations can be 'theoretical or practical', the clear emphasis enshrined in the module title is on 'introducing communication practice'. It might be possible to research academically the best way to haggle over the price of a pair of jeans with a market trader. It would be more relevant to the spirit of this unit to observe the process at first hand and to draw some conclusions about what is going on.

The module offers a wide range of choices and the difficulty comes in heeding our earlier advice – be modest. You are asked to consider skilled (or unskilled) communication wherever you may find it. The list of example skills here is both general and only a starting point. So, when looking at this list, treat the advice 'be modest' as 'be focused' or 'specialise'.

- Speaking, listening and empathising
- Reading and observing
- Identifying and using sources of information
- Drafting and writing
- Planning and structuring a presentation
- Oral presentation skills
- Dealing with questions
- Reviewing own performance
- Using IT to communicate

This is a general list of communication skills rather than a list telling you precisely what to investigate. This is positive as, in the best traditions of coursework, it throws both choice of content (the human text) and task open to you the candidate. Clearly, an investigation of 'speaking' as a skill could hardly be condensed into 500 words. On the other hand, the study of an individual speaker in an individual context or an investigation into strategies by which conversations are joined or started would be focused, individual and thus ideal. The emphasis here is on the specific, on the observed, the experience of communication and the skills and methods of the researcher. Sometimes it is best to start with a context and work back to a skill. The examples of context given in the specification are quite predictable and not particularly unusual:

- classroom
- interviews
- the workplace
- the family
- leisure activities
- shops
- media texts.

If one takes these as starting points, infinite possibilities begin to reveal themselves. 'Leisure activities' includes all manner of genuinely interesting communication locations: night clubs, sports grounds, concert venues, even the back seat of your car. All of these in all their permutations have their own dynamic. 'Media texts' also turns out to be a goldmine. The opportunity offered here is to open up film clips, television episodes, even newsreel to a communication skills analysis. What were the problems with Robert De Niro's character's communication with the Cybil Shepherd character in Martin Scorsese's *Taxi Driver*? What are the key communication skills required by a vampire slayer given the evidence of Buffy?

REAL LIFE CONTEXTS, REAL LIFE TEXTS

In keeping with the whole of AS, the starting point must be to start from where you are. AS Communication Studies is essentially about your immediate experiences of communication; as sender and receiver of messages; as a member of a modern society surrounded and bombarded by communication texts; as a student of communication, investigating its forms and functions. A key to understanding communication practice is to make the connection between real life contexts and real life texts. Two sets of 'real life' experiences are privileged here.

- **Real life contexts**: places and situations in which communication takes place.
- **Real life texts**: the extra, McLuhan would say 'extended', experience we have of communication, both directly and indirectly, as a result of our interaction with texts – films, television, music CDs, virtual reality, various forms of advertising.

Marshall McLuhan (1964) incisively described the mass media as 'an extension of our senses' and it is in this spirit that texts are here engaged. We consider them not as text but rather as repositories of communication data, as stores of communication experience. We consider them not as representations but rather as presentations. In this sense a film like *Titanic* can be used in the same way as a family home video, or as CCTV footage can be used as a means of looking at people in town centres making out or fighting.

Clearly, there is some difference between communication in our lives and communication in media texts. Partly it is a difference between undirected and directed performance. However, the essence of this difference is not easy to identify and, as we shall see in Part 4, a leading account of 'self-presentation' (the processes by which we bring ourselves to the world) suggests that when we communicate we are always staging a 'performance'. The theorist Erving Goffman, whose work is discussed in detail on pages 211–218, expressed it as follows: 'All the world is not, of course, a stage, but the crucial ways in which it is not are not easy to specify' (Goffman 1990).

The stimulus of 'real life' leads you in two directions: to a method that is genuinely investigative and exploratory (which really wants to find something out) and to a content that is found in your life and your experiences. If you are wondering where precisely to look, the following 'lives' might prove useful.

- **Home life**: what do you do when you're home alone; the things you watch and think about and listen to and write; the games you play.
- **Family life**: your immediate home context; your primary group; those people with whom you live and to whom you are connected.
- **Working life**: where you go to do what you have to do; the work you do and the people you do it with.
- **Social life**: where you go to do the things you like to do; the people you like to see; the places you like to go; the things you like to do.

ACTIVITY . . .

Make simple lists of possible investigations into each of the following lives, alongside ours.

continued

Home life

- What are the communication skills needed to use a PC effectively?
- Which communication skills, if any, does playing computer games develop?
- What skills are demonstrated by successful television presenters?
- What is the difference, skillwise, between an effective performance of a song and an ineffective one?

Family life

- How effective are members of your family at listening to one another?
- What techniques does your brother/sister use when avoiding or arranging dates on the phone?
- How could you communicate more effectively with all or any of your family members?

Working life

- Examine the different ways your teachers use questions.
- What communication skills does an effective teacher/student need?
- How does the way in which you speak differ between work and home (both in what you say and in how you say it)?

Social life

- What communication skills do you need to attract potential partners in a crowded nightclub?
- What sorts of communication skill do bands employ between and around performing songs?
- What do you need to become an enthusiastic and committed sports spectator?

TITLES, QUESTIONS AND HYPOTHESES

Having arrived at some kind of focus, the investigation can begin. The AS specification suggests that candidates will 'formulate an appropriate title, question or hypothesis'. It may be as well to hedge your bets and go for all three, given that they can each be potentially used to tighten the focus of the investigation. The title is simply a signpost which tells of the general area of concern, for example 'communication in nightclubs' or 'my mum's phone technique'. The question, in keeping with much of this part's advice, takes this a step further by first asking you what you want or need to know. It then provides an answer in the form of an avenue of enquiry: 'How important are verbal skills in the nightclub context?' or 'Is my mum's telephone technique skilful?' The hypothesis is a step further still in that it asks you to make public your expectations for the investigation and to offer them to be proved either sound or mistaken. A hypothesis is a theory offered in the form of a proposal put forward to be examined for its validity. In the quoted examples, sample hypotheses might be 'verbal communication in nightclubs is almost entirely phatic in function' (it opens channels and maintains them) or 'my mum is a very skilful communicator by phone'.

ACTIVITY . . .

Formulate questions and hypotheses for the following investigations.

- A teacher's questioning skills.
- Skills for interviews.
- Mr Bean's communication problems.
- Listening as a skill for students.
- Computer games and communication skills.

It is important to know why you are working and what you are working towards. This coursework project is concerned with observing communication in practice, so it is vital to know what you are looking for and where you are looking from. Like much of communication practice, the key is good preparation. If you need to observe communication, you need to be prepared to record the available evidence effectively and at the same time be aware of the limitations of any such observation.

OBSERVATION: THEORY AND PRACTICE

Every investigation will be different and each investigation will require its own specific approach. However, there will be general principles that apply across most cases. The first is an ethical issue concerning the obligations you, as a researcher, have to the subject(s) of the investigation. The British Psychological Society has a code of practice which relates to psychological research and which states that 'Psychologists shall normally carry out investigations . . . with the consent of the participants.' It goes on to suggest that participants should have 'adequate knowledge of the nature of the investigation or research'. Even where it is not possible to give full information about the work in advance (for example, where this would interfere with the research), researchers are expected to 'provide such full information retrospectively'. Research into people's communication skills is unlikely to be as sensitive but these are sound principles from which to work.

Working with your subject(s) is a good place to start your plans for observation. Having participants who are at their ease being observed is likely to make the observation more comfortable and thus more successful. Clearly, your methods of observation will be determined by your subjects and context, but all methods have their advantages and disadvantages. We must start by recognising that observers do have an influence on what is observed and then think of ways in which this can be minimised, controlled or taken into account. Here are a number of ways you can improve the quality of your observations.

- **Become a participant in the observed activity**. Participant observation puts you into the thick of the action and allows you to see the demonstration of skills first hand. It also potentially puts the subject at ease in that the observer is not a conspicuous external presence. The disadvantages have to do with the difficulty of trying to observe an activity while taking part in it (this might be helped by recording the activity on video, or minidisc or audio cassette).
- **Allow the subject to site the observer**. 'Where do you want me to sit?' is often a productive starting point. It allows the subject to deal with their own difficulties in their own way (and being observed is always to some extent 'difficult'). This might not allow the best view of the activity but it will help to create a conducive atmosphere.
- **Observe over a long period**. Even if your intensive observation is to be over a short period, an extended attendance at the observed activity will break down barriers. Hopefully you will become a fixture of the situation and thus less of an obstacle.
- **Record your activity**. A recording is a useful prompt to memory rather than something to analyse in itself. A minidisc or Walkman recorder is an unobtrusive way to collect evidence of verbal communication and the sequence of events. Video cameras seem especially intrusive at first, but if left on they tend to 'disappear'. However, it's worth recognising that video cameras only see what is in front of them, so you do get a significantly limited view.

Obviously this is not a problem if you have chosen to analyse behaviour displayed in a film or video, though you are of course watching communication that knows in an obvious way it is being observed. With or without these interventions, the other significant factor in the quality of observation argument is the preparation you make for the kind of evidence you need to collect. An observation will need an observation sheet, a purpose-designed piece of stationery that will help you collect good-quality information. Partly it is a matter of knowing what you are looking for and partly a matter of allowing yourself opportunities to record what's actually going on. What this means in practice is allowing yourself a set of prompts which includes 'other'.

The purpose of the observation sheet is to collect data or evidence on which you can base your research essay or report. It is useful to differentitate between two different types of evidence that might be collected during an observation which are themselves the results of two different kinds of response to the experience of observing. Both are equally valuable.

- **Statistical evidence**: This results from analysing the content of the activity. How many questions were asked? What kinds of questions were asked? How often was eye contact found with members of the audience? How often were the subject's arms folded and unfolded? These are important facts if you hope to come to conclusions which can be proved. As far as any data collected by human beings may be considered to be objective, these will tend to be objective.

- **Critical evidence**: This is the result of considering the meanings and motivations of the observed behaviour. What is the function of eye contact in this context? What is the effect of open questions on this audience? What does folding arms mean in each case? This is the first stage of analysis, which must begin while the subject is still warm. It is a reflection of how it seems to you at the time and is thus honestly subjective.

These two kinds of data should ideally support each other or at least provide a check which will prevent you from drawing bizarre conclusions from what you've actually observed. The feeling you have that your subject finds it difficult to hold or maintain eye contact might be confirmed by a low tally of observed eye contacts. A high tally might similarly confirm your experience that your subject was working hard to engage with audience members individually. The relationship is mutual and therefore provides a double test for any hypothesis; it asks 'Where's the evidence?' twice.

Do not attempt to observe too broadly. The essence of this investigation is 'focus' and your observation should reflect this. Observation sheets should not normally exceed an A4 side. To make this format usable means limiting the number of observation categories or fields. It is important to begin by recording the details of the context of the observation efficiently and then to keep track of the sequence of events. An observation sheet might usefully start with a set of prompts which addresses the key elements of what you're observing ('Who? When? What? Where? How?' are as good as any, together with an implicit 'Why?').

Sample Observation Sheet Header

Subject (who):	Context (where):	Method (how):
Activity (what):	Observer:	Start time: End time:

It may seem tempting to fill the sheet with prompts but it is much better to layer your observation. You might, for example, begin by looking for and at non-verbal elements, then move on to identify linguistic features before finally concentrating on strategies (those rehearsed routines of communication we use on a day-to-day basis). This would allow you to use a sort of scrolling A4 to cover the various stages of an observation. The example on the sheet printed below was used to observe (the interview was conducted over the telephone) the verbal communication of a university teacher, who was acting as an expert for a Communication Studies student's A Level project on 'children and TV violence'.

Subject (who):	Context (where):	Method (how):
Activity (what):	Observer:	Start time: End time:

Content	Comment
Phase:	Start time:
Register/mode of address (how are we being spoken to?):	
Vocabulary (what sorts of words were used?	
Paralanguage (tone, pitch, volume, etc.):	
Phase:	Start time:
Register/mode of address (how are we being spoken to?):	
Vocabulary (what sorts of words were used?):	
Paralanguage (tone, pitch, volume, etc.):	

There is nothing particularly surprising about this sheet, nor should there be. Essentially we are looking to identify the key elements of interpersonal communication and then see what influence they have in particular situations. See how the observation sheet offers a grid for you to work in. The vertical axis is divided into five-minute phases and the horizontal axis is divided into statistical and critical modes (you collect data on the left and you make comments on the right). Perhaps it would be useful to see this sheet after use.

Subject (who): Jane	Context (where): 'Home' (both)	Method (how): Telephone
Activity (what): Expert interview	Observer: Me	**Start time:** 6.30 pm **End time**: 6.45 pm

Content	Comment
Phase: opening	**Start time**: 6.30 pm
Register/mode of address (how are we being spoken to?): friendly, engaging, informal, very relaxed teacher pupil.	Jane was pleased to hear from me and very supportive. The conversation began with pleasantries.
Vocabulary (what sorts of words were used?): Sophisticated and academic. Restricted code in the sense of a technical language (social science). 'Uses/gratifications', 'magic bullet'.	Jane is clearly well-educated and intelligent; her use of language is precise and self-confident (in the same way that she is).
Paralanguage (tone, pitch, volume, etc.): Accent is very 'posh', intonation is musical and pleasant on the ear, there is plenty of variation.	Jane's accent signifies her social class (she is a colonel's daughter). She makes good use of an attractive and flexible vocal range.

This observation sheet can also be used when addressing examples on video or tape/CD. The facility offered by these formats to pause, to slowly advance, and to rewind gives greater scope for detail on the sheet and considered comment. Clearly, a single observation is of little use and any findings will need to be checked by at least one further visit. If a subject is performing in a media text, a second extract from the text would serve this purpose. There is an unwritten rule of proportion in these cases which considers the length of observation alongside the intensity or concentration of the action. Media texts, as conventionalised representations, will work in fairly short extracts, whereas the less precise character of live communication requires significantly longer periods of observation. Real world observations should be limited, except in exceptional cases, to an upper limit of 30 minutes.

If you had decided to observe your teacher to determine if they were a skilled communicator, three 20-minute observations will be of far more use than a single 90-minute marathon. Don't be afraid to bring your previous experience to bear on this or any other case or to imagine your common sense has no role to play. Communication Studies is always reminding you of the importance of context and yours is of utmost importance here. Your investigation begins and ends with yourself: what you know, what you believe, what you have found out. As a student of communication, it is inevitable that you will want to make reference to available theory, either in terms of what you have been taught here or elsewhere, or in terms of further reading and academic research.

The key to using 'theory' is that it must inform your investigation and ultimately understanding of communication in practice. What merits the title 'theory' is after all the result of investigations much like yours and the drawing of conclusions from these. The philosopher and philologist Friedrich Nietzsche claimed 'There are no facts, only interpretations' and this is nowhere more true than in social science research. We can offer only our 'treatment' of material, supported by detailed reference to available evidence and research, which is in itself a treatment based on similar grounds. This is the spirit of investigation – at best it is open and flexible and sure of itself.

WRITING IT ALL UP

When you come to write up your findings, it is likely that you will find 500 words limiting and that you will need to edit down to the required number. Drafting is therefore essential. While there will need to be a degree of formality in the style of this essay, a greater need will be for the writing to have a balance and a shape that reflect both its status as an essay and the priorities of the mark scheme. In the mark scheme for AQA's Unit 1 the key phrases are 'critical, analytical thinking', 'range of appropriate examples', 'focused' and 'conclusion'. This is describing a well-structured piece of writing which gives priority and thus space to a detailed and analytical account of the work undertaken and which draws conclusions from this work. The five-paragraph essay, a format which is detailed on pages 257–259, will likely serve as a blueprint here:

- **Introduction**: State your case and methods briefly; include your working hypothesis. [50 words]
- **Main point 1**: Try to make a point (in this case draw a conclusion from your investigation) and then support it with evidence from your research and reading. [100 words]
- **Main point 2**: As above: quotation from and reference to primary sources is valuable (your actual observations). [100 words]

- **Main point 3 and other comments**: As above, but you've only got 500 words so any other comments will be welcome. [150 words]
- **Conclusion**: Given that the mark scheme refers directly to a conclusion in the three highest mark bands, make sure yours is formal and evident; reflect on your investigation as a whole in terms of its strengths and weaknesses; summarise what you have learned and, by implication, what the audience can learn from this. [100 words]

Given that the assessment objective tested in this task refers to the ability to 'demonstrate knowledge and understanding of key concepts, conventions and theories', your writing style is a secondary issue. It might be best to address the matter of style in terms of efficiency. You need a way of writing that allows you to pack the maximum amount of analysis and comment into 500 words. But you must not lose clarity or comprehensibility. The case study below may help to point the way.

CASE STUDY: BASIL FAWLTY AS THE 'HOTELIER FROM HELL'

My investigation was into the communication skills required by a competent hotelier by examining John Cleese's presentation of 'the hotel manager from Hell' across two series of *Fawlty Towers*. My hypothesis was that servicing the needs of customers depends on appropriate motivation, a strong sense of empathy and active listening: Basil Fawlty proved to have none of these. I watched Fawlty 'live' with an appropriate set of observation sheets, detailing his verbal and non-verbal communication along with his relationships with others. These are my findings. [85 *words to set the scene*]

Birtwhistell (1970) has suggested that some 65 per cent of meaning in dyadic (two-person) communication is carried non-verbally. If this is so, then Basil Fawlty is giving out all the wrong signals. His non-verbal leakage is so 'heavy' as to suggest a kind of communicative incontinence rather than competence. His orientation is often distancing and contemptuous, his paralanguage is dismissive (with an intonation which signifies sarcasm) and aggressive (inappropriate volume and emphasis), and his use of his height and a lack of understanding of Hall's (1959) notion of 'personal space' means guests are too often intimidated. Clearly, his physical appearance is an aspect of this problem but it is aggravated rather than alleviated by his behaviour. [110 *words on my first major point: use of* NVC]

He equally lacks sensitivity in his use of language to guests, rarely finding an appropriate register. He was found to range wildly from the ridiculously self-deprecating and fawning for those he considers his 'betters' (such as the self-styled aristocrat in 'A Touch of Class') to the downright abusive (telling guests to 'Shut up!', even shouting this or at one point ordering all the guests out of the hotel). His language is sophisticated, if a little ostentatious, a wide-reaching elaborated code, which in itself often functions as a barrier to communication.

continued

Guests are more often put off by the torrent of words than engaged by them. [106 *words on my second major point: use of language*]

However, the singular skill that Fawlty most lacks is that of empathy, the ability to see and feel as others do, to put oneself in another's shoes. Fawlty is ill at ease with himself and thus with other people. His attempts at social one-upmanship suggest a fragile self-concept and this is directed against his hapless guests, who are made into 'riff-raff' by his failure to understand himself, a classic case of 'projection'. To genuinely get on with the guests of this modest hotel, Fawlty would need to recognise it as being modest. Without this he will always lack the necessary social skills. [102 *words on my final major point: empathy*]

By deduction it is possible to construct something like a model of the ideal, or at least a potentially successful, hotelier. It would probably start with motivation, having a clear idea that managing a hotel is what you really want to do; this probably outweighs any consideration of skills. Wanting to be effective in itself ought to inform your non-verbal communication and help to promote a positive impression. Given the primacy effect (that first impressions count), this should allow verbal communication a constructive context and further encourage engagement and empathy. Fawlty lacks appropriate motivation (he is concerned only with himself) and, as a result, all the skill he has is pitifully misdirected. [110 *words in conclusion*]

[Total words: 513]

As something clearly written for a purpose, to demonstrate an approach, this 'Basil Fawlty' investigation is a little forced, a little formulaic. It is not a blueprint; rather it is a 'rule of thumb', establishing the nature of the investigation as something that should be more properly called 'Investigation findings'. It demonstrates in a faintly cynical way the essential truth that the marks are available for 'discoveries', understandings and interpretations, and not processes, actions or even interactions. In 'live' investigations this is hopefully a more organic process, and the style and register of the essay will most often reflect the nature of the 'project'. The two examples that follow will hopefully give a flavour of this and represent something of the variety and diversity of work in this excellent unit. All the examples that follow are taken from the work of real students who have submitted the quoted work for assessment in unit CMS1.

Musician Naomi McMaster took her own day-to-day experiences as the prompt for a successful investigation, choosing to make sense of the communication codes employed by her conductor, Tildy Horton. Here the background is clearly significant experience and observation, but the focus of the writing remains the interpretation of the 'behaviour' in the terms of the Communication Studies Specification.

My investigation is into the skilful communication of Sandwell Youth Jazz Orchestra (SYJO) conductor, Tildy Horton, during rehearsals. These are my findings.

My hypothesis is that conducting isn't just a straight set of rules. Although there is an agreed code or 'official language' of conducting, there is more to good conducting than this. There's a kind of in-built sense/feel for the music that makes you better. It's not what you do, it's how you do it: there's almost a paralanguage of conducting.

Tildy's techniques complement the style of jazz in the same way that a classical conductor might enhance classical music. Her hand movements while conducting are not straight and rigid but more relaxed, and often she will just click her fingers to the beat of the music.

Conducting is non-verbal communication by necessity because the music's volume creates a mechanical barrier (it is also improper to talk during a concert). However, Tildy will often use her only physical opportunity to use verbal communication when starting the band. She turns her head to the tempo of the piece making eye contact with various members of the band in accordance to the beat as she says 'a-one a-two a-one two three four'. The volume at which Tildy speaks indicates the type of piece we're playing; for a slow chart she will talk more softly and for an up-beat piece her voice will be louder. Tildy's tone fluctuates in a jovial way as she speaks, making both watching and playing a more enjoyable experience. In fact, much of Tildy's technique is about flouting the rules of classical musical, and thus undermining its stuffiness and seriousness.

Proxemics come into play when we are going through a whole piece of music. Tildy walks around as if trying to determine how we are playing, how we can improve our techniques and how we would come across to an audience. She will then move back to the centre of the band and bring us all 'together' at an appropriate time.

Standing next to someone is seen as a much friendlier position, and suggests closeness and support. Tildy adjusts her orientation to help individuals; standing adjacent to someone communicates that she knows they're genuinely struggling and wants to help them. When she directly faces you and simply points at the sheet music she infers that that you are making a simple mistake.

Eye contact is also important when the band is playing, usually to point out a wrong or 'strange' note. In doing so Tildy does not point out the mistake to the group but to the individual and you know for next time not to make the same mistake again.

Some people may think that a conductor's role in our band is not necessary or as important as it actually is. Having Tildy stand at the front of the band serves a major role in the way we play through our communication. Her indications and directions ensure that the band plays to the best of its ability.

[Total words: 501]

Psychology student Leanne Tomkins took an altogether more removed and extreme stimulus for her investigation, and her response is appropriately intense and academic. The film *Girl Interrupted* is based on a first-hand account of life in an old-fashioned 'asylum' in the 1960s: Angelina Jolie won an Oscar for her portrayal of the psychotic Lisa Rose. For Leanne, though, it is chiefly an opportunity to observe communication in extremis, at the limit.

My investigation is into the communication skills used when manipulating a person's thoughts and consequent actions. I did this by observing Angelina Jolie's role 'Lisa Rose' in *Girl Interrupted*. These are my findings.

How successful a person is at mentally manipulating another person depends on the choice of both verbal and non-verbal forms of communication from appropriate paradigms. The syntagms the person creates with these signs determines the extent to which the person feels manipulated. If the appropriate forms of communication are used the victim will be successfully manipulated. Lisa Rose is very successful in her choice and methods of communication, and consequently manipulates Daisy into hanging herself. This is an extreme version of a common situation and is therefore useful in clarifying the basic rules. Persuasion is about two people and a context, which is emotional and social as well as physical. The psychology of it is to do with the imposition of the will and the exploitation of weakness. Daisy has a fragile self-concept and low self-esteem; Lisa Rose's communication skills do the rest!

Throughout the scene, Lisa glares at Daisy with eyes that burn with hatred. It is obvious from Daisy's body language as she increases the distance between them that this petrifies her and she feels unable to escape it. Proximity is a key indicator of attitude. Lisa's locked intimidating glare makes Daisy very nervous and her limbs twitch showing how uneasy she feels. This immediately puts Lisa in control; she is already manipulating her body language.

Lisa's weak, frail, framework contrasts with the strong, taunting comments that come from deep inside her. She continually taunts Daisy and insinuates accusations of a sexually abusive nature using explicit language. Taboo language both breaks down and reveals a psychological barrier made stronger by conventional social attitudes which see this as unfeminine.

The use of language allows us to talk of abstract concepts such as truth and emotions – i.e. pleasure. In this case using a raised voice in an intimidating manner, Lisa suggests to Daisy that she enjoyed the abuse from her father because she had never known any different. Paralanguage is a flexible set of codes with a prime modifier of modes; here she moves from the aggressive to the sarcastic.

The tempo of Lisa's voice varies throughout the scene. When she shouts at Daisy it is very loud and fast, then this taunting ends with a rhetorical question whereby the silence following the question lets the obvious answer sink deep into Daisy's soul.

> Piece by piece Lisa breaks down any defences Daisy once had from the truth by using carefully developed strategies, and consequently Daisy acts out the self-fulfilling prophecy that Lisa saw for her and that night commits suicide by hanging herself.
>
> [Total words: 458]

The essence of the success of both of these very different investigations is a genuine sense of engagement with their subject matter. This in turn translates into a real engagement with the reader of the 'report' in the form of a desire to share with us what they have discovered or deduced. This is hard to fake, but relatively easy to find given the potential scope of the investigations. An informed and supported free choice is the basis of this unit of work.

MAKING A PRESENTATION

A presentation is a formal talk made to a group of people and usually requires the support of visual aids, such as overhead transparencies (OHTs). For the AS Communication Studies Unit 1, you are expected to give a talk lasting approximately ten minutes, with a question-and-answer (Q&A) phase of up to five minutes. Your presentation will be based on an investigation you have made into some aspect of personal communication skills. This means that most of the information you need to communicate as part of your presentation should have been collected and organised into a written form. In making your presentation, you will need to assimilate this material into a form appropriate to a verbal presentation.

This essay will form part of the basis for the oral presentation, but do not think that this is merely a translation exercise where you squeeze the essay into the presentation. The oral presentation is about the investigation and not the research essay. The key here is *audience*. The essay is written for an examiner; therefore it will be written in a kind of formal written style. The presentation is for your peers – fellow students and learners. Not only will this probably mean you modify your style to go with the modification in form, but also it will mean you modify the content. What is selected for one audience will be very different to that selected for another. Your essay is likely to have little room for the flavour of the observation or the humour whereas in the oral context features such as the character of the observation or humour will be useful ways to alleviate tension and thus making your audience more appreciative of your message.

You should have realised by now that one key to achieving this is organisation. In preparing your presentation it will help if you start by deciding on how you intend to structure it. Begin by making an outline plan of how your presentation will evolve. You are not necessarily bound by this plan – you can go back and change it if you need to. By having such a plan, you will at least have a framework that should enable you to structure your talk so that you can communicate the important information within the ten-minute time limit. The advice on written communication about jotting down the points you want to make and numbering holds good here. Remember too the importance of creating logical links between your points. You should consider carefully how you might control the flow of information to your audience in such a way as to hold their attention throughout.

USING VISUAL AIDS

Many speakers nowadays like to support their presentations with visual aids. A programme such as PowerPoint will allow you to generate high-quality, professional-looking overhead transparencies with quite minimal design skills. Alternatively, it is possible to use a fairly basic word processing package to produce less ambitious OHTs that will still be far more clear than those produced by hand. The danger is that as transparencies become easier to produce, speakers will use them without thinking of what advantage they offer. Another danger is that audiences think that the more effort presenters put into their visual aids, the less effort they will put into the content of their presentation.

In deciding what aids you intend to use, a good starting point is to ask what work you expect the visual aid to do. The content of the presentation must precede the visual aids. Visual aids must aid, they must help, they must assist. At worst visual aids can be a distraction from what you are saying. A good visual aid should be seen as a reinforcement of what you are saying. It is always a good idea to ask yourself 'What work is this visual aid doing?' You should be able to come up with a clear answer to this. If you cannot, then it is probably best not to use the aid at all.

There are a number of pitfalls in using visual aids that are obviously to be avoided. A common mistake that people make is to use visual aids that are too small to be read by the whole audience. If you are using an OHT or a poster, for example, make sure that the smallest point size is at least large enough to be read from all parts of the room. A common reason for using type that is too small is the attempt to get too much information on to a visual aid. This should be avoided at all costs.

Always think carefully about why you are using the aid. Too many presenters seem to think that all they have to do is to read what an OHT says. This is not only pointless, it is insulting to your audience as it may suggest that they cannot read. A good OHT should be a method of reinforcing a point in such a way that it gets the attention of the audience and also helps it stick in their mind.

One particularly effective way of using an OHT is to divide it into sections and mask each of these. As a speaker, you can then reveal the OHT section by section simply by lifting the masking from each. This strategy helps keep the attention of the audience both by avoiding giving it too much information in one go and also by providing some element of suspense as it waits for the next section to be revealed.

Using a programme such as PowerPoint to develop your OHTs also allows you to develop hand-out materials that you can use to support the visual aids. For example, the audience can have a print copy of the transparency to save them the trouble of copying it. At the same time it is possible to provide a space at the side of this for additional notes. Any such attempt to make the work of the audience easier is likely to be well received. If you are going to provide a hand-out at some point in your presentation, you should tell your audience in advance; this will save audience members wasting time taking notes.

Another type of visual aid that you may wish to use is a short video sequence. For example, a short extract from a television soap opera may provide a useful illustration of a particular point you are making. A well-chosen clip used appropriately can have a telling impact on your audience. Again, however, don't allow the visual aid to become a distraction. Leaving the television set switched on when nothing is playing is almost guaranteed to distract an audience. Some people are so conditioned to television that they will watch white noise on the screen rather than listen to a live speaker. So be prepared to switch on the television only at the point when you intend to introduce the clip into your presentation and switch it off again immediately afterwards. Obviously it is a good idea to make sure in advance that the video you intend to use is cued up and that the equipment will function at the push of the appropriate button. Better still, get someone who is familiar with the equipment to help you.

It is always a good idea to practise your presentation before you actually deliver it. You can do this in front of a friend or family member if they are willing to help and you feel confident. Otherwise you can simply use a mirror as your 'audience'. This practice session will help you to identify any problems that you may encounter and allow you to address them before your actual performance. A common difficulty is mistiming your presentation. Make sure that your practice run-through is at the same pace as you intend to deliver your presentation and use a stop-watch to time it. If necessary you can then adjust your timing accordingly. Make sure that you are fluent in your presentation. If there are any sections where you find yourself faltering, try to find out what is causing this. It may be that simply changing some of the words on a cue card will cure the problem. Finally ensure that your delivery is going to be clear and confident while remaining sensitive to the needs of your audience.

You will often hear it said that a good presentation has a beginning, a middle and an end. Similarly, advice on public speaking is often given in the form of 'stand up, speak up and shut up'. Often too little attention is paid to the way in which you should 'shut up'. It is important that you signal the end of your presentation. Otherwise the audience may be left in doubt as to what is happening if you simply allow it to drift to a close. One way in which to close is to announce that you have finished and are now happy to answer any questions. This approach also has the benefit of making it clear to the audience that they now have a role to perform.

The Q&A phase of a presentation is a chance for you to impress with your knowledge and grasp of your chosen topic. It is important, however, that you see this phase as an extension of your presentation; that means that you must stay in control of this phase of the presentation at all times. You must learn to control any discussion through yourself, rather than allowing members of the audience to discuss issues between themselves.

You can help make sure that you remain in control by using your position at the front of the group to control the proceedings. Make sure that it is *you* who decides who will ask the question by making it clear who you want to speak next. Ask people to raise their hand if they wish to ask a question. If several people do so at the same time, indicate the order in which you want them to speak.

When someone asks a question, give yourself time to respond properly. Don't just say the first thing that comes into your head. Try to frame a considered response that will answer the question fully. At the same time look for the opportunity to develop the point further by steering it towards an issue that you feel confident about or would have liked to have developed in your presentation.

There are several strategies you can use to give yourself time to think when you have been asked a question. A stock phrase such as 'Well, that is an interesting question' is a useful tactic to employ. Another method of playing for time is to repeat the question back with some slight rephrasing. You can say: 'So the question you are asking is . . .' Summarising the question is also an effective way of checking you've understood the question asked of you.

Usually there is a time limit on the Q&A phase of a presentation. One test of your skill in maintaining control is how well you bring the phase to its conclusion. Keep an eye on the clock. In the heat and excitement of debate, it is easy to lose track of time. In good time indicate that questions will have to come to an end. For example, you may indicate that there is time for just two more questions. At the same time you can identify who the questioners will be. In this way you can bring your presentation to an orderly conclusion.

Finally at the end of your presentation, make sure you put all your notes and visual aids back together in a logical and organised fashion. This way you will have them ready for the next time you give the presentation as well as being available for assessment, if this is required as part of your course.

TURNING THEORY INTO PRACTICE: PREPARING FOR A COMMUNICATION ORAL PRESENTATION

This oral presentation requires you to invite an audience and rewards you for your necessary preparation and visual aids. Both of these dimensions need a mature response. The oral presentation is a practical examination, an assessed performance. You must select people in front of whom you are happy to perform. You simply can't afford to be shy in this context so don't invite those audience members who will make you shy (or in front of whom you will be too 'cool' to perform). Similarly, this is a Communication Studies examination in which you will need to be asked intelligent questions. There is no room for sentiment, for an 'I'll be in your presentation if you'll be in my presentation' approach. Choose those who can, not those you fancy.

In terms of rewarding preparation, there is again a need for an awareness of context; this is real but it is also academic. It may well be true that many excellent presentations have been done without recourse to either notes or visual aids, and that many presentational catastrophes are accompanied by a sheaf of notes and impeccable OHTs. This is not the point; marks cannot be given for the quality of nothing. Put simply, you are actually being asked to prepare notes for a talk with visual aids.

Preparation, then, is likely to be a place where you turn the 'theory' of the report into the practice of the oral presentation by working through issues which are central to Communication Studies such as audience, channel, status of sender, negotiation and barriers. You will perhaps notice that the coursework is making some key links here with other elements that you will have met on the course. There is a simple but important step from analysing texts to creating them.

WHAT DO YOU MEAN BY PREPARATION?

In order to score good marks you need to show what you have done by way of preparation. Put simply, the key components are:

- a running order/simple script
- room plans and layouts
- a commentary in which you justify the decisions you have made
- a set of appropriately chosen visual aids
- materials made especially to aid the efficient presentation of your material (cue cards, formal notes and so on).

Good preparation should result in a good presentation. Don't see it as an end in itself. How much detail you decide to include in your preparatory materials will vary according to the content of your talk. Don't forget that the main purpose of your preparation is to help you make an effective preparation. A sound preparation is all about structure, knowledge and confidence. Good preparatory materials can give you practical help in ensuring you achieve these qualities in your presentation. A simple running order, for example, is an invaluable aid to shaping a presentation. Here, Jenna Rushton is planning to deliver her verdict on *Trainspotting*'s Begbie (the Robert Carlyle character in the film) and his attempts to 'do' the message 'masculine'.

Running order

- **Introduction**
  'Good afternoon . . . '

  OHP 1: *Question 'How does Begbie's NVC attempt to display Masculinity?'*
- Investigation
  Original thoughts.
  Why Begbie?

  OHP 2: *Begbie's character.*
- Definitions
  Explain difference.

  OHP 3: *Definitions of 'Masculine' and 'Macho'.*
- Hypothesis
  What I hope to find.

  OHP 4: *Break down hypothesis.*
- Explanation of three scenes.

- What I was observing in NVC.
- Birdwhistell
  Quote explained.

Video Clip 1
> **OHP 5:** *Explanation of* NVC *– emphasis on orientation leading into his initial seating position and what he holds.*
- Props
  Connotations of each prop: Beer glass, cigarettes, seating position.

Video Clip 2
> Explanation of leakage – emphasis on paragraph 3, 'His eyes are constantly glancing' (leakage).

Video Clip 3
> Instant reactions. Demonstrate by knocking something off table. Audience will look. Proves point of leakage and also that Begbie intends no harm, as he doesn't look over balcony.
> Expand on paragraph 4.
- Accent
  Last clip, hard to understand dialogue, translate.
  Expand on pitch, speed tone, language use, etc.
  Role-play with model?
- Conclusions

OHP 6: *Picture of Begbie.*

This is an effective single-side A4 summary of the whole talk which identifies the natural breaks in the material, the need for regular visual aids to maintain interest and the significant stages of the 'narrative' or argument. It also signals in a more subtle way the importance of using a subject-specific vocabulary appropriate for addressing Communication Studies issues.

This running order should be all you need to give a detailed, specialist presentation. It is rarely a good idea to write out a verbatim script. However, many presenters will seek a half-way house, whether this be in a detailed set of notes or cue cards, which are in effect notes reprocessed as a smart, but small, deck of prompt cards. Jenna chose the latter and it might be useful to see the degree to which she found extra support useful. For example, here are her running order prompts.

- Explanation of three scenes.
- What I was observing in NVC.
- Birdwhistell
  Quote explained.

Video Clip 1
> **OHP 5:** *Explanation of* NVC *– emphasis on orientation leading into his initial seating position and what he holds.*

This became a set of cue cards with the following support.

■ What I was observing in NVC.

NVC stands for non-verbal communication. This is carried in forms of body language such as eye contact, which is phatic and it opens up channels for other communication.

Facial expressions – the smile/laugh/frown.

Also orientation. Seating and standing positions.

Proxemics. Hall's notion of personal space.

Open or closed. Arms folded, or casual.

Hands used for emphasis while voice is engaged.

■ Birdwhistell

He said, '65% of social meaning in communication is carried non-verbally.'

This is apparent through Begbie. All of us are communicating non-verbally right now, through stance, seating positions and facial expressions. Body language is our biggest give away, yet is important when communicating.

Video Clip 1

Point out his seating position. Sits central – attempt to be centre of attention.

Tells story, relives events with body movements

Breached chest – attempt to look masculine, fearless and intimidating.

Square up. Intimidation. Invasion of personal space.

Hands for emphasis to accompany tone of voice.

Higher pitch, quick speaking. Accent hard to understand.

Example. 'Come on then, if you think you are hard enough.'

Face – eyebrows, wide eyes, high pitch, chest and shoulders breached.

Cue cards have the added advantage of also functioning as a sort of primitive clock, laying an elegant paper trail from the beginning to the end of the presentation. This physically reinforces the good practice of always knowing where you are, where you've been and where you're going – something that confident speakers often share with their audiences. Once a card has been used it can be returned to its place, or joyfully discarded, and you are one step closer to the end! The only real danger is to confuse the functions of cards with the functions of scripts: cue cards 'cue'; they are prompts, not theatrical 'prompters' which feed you line by line the play you have forgotten. For ten minutes, ten cards is probably excessive so if you prepare over a hundred, like one student, you can only expect to be turned into an anecdote: his first two cards read HELLO and MY NAME IS . . . (but that would be telling).

The other natural clock is the sequence of visual aids with which you will use to brighten up your presentation and through which you will try to illustrate and develop your arguments. These may range from spectacular multi-media PowerPoint presentations to hand-drawn communication models, from cleverly edited video clips to live action role-play demonstrations. Their primary function, however, is crude and simple. They serve, if successful (or spectacularly unsuccessful), to divert attention from the primary text (you) to a series of secondary texts and give you a welcome break from the heat of the persistent eye contact of your audience.

Doing this may merely involve titling, marking out the boundaries of the presentation by revealing its structure. Rajiv Nath's tenth slide has style, impact and humour but it is still only a sub-title, albeit a very effective one.

Figure 2.4 *Comparisons between Anne Robinson and a pedagogical* figure*

* Technically, of course, the comparison is with an andragogical figure since the teacher is teaching adults.

Usefulness and effectiveness are again the chief criteria rather than sophistication. Successful visual aids visualise and prioritise key information in with impact and in a memorable way (in the context of a ten-minute talk!). Here the Begbie dilemma gets a simple but useful reinforcement.

My hypothesis is that in trying to perform the idea or construction 'masculine'

Begbie merely manages the rather limited ideological version 'macho'.

Figure 2.5   *Visual presentation slide – Begbie*

In a similar way considering your room layouts as a series of diagrams – one could call them 'models' – may allow you to better identify the issues. David Dean chose the following layout for his presentation on the effects of the gender of the receiver on skilful communication. The plan is crude and colourful but very useful for identifying problems both before and after the presentation. Here, for example, the audience is an issue, beyond the simple logistical problem of making sure it can see everything.

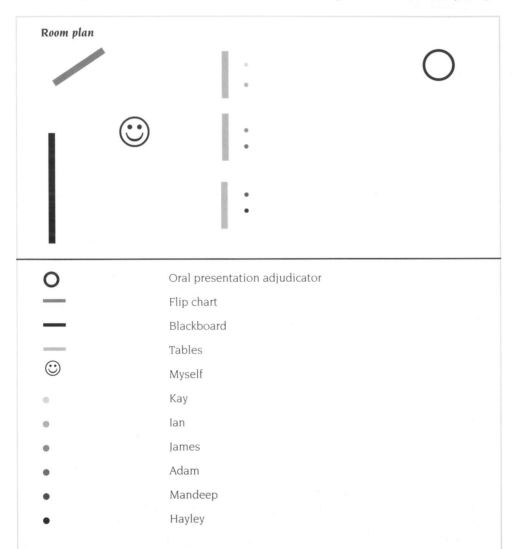

Room plan

O	Oral presentation adjudicator
—	Flip chart
▬	Blackboard
—	Tables
☺	Myself
•	Kay
•	Ian
•	James
•	Adam
•	Mandeep
•	Hayley

I chose this plan because I found it was the most accommodating. Everyone in the audience can see both the flip chart and the blackboard. I have room at the front to move, talk and take volunteers. And I'm not too close to the audience to seem intimidating and not too far away to seem rude.

Diagram 2.3 *Oral presentation plan*

The room plan is, in this way, an integral part of what is sometimes called the 'Preparation essay' or 'Commentary', a sort of thought-diary of evaluative decision-making, which is the best way to ensure you get good marks for preparation. Again there is no specified format for this, though a question-and-answer approach is one of the better options along the lines of that used by Satdip Kaur for her presentation below on David Beckham's self-presentation skills.

WHO HAVE I INVITED, WHY AND WHAT ARE THEIR NEEDS AS AN AUDIENCE?

I have invited Inderjit, Jasmina, Randip and Laura to my presentation. The main reason why I have invited this audience is because all of them are Communication students and so will be able to understand the technical terms that will be used and they will be able to ask me relevant questions. Also I feel confident standing up in front of them, as I know them well. Inderjit, Jasmina and Laura are all in my Communication class, and when we have group discussions I can convey my thoughts and opinions easily in front of them. Randip is my sister and I will be able to talk in front of her as I talk to her every day of my life.

Significantly, all of my audience have different opinions about David Beckham. Hopefully by having a varied audience I will be able to retrieve different views of the presentation as a whole and different types of questions will be asked. Inderjit, Jasmina and Randip all dislike David Beckham, whereas Laura likes him.

The presentation itself won't last too long so the audience won't get bored, but there will be a video clip to show my findings, and the presentation will become more interesting than if it were just continuous talk. My presentation will be presented on Microsoft PowerPoint, which will use pictures relevant to my coursework.

A set of relevant questions can invite that thinking aloud which is often the prelude to making sound decisions. It is an exercise in visualising the ideal presentation and then interrogating yourself so that you identify the key elements of this ideal performance. The following prompts might function as a reasonable starting point.

- Who will you invite and why?
- What are the dynamics of the group you have just formed (your audience)?
- How will you address them (register, mode-of-address)?
- What do you want them (privately) to say about your presentation? Choose five adjectives (beyond 'superb' and 'fantastic').
- What are the aims of your presentation?
- How will you achieve them?
- How will you arrange the room?
- What equipment will you need?

REVIEWING YOUR PERFORMANCE

Finally you are asked to review your presentation and investigation in the light of your performance as a communicator. This is an important stage educationally and, as a bonus, you are given a 30 mark incentive to do it. Essentially the review asks: 'What can you, as a student of communication as a skill, say usefully about your own skill as a communicator in the context of a ten-minute oral presentation?' Remember, the focus of the review should be the presentation itself. This brings the reviewer to the next stage of evaluative decision-making, the simple test to see whether the preparation decisions were really the right ones. Did the room work? Was the style appropriate? How good was the audience?

However, central to the process still is the question: 'What have you learned about communication skills/skilful communication?'

Five hundred words in five paragraphs would plan out like this.

- **Introduction:** Opening comments reflecting overall success/failure of presentation. [around 50 words]
- **Review of personal performance:** What worked and what did not; assessment of the significant barriers and attempts to overcome them. [around 100 words]
- **Review of stylistic decisions:** How fluent was your presentation? Did you get your message across? [around 100 words]
- **Review of paraphernalia:** How useful were the materials? How responsive was the audience? How did the questioning go? [around 100 words]
- **Conclusion:** What would you have changed? What have you learned about communication? What would you do next? [around 150 words]

The case study below helps to illustrate how to do this,

CASE STUDY: REVIEW OF BASIL FAWLTY PRESENTATION

I adopted an 'all or nothing' approach to my oral presentation and got in return a bit of both: at best I received laughter and understanding, and at worst an embarrassed bewilderment. My decision to do the oral as Fawlty, complete with stick-on moustache and domed forehead, proved at least uncontroversially to be the most significant decision I made. [59 *words to set the scene*]

    At some level the disguise certainly helped me to start: it had an effectively phatic function, engaging the audience even before informing them. This offered a considerable psychological boost to me, though this was too quickly followed by anxiety as I slowly realised how difficult it was going to be to keep this act up for ten minutes. As a result I was soon compromising my original plan and using the Fawlty paralanguage only when I was demonstrating a point. [80 *words of heartfelt personal response*]

I guess that what I was discovering word by word and line by line was the real difference between theory and practice. In my preparation commentary I had addressed the question 'What style of talk will you deliver?' and had conducted a decent discussion involving factors such as formality, technicality and 'humour'. This proved to be much easier in theory than practice, and I did feel some jarring between the quite technical analysis of Fawlty's behaviour and my desire to keep it motivated and 'light'. In fact, there was a sense in which I'd missed the point and that the only way to really 'compete' with what was essentially a densely written script would have been to have worked from a densely written script. The point is that life, unscripted, does not make such demands. [135 *words on the 'text'*]

Obviously the 'real' Basil Fawlty was a considerable ally and I was able to project a short segment onto a screen about halfway through when they were beginning to flag. The presentation itself was greatly helped by the audience's familiarity with the material and love of it. However, this in itself was a kind of barrier since it ruled out a genuinely critical response. In fact, looking back the impact of the clip was a mixed blessing, for it interrupted the flow of the presentation and I never really got that momentum back. At worst it could be said that 'post-clip' I was merely winding down to the questioning phase, which thankfully produced some good questions and was genuinely engaged and surprisingly enjoyable. This, at least, confirmed that I'd chosen my audience well. [133 *words on doing the oral presentation*]

As this review implies, I have learned both general and specific things. The general lessons have been largely to do with organisation, or sometimes the lack of it. More specifically I have greatly benefited from seeing communication theory evidenced in practice. In a sense my study of Fawlty emphasised the dangers of taking basic communication skills too lightly. In being asked to practise what I had otherwise analysed, I have learnt much about the precarious nature of most interpersonal communication and of the need to 'improve the odds' by careful preparation. To an extent this is also the message of Goffman's so-called 'dramaturgical' model, where elements such as 'role' and 'teams' and 'setting' combine to produce those 'performances' which constitute our social lives. At the core, as Goffman suggests, is self-presentation and this is something that I was painfully aware of throughout my partly cynical, partly sincere, performance. [149 *words on what has been learned*]

[Total: 511 words of review]

Bibliography

Goffman, E. (1990) *The Presentation of the Self in Everyday Life*, Harmondsworth: Penguin.

The paradigm of performance with its tendencies towards cynicism and sincerity is also a useful context in which to site your review, which must find its place with an eye to both theory and practice. Honesty about what occurred is a prerequisite; it is not an exercise in recreating a better presentation than you actually did! Conversely, there is much evidence to suggest that problematic presentations prompt the better reviews (or at least the easier!). Beyond being as hard as you can with yourself, which often gives your writing a cathartic energy, it is also useful to see your experiences as a case study and think what might be learned by yourself and ultimately the reader. This is partly about letting the piece have its own momentum and partly about letting it find its voice. Good reviews, like good investigations, vary greatly. As such they cannot easily be faked. To mark out some of the ground it might be useful to consider reviews of very different qualities of presentation.

Rachel Neate's presentation had an easy confidence and progressed very much as she would have liked. Dealing with those communication skills necessary for a 'normal life' by considering novelist Iris Murdoch's battle with Alzheimer's Disease in the film *Iris*, Rachel used sharply edited clips to punctuate her presentation. Her register expertly negotiated the sensitivity of much of the material and created an excellent context for discussion and debate. The problem of the review then is how to be pleased for 500 words.

I feel that overall the presentation that I delivered went extremely smoothly. The feedback that I have received was very positive, and so suggests that my audience are in agreement with me. Throughout my performance I was relaxed and I got the impression that my audience were at ease with the situation. Most of this feedback was non-verbal, 'given off' as Abercrombie would say as well as 'given': 'leaked' as well as meant.

Nevertheless, there were certain aspects of my presentation that didn't go entirely to plan. I had envisaged myself being seated throughout. However, this was not so. The flip chart that was made available was rather large. This made me work a little harder and added an unintended extra rhythm to the presentation. It also perhaps made the presentation more personal/natural. I had to alter my original room plan to accommodate the practicalities of the visual aids. An extra table was added, which also prevented me from remaining in my seat throughout. One factor that some people may have viewed as a problem, but I viewed as an advantage under the circumstances, was that my room was quite dimly lit. All natural light had to be banished, because I was going to project my video images onto the wall, and the only significant artificial light present came from the corridor outside. However, everything that needed to be seen (video clips, visual aids, myself) could be viewed clearly. I felt that the lack of brightness enabled me to break down many barriers that were inevitably going to exist between the audience and myself. My audience were comfortable in the room and seemed to be relaxed by the tranquillity of the whole environment. I found that the absence of the harsh lighting appeared to dispel some of the pressure and make the entire experience far less daunting. Goffman stresses the importance of 'setting' in self-presentation.

I was extremely content with my choice of visual aids. The flip chart allowed me to explain important points to my audience. Their reaction showed that they understood my points, and the flip chart did hold their attention and engage their thoughts in a way that I knew OHP sheets never could. My interaction with the flip chart prompted me to elaborate and clarify certain points. My video clips also worked well, and I felt that they were the correct length. They were long enough to be easily digested, but not so long that the intended message was lost. My audience responded well to the running order. The informal style that I opted for was the correct choice and I think that the way I varied my use of the video clips and flip chart helped to keep my audience focused and interested.

For the questioning phase of my presentation I sat down, as this is the style that I had initially opted for. Being seated made me less imposing, and because I was at their level I thought that the audience would find it easier to offer their questions. During the question-and-answer session the atmosphere was relaxed, and I answered all questions as thoroughly and detailed as I could manage. Overall I feel that I was triumphant in my endeavour to deliver a worthwhile, thought-provoking presentation.

[Total: 547 words]

David Clayton's problem is the reverse. Having completed an objectively disastrous presentation, which lasted a mere 6 minutes and included a lengthy film clip, he needed to salvage the portfolio through the review. His investigation was into the skills of seduction as evidenced by the Ryan Phillippe character in the film *Cruel Intentions*: his presentation to an all-male audience degenerated into a social event. As a review what follows is probably better than Rachel's incredibly literate survey on pages 86–87, but it would be interesting to speculate whether David simply has more to get his teeth into.

My presentation on seduction did not go according to plan. I prepared my visual aids, room layout and order of speech so I could stand up and feel confident that I knew what I wanted to say and the way I wished to say it. I also carefully selected my audience so that I felt relaxed, not embarrassed, talking about such a potentially embarrassing subject. The deliberate decisions I made unfortunately did not pay off. I felt rushed, unsure and very alone. As I began my talk I wanted my audience to feel as relaxed as possible, hoping that their comfort would ease my nerves, allowing me to conduct a better presentation. The informal register I used did little to help the mood of my audience. With this, I paid more attention to how I was coming across to my friends, instead of focusing on the theory of my presentation, and was desperate to use the video clip to give myself a breather and gather myself (hoping for an improved performance in the second half).

continued

The arrangement of the room was easy; my audience and I were both sat on tables in a normal, casual, everyday manner. All of us were at equal eye level; therefore nobody was superior. However, my proximity was wrong. I was closer to the audience than I would have preferred being, which added further pressure. The atmosphere the layout created was natural, but my task was not a natural one; it replicated sitting in a pub, where you do not stand up for 10 minutes and talk about how a male movie star uses his good looks to attract girls. A formal atmosphere would have been much more enabling for me, as I could have talked more formally and as a result talked more. Formality works as a brake; without it the presentation simply ran away.

Among my problems was my inability to use carefully prepared visual aids merely because my audience did not seem initially engaged. I suffered from a classic case of role conflict: who I was meant to be in the oral clashed with who I wanted to be for my friends. I intended to give each member of my audience their own hypothesis as I felt it would be more beneficial for them to have something 'to hold', instead of simply being given visual after visual. This was the crux of my presentation. However, when I showed them the clip of Phillippe 'in action', to give them an introduction to him while backing up my analysis of him, it seemed like a film trailer. The clip ran too long and had no semantic purchase.

I do not believe I gave my audience enough theoretical information; I did not make reference to paralanguage, vocabulary levels of signification – all of which are important characteristics in seduction. The audience were my 'laddish' mates, who fall into the 'sporty/lad' sub-cultural group. Because of their expectations I was not allowed to display my knowledge, to perform artistically or show off what I'd found. Their NVC (slouching, smirking and bouncing a football) had an effect on my NVC and enthusiasm. I assumed from their NVC that they embodied psychological barriers and were unwilling to listen or take my presentation seriously. Whether true or not, this created a psychological barrier. I felt I had to 'match up' with them and began to direct a lack of enthusiasm through my NVC.

[Total: 570 words]

And so the 'oral from hell' becomes an engaged and fluent triumph in a way that the presentation never was.

Hopefully these authentic examples of coursework will give you a better understanding of the character and level of Communications AS practical work. Special thanks must go to the students of the Rowley Regis Centre of Dudley College and to their teachers – Andrew Hickman, Nigel Ward and Cara Wheatley.

FURTHER READING

Allen, R. E. (1990) *Oxford Writers' Dictionary*, Oxford: Oxford University Press.

Barrass, R. (1984) *Study! A Guide to Effective Study, Revision and Examination Techniques*, London: Chapman & Hall.

Carey, G. V. (1971) *Mind the Stop*, Harmondsworth: Penguin.

Chambers, E. and Northedge, A. (1997) *The Arts Good Study Guide*, Milton Keynes: Open University Press.

Drew, S. and Binham, R. (1997) *The Student Skills Guide*, Aldershot: Gower.

Fowler, H. W. (1998) *The New Fowler's Modern English Usage*. Oxford: Oxford University Press.

Fry, R. (1997) *How to Study*, London: Kogan Page.

Gowers, E. (1987) *The Complete Plain Words*, 3rd edn, Harmondsworth: Penguin.

Orwell, G. (2000) 'Politics and the English Language', in *Essays*, Harmondsworth: Penguin.

Partridge, E. (1999) *Usage and Abusage*, Harmondsworth: Penguin.

Roget, P. (2000) *Roget's Thesaurus of English Words and Phrases*, ed. B. Kirkpatrick, Harmondsworth: Penguin.

PART 3: TEXTS AND MEANINGS IN COMMUNICATION

In this part of the book we will deal with the ways in which communication texts generate meanings.

- We will define, identify and undertake practical work on communication texts.
- We will introduce two useful approaches to the study of text – the semiotic approach and the process approach.
- We will explore these approaches practically and in some detail to provide you with an analytical toolkit.
- We will address the limitations and the strengths of both the semiotic and the process approaches.

▼ 1 TEXTS AND MEANINGS

In this section we will begin to look at how communication texts work.

- ■ We will introduce key concepts such as representation, genre and convention.
- ■ We will consider the potential of certain texts to have multiple meanings, while other texts are deliberately more focused.
- ■ We will explore the different kinds of readings which texts might encourage or allow.

'WHERE DO I BEGIN AND WHAT SHOULD I PRESUME?'

Having established what a communication text is (see pages 5–12), it seems appropriate to address what they do, how they are constructed and, most importantly, how we respond to them. We might usefully start simply by looking carefully at what is in front of us, or in certain contexts, by listening carefully or by paying particular attention to the material used. This is what this section will help you with. It will, within a limited technical vocabulary, offer you ways of approaching texts for the first time.

Let's have a look at the advertisement on page 93.

Our primary concerns are to describe what is there, what is represented in, on and by this particular text. What the text clearly does is to give physical form to a message, a meaning, a set of ideas. These ideas have been conceived in the form of this text: having presented themselves to the author(s), they are being re-presented to us (i.e. presented again, for a second time).

KEY TERM

REPRESENTATION Usefully defined by O'Sullivan *et al.* in their important book *Key Concepts in Communication and Cultural Studies* (1994) as 'the process of putting into concrete forms . . . an abstract ideological concept'. Thus communication texts must be addressed in terms of their representations and the degree to which these leave room for the reader to explore meanings.

For your *FREE* game, *FREE* delivery* and money saving opportunity, subscribe to *PC FORMAT*

PC FORMAT

*Free in the UK

Figure 3.1   PC Format postcard. Courtesy of PC Format

In this case what is represented are four women and four 'props': some spectacles, a video camera, a brain in a bubbling jar, and a mini-computer, complete with mouse. The women are all looking out, in different ways, towards the reader/receiver/camera – in this case, us. They are surrounded by a sort of white light which crudely highlights them and binds them together against a polished black background which carries a logo 'PC FORMAT' and some indication of what it is we are looking at – a promotional card for a computer magazine. The women seem superficially to be different but there are obvious ways in which these representations of women, because that's what they are, are alike.

ACTIVITY . . .

List the similarities and differences between these representations of women. These may be to do with their physical appearance, the way in which they are photographed, their costumes or simply their presentation on this page.

You may find that these representations of women fit into a broader social 'model' of how women are usually represented and thus perceived. You may decide that with their consciously styled appearance, their careful make-up and their almost seductive glances, they conform to a stereotype of women often used in the media.

STEREOTYPE A stereotype is a mould into which reality is poured, whatever its individual shape. A stereotype is a simplified and generalised image of a group of people, which is created out of the values, judgements and assumptions of its creators, in most cases society itself. A stereotype of women might suggest their motherliness or, in this case, their function as decorative aesthetic objects to be appreciated for their beauty and allure.

More importantly you may begin to ask yourself: What are the connections between four attractive young women and a personal computing magazine? This can be addressed in at least two ways – logically (by systematically identifying in detail what is there) and imaginatively (by imagining what kind of story the text is telling).

In 1970 the American Communication theorist George Gerbner suggested that in order to establish the potential meaning of any piece of media content or output it is useful to consider the following aspects.

- **Existence**: what is there.
- **Priorities**: what is important.
- **Values**: what is valued.
- **Relationships**: what is related to what else.

Subjecting PC *Format*'s postcard to this formula quickly produces results, which could be represented in this way.

- **Existence**: four 'girls', four props, a black background, words.
- **Priorities**: their glamour, their beauty, the aesthetic dimensions.
- **Values**: the glamour of the girls is an index of the magazine's values.
- **Relationships**: the advertisement is designed to appeal to our sense of ourselves in terms of our status, our intelligence, our sex appeal.

CONTENT ANALYSIS Gerbner's formula arose out of work he was doing on the content of American television. For example, Gerbner looked at violent acts and suggested that an average week produced 400 victims of violence. This is a statistical approach to analysis, which is useful for establishing trends within media output (e.g. the roles women have in television advertising compared to those of men).

In this case, the logical approach is a little longwinded because the message, though potentially patronising (not to say sexist), is easy to understand. We know where this text is coming from and to whom it is speaking. The imaginative approach to textual analysis would suggest that we engage with the form, style and content in an unaffected and open way, but even this gives little significant extra information. What we know about this text is heavily dependent on the way it functions within the conventions of a genre.

GENRE This term describes the subdivisions of the output of a given medium (e.g. television, film, in this case magazine publishing). A genre is a type, a particular version of a communication medium. For example, soap opera is a television genre, for it represents a particular approach to theme, style and form.

ACTIVITY . . .

Consider the different genres of magazine available in your local newsagent. Identify three significant genres of currently available magazines and list their apparent characteristics. Select one genre, which might usefully be 'computer games magazines', and devise an A4 cover mock-up for a new addition to this genre.

Selecting examples from the genre of 'computer games magazines' makes the story of our original much clearer. What we are seeing from looking more widely at the genre of the text is the degree to which the production of any text is guided by particular ways of presenting and representing reality. The example that follows confirms that our original text contains a compilation of images which almost certainly featured on the magazine's cover at some point. In essence the text is delivering exactly what its readers expect – a predictable collection of reviews, previews and advice presented in an exciting and visually glamorous fashion.

CONVENTION Where people agree to follow guidelines in the practice of communication. These guidelines may be stated or unstated, explicit or implied. To represent 'real life', a communication medium is necessary. For the communication medium to make sense, it must be ordered by conventions. In the case of a magazine cover, conventions of illustration, typography, colour and content are used.

Concluding that our original text is highly conventional is not to deny other interpretations but rather to identify the most likely intention of the piece. In terms of the possible things the text could say, one stands out as most likely, as most desired by the text itself. The conversation a text offers is called a discourse. This is

Figure 3.2 *Cover of PC Format, July 1998. Courtesy of PC Format*

conventionally referred to as the 'dominant discourse'. Julian MacDougall (2000) explains it like this: 'What the text tries to do is offer a winner – a discourse that is privileged over others.'

The dominant discourse of the PC *Format* text privileges a context in which the audience is assumed to be young, heterosexual men who will easily make connections between slick, fast women and slick, fast machines. It is not necessary to be a feminist to find this depressingly immature but it is important to understand that any such response goes against the grain of the semantics of this text.

SEMANTICS The study of the relationship between signs and meanings.

The conventions of a particular format are often most apparent when that format is subjected to criticism and especially via parody or pastiche. When a young female reader of PC *Format* wrote in to complain about 'scantily clad females canoodling about new PCs' and suggested that perhaps one of the male reviewers should appear instead, the magazine mocked up a version of a cover which featured a young Scottish reviewer (see Figure 3.3). This self-parody successfully apes the conventions of the format but only goes some way to understanding the issues of representation.

It's not amusing; it's chilling. In a few years, once Colin has graduated from Butcher School and wrestled the Editorship from Dave Bradley, this is what *PCF* will look like.

Figure 3.3 PC Format, no. 84, July 1998, p. 200. Courtesy of PC Format

Compare and contrast the two covers (Figures 3.2 and 3.3) with those featured earlier in this section. List the similarities and differences, and consider the reasons why the role-reversal did not produce exactly the same results.

Clearly, all readings of these texts are being made in relation to the dominant discourse; even if we reject it out of hand, we can't ignore it. These are classic examples of what Umberto Eco (1979) has called *closed texts*, texts in which one reading is significantly privileged. Other readings can be offered but they do not enhance the experience of the text, rather they are likely to frustrate readers and/or lead them to reject the text. *Open texts*, by comparison, are those in which individual readings are not significantly 'preferred' and in which the potential polysemy of the text is emphasised, even celebrated.

KEY TERM

POLYSEMY/POLYSEMIC Refers to the capacity of a text or part of a text to be read in several different ways. For example, a red rose might communicate love, a fondness for horticulture, a political allegiance or Lancashire.

The image on page 99 was originally a painting by Edvard Munch. It, like many of the texts in this part, represents a woman but, unlike most of what we've observed, it is very much open to interpretation. Here the imposed discipline of Gerbner's formula (Gerbner 1970) might produce useful results, by asking key questions about what it is we are seeing. Some degree of emotional and imaginative engagement might also add to our understanding and response. Here is a text that demands a reading. This is not a criticism of those rather transparent mass media texts we looked at earlier; it is simply a reminder of the range of communication texts. This text has a very different function and context. Munch's painting, which he called *The Scream*, is clearly a communication text, albeit a sophisticated one, which employs artistic conventions to represent a particular kind of reality.

Use Gerbner's formula to respond logically/systematically to Munch's text. Briefly add your own personal response to this text. What do you feel and think about it?

Figure 3.4 *Edvard Munch, The Scream, 1893. Photo: J. Lathion*
© *Nasjonalgalleriet, Oslo, 1999*

It is difficult to talk in this context about 'dominant discourse' because beyond the
interpretative title, which sort of tells you what is going on, there are few clear clues.
This text is open in the way that most mass media texts are not; it has no clear editorial
position. This text has alternative readings but it would be difficult to categorise or
even explain them in the way that Stuart Hall, among others, has done for media texts.

In their 1980 book *Culture, Media, Language*, Stuart Hall and his co-authors present three main types of reading of media texts, each of which has to do with the reader's social context (i.e. where the reader is in social terms). These are as follows.

- **The dominant-hegemonic**: the reading that the text prefers; the dominant discourse; the reading that relates the text to society's ideological norms.
- **The negotiated**: the reading that broadly accepts the dominant discourse but which modifies it according to personal circumstances.
- **The oppositional**: the reading that contests the dominant discourse and takes some alternative and opposed meaning from the text.

Hall is interested in the ways in which communication media reflect particular social and cultural views, which he argues are those of dominant groups and classes in society. The adjective hegemonic is chosen to reflect this perspective, since hegemony, a term used by the Italian writer Antonio Gramsci, represents the way the ruling classes maintain their power by manipulating the way we think about ourselves and our world. In simple terms Hall would argue, for example, that our 'harmless' magazine promotion is implicitly promoting all manner of social and political propaganda – about the desirability of consumerism, about social and intellectual elitism, about the position and value of women. This is not just about what the text intends to say but about the ways in which all texts fit into a pattern of social communication, which on the largest scale is about society talking to itself.

KEY TERM

HEGEMONY Gramsci explained why the majority of people in a culture do not adopt the values and beliefs of their own class. He argued that the dominant minority within cultures present the values and beliefs of their own class as somehow 'natural' and thus universal. In this way people end up promoting the values and beliefs of the dominant or ruling class rather than of their own class.

It is possible to see *The Scream* in these terms, with the dominant-hegemonic as the need to see the text as a work of art (and thus in some unspecified sense valuable) and an oppositional reading as one that rejects these notions of cultural value. Most practical readings of text are negotiated, a compound of the two previous positions mixed with significant personal response. With this sophisticated example still in mind, let us turn to a common case of media-manipulated response, of moral panic in action.

KEY TERM

MORAL PANIC Cohen has described moral panic as what occurs when 'a condition, episode, person or group of persons emerges to become defined as a threat to societal values and interests' (Cohen 1980: 9). Classic cases would include media coverage of issues such as AIDS, punk rockers, or the 2000 campaign by the *News of the World* to 'name and shame' paedophiles.

Recently statistics for teenage pregnancies were published for Western Europe and Britain was once again top of this league. A quality Sunday newspaper ran a full-page article entitled 'Too Much Too Young'; this was accompanied by a still from a Channel Four documentary on the same subject. The image was of two young people in school uniforms, the boy with a loosened tie and a depressed or uninterested gaze, the girl with a short skirt and a heavily pregnant stomach. The fact that we could not get permission to show you this image does much to support the brief reading that follows. Channel Four, which owns the image, simply said that this image had been especially commissioned by them to advertise a forthcoming documentary. The 'stories' told by the photograph and the article become more interesting to us as students of communication from the moment that permission is denied.

In the case of the newspaper article, the dominant-hegemonic reading is fairly clear: we are being encouraged to share the newspaper's shock, horror and outrage at ever more precocious and promiscuous children, and the inevitable outcomes of under-age sex. The preferred reading thus runs something like this: here are two *children*, not yet out of school uniform, who have experimented with sex and who are now in considerable trouble – which is nobody's fault but their own.

For many of us this is not an entirely convincing reading, though the gist seems plausible enough. There is plenty of room in their unspecified non-verbal communication (their postures, facial expressions and gaze focus are all relatively open to a range of interpretations) for negotiated readings. Partly these will be informed by our 'relationship' to Britain's 'child sex' statistics; we possibly all know, know of, or are people who have had under-age sex or even teenage pregnancy. All of these experiences elaborate the dominant-hegemonic reading, which offers the issue of child sexuality as a fuel for a moral panic.

Oppositional readings might start in an examination of the physical evidence provided, where the slightly-too-well-composed image, with bulging belly in a central position, might prompt an accusation of contrivance. This is validated by the suspiciously 'old' girl/model, her make-up, the way she is strategically lit and the amount of thigh she is showing to us. One reading therefore runs: this is a set-up, an opinion masquerading as a fact, an assertion disguised as a truth. What if the 'problem' of under-age sex is not a moral but a practical problem? What if this demonising of girls with 'inappropriately' womanly bulges (and the girl is the principal focus) is part of the problem?

These are the kinds of readings which Communication Studies will ask you to consider – not to convert you from a moral to a pragmatic view of under-age sex, but rather to get you to understand the potentially polysemic character of communication at most times in most places in your life. All meaning is thus 'up for grabs'.

▼ 2 DECODING AND DE-CODING

In this section we will consider two basic approaches to the study of communication, the semiotic and the process approaches.

■ We will provide broad definitions of the two schools of thought.
■ We will consider a simple but useful process model.
■ We will set out the foundations of semiotic analysis.

How can it be that different people make different readings of the same text? Why is it the case that people who think in the same way about communication group together to support each other in their interpretation of what communication is, how specific texts should be read and how they view the world?

As stated on pages 15–17, there are two main schools of thought of communication theory. The process and the semiotic schools constitute two different approaches to the study of communication. They offer us tools with which to systematically analyse communication texts. Let's look at the process and semiotic schools and, in so doing, further explore key ideas of representation, genre and convention.

As the only real test of explanations is through their practical application, let's examine another text. This text is the cover of the DVD of the 1998 film *The Truman Show*, directed by Peter Weir and starring Jim Carrey.

How are we to understand it? What might it mean? Let's use process and semiotic approaches to try to understand what it means and how it makes its meanings.

PROCESS SCHOOL

■ Sees communication as the transmission of messages
■ Is concerned with how senders and receivers encode and decode
■ Sees communication as a process by which one person affects another
■ Is concerned with matters such as efficiency and accuracy
■ Evaluates the success of communication in terms of 'delivered signal'

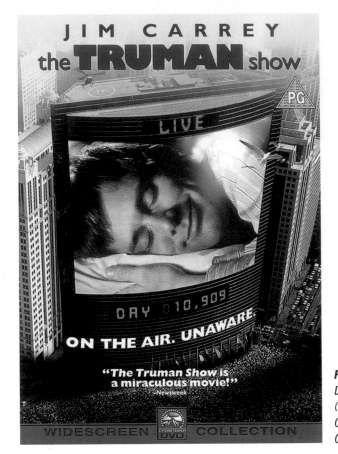

Figure 3.5 *Cover of the DVD of The Truman Show (Paramount 1998). Courtesy of the Kobal Collection*

SEMIOTIC SCHOOL

- Sees communication as the generation and sharing of meanings
- Is concerned with how messages and texts interact with people
- Sees the study of communication as the study of text, context and culture
- Does not see misunderstanding as evidence of communication failure

Put simply, the process explanation of our film capture would see it as the encoded version of a desire by Paramount Studios to publicise its film among a specifically targeted audience who would then decode this message and either comply with or reject or ignore its efforts. The significant issues here are the assumption that the text is a version of some predetermined intention, that the message is therefore essentially singular, and that the effects of communication can usually be quantified.

The significant elements – intention, sender and audience – are often obvious, but it is sometimes necessary to tease them out. Process models of communications, like Lasswell's Formula below, can serve as useful prompts for this exploration. In 1948 Harold Lasswell offered a five-point plan for identifying the significant features of communication processes. Lasswell's Formula asks five questions:

- Who?
- Says what?
- To whom?
- In which channel?
- With what effect?

This formula is immediately useful since it clarifies areas of investigation which we recognise as the sender, the message, the receiver, the channel (and medium) and the outcome.

CHANNEL/MEDIUM It is important to distinguish between these sometimes confused concepts. While a medium is a means of communication, a way of communicating (a technological medium like television or film or a human medium like speech or gestures), a channel is a physical connection between communicators, a route (like sound waves or the electronic type that is carrying this message to you).

KEY TERM

Lasswell insists that we find a specific context for communication texts and then implies that the narrow context he has identified is the only one that counts. We will see later that the semiotic approach also privileges context, but in a very different way, to describe those wider cultural, social, political and historical conditions within which texts might be located and made meaningful.

Let's apply the Lasswell Formula to, for example, the DVD cover of *The Truman Show*:

- **Who?** Paramount/Jim Carrey
- **Says what?** This is a film called *The Truman Show* with . . .
- **To whom?** Those who saw it and those who missed it
- **In which channel?** A DVD cover
- **With what effect?** It is seen, touched and, it is hoped, bought

The Lasswell Formula has served its purpose in efficiently identifying the text, its context and its intention. As an instrument for further analysis, however, it is limited – beyond a discussion about who the sender is. What's more, different texts produce different sets of results, with varying degrees of usefulness – even within the same genre.

Apply Lasswell's Formula to the text below (the DVD cover of *The Italian Job*) and compare your results with those given for *The Truman Show*. What differences do you notice?

THIS IS THE SELF
PRESERVATION SOCIETY

MICHAEL **CAINE**
NOËL **COWARD**

THE
ITALIAN
JOB

"THE MICHAEL CAINE
CRIME CORKER IS BACK...
A CLASSIC... NOT TO BE MISSED"
IAN FREER - EMPIRE
★★★★★

PG

WIDESCREEN DVD COLLECTION

Figure 3.6 *Cover of the DVD of* The Italian Job *(Paramount 1969)*

The problem here is partly caused by a more sophisticated text, or at least a more open text (or a text that is differently closed). While the preferred reading/dominant discourse of *The Truman Show* text runs along the lines of 'Jim Carrey, he's a funny man/top star/guarantee of quality', *The Italian Job* text is much more diverse. It is clearly offering explicitly alternative readings which may be modified to suit the reader's interests: to do with Caine as an actor/cultural item; to do with the film as a classic of sorts; to do with those other classics, the Minis; to do with the 1960s and certain kinds of chic or cool; to do with technical qualities never seen before.

It is possible that the combined effect of these 'alternatives' in fact ironically makes oppositional readings less likely, that they are all in fact in their ways preferred readings. If you are opposed to the premise that Jim Carrey is a kitemark of quality, you are liable to reject the whole package, whereas if you reject Caine's claims you are offered alternative reasons to respond constructively – the text is in active negotiation with you.

NEGOTIATION This concept is at the very heart of the semiotic approach to the study of communication, implying as it does that texts do not have meaning except through the process of negotiation between text and reader.

Very much in the manner of the logical approach we used in the previous section, the semiotic approach is concerned to consider systematically those elements that constitute communication texts. This process is sometimes referred to as deconstruction because, simply speaking, what is being done is breaking texts down into their constituent parts. For example, we might recognise that the following film still is constructed from elements including setting, costume, lighting and actor performance.

Figure 3.7
Still from
Trainspotting
(Figment/
Noel
Gay/Channel 4
1996).
Courtesy of the
Kobal
Collection

CODES Consist of signs. Signs are anything that has the potential to generate meaning, to signify. When a sign has generated meaning, it is said to have achieved signification. This is fundamental to the semiotic approach to the study of communication.

Identifying the contributing codes of communication is a very useful step in the analysis of any text; it is very like discovering the spectrum of colours from which all others are made. Codes are the languages of communication; they are the systems through which communication operates. John Fiske (1990) argues that it is important to distinguish between two types of code, which he calls representational codes and presentational codes. Representational codes are those that produce texts like the one above; they are used to create messages with an independent existence. On the other hand, presentational codes are used to provide information about senders and contexts; they are primarily concerned with self-presentation. Clearly, the still from *Trainspotting* theoretically has examples of both types of code, though its very presentation as a still makes it essentially representational rather than presentational. The presentational elements – notably the non-verbal communication offered by the above character's posture, appearance and facial expression – are all explored in detail later in this text.

It is enough here that we take on board that at the heart of the semiotic approach to the study of communication is the recognition of codes as the organising systems of communication. Implicit to this understanding is the notion that all communication is encountered and interpreted in a social and cultural context, in other words through interaction with other human beings. Systems and structures, like the conventions of a language, make the generation of meaning possible, but it is at the level of interaction and context that individual meanings are made.

Codes are, in essence, convention-governed systems that are agreed to by members of a community or culture or society. Codes may be behavioural, signifying, technical or cultural; in other words they might be used to determine how we behave, make meaning, use media or even maintain our way of life. They organise what we do, what we see and what we say. They constitute our lives and are the various languages in and through which our lives are expressed.

ACTIVITY . . .

Identify and list the codes likely to be active in a simple activity like walking to a local shop to buy groceries. Classify these codes in terms of (a) those that condition or control our behaviour and (b) those that affect the way we make meaning or communicate. You may wish to start by considering the code that determines which bits of the built environment we walk on and which bits we generally avoid.

If our lives are literally described by a network of codes, the next useful step might be to look at points of intersection. Codes are all very well as organising principles of communication, but to us as students of communication, interested in the interaction of text and reader, the particular will always be more important than the general.

Let's think about the CD, the cover of which is reproduced opposite. Although it is quite interesting to see the CD pictured opposite in terms of a set of coded conventions –

representational and technical – we are always likely to be more interested in what it particularly is and, in this case, how it particularly sounds. What is encoded here is a piece of communication that works through a number of codes, some of which we are unable to access in this format, except in our auditory memories if we have the knowledge and inclination. The picture of the CD below is not a CD but rather it is a representation of one. It is an idea given concrete form. It cannot be played.

Figures 3.8 and 3.9 SClub7, Bring It All Back *CD and CD cover.*
© *Polydor Ltd. Courtesy of Polydor Ltd*

A code is a system of signs agreed by the users. Given signs are selected from within given codes. There is, therefore, clearly a code within which 'Bring It All Back' can generate meaning and another, which can distinguish between the 'S' sign and 'CLUB 7'. The background, too, is a significant sign, a foundation on to which other signs are locked.

Without needing to access the musical content, we are aware that communication is taking place: an encoded message is being offered for decoding; an invitation to negotiate meaning has been posted; a collection of signs is doing all it can to signify. Whichever way you choose to describe this situation, this is the essence of all text-based work.

Before we go any further, it might be important to register your first impressions of and personal response to this basic text.

ACTIVITY . . .

What is communicated by the SClub7 CD? Look at every component and comment.

While the approach we are adopting here is essentially semiotic, it does not differ that much at this point from the process approach. Do not see these approaches as mutually exclusive (as a matter of either/or). At a practical level, let them both inform your critical work. Process simply puts much greater store by the role of the encoder and what their intentions are, while semiotics tends to privilege the receiver.

If we move now from the CD to its cover, we can take another step towards understanding how codes operate and how signs are selected and combined.

This arrangement of signs (group members, facial expressions, costumes, setting) is clearly a selection from a vast number of possible selections and combinations. The number of different ways seven people can be arranged in a straight line is staggering. The signs that appear can only be understood in terms of their relationships both with one another and with all the selections that have not been made (the choice of a light background, for example, precludes the choice of a dark one). These relationships are what the Swiss linguist Ferdinand de Saussure (1983) called the syntagmatic (or horizontal) relations and the paradigmatic (or vertical) relations of a code, a language, a set of signs.

KEY TERM

SYNTAGM In semiotics a syntagm is a chain of signs, a unique combination of sign choices. Units may be visual, verbal or musical. The scale of the units and syntagms may range from the very large (the nine planned episodes of the *Star Wars* triple trilogy might constitute a syntagm) to the very small (as in the syntagm 'small', which consists of the signs 's', 'm', 'a', 'l' and 'l'). The important point is that syntagms invite negotiation as a whole; they are bigger units of potential meaning.

PARADIGM   A set of signs from which one might be chosen to contribute to a syntagm. Paradigms define their individual members with reference to all others in the set. To select from a paradigm is at that moment to reject all other signs in that set, just as by selecting something (or nothing) to cover your feet today, you have rejected all other possibilities; this choice from a paradigm of 'foot coverings' has contributed to the syntagms which constitute the things you are wearing today. When Peugeot's 'lion' went 'from strength to strength', it got its strength partly from the paradigm of 'elite animals' from which it was chosen and partly because that paradigm does not include 'weasel', 'frog' and 'sloth'.

ACTIVITY . . .

Look at the SClub7 CD cover and identify SIX significant paradigms which have been used to create the syntagms offered.

- Which of these do you consider to be the most important to the meaning of this text?
- Which choice turned out for you to be the most significant?
- What are the dominant signs in these syntagms?

The important thing to remember is that, as students of communication, we are interested specifically in engaging with texts in an attempt to work out their meanings. It is not technical terms which unlock texts but rather the issues these concepts and methods raise. The two-dimensional grid which Saussurian linguistics imposes on any text is useful only, ultimately, if it delivers more than the lay and naked eye.

In the case of SClub7, a very conventional text is further clarified by reference to such paradigms as 'settings for bands', which here directs attention to the cleanness and/or blandness of a photographic backdrop and from there to the banal realisation that it's sand they're in and that the backdrop is clearly meant to represent the sky and/or sea. For an 'enjoy-it-while-you-can' teeny-pop sensation, this is a snapshot of their best summer ever with as much sincerity and irony as the sender and receivers will allow. Given that all the human figures are taken from that specialist paradigm 'members of the pop group SClub7', it is their arrangement and presentation that are important. Here, in fact, is an excellent example of the overlapping of representational and presentational codes, where the self-presentation of individuals is set firmly within the representation of the group itself. The individual syntagms that represent the seven individuals are in themselves part of a larger syntagm whose meaning is 'SClub7'. The male figure at the top of the cover, for example, is communicating discretely through various non-verbal signs, such as his facial expression and his posture, but he is also himself a significant component of the representation of the whole group.

In all of this, broader issues of representation are also being addressed; for, although such factors as gender, ethnicity and even sexual orientation are clearly inscribed, the meanings assigned to and through them are very much open and available. At a superficial level, for example, we notice that three of the 'girls' are sitting upstage (in the foreground) at the base of a pyramid that has a black male and a (too-conveniently contrasting and slightly subordinate blonde) white female at its apex, as a kind of symbolic master and mistress. In seeing some of this, we are allowing ourselves the opportunity to explore the very idea of convention, or rather ideas of it, and to see the levels at which formulas work. It also reminds us that blandness and conventionality are neither necessarily neutral nor harmless. Too much public communication plays these games and carries a significant ideological impact simply because it goes unnoticed and unchecked. This is the point the writer George Orwell was making when he remarked of advertising that it 'hits below the intellect'.

▼ 3 WORDS AND PICTURES: SIGNS AND SIGNATURES

In this section we will further examine the semiotic approach to the study of communication.

- We will look at the composition and operation of signs.
- We will examine the different levels at which signs can have significance.
- We will consider Charles Peirce's ideas about the sign categories icon, index and symbol.

Now that we have established the two principal approaches to the study of communication, we can begin to look more closely at their claims to explain the character of communication in practice. This section will further explore the semiotic approach to texts while the next section will take the process further.

INTENTION

When we are examining texts in which the sender, message and receiver are clearly identifiable, it is a relatively easy job to frame a response. However, it can be a very different matter if the text is a little elliptic or enigmatic. The A6 flyer on page 114 was discovered in a Cambridge library and attracted with its Japanese cartoon-style aesthetic. It features, almost uniquely in advertising, the word 'ordinary' and a striking image.

ACTIVITY

Examine the flyer depicted in Figure 3.10.

- What might the purpose of it be?
- Who might send this text? Give two or three possible options.
- Who do you think the intended audience might be (in terms of age profile, personality, etc.)?

WORDS AND PICTURES **113**

Figure 3.10
Cambridge Youth Project 'Ordinary' flyer. © The Cambridge Youth Project. Courtesy of Selina Dean

As far as the process approach to communication is concerned, the answers to the above questions are found on the flyer's reverse side:

- **Purpose**: 'why not write . . . for *Gunge* newspaper'.
- **Intended audience**: 'between the ages of 14 and 25'.
- **Sender**: The North Cambridge Youth Project.

However, what they add up to is a list of intentions, a notion of what the designers or compilers or sponsors hoped they were communicating to their target audience. They do not necessarily do justice to the quality of the design or to that of the companion piece (below) in which the man is replaced by a woman and 'ordinary' is replaced with 'quiet'. These may be male and female versions or perhaps versions for males and females. They share reverse-side texts and have clear generic links: the floating background texts, the style of illustrations and the arrangement of elements. Despite the clearly stated intentions, the reverse side clarifications do little to identify a preferred reading of either of these striking designs.

Figure 3.11
Cambridge Youth
Project 'Quiet'
flyer. © The
Cambridge Youth
Project. Courtesy
of Selina Dean

In the majority of print advertising, readings of largely visual texts are prompted, supported, privileged, even prescribed by a variety of verbal arrangements: headlines, captions, slogans, titles. Roland Barthes, the French semiotician, devised the term 'anchorage' to describe the ways in which texts, or parts of texts, are anchored to particular meanings (Barthes 1967). In this way the creator of a communication text can steer the reader to the meaning that they prefer them to make of the text. In the crudest sense, this process can be exemplified with reference to the following simple illustration.

> **ANCHORAGE** The process by which the meaning of a text is fixed, usually by means of a caption or voice-over to visual images.

Figure 3.12   Dog/cat/horse?

In Figure 3.12, assigning any of the animal titles to this drawn animal is tantamount to investing this crudely made sign with meaning. While it is fair to say, with process theory, that at the point of conception, this collection of marks had a conscious intention, its polysemy (its capability for different meanings) is also difficult to dispute. In fact, the issue is made more problematic and interesting by its context as an illustration from a textbook in a chapter addressing explicitly the ways in which words work upon visual material and in so doing limit the possibility of multiple meanings. Its genuine intention (and therefore one of its readings) is thus 'something drawn that might be variously interpreted' or more specifically 'something drawn that might plausibly represent "dog", "cat" and "horse"'.

Perhaps the crudest example of this is the visual joke, where words, a punch line, allow readers to discover something in an image they have not seen. When we were young we might have been presented with this visual puzzle.

What is this?

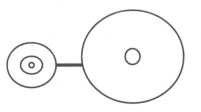

Figure 3.13

The answer – a bird's-eye view of a Mexican frying an egg – is a classic anchoring statement because it literally activates the given sign and answers our need for explanation, for a meaning. On the page is a series of circles and a line. Words link this to a situation, if somewhat stereotypically and surreally. What we are seeing here – in a very stark way – is the relationship Saussure identified between the two parts of a sign – the signifier and the signified.

> **SIGNIFIER/SIGNIFIED**   According to Saussure, the basic unit of communication is the sign. The sign is composed of two elements – the signifier and the signified. The signifier is the label that people attach to objects when they want to communicate about them. The signified is the object or the mental concept of the object to which the signifier refers. The signifier and the signified unite to form the sign, but the relationship between the two elements is an arbitrary one – that is, there is no logical or necessary relationship between them. That's why it's possible to change which signifier relates to which signified; there are no absolute rules connecting the signifier and the signified.

KEY TERM

In the Mexican gag the signifier is anchored to its comic purpose by the words of the punch line and at the same time other explanations (other signifieds) are downplayed or eliminated. The circles and line might, for example, have had a scientific, paranormal or anthropological significance. Anchorage lessens or even removes the 'might' given that its function is, in Barthes' words 'to fix the floating chain of signifieds'. This fixing is clearly evident in the cover design of the FilmFour listings magazine (see Figure 3.14), which features a still from the British film *Elizabeth*, together with a couple of substantial 'anchors'. This is obviously a publicity shot for the film. The photographic backdrop suggests this, but FilmFour has fixed its meaning in a particular way. This is

Figure 3.14 'Killer Queen' poster. Courtesy of FilmFour

a potentially open representation of a complex historical character, partially closed by the twin captions: 'KILLER QUEEN' and 'ELIZABETH RULES OVER A MONTH OF BRITISH FILM'.

ACTIVITY . . .

What readings of the image are being suggested by the captions? What alternative readings become possible if the words are taken away? (What has been done to the image to make it more effective?)

As we begin to consider the potential readings of any image, it is noticeable that images are capable not only of different meanings but also of different types of meaning. Put simply, and with direct reference to the *Elizabeth* still, there is a significant difference between the designation 'Cate Blanchett in the film *Elizabeth*' and the designation 'Killer Queen' or even 'a woman who needs to have her wits about her'. Barthes addresses these different kinds or levels of meaning in his notion of 'orders of signification'. These are levels at which signs might be significant or signifiers may connect with signifieds.

The first order of signification is *denotation*. Connections are made between signs and objects. It is agreed that specific signs will signify specific objects at a general societal level. In the *Elizabeth* example, what is denoted might include 'the actress Cate Blanchett', 'a woman in period costume' or 'the film's central character Queen Elizabeth'.

The second order of signification is *connotation*. If denotation describes the way in which signs signify at a general societal level, then connotation describes the way in which signs signify at a specific individual level. Connotations describes the way in which groups of people share meaning at an associative level. By virtue of the groups we are members of, we share in the connotative use of signs. In the *Elizabeth* example, the particular ways in which this image has been presented might provoke particular sorts of personal response, connoting aspects as diverse as vulnerability and danger.

Myths are, according to the authors of *Key Concepts in Communication and Cultural Studies* (O'Sullivan *et al.* 1994), a culture's way of conceptualising an abstract topic. A myth consists of a collection of concepts bound together by general acceptance and significant in our understanding of particular kinds of experience. The image we have been examining contains within it a very specific kind of myth, that of Elizabeth herself, however she is represented, and the age she names. This is connected to notions of national identity and pride as well as the perpetuation of another significant myth, that of monarchy as a natural repository of the nation's hopes and dignity.

The third order of signification is *ideology*. Fiske and Hartley (1978) have suggested that myths and connotations are in themselves evidence of a deeper, hidden pattern of meaning which they label ideology. This is ideology as a description of the various ways in which society, or those controlling it, organise and control the ways in which meanings are generated – what Marxists would call the intellectual means of production. A final visit to our example will reveal that part of the meaning system in which the text is active has to do with gender. It is hard to avoid understanding this image of a woman without reference to the connotations of the female, not to say myths about femininity, and this is partly a response to the text's implicit ideology. Here the woman is strong but only in the ultimate context: that women are weaker, more vulnerable and conventionally not like this.

ACTIVITY...

Looking at the images below and on page 120, demonstrate your understanding of denotation, connotation, myth and ideology by suggesting at least FOUR supporting captions.

It is clear that some signifiers, by their character, need far less anchoring than others. This has partly to do with the open or closed character of texts but it is also related to two other ideas, one from each of the process and semiotic approaches, which it may be useful to introduce at this point.

The first idea is that of *redundancy* which derives from Claude E. Shannon and Warren Weaver's process model of communication (1949). Shannon and Weaver, in a development of the Lasswell Formula we used earlier, proposed a model of communication which, while linear (a straight line), addresses the issue of inefficiency in communication, here described as noise source.

REDUNDANCY/ENTROPY A communication that is low on new information and which is highly predictable is said to be redundant. A communication that is high on new information and that is highly unpredictable is said to be entropic.

KEY TERM

If we meet someone every day and they always say the same thing to us, that communication can be characterised as redundant. Our knowledge of the conventions of film in general and of specific film genres in particular makes much of film narrative being easy to predict – that is, to make them redundant. Astute communicators will try to wrap up the entropic elements of a communication with redundant elements to make it more easily understood. It could be said that the objective of an effective communicator is to make the entropic redundant – that is, to make the unpredictable, the difficult to understand, easy to understand.

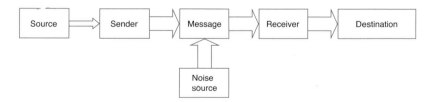

Diagram 3.1 Shannon and Weaver's Mathematical Theory of Communication

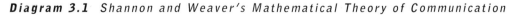

Figure 3.15 Angelina Jolie as Lara Croft in Tomb Raider (Paramount 2001). Courtesy of the Kobal Collection

Figure 3.16 Saddam Hussein as Veronica Lake. Courtesy of Worth100.com

In recognising the potential for interference between the intended message encoded by the transmitter and the received message, Shannon and Weaver (1949) are partly acknowledging the polysemic character of texts. However, within the process tradition to which they are significant contributors, polysemy is not really an issue. Shannon and Weaver are concerned only to establish those inefficiencies which might limit the transmission of intended meaning to the receiver, and through this to suggest ways in which these inefficiencies might be countered. They are concerned with accurate decoding and how it might be achieved. The Shannon and Weaver model is often referred to as the Mathematical Theory of Communication. They were trying to devise a system to eliminate the deterioration of communication using telephones. They discovered that if a mathematical value could be placed on the noise source, then the telephone engineers would know by how much the signal would have to be increased to overcome the noise source.

Redundancy refers to the level of predictability that can be built into a message or a text. Genre, for example, assists redundancy in that it offers a series of expectations which are to a large degree predictable. When we choose to see a horror film, we do so in the secure knowledge that significant parts of the text will be already familiar to us from our experience of other horror films. This familiarity makes us secure and confident.

BROADCAST/NARROWCAST   To broadcast is to transmit highly predictable (redundant) information to large, heterogeneous (i.e having nothing in common with each other in terms of age, gender, sexual orientation, income, geography, disposable income, lifestyle or interests) audiences. To narrowcast is to transmit highly unpredictable (entropic) information to small homogeneous (i.e. having much in common in terms of age, gender, sexual orientation, income, geography, disposable income, lifestyle or interests) audiences.

KEY TERM

In order to communicate with a general public audience, most broadcast communication has a large degree of redundancy, in that it conforms to predetermined conventions. New situation comedy on television, for example, will be keen to reference its original comic situation, its cast of soon-to-be-familiar characters, and its cumulative punch lines in the context of the genre as a whole. Redundancy, rather than anchorage, is the key to identifying intended meanings and preferred readings in this case. Redundancy is, in effect, an implication of generic or even formal conventions, a sort of insurance policy taken out by the sender to guard against potential audience misunderstanding or bewilderment.

In contrast, unpredictability in the content or form of a message is described as entropy. Entropic content concentrates information in a demanding way, while entropic form usually breaks existing conventions. Entropy opposes redundancy and calls for a plurality of response rather than a conventional singularity of response. In time, of course, as broken conventions become the new conventions, the entropic becomes redundant and the process begins again. An example of this process would be Channel Four's *The Big Breakfast*, which set out systematically to break all of the conventions of breakfast television and ended up being successful and greatly imitated.

Conventions are also at the core of the relationship between signifier and signified, as one of the principal influences on the ways any reality can be represented. For example, if we want to communicate the idea 'baby', we might choose a conventional way of representing this by speaking or writing the English word that is formed 'b-a-b-y' or 'B-A-B-Y'. In fact these are only two of the vast number of ways this word might be represented in written or printed form. Others include 'baby', 'Baby' and 'BABY', each of which carries its own particular connotations. What must be grasped, however, is that, whatever the typeface, there is no logical or necessary connection between this sign (these signs) in its physical form as signifier and any idea or reality we might associate with it – that is, any signified. The connection is artificial and arbitrary, a matter of agreement. Language then is highly conventional in the same way that it is highly redundant.

Collect or compile TEN different ways or forms of representing the concept sometimes represented by the word 'baby'. These representations may be made by you or collected from outside sources. Arrange them in order of greatest convention, in terms of the degree to which their meaning is dependent on 'outside' knowledge of the language, society and culture in which they were made. A word is therefore highly conventional, whereas a photograph has a low degree of convention.

Clearly, you will have found representations (signs and syntagms) in which the relationship between the signifier and signified is other than arbitrary. Photographs of babies, for example, do not represent 'baby' simply by a matter of agreement, but rather through a closer (albeit technologically aided) relationship between signifier and signified. These representations take their form largely from the character of the signified. In the case of baby photographs, the shape and size of the baby pictured is largely determined by the shape and size of the baby photographed. The signifier is thus said to be motivated to some degree by the character of the signified: the more significant the determination, the higher the *motivation* is said to be.

KEY TERM

MOTIVATION   In semiotics this refers to the relationship between a sign and what it represents. Specifically it describes the degree to which the form a sign takes (word/symbol/drawing/photograph) is determined by the subject being represented. Thus the horse in a colour photograph is said to have high motivation simply because, as a sign, its form (what it looks like) is very like the horse it is representing. Similarly, a word sign has very low motivation because its form/shape/appearance usually has next to nothing to do with whatever it is representing.

Figure 3.17a
*Baby drawing
(Paul Mendez)*

Figure 3.17b *Norman
Rockwell, detail from
'The Tantrum',* cover of
the Saturday Evening
Post, *24 October 1936*

Figure 3.17c *Baby
photograph. Courtesy of
www.digitalvisiondownload.com*

This is not to say that any representation is free from convention, for no sign is totally motivated (though some are totally conventional). In any representation, even photographic, there is room for the sender to impose perspective, focus, distance – in other words, there is room to conventionalise the representation. The more consciously the images are being produced for specific contexts, the greater the degree of convention bearing down on the motivated image.

The three images on page 124 appeared in a brochure for a day nursery/crèche (Figure 3.18).

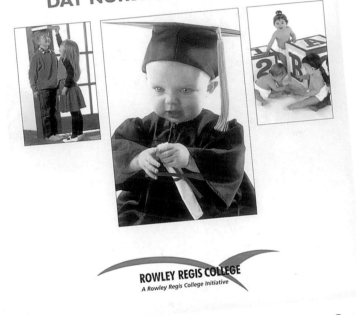

ROWLEY REGIS COLLEGE
A Rowley Regis College Initiative

Figure 3.18 The Toy Box. Courtesy of Rowley Regis College

These three images/signs/syntagms are clearly highly motivated (they were originally glossy, full-colour representations). Examine the degree of convention in each of these and suggest what sorts of meanings are delivered in this way. Another way to do this is to look at the level of redundancy or predictability of them as messages.

If we now look at the front cover of the brochure which featured these images, we can see more precisely – owing to the anchorage provided by words – the context for these images. We can also identify a number of significantly conventional signs to support and contrast with these significantly motivated ones. This is useful up to a point, but it does leave a rather large grey area somewhere between highly motivated and highly conventional. While Saussure was content with the dichotomy of signifier and signified, of motivation and convention, Charles Peirce went further. Rather than a dichotomy, Peirce (1966) proposed a trichotomy – three elements in the composition of the sign, three different types of sign. He labelled these three types of sign as icon, index and symbol.

The cover on page 124 contains good examples of Peirce's three sign categories which, he stressed, were tendencies and not mutually exclusive designations.

Peirce first identified those signs that communicated their signified through resemblance, in other words by looking like their signified, or in certain cases by sounding like or smelling like their signified. These are essentially motivated signs and he labelled them *icons*. The representations of the children and the toy box clearly fit into this category.

Second, Peirce talked of *indexes*: signs that communicate their signified by association; in other words, because one thing exists, another thing is assumed to exist. We see smoke, we assume the existence of fire. Therefore the character of the relationship between indexical signs and their objects is said to be existential. The cover on page 124 provides a range of examples – from the mortar board and gown as indexes of education to the toys and toy box as indexes of childhood and fun. A mortar board does not resemble education; rather it is in some sense a part of education as a broad concept. Notice also that the toy box has been described as both iconic and indexical, reflecting the different ways in which it is communicating.

Peirce's third sign category, *symbol*, was reserved for signs where the relationship between sign and object was a matter of agreement. There is no logical or necessary relationship between the signs 'toy box' and the object we recognise from the picture; it is a matter of social convention. If we follow the social convention, we will get along with fellow human beings. If we don't, we will not get along; we will most likely be shunned by them. All the words on this cover and the college logo are typical examples of symbolic signs.

In uncovering the categories of sign we find we are, in fact, engaging with the very act of signification, examining how signs mean even before we examine what they mean. In the whole of this section we have been trying out explanations of the way texts work in order to find out more about what they might have to say. Our next text carries with it a significant challenge: to communicate your understanding of sign categories with reference to a specific live text.

Figure 3.19 *AXA/Sun Life leaflet*

TEXTS AND MEANINGS IN COMMUNICATION

Plan, in note form, a five-minute presentation entitled 'Icons, indexes and symbols' aimed at your fellow students. Exemplify your explanation with detailed reference to the leaflet cover on page 126, paying particular attention to:

- the prominent logos
- the trailing hand
- the child and his 'costume'
- the choice of typefaces.

▼ 4 TAKING THE PROCESS FURTHER

In this section we will examine the process approach to the study of communication.

■ We will look at Gerbner's model of communication.
■ We will examine the character of the sender in communication in terms of status and in terms of a gatekeeping role.

We have looked at the semiotic approach to the study of communication where meaning is a matter of negotiation within a specific cultural context. We will now attempt to address some of the issues thrown up by the process approach. Let's start with the significantly more sophisticated process model of George Gerbner. Gerbner moves the basic linear model offered by Lasswell and Shannon and Weaver into a second dimension, making a distinction in the process between the act of perceiving the world ('seeing') and the act of communication itself ('saying').

Gerbner's model is an attempt to provide a general-purpose model of communication, and as such it is perhaps doomed to failure. However, it does provide a useful context in which to discuss aspects of the communication models and ultimately the limitations of models. Gerbner's model works best for communication that is genuinely informative, which provides the receiver with information of which they are previously unaware. To understand Gerbner's model, let us look at Pete's story as presented in the case study that follows.

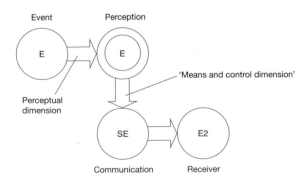

Diagram 3.2 *Gerbner's model of communication*

CASE STUDY

In December 1980 I was awoken, as an undergraduate student, in my hall of residence by my roommate to the news that John Lennon, the former Beatle, was dead; in fact, he had been killed. My roommate, Mike, had heard this 'news' on early morning radio. In Gerbner's terms he had made a selection from the range of potential news available to him in his context as a radio listener for whom only one radio channel was available at that time; the one to which his radio alarm clock was habitually tuned. In fact the event was so newsworthy it would not likely have mattered which radio station he was receiving. This news selection (in Gerbner's terms this perception of an event) had most likely been prompted by a number of factors: the insistence of the radio announcer that this was *the* news story; the peculiar social and cultural relevance the Beatles had to anyone like the two of us, who were born at the very beginning of the 1960s; the fact I was, to him, 'a long-haired hippy'; the fact Lennon was only 40 years old. None of this plays a significant part in Gerbner's version of communication, save in a stretching of context to a much broader 'where we're at (man)'; emotionally, socially, culturally. Gerbner suggests we select what we 'see' (hear, think, taste) from a range of available stimuli and that, when we have selected, we deliver this perception to our receiver(s) in the most appropriate way; for us, for them and sometimes for both.

As Mike moved that day from his bedroom to mine, through the shared living space, he probably was converting an idea/surprise/shock into a communicable form, just as I now in this retelling am finding appropriate means. Mike was entering Gerbner's 'means and control' dimension, and my bedroom, awaking me with a noisy door, a phatic shoulder shake and a clear message: 'John Lennon's dead'. There was no room for misunderstanding, little for selection. My context as receiver probably made the message more believable, the very fact that I'd been woken up was an index of the importance of this news. What was available to me was partly this fact dawning on me and partly the urgency of the communication: the voice, the face, the words. The follow-up was, 'He's been killed', but by then the message had been received, perceived, understood. In this case, Gerbner's model, if necessarily imprecisely, does offer a meaningful account of communication in practice. The world is perceived, and that perception is passed on to a receiver, at which point the act of communication is over.

How different it is, then, if we examine a very similar message in a very different context – largely pictorial, public, political and nearly a thousand years old. The most famous section of the Bayeux Tapestry contains the following words and images.

Figure 3.20 *The death of Harold. Detail from the Bayeux Tapestry*

Applying Gerbner, the event is clear – an incident from a battle in 1066. However, this is the point at which the model begins to break down. It is fair to say that this section of the tapestry is an attempt to represent the death of King Harold, the English leader; this is anchored by the Latin text, 'Harold Rex interfectus est' (King Harold is killed). There are probably interesting things to say about the 'means and control' dimension, given this is the victor's version of the event and was constructed some 30 years after the battle, ironically by English seamstresses under the commission of William's half-brother, Odo. Nevertheless it is difficult to see Gerbner's model as usefully clarifying this process, which was prolonged, celebratory and clearly propagandist. In fact, it is difficult even to argue for the tapestry as a coherent perception, then representation, of a far-off event. It reads much more like the conscious coining of a new mythology. Its bias and perspective are clear, it certainly has intention, but its form and style expect a much fuller response. This openness is partly shown in the above section which the Bayeux-bought guidebook describes, appropriately in French, as 'Harold est tué d'une flèche dans l'oeil' (Harold is killed by an arrow in the eye). This is prompted by the figure straddled above by the word 'HAROLD', who appears to be removing an arrow from his face or head: it is the stuff of legend. Scholars, however, with other ways and more experience of reading texts like this, inform us that the convention is to depict the victim at the point of death, crudely, under the word 'killed' or 'dead' or whatever. This would make Harold the victim of the stooping, mounted Norman knight to the right and would neuter the joke that has Harold's last words as 'Careful with that arrow; you'll have somebody's eye out'. This is not a History lesson, but rather a lesson in the precariousness and potential inefficiency of communication, even communication of a very contrived, considered and artificial kind.

In the case of Pete's learning of John Lennon's death, the immediate sender was both obvious and identifiable, though in a more profound way he was the last in a chain of gatekeepers, which stretched back to those who witnessed Lennon's fatal wounding. Mostly this was a matter for mass media news organisations, save at the final stage when it became a stimulus for interpersonal communication. There is a theory that the more important the news item, the more likely we are to receive the news from an interpersonal source – a friend, a family member, a colleague. A more contemporary example might be to think of how you found out that Diana, Princess of Wales, had been killed. Was it from a mass media source? King Harold's death is told in a much less immediate way and it is highly unlikely that any of its intended audience would have had to wait until 1096 to find out what happened at Hastings. The relationship between the teller, the tale and the audience is less than straightforward and yet in many ways it has immeasurably more in common with the modern mass media than did Pete's friend's important news of 8 December 1980.

ACTIVITY . . .

Identify the sender(s) in the following communications:

- the *Sun* newspaper
- the film *Mission Impossible* 2
- the campaign of TV advertisements for Budweiser beer
- the new album from The Darkness
- the book *Harry Potter and the Order of the Phoenix*
- the television cartoon series *The Simpsons*.

Identifying senders is significant in the sense that it has an impact on the way we respond to messages. This is why when advertisers choose to write advertising copy in the style of newspaper or magazine journalism, the words 'ADVERTISEMENT' or 'ADVERTISING FEATURE' declare this to be the case. Mass media communications are usually produced by complex teams but the industry is forever asking us to individualise and personalise its communications. Promoting films by means of their directors and stars is an example of this. It is easier to relate to Stanley Kubrick as sender than to the large numbers of people who were responsible for making *Eyes Wide Shut*.

Senders, in terms of their status and authority, are one factor that contributes to the building of audiences. Status here has a phatic function; it attracts attention. There are clearly types of text that are sold on the basis of the sender's identity. Advance orders of the latest release from popular bands, popular novelists or a film featuring a particular star are proof that sender status is a vital ingredient in mass media marketing.

Audiences are also built around certain kinds of message. We have previously discussed genre as an example of this, but the ways in which messages are composed work at more subtle levels as well. The process approach is always concerned to explore how communication can be made more efficient. For example, Gerbner's model focuses on the relationship between two aspects of a message: its form and its content. This explicitly acknowledges that there are a number of ways of communicating a given content, at the level of both medium and channel. What process theory is keen to suggest is that some forms are in specific cases better suited than others, and therefore that the job of the communicator is to find the best formal match for a particular content to a particular audience.

When evaluating the effectiveness of any piece of communication, we are partly engaging in this debate, placing the particular text in a paradigm of appropriateness for a particular context. It is clear that most communication texts are targeted at a specific (although not always specified) audience and equally clear that this is a contributing factor to the way in which texts and messages are composed. Equally clearly, this cannot be the last word on a process that is human and creative. Process models are used to evaluate communication in terms of its intentions and the degree to which those intentions are fulfilled. This may function as a useful starting point but it can all too easily limit both our response to texts and our understanding of their impact and effectiveness. What is intended is often clear or is easy to guess but what is achieved in and by a text is very often both more and less than its intention. There is a character in Ian McEwan's novel A *Child in Time* (1987) whose first novel becomes a surprise success just because it ends up on the wrong desk at a publisher and is released as a novel for teenagers and not, as intended, for adults. This is the problem with assuming that what was achieved in communication is what was intended to be communicated. Communication is invariably achieved, but there's often a big difference between the desired objective (intention) and the achieved result (outcome).

ACTIVITY . . .

Consider the intended meaning of the promotional leaflet, Figure 3.21, issued by Coventry University. What do you think about this as a piece intended for students? What do you think the creators of this advertisement wanted to achieve?

Clearly the audience is being asked to identify with the images offered either literally or in terms of a style to which it can relate. In its original form the text was printed on a glossy two-sided card. The background is a flat white which gives a certain equality to the six foregrounded figures who, anchored by the tagline 'Ideas as big as your head', compete for our attention, as if our heads as well as theirs are involved in the game. We are actively invited to decode these figures, to actively engage with the text.

The degree to which this engagement is the norm in media communication gives the lie to arguments about audience passivity. In many adverts, for example, the audience is asked to find the desired meanings for itself.

Figure 3.21 '*Ideas, as big as your head' leaflet, from the Media Degree Show. Courtesy of Coventry University*

The increasing popularity of phone-in competitions and popular referendums on all manner of subjects is further proof of the activation of the mass audience. Because feedback is being built in here, there will be a crude increase in the effectiveness of communication. Within the terms of reference of the process school, feedback gives encoders information on how their messages are being received and therefore notionally the opportunity to improve them.

Feedback to print-based texts can be expressed in two main ways: the direct way, which takes the form of filling in reply slips, donating money or buying a book (for example); and the indirect way which sees the text as a starting point for various kinds of interpersonal and medio communication. This is partly the reason why shock and scandal are so effective because they stimulate indirect publicity. The advertising for the clothes firm Benetton has often courted such publicity, offering controversial campaigns which prompt massive amounts of indirect (and some direct) feedback.

Moreover, developments in technology, and particularly the emergence of the Internet, have offered much greater opportunities for texts to be interactive because of the very fact that even with mass media texts the feedback can be almost instantaneous.

The phenomenon of *The Blair Witch Project* is a case in point, where a campaign begun by an Internet film reviewer almost unwittingly hyped this low-budget film to notoriety and international success. Here was a film which explicitly involved its audience in its promotion, its merchandising and its communication.

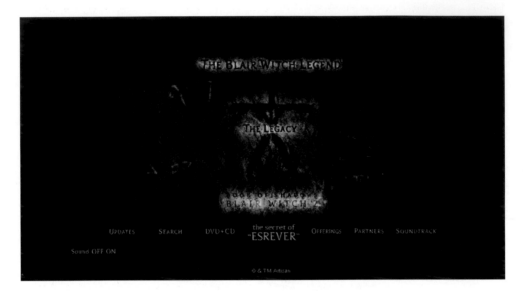

Figure 3.22 *Blair Witch website. www.blairwitch.com*

ACTIVITY . . .

Consider the specific ways in which the above website identifies and communicates with its audience. Who makes up this audience and how are they addressed?

For Gerbner the whole Blair Witch 'project' is a classic case of operations in the 'means and control' dimension. In Gerbner's terms the film's producers are simply selecting the most appropriate channels in the same way that any film is marketed. Gerbner's model cannot allow for (nor should we expect it to) the ability, granted largely by an unlicensed new medium, of the film's audience to 'hijack' this process and do it for themselves. Partly the audience for this reading comes from the difference in register between the website quoted and the conventional language of film promotion. They are almost different languages.

Halliday (1978) defines a register in three dimensions:

- formality/ informality
- technicality
- character as an essentially written or spoken 'dialect'.

The register of the *Blair Witch Project* website is somewhat informal but significantly technical; it demands specialist knowledge. While it is in a real sense written, it is more properly a version of a spoken register, copying the patterns of speech. The extract below, taken from the video cover of the film *Titanic*, might stand as an example of a more conventional film promotion:

> Nothing on earth can rival the epic spectacle and breathtaking grandeur of *Titanic*. Winner of eleven Academy Awards® including Best Picture, this sweeping love story sailed into the hearts of moviegoers around the globe, ultimately emerging as the most popular motion picture of all time.
>
> International superstar Leonardo DiCaprio and Oscar®-nominee Kate Winslet light up the screen as Jack and Rose, the young lovers who find themselves on the maiden voyage of the 'unsinkable' R.M.S. *Titanic*. But when the doomed luxury liner collides with an iceberg in the frigid North Atlantic, their passionate love affair becomes a thrilling race for survival.

ACTIVITY

Define the register of this piece in Halliday's terms. What differences are there between this and the website register of Figure 3.22?

Register is intimately connected with the notion of mode of address, or the recognition that texts 'speak' to readers from predetermined positions using specific codes and registers. In choosing a register or even setting a register, a certain kind of relationship is being established, a set of conventions is being activated around which the text invites us to respond, even to judge. In the case of *The Blair Witch Project*, the mode of address is related to a documentary tradition of home-made film and thus our otherwise critical eyes are drawn away from technique and towards content. Its register is a strange mixture of the extremely informal, not to say amateurish, and highly technical in that the film is in fact engaged in a sophisticated discussion about the techniques and conventions of the horror genre itself.

REFLEXIVITY This describes what it is to be self-conscious, to be self-aware, and to reflect on who you are, what you're doing and how you present yourself in the world. It is a feature of much of contemporary communication that it is similarly conscious and aware. It is self-reflexive. In this way, for example, we are used to seeing films about the making of films, advertisements that play with the conventions of advertisements, and comedies that refer to the 'rules' of comedy.

KEY TERM

In a process sense the film simply (and luckily) hit upon the most appropriate form for its treatment of its content. In a semiotic sense its reflexivity and openness as a text allowed a significant range of readings which in turn built an audience. One model that goes some way to integrating these positions is that of Roman Jakobson. Jakobson (1962) identifies six elements in communication. He arranges them in a primarily linear fashion.

	CONTEXT	
	MESSAGE	
ADDRESSER	CONTACT	ADDRESSEE
	CODE	

Diagram 3.3a *Jakobson's elements of communication*

He goes on to link these six elements to the functions of communication by suggesting that within each communicative function a different element is dominant. He then arranges his six functions to correspond to the dominant element in the arrangement above.

	REFERENTIAL	
	POETIC	
EMOTIVE	PHATIC	CONATIVE
	METALINGUAL	

Diagram 3.3b *Jakobson's functions of communication*

- **The emotive function** communicates the sender's emotions, attitudes and status.
- **The conative function** prompts the receiver's response to the act of communication and encourages participation.
- **The referential function** communicates the relationship between the text and the wider reality, truth and fact.
- **The poetic function** communicates the text's formal and stylistic qualities.
- **The phatic function** establishes and maintains channels of communication.
- **The metalingual function** identifies the significant codes of the text.

Jakobson argues that while all of the above functions are co-existent in any act of communication, their importance varies according to the character of the individual act of communication being considered. A chat show guest's reminiscences of their childhood would be principally emotive; a stand-up comedian would hope to be chiefly conative; our experience of the news is likely to be referential; our enjoyment of an adaptation of a classic novel ought to be poetic (otherwise described by Jakobson more broadly as 'aesthetic'); much embarrassed communication on public transport with strangers is phatic; whenever we enquire of the geographical origin of an English speaker we are engaged in the metalingual function of communication. Jakobson offers a structuralist insight into the character of communication in a linear context and offers us as readers a useful and, in terms of the two approaches, a largely non-partisan approach.

Figure 3.23   *Halifax Building Society leaflet*

Identify Jakobson's six elements and six functions within the Halifax advertisement (see Figure 3.23). Which do you personally consider especially significant in this example?

▼ 5 PUTTING IT BACK TOGETHER

In this section we will demonstrate the use of techniques of textual analysis on actual texts.

- We will take you through an in-depth analysis of a couple of print texts.
- We will give you advice on planning and writing responses to texts.

We have broken down the communication process into its component parts. It is now time to start putting it all back together again. This section will offer you examples of the sort of analysis you will be asked to undertake as a student of communication. This section is principally about demonstration – of a method, of a way of thinking, of a critical process. It will deal with a range of texts and the principal tasks you will face.

The process of looking at, engaging with and ultimately analysing texts is a logical and straightforward one. It requires you first of all to examine what you are offered in an open, honest and personal way and then to use that information along with the specific knowledge and experience provided by your course of study, and/or this text, to push that response further. It is a subjective and objective approach, usually in that order but most often in an integrated fashion. Having asked 'What do I think about this text?', you are expected to consider 'How else could this text be considered or interpreted?' Sometimes this 'how else' makes you reconsider your own initial position, sometimes not. It is perhaps useful to see this process in terms of a series of actions, as follows.

- **Look**: What is it? How does it impact on you?
- **Read**: What does it say? What does it consist of?
- **Explore/analyse**: How is it structured? How does it work?
- **Review**: What do I think of it now? Is it as I originally thought?
- **Respond**: Here are my considered thoughts, feelings, opinions.

FIRST IMPRESSIONS

It is vital to record your first impressions of the texts you are asked to work with. In most cases this initial engagement is all a text has in its original, 'real world' context. Because much of the material produced by the mass media is genuinely ephemeral (i.e. here today and gone tomorrow), first impressions are sometimes all that a text is intended to receive. The article on page 140 appeared in Q magazine, taking up approximately one-third of page 28 within an issue of 164 pages. What is your first impression?

It is likely that your first impression was some kind of response to the striking, full-length image of an attractive young woman. This is clearly the intention of the article's designer, given that the girl's picture takes up more than half of the allotted space, is head and shoulders above the accompanying text, and is photographed in a way that accentuates her prominence, dominance and her literal length. You may also have been struck by the reference in the headline to Ted Hughes, the former Poet Laureate. Stereotypically we are perhaps being asked to be surprised at the juxtaposition of this attractive young woman and poetry.

At this point it is useful to be able accurately to classify the text with which we are dealing. Lasswell (1948) is useful in this respect, inviting the identification of sender, message, receiver, channel and effect. In the case of the Q article, the responses could be:

Who?	Q magazine
Says what?	Jewel's book of poems is out in May
To whom?	Q readers, contemporary music enthusiasts
In what channel?	A news/feature article
With what effect?	They know about, are amused by, or have received opinions about Jewel's poetry

These responses can then be supported or challenged with reference to conventional communication practice within the identified medium and/or channel. The confirmation question runs something like 'What makes this an article in a music magazine?' (If we didn't know, on what basis would we guess?) In this case our evidence might include: the relationship between images and text; the way in which the central image breaks the border; the bold text headline; the hierarchy of types; the caption image; the youthspeak vocabulary; and the energetic and economic register of the text.

It is not always this straightforward, but the process is always about looking for those aspects of a given text which it shares with other texts you have looked at. Moreover, it is important to remember that the sort of critical analysis you are engaged in is not about producing correct answers but rather about producing meaningful responses. Dealing with anonymous texts is a matter for intelligent deduction, not hopeful guess-work. To identify the precise source is not the issue; to appreciate the characteristics of a text is far more important.

We are now becoming interested in this Q article, given we have engaged with it both in terms of the initial impact and in terms of how it fits into a genre. The next stage is to consider in detail what we are in fact being offered. It is useful here to think in terms of the dominant signifiers, the dominant syntagms and the significant paradigms, and codes that are at work in the text.

Who Needs Ted Hughes?

When a ropey pop star poetry book sells two – yes, that's right – *two* million copies.

A Night Without Armor, Jewel's book of poetry, has now sold over two million copies in United States.

According to the preface, the Alaskan-born singer "explores the fire of first love, the fading of passion, the giving of trust, the lessons of betrayal and the healing of intimacy" in the book. A sample poem is A Couple Sitting On A Beach which consists of four simple lines: "He's the skinny one of the two/He reminds her of it constantly/He's a very funny guy that way/Ha-ha as she wobbles-to-walk wobbles-to-walk."

A Night Without Armor is published by Harper Collins in the UK in May. Meanwhile Jewel is also making her acting debut later this year in a new Ang Lee film, Ride With The Devil.

Jewel: Shall I compare thee to, like, a really nice leaf?

Figure 3.24 'Who Needs Ted Hughes?', *Q* magazine, no. 151, April 1999, p. 28. Courtesy of *Q* magazine

In an almost arithmetical way we are considering the different ways in which the meaning of the article might be calculated or totalled. This process might start at a formal level in the equation:

$$IMAGES + WORDS = TEXT$$

In the text in question, this bears considerable fruit, for it asks us to see a relationship between the dominant image (full length, colour, half article size), the secondary image (close-up, black and white, miniature inset) and the words. A single reading of the article is enough simply to reveal this relationship.

This is, in essence, a narrative – a story that transports us from image A to image B, or crudely from a state of ignorance to a state of knowledge. Having got the formal structure worked out, we can get into the detail: of the significant syntagm which is the first image; of the text in terms of its register, its vocabulary, its mode of address, its bias; and of the book cover as a conventional representation of 'serious' writing and 'serious' writers. This stage, however, is simply setting the agenda, uncovering interesting issues of representation, of narrative and of genre. It is also appropriate at this stage to identify the dominant codes, which in this case are largely non-verbal and verbal.

NARRATIVE The way in which a text reveals information to the audience in order to create a 'story'.

KEY TERM

HOW SHOULD I MARK UP (ANNOTATE) THE TEXT?

Clearly, this preparatory work on texts requires significant annotation of the texts themselves. Start on a separate sheet and sketch the general relationships – for example, the proportions of text and the positions of images. Once you approach the details of a text, the most appropriate place to work is on and around it, exploding general points to either side, above and below.

DECODING WHAT'S THERE

Paradigms are those collections of signs from which we make selections. The signs chosen are then ordered into chains that we call syntagms. Identifying these paradigms is therefore a useful way of revealing something of the process of construction. In the Q article two images are used which are taken from the same paradigm – the paradigm of available images of the singer Jewel (this paradigm is in itself part of a broader paradigm of representations of women).

Clearly, these images, be they of Jewel or of women generally, come from very different parts of these respective paradigms. In fact, the preferred reading is probably to see them as opposites, a fact that is reinforced by the use of technical codes (colour versus black and white; medium shot versus close-up). It is our job, however, to explore beyond the dominant discourse, to refuse to take the stereotypes at face value. For while the cover of Jewel's book is a study in understated convention (serious facial expression, face cleared of unruly hair, dark clothing, wordy backdrop, title positioned to avoid any hint of cleavage), the full length 'Girls just want to have fun' shot has more to say if we are prepared to look.

Unanchored this could easily be a fashion catalogue shot or even part of a sequence for a Lads magazine. In the context of an article amazed at the success of Jewel's 'ropey pop star poetry book', it is simply meant to describe the antithesis of 'poet'. The caption ('Shall I compare thee to, like, a really nice leaf?') makes this clear. Jewel is just an ordinary girl – vain, superficial and unsophisticated. What this anchor activates is one set of dominant signifiers which adds up to 'silly girl out to have fun' or worse. At the same time it de-activates any part of the image which might contradict or oppose this reading, any factors which might in fact empower Jewel or suggest she is in control of her own communication. Yet these elements are present if we care to look for them and the conversation between 'Jewel as fool' and 'Jewel as cool' can be referenced in practice in this way:

Jewel as fool:	**Jewel as cool:**
Flick of hair across the face is flirty	Hair unkempt suggests refusal to conform
Blondish hair connotes stereotype bimbo	Facial expression is defiant, confident; challenging gaze engages reader
Open coat reveals breast	Clothing is deliberately and ironically trashy
Navel is exposed	Disguised thumbs-up is indication of knowingness
Short skirt has stereotypical connotations	Slouching posture: refuses to be pin-up
Plastic mac is sexy in an obvious way	Long legs are accentuated
Posture is open-legged, available	Posture is confident
Active foot indicates playfulness, coyness	Trainers are a key signifier, denying the stereotypes of girls in short skirts: they are practical, enabling
Jewel is just another pop bimbette	**Jewel knows what she is doing**

Thus we can see that the image is in fact potentially more problematic than the pre-ferred reading will allow, and we are learning a little more about mass communication. At this point you usually have a couple of sides of notes and hopefully half the time allotted for the task left for presenting your response. The starting point for this phase should be your review of the evidence you have uncovered, from first impressions onward, arriving ultimately back at your considered impression of the text. Sometimes your opinion has not significantly changed; either way this kind of general response is a sound place to start your written critique.

Figure 3.25 *Cover of the DVD of* Bart Wars. *Courtesy of Fox*

Rather than labouring a point, let's review the process by quickly responding to a new text – (see Figure 3.25). Here are the key questions or prompts with some suggested responses (these responses are not exclusive; they are not the only valid responses).

- **Look:** What are my first impressions? It's amusing – a *Star Wars* spoof; there is that play on words and the Vadar/Skywalker duel.

  What is it? It's a DVD cover saying 'Here are some episodes of *The Simpsons*' to a youngish/young at heart audience. It wants us to buy the DVD. The sender is whoever makes *The Simpsons*.
- **Read:** What does it consist of? Formally, some cartoon art and some words. In terms of content it offers some familiar characters and some familiar mythic film characters. Colour is clearly important: clear, bright, well defined.
- **Explore:** The dominant signifiers are the words and the human figures. A dominant code is intertextuality. Much of the intended meaning of the cover depends on various degrees of knowledge of the *Star Wars* films and mythology – for example,

'the Simpsons strike back' is a variant of 'the Empire strikes back'. Moreover, and more significantly, the fact that Bart is shown duelling with his father, Homer, refers to the moment in the first trilogy where Luke Skywalker discovers that Darth Vadar (Homer in this parody) is in fact his father. This is a scene from the third film *Return of the Jedi* and thus the whole trilogy is parodied on the cover. Essentially the representations are iconic, though with fairly low motivation, and this allows a range of visual humour and an informal register. The costumes are exaggerated but recognisable, the facial expressions dramatic but in this context amusing – partly in the context of the style of presentation and partly, to *Simpsons'* cognoscenti (those in the know), in the context of Homer and Bart's ongoing relationship and beyond to the father–son relationships on which both these texts draw.

■ **Review**: A clever and amusing text, whose function is principally phatic. It is doubtful if any of the episodes referred to in the lower part of the cover are substantially related to the Star Wars phenomenon. The PG logo, which is an index of suitability and security, has an irony in the context of a son and father fighting to the death, which can surely be no accident, particularly as Bart is reputedly ten years old.

KEY TERM

INTERTEXTUALITY This is defined by John Fiske as follows: 'The meanings generated by any one text are determined partly by the meanings of other texts to which it appears similar' – more simply the ability of one text to refer to another.

WRITING IT UP

Having made a structured response to any given text, you will be required to present this. We will deal later with the specifics of this (see pages 257–264), but a brief 'walkthrough' with an analysed text will do no harm here.

In all of these cases it will be important to plan your response so that you offer your reading in the most convincing way and so that you miss out nothing important. It will be important to read the task carefully to discover what precisely is required. The best way to do this is physically to underline the key words of the task and then, more importantly, write down the implications of each of the words or phrases you have underlined. In other words, write in your own words what bearing each of these words should have on your response.

In the AQA Communications Studies AS unit 2, for example, the first task is always a variant of 'Using the techniques of critical analysis explore the ways in which this text communicates with its audience(s)'. Clearly, the twin keys are 'techniques of critical analysis' and 'explore the ways' and the implications run along the lines of 'We should use technical and critical terms to examine the meanings of the text in detail'.

The important thing is to avoid mere description and ensure significant analysis. This can be aided by the way you structure your response, which will of course be into a series of paragraphs. The first and last paragraphs largely take care of themselves – the first providing an overview and/or an account of your initial impressions, the last leaving the examiner with your considered opinions on the qualities and effectiveness of the text, not always the same thing. In between, the body of the analysis needs to detail the three significant stages of analysis: classifying the text, deciding what's communicating and decoding/exploring meanings. If you work on 50 words at each end and 50 to 100 words in each paragraph in between, you'll get a feeling for the proportions of your piece. A response to *The Simpsons* cover might have the following plan.

1	**First impressions**	humour, colour, *Star Wars*
2	**What's there?**	syntagms: words and pictures representation: father-and-son icons setting: index of sci-fi/Star Wars anchorage: sets agenda
3	**What does it mean?**	dominant code: intertextuality cross paradigms: Simpsons/Star Wars signification. connotation/myth
4	**Final thoughts**	PG logo: irony sophisticated text, skilful, successful

If you prefer, this planning may work through a slightly more developed note form which forces you to think through the detail before you write. It is vital that you understand that this is the nature of the game; the essence is your analysis of the text, the note form being a way of getting to that analysis in a quicker and, it is hoped, clearer way. The hope is that you will cut through the verbiage to the key critical and technical vocabulary, not that you will limit the analysis by limiting the vocabulary.

For example, note form analysis of DVD cover

First impressions:	colourful, engaging (phatic device) title is pun (play on words) humorous (words and pictures)
What is it?	Who?: 20th Century Fox Says what?: Here's a new *Simpsons* DVD To whom?: the DVD-buying public, especially *Simpsons'* fans In what channel?: a DVD box cover With what effect?: we see it, we buy it

What does it consist of?

SYNTAGM 1:	some words (anchors and puns) some figures (iconic – Bart/Luke, Homer/Vadar) a background (index of Star Wars/sci-fi etc.)

In all cases, remember that what is being tested is your knowledge of critical techniques and your ability to respond to texts.

▼ 6 SOME PRINT TEXTS AND SAMPLE TASKS

In this section you will have the opportunity to respond to a range of print texts for yourself. Each text is accompanied by a set of prompts.

In the final section you will have the opportunity to try out your developing critical skills on a range of print-based texts. In each case you will be provided with a series of prompts to stimulate your response and then one or more examination-style tasks.

What you will realise, looking across a range of very different texts, is that it is experience of the method, of the specific tools, that is needed and not necessarily experience of the potentially vast range of texts. In other words, it matters that you have looked at texts, not that you have looked at a specific variety of text. What you also need is genuine and honest engagement with texts and this is clearly helped by them being unseen and unprepared.

Figure 3.26 'Tolkien Trail' information leaflet

Prompts (for Artefact A, figure 3.26)

■ What is the dominant signifier?
■ What potential barriers to communication are there here?
■ How do the design elements work?
■ Who is the intended audience?

ACTIVITY . . .

Prepare an Overhead Projector Transparency (OHT) which sums up the strengths and weaknesses of this leaflet cover as a piece of effective communication.

ARTEFACT B: COMIC BOOK PAGE

Prompts (for Artefact B, figure 3.27)

■ How does this text work?
■ What are its chief components?
■ Comment on representation in this text.
■ Comment on the register of this text.

ACTIVITY . . .

Prepare a set of notes for a five-minute presentation to your fellow A Level students entitled 'Comic Book Communication' which uses page 149 as your only source of evidence.

A very different kind of cartoon communication is provided each day in all newspapers – the political cartoon. Here the issue of representation is made more interesting by the fact that many of those represented are 'known'. The first task of the cartoonist is therefore to create a likeness or exaggerated caricature of the public figure which the audience will recognise. This is often achieved by a combination of iconic and indexical features, wherein the exaggeration of key features (e.g. the ears of Prince Charles) and the use of significant props (e.g. the Queen's crown in an inappropriate context) combine to create a signifier that is identifiable with its intended signified at the level of denotation but which also carries with it implicit connotations.

Figure 3.27 *Illustration from Alan Moore and Dave Gibbons, The Watchmen (Titan Books Ltd, 1987)*

Figure 3.28 *Political cartoon by Steve Bell. © Steve Bell 2001. Courtesy of the* Guardian

Prompts (for Artefact C, figure 3.28)

- Comment on the presentation of the context (where we are and how we know).
- In what specific ways are the Americans (and the USA) represented?
- What is the effect of the speech bubble?
- What attitude to the so-called 'War on Terrorism' does this cartoon have?

ACTIVITY . . .

You have been asked to explain Peirce's three sign categories (icon, index and symbol) for a Communication Studies textbook like this one. You have been allowed 150 words in total, and the above cartoon has been provided as evidence. You should take your illustrative examples from here only.

ARTEFACT D: PROMOTIONAL POSTCARD

Figure 3.29 *Butlins promotional postcard*

Prompts (for Artefact D, figure 3.29)

- What is each window communicating?
- What is the purpose of the division of the card?
- What is the meaning of the settings and props?
- What are we being offered here?

ACTIVITY...

In 250 words justify the design of this postcard, pointing out the ways in which it positively represents Butlins and the experience of a Butlins holiday.

ARTEFACT E: GREETINGS CARD

DAD

HEY –
Christmas is here !
Now, ain't that great ?
Time to get down
and celebrate !

Figure 3.30 Greetings card

Prompts (for Artefact E, figure 3.30)

- Comment on the way the words are arranged on the page.
- What sort of representation are we being offered?
- What is the function of the coloured stars?
- What is the register and function of this cover?

ACTIVITY . . .

Prepare a design for a 'Rappy Christmas, Mum' card and annotate semiotically to demonstrate the nature of the communication you are conducting. Identify the significant paradigms, the character of the signs used, and the preferred reading. Present your design and analysis within a single A4 side.

Figure 3.31 Cover of Decathlon *fitness catalogue*

Prompts (for Artefact F, figure 3.31)

- Comment on the ways in which the text uses space.
- Examine the ways in which the two people are represented to us.
- Explore how words are used on this page.
- Who is the target audience?

ACTIVITY . . .

The cosmetics millionaire Charles Revlon once said: 'In our factories we make lipstick, in our adverts we sell hope.' With this in mind what is being sold here in addition to health and fitness equipment, and how are these 'other things' delivered?

Figure 3.32 Website for fans of popular culture, www.theory.org.uk

Prompts (for Artefact G, figure 3.32)

- In what ways is the experience of the web page different from that of this book?
- What are the primary conventions of a website home page?
- In what ways does the text establish its authority?
- What are the weaknesses of this format?

ACTIVITY ...

Select a website home page and consider the different ways in which it attempts to target its audience. Consider also the barriers it might be putting up to those it does not wish/intend to target.

FURTHER EXAMPLES

It seems corny to say so, but if you want examples just look around. Communication texts are around you and among you – from the cereal packets you absentmindedly read at breakfast to the books or magazines you read before you go to sleep. All have their messages, their devices, their conventions and their idiosyncrasies. All await the careful reader. A list of places to start might include the following.

- Leaflets: look at a range from those which inform you about sexually transmitted diseases to those which offer you *English Heritage* or *The National Trust*
- Flyers: from adverts for Dial-a-Pizza to local band promotions
- Brochures: from college prospectuses to luxury car specifications
- Magazines: from FHM to *The People's Friend*
- Newspapers: from free papers to 'The Free Press'
- Advertisements: from matchbooks to billboards
- Posters: from Che Guevara to Baby Spice
- Book jackets: from Harry Potter to Dennis Potter
- CD covers: from Westlife to Parklife
- Websites: from *The Blair Witch Project* to Tony Blair.com
- Scripts: from screenplays to school plays
- Storyboards: from *Chicken Run* to *Logan's Run*
- Postcards: from college promotions to seaside humour
- Greetings cards: from 'It's a Boy!' to 'With Deepest Sympathy'
- Packaging materials: from cereal packets to shop liveries

This is not a list to alarm you but rather to remind you of the vital part played by communication texts in our lives. To be aware of this is in itself a step towards being an effective critic.

FURTHER WORK . . .

1 Consider the ways in which an organisation with which you are familiar (e.g. your school/college, place of work or worship, your preferred nightclub) presents itself in terms of the texts it offers wittingly and unwittingly to be read. Contrast the formal/direct communication (prospectuses, open days, slogans) with the informal/indirect communication (relationships, premises, reputation). Suggest ways in which your chosen organisation might improve its communication.

2 Using any medium or combination of media, present a guided tour of a specified part of your local area. Present the material in the manner of a reading, offering interpretation that might be historical, cultural, political and/or aesthetic, that is, choose what you want the guide to do – inform, entertain, persuade, advertise, or all of these. Present your new text to an audience of local people and evaluate its impact.

3 Responding to and interpreting practical texts is an essential way of drawing

continued

together the various elements of a Communication Studies course. By considering the variety of communication, you are implicitly responding to the cultural question 'What is communication?' Which definition of communication best fits the experience you have of the range of texts we have considered, from the built environment to body modification?

4   The writer Virginia Woolf claimed that 'what a female writer writes is always feminine: the difficulty is in defining what is feminine'. How far do you think it is useful to talk about communication texts as masculine and feminine?

5   The whole pattern of social life is being radically altered by developments in Communication and Information Technology, particularly in terms of the Internet and e-mail. To what extent has this changed the character of our experience of communication texts? (What difference has it made to our social lives, working lives and relationships to traditional mass media?)

FURTHER READING

Fiske, J. (1990) *Introduction to Communication Studies*, 2nd edn, London/New York: Routledge.

Guiraud, P. (1975) *Semiology*, trans. G. Gross, London: Routledge & Kegan Paul.

Hawkes, T. (1977) *Structuralism and Semiotics*, London: Routledge.

O'Sullivan, T., Hartley, J., Saunders, D., Montgomery, M. and Fiske, J. (1994) *Key Concepts in Communication and Cultural Studies*, 2nd edn, London/New York: Routledge.

PART 4: THEMES IN PERSONAL COMMUNICATION

In this part we are going to look at a wide range of themes, ideas, concepts and issues in personal communication. We have grouped them together under three broad headings: Verbal and Non-Verbal Communication; Intrapersonal Communication; and Group Communication.

▼ 1 VERBAL COMMUNICATION

In this section we look at verbal communication.

- We consider what language is, how it can be defined, and how human language is different from animal communication systems.
- We look at the formal study of language.
- We consider language in relation to gender.

Without language, human beings would probably lead less complex lives than they do. The capacity to use language is one key factor that separates the human animal from other animals. Imagine a world in which language did not exist; consider all the things that we would be unable to do (for example, this book could not exist). It would be impossible to express our ideas. The range of feelings that we could express would be much more limited. The seemingly simple process of communicating with other people would be much more time-consuming and imprecise. Passing on our experiences to other people and to the generations that follow would be impossible. Similarly, our awareness of the experiences of previous generations would be quite limited.

There can be little doubt that language is a central part of our experience as human beings and has contributed to human animals dominating planet Earth. Of course, there are people who would question whether this domination is a good thing. Civilisation might well be an elaborate dead-end in the process of evolution, but the fact remains that the capacity to use language as a means of communication is largely responsible for the development of the peoples who occupy planet Earth.

WHAT IS LANGUAGE?

Language is a complex sign system. The signs it uses are composed of either sounds or symbols in the form of letters. These sounds and letters are put together to form words. Words in turn are combined together to form sentences.

As you saw on pages 92–127, where we looked at textual analysis, the function of a sign is to signify an object or concept that has an existence in the real world. The sign stands in place of that object or concept and is used to represent it.

Language is composed mainly of symbols. A sign that is symbolic is one that has no direct connection with the thing it stands for. The word 'cat' has no real link to the furry animal that it represents. We could just as easily use the word 'wood' to describe the furry quadruped. The use of the word 'cat' is arbitrary. It represents a cat because everyone agrees that that is what it represents. Unless of course you live in France, where you would call it a *'chat'*. It's when you think about the fact that there are thousands of languages in the world which all have different signs to represent the furry quadruped that you realise that there is no essential, logical or necessary connection between objects in the world and the signs that we use to represent those objects.

Most written and spoken signs are symbolic. A few words that we speak are in fact iconic. They work by being recognised as similar to what they represent. These are called onomatopoeic words, where the sound of the word imitates what it represents. 'Squelch' or 'quack' are iconic rather than symbolic. Some languages are written in an iconic fashion. Chinese employs ideograms which are a type of word picture.

In his ABC *of Reading* (1951) the poet Ezra Pound explained how simple ideograms function, for example:

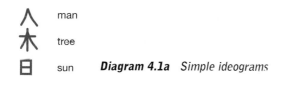

Diagram 4.1a *Simple ideograms*

Here we can clearly see how these iconic signs relate to their objects. Pound then explained how simple ideograms could be combined to form more complex ones, for example

 sun tangled in the tree's branches, as at sunrise, meaning now: the East   **Diagram 4.1b** *Complex ideogram*

WHAT DO WE DO WITH LANGUAGE?

So what is the value of this complex sign system that allows us to communicate with one another? What are the uses to which human beings put this great skill? After eavesdropping on a few conversations or listening to people on their mobile phones, you may be tempted to reply 'not a lot'. It is possible, however, to categorise some of the functions of language to identify how it is used. These functions would include the following.

- **The communication of our experiences of the outside world**. Using language is an important way of letting other people know about the world and our experiences of it. For example, we can tell people of dangers that exist as well as the pleasures to be had. In this way, language allows us to explain our emotional response to our experiences of the world.

- **The capacity to communicate ideas**. You will see that this is linked to the previous function. However, language does not limit us to describing our experiences of the concrete and tangible. It allows us to talk about abstract concepts, such as love and truth. It also allows us to speculate on the very purpose of our existence.
- **The capacity to be creative**. We can sing songs or recite poetry using language. This is sometimes referred to as the aesthetic function of language.
- **The capacity for making reassuring noises to each other**. This is called the phatic function. It implies that many of the utterances that we make carry little information. They are designed simply to help with social interaction. They have been described as ritualised exchanges. For example, the question 'How are you?' requires the ritualised answer, 'Fine. Are you OK?', rather than a detailed audit of the receiver's state of mind and body.

ACTIVITY . . .

Spend some time listening carefully to someone else speak. Try to identify examples of each of the above functions in their conversation. Which of the functions do you feel predominates? Do you think this is likely to vary from person to person?

You can see from the above examples that language is important to human beings in determining how they communicate their experiences. If language is such an important factor, it follows that to some extent the view that we have of the world is likely to be determined by the language that we use. Indeed, an important philosophical debate is concerned with the relationship between thought and language. Put very simply, the question is how does language affect the way in which we think? Do we in fact use language to think with? If so, then language obviously must determine and define what we are able to think.

The term used to describe this concept is linguistic relativism. In essence it means that the language we have learned to speak determines the way in which we see the world. So for example, if we have grown up using German as our first language, we will interpret the events that take place in the world differently to a person who has grown up using French or English.

Language in this way positions us to take a particular view of the world and our experiences in it. This theory was put forward by Edward Sapir (1956) and Benjamin Lee Whorf (1956) and is called the Sapir Whorf Hypothesis. A hypothesis is a theory and, like many theories about the human mind, it is hard to prove whether it is true or not. However, it may be useful to look at an example of how the hypothesis might work.

English people have a reputation for being embarrassed about sex and bodily functions. It may well be that this embarrassment is in part due to the fact that the words we use to describe these activities and the related bodily parts are all taboo words in English culture. Indeed, most of them are swear words and many are used as a means of verbally abusing people we do not like. If we look back to the medieval period in this country, a poet like Chaucer was happy to use such vocabulary, in its original meaning, in a poem like *The Canterbury Tales*. It was in the Victorian era, famed for its hypocritical prudery, that such language was outlawed.

The question is the extent to which social prohibitions on the use of this language have created this furtive attitude to sex and bodily functions among English people. Certainly our European neighbours seem to be far less inhibited about these issues, as a glance at their television programmes will reveal.

Another example of the way in which language can be said to frame our thinking is in the issue of race, where 'white' is assumed to have positive connotations and 'black' to have negative connotations. Many English people still use forms of or synonyms for 'black' to connote negative ideas. For example, people use a phrase such as 'giving someone a black look' to describe an intimidating or threatening gesture. 'Black sheep' is used metaphorically to describe someone who does no good. White, on the other hand, has connotations of purity and cleanliness. A white Christmas is much hoped for. White weddings are symbols of chastity and purity. At funerals people are expected to wear black. On the other hand Chinese culture associates white with death. (If nothing else, the fact that different cultures employ the same sign in different ways reinforces the notion that there is nothing essential about the signs we use to represent objects; there is no essence of cat about the sign 'cat'; there is no essence of purity to the sign 'white'.)

It can be argued that the connotative power of black in our language serves to determine our thinking about blackness in a negative way.

You may like to consider the way in which language is also said to reinforce attitudes to gender. This issue will be discussed at greater length later in the section.

SOME USEFUL TERMS IN LINGUISTICS

The study of language is called linguistics. It is useful at this point to introduce some of the terms that are commonly used in linguistics.

Semantics

Semantics is the study of meanings. One of the complexities of language is that the same word can have different meanings. In the same way, similar sounding words can be spelled differently and also have different meanings. Moreover, the meaning of words can change over a period of time.

> **SEMANTICS** The branch of linguistics that is concerned with the meaning of words and how these have changed. It is concerned with the relationships between signs and meaning.

KEY TERM

As we have already stated, the meaning of words is arbitrary. Words mean what they mean because of agreement within a culture as to their meaning. Of course, in reality, semantics is not quite such a precise science. If, for example, we use the word 'dog', we all have a mental concept of a mammal with four legs and a tail. However, each of us is likely to have an individual picture of a dog. Perhaps it is our own pet dog of which we are particularly fond, a small black poodle for example. As you saw in Part 3, words, like other signs, carry with them denotative and connotative meanings. The word 'dog', while representing the concept of the animal, will carry with it meanings that will be interpreted in different ways by individual members of a culture. Not only will each have a different mental picture of a dog but also the word will carry emotional connotations for many people. For example, some will experience great feelings of warmth and affections towards the pet waiting to greet them when they arrive home. For others it may be fear, hatred and anxiety after an unhappy experience with an aggressive dog.

For this reason many people see words as imprecise tools for conveying meaning. In the above example, we considered a word that is a concrete noun. Such words refer to objects that have a tangible existence in the real world. A dog is something that you can perceive with your senses. Many words that we use are, however, abstract. They refer to ideas. Truth, love and beauty are examples of abstract nouns. If it is difficult to fix the meaning of words that relate to real objects; it is clearly even more difficult to agree on the meaning of words that describe things that exist only as ideas.

Syntax

Syntax is a way of describing the conventions of how words are combined to form meanings. Syntax is in fact the rules of language or its grammar. We tend to observe these conventions much more carefully when we are writing than when we are speaking. For example, it is quite common in speech to miss out the verb from a sentence. In writing this is traditionally assumed to be a serious omission.

Phonology

Phonology is the sound system of language. The basic unit of sound is called a phoneme. This represents an individual sound, such as that made by the letters 'th' in English. Although the sound 'th' exists in English, it is not found in other European languages such as French. Consequently, one way of identifying a person speaking English with a French accent is that they will pronounce words containing these letters awkwardly.

Phonetics

We call the study of the sounds of language phonetics. Systems for writing shorthand such as Pitman use phonetics. In Pitman shorthand the symbols for 'sea' and 'see' would be identical because they sound the same. Of course, when reading back shorthand notes, the actual word would be determined by the context.

Discourse

Discourse is another term that you will find useful in your exploration of the nature and use of language. In fact this is a good example of a word that has taken on new and different meanings to meet a range of different needs. In *Key Concepts in Communication and Cultural Studies* (O'Sullivan *et al.* 1994) its meaning in linguistics is defined as 'verbal utterances of greater magnitude than one sentence'.

The term is more generally used in Communication Studies to describe a particular type of speech used by a group of people. Lawyers, for example, are said to use the discourse of the law. This is a vocabulary and way of speaking specific to legal circles. Media forms such as television have their own discourse or way of speaking.

Each of us is likely to be able to use a range of different discourses in our daily life according to the context in which we are speaking. The discourse of the Communication Studies classroom is likely to be rather different to the discourse of love, for example.

RESTRICTED AND ELABORATED CODES

In an important study of the use of language published in 1971, Basil Bernstein suggested two categories that are used according to the situation in which we find ourselves, namely the restricted code and the elaborated code.

The restricted code is used mostly in group situations when we are speaking to people who are likely to share our interests and experiences. It is characterised by a limited vocabulary and a basic use of syntax. Restricted codes are also likely to have high levels of redundancy (or predictability) in the words that are used to encode a message. Bernstein argued that restricted codes reinforce the sameness of people communicating within a group. One way in which you can readily identify the use of a restricted code is if you are listening in to a group of people and find yourself feeling excluded by the way in which they are speaking. For example, if you listen to a professional group such as lawyers or doctors, they will employ a restricted code to discuss issues relating to their work which many of us would find hard to understand. Similarly, a lawyer or a doctor might feel excluded if they were to listen to a group of Communication Studies students discussing semiotics or even restricted and elaborated codes.

Elaborated codes use a wider range of vocabulary, more complex syntax and are much harder to predict (they are more entropic). The elaborated code is less concerned with group relationships and more appropriate to the expression of individual ideas. In fact using an elaborated code is in many ways an assertion of a person's individuality by identifying differences between speaker and listener. Just as the restricted code assumes a background of shared interests, assumption, even a common view of the world, so the elaborated code is about uniqueness and individuality.

Clearly, an individual is not limited to the use of just one of these codes. A surgeon who might spend much of his or her day speaking in a restricted code to colleagues about clinical matters may well go out for a social drink in the evening and employ an elaborated code to express views on the current political situation or the appointment of the new England football manager.

In Bernstein's original research his focus was on the language of children and identified how social class directly affected the use of these codes. In general working-class children were found to use restricted codes, largely because working-class communities are characterised by social relationships that are close-knit and inward looking. Middle-class children, however, employ an elaborated code because social relations within this group are more mobile and more outward looking. In fact a characteristic of middle-class language use is the capacity to move between restricted and elaborated codes in response to the demands of the social situation.

ACTIVITY . . .

It has been suggested that the words 'restricted' and 'elaborated' imply a value judgement about the language codes people employ. Do you think there is evidence to suggest that we value the use of elaborated codes more highly than restricted codes?

Compare and contrast the use of language by characters in the British situation comedies. Pay particular attention to such aspects as education, family background and social position.

The study of language is obviously a complex and difficult business. This study is further complicated by an important distinction made by Ferdinand de Saussure (1983). He used the term 'langue' to describe the rules of language, or more accurately the system of language that allows us to communicate with one another. The term 'parole' is used in contrast to this to describe individual use of language, or the single utterances that people make. However, it is only possible to study the notion of langue by looking at individual uses of it in the form of parole.

Most people have the competence to use language. By this we mean that they can construct sentences in order to communicate with other people. An important question in linguistics is where does this competence come from. Or, put more simply, how do we learn language?

As we have stated, human language is a sophisticated means of communication that separates human beings from other animals. An obvious question to ask is how this ability evolved. The work of Noam Chomsky (1968) is particularly important in this context. Chomsky's work spans many academic disciplines, but his particular contribution to Communication Studies is his exploration of how language is learned. In the process of researching this issue, Chomsky attempted to teach language to chimpanzees – with somewhat limited results.

The arguments that he puts forward are both complex and difficult. In a simplified form his basic argument is that we are all born with an innate or inborn ability to learn language. This innate ability might be compared to our walking on two legs, in that it is a skill that distinguishes us from most other mammals. The question that may have sprung into your mind might well be why different nations speak different languages. To explain this, Chomsky makes an important distinction between syntax and vocabulary.

It is a capacity to learn the conventions of language (of grammar and syntax) that we are born with. Research indicates that these conventions are basically very similar for all languages. The differences between the conventions of different languages are trivial in comparison with their similarities. Chomsky uses this fact to argue that the capacity to learn language is an ability that we are all born with. What distinguishes one language from another is the vocabulary that we learn. If you grow up among people who speak English, you will learn an English vocabulary. In France, you will learn French. Children growing up in bilingual households generally learn both.

Speakers of a first language are sensitive to the conventions of their language. Someone for whom this language is a second (or third) one will often be identified when they don't observe the conventions of that language. If someone says 'I have been in England since five years' we know what they mean but we also appreciate that they have literally translated from their first language (in this case French) into their second language, English.

Our working knowledge of syntax allows us to use vocabulary to generate sentences. The number of sentences we can generate is potentially limitless. Of course, not all of them will make sense, although they may conform with conventions of grammar.

Chomsky's argument is a complex one but one of his prime concerns is the issue of what he calls 'deep' and 'surface' structures in language. These allow us to do the same thing in two different ways or to create a sentence that contains two different meanings. For example, a sign outside a pharmacist's shop that reads 'We dispense with accuracy' is capable of two different interpretations. On the other hand we can create two sentences (e.g. 'The child kicked the ball' and 'The ball was kicked by the child') which both convey the same idea. For Chomsky this competence in generating language that contains both of these structures is the basis of how we communicate. In fact, it can be argued that creating meaning is a feature of the human condition and a function that we are all predisposed to do.

ACTIVITY . . .

Chomsky gives the example of the following sentence which, although grammatically correct, makes little sense:

Colourless green ideas sleep furiously.

Try to generate sentences of your own that have this quality.

Interestingly, a lot of research into the acquisition of language has centred on the use of sign languages. There is a commonly held belief that sign language is a basic iconic language that is a poor substitute for spoken language. However, studies of signing have shown it to be a complex system of communication with its own syntax as well as its own vocabulary. Although the UK and the USA generally share a common verbal and spoken language system, they have completely different sign languages, neither readily comprehensible to a native signer from the other country.

People using sign language are capable of engaging in the same abstract debates and discussions as those who use verbal means of communication. Clearly, sign language has freed itself sufficiently from relying on resemblance to express such complex and abstract ideas.

Patterns of language learning are also regional as well as national. In the same way that we learn the vocabulary of the culture in which we grow up, so we also learn to imitate the speech patterns and pronunciations of the people in the area in which we live. We learn to speak the dialect of the place where we develop our language skills. In this way, in the UK we can identify people by their accent. People from Yorkshire, Merseyside and London all have specific patterns of speaking that help us to place them geographically.

There are also specific variations in vocabulary between regions used to describe everyday items. Small pieces of bread, for example, can be called rolls, cobs, balm cakes, breadcakes or batches, according to the area of the country in which you find yourself.

For the first 60 years of the twentieth century a regional accent was considered a distinct obstacle to advancement in certain careers. 'Received pronunciation', or RP, is the term used to describe English spoken without any trace of regional accent. It is the type of English spoken traditionally by BBC newsreaders and for many people it is a voice that connotes authority. Most of the films and television programmes made before the mid-1960s feature lead actors and presenters speaking RP; indeed, regional accents tended to be reserved for people of a socially inferior status – for example, the chirpy Cockney private you'd always find in British films about the Second World War. Up until the 1960s, whatever region of the UK young actors came from when they went to drama school, they would be trained to speak RP. It was only the popular acceptance of naturalistic drama that enabled actors such as Albert Finney, Rita Tushingham and Michael Caine to keep their regional accents (although in *Zulu*, Caine's first film in a leading role, his accent was distinctly RP).

Nowadays an RP accent doesn't have anywhere near the value it once did. A number of regional accents (such as those associated with Yorkshire, Lancashire and Scotland) and adopted accents (such as Estuary English) are now felt to be a distinct advantage when trying to gain employment as, for example, a British breakfast television presenter or British children's television presenter.

How important is dialect in modern British society? Do we value people with regional accents as highly as those who speak RP?

- Examine TWO serious news/documentary programmes (e.g. *Newsnight*, *Panorama*, ITV *News*) for the accents/type of language used by the presenters/ interviewers. Does this affect their image and the importance that we as the audience attach to what they are saying? Who is likely to be the target audience of this sort of programme?
- Examine TWO long-running soap operas and note the accents and language of the main characters. What does it tell you about the social class of the characters and their likely education/jobs/etc.? Who do you think is the target audience for this sort of programme?

Human beings and animals

The philosopher Rene Descartes said that animals are mere machines and that Man stands alone. His basic argument is that, unlike animals, human beings are rational creatures gifted with a number of abilities which distinguish them from and raises them above the animal world. One of these abilities is the skill of using language to communicate. Clearly Descartes' argument is ultimately a theological one but the idea that language is a uniquely human capability is central to any study of Communication.

No one would deny that animals have a complex system of communication. We marvel at the way in which whales and dolphins among other animals communicate as part of their own patterns of social behaviour. Obviously animals living together in social groups will need a system of communication that enables them to function together as a social unit and work in the best interests of the group. Primates, considered to be Man's closest relatives in the animal world, have been the object of study for many years, both in terms of their patterns of social behaviour and the capacity for communicating within their social groups.

It has been observed that most primates have a reasonably elaborate system of calls which are used for such things as establishing territory, signalling distress and warning of imminent danger. One species of primate, the vervet monkey, has been observed to distinguish different types of danger in the calls that it uses. The calls it emits inform other members of the group whether the danger is from a snake, a hawk or a leopard, for example, and allows them to take the necessary evasive action.

Even the most sophisticated of animal communicators, however, only communicate in this way when they are in an emotional situation – for example, if they feel threatened, want to mate or have found something to eat. In contrast to this, human beings have the capacity to use words we have created in the absence of the things we are talking about. Indeed, we can readily talk about ideas that we may not have experienced first hand – for example, a foreign country we may never personally have visited. This capacity is called displacement. It is central to our ability to share and collect ideas and information about the world at large. Our own experiences of the world may be limited by the language we inherit from how other people speak about the world. In consequence we can have quite detailed information about places we have never visited and times before we were alive. In fact, human beings' capacity to be creative in the use of language means they can talk about the future, even though none of us may have actually experienced it.

Chomsky argues that language is a uniquely human capability because human beings are born with the potential to learn and use language. Their brains are in some way hardwired to learn and develop language skills in a way that animals' brains are not. Put simply, Chomsky believes that the rules of language, grammar or syntax, are an innate human capability. There are, he argues, universal rules that apply to all languages. What we learn is a vocabulary to apply to this set of rules and this allows us to created or 'generate' sentences which are the basis of our language. The vocabulary which we learn and apply will depend on our upbringing and culture – for example, most people will learn the language of the country or region where they grow up. Children growing up in bi-lingual household will most likely learn two sets of vocabulary. The rules of how to combine the words in these vocabularies into a sentence, however, are something we do not have to learn; they are an in-born skill, just like walking on two legs.

Chomsky is signalling a fundamental difference between human and animals systems of communication. The animal system is ultimately closed, in that there are a limited number of messages that can be sent. This is partly due to the fact that for even the most sophisticated of animals each sign has just one function and its meaning can only be expressed in that one way. In consequence, animals are not able to use sounds in a novel or creative way. Human beings, on the other hand, are capable of generating an unlimited number of messages because their grammatical rules, or syntax, allow us to do just this. Chomsky uses the sentence: 'Colourless green ideas sleep furiously' to demonstrate how we are even able to generate messages that have no obvious meaning but which we accept as conforming to the rules of grammar. Each and everyone of us is capable of sending messages that have never been sent before. Many of us will do so as we adapt to new situations that we meet.

Additionally, the signs that we use for human language are often given multiple functions. This allows us to express one meaning in a whole series of different ways, each with perhaps a slightly different nuances. In this way we can be creative with our language and use it to adapt to new and different situations. Look, for example, at the ways in which new technology such as e-mail and text messaging has required us to modify creatively our use of language. These changes can be effected very quickly in our culture; changes in animal communication are extremely slow and usually limited to the speed of genetic rather than cultural evolution. As we have noted elsewhere the system of sounds and signs that we call 'language' is largely culturally agreed. The system only works through our implicit cultural agreement as to the agreed meaning of these sounds and signs.

Interest in how language is acquired has fascinated scholars through the ages. One way of looking at this has been through so-called wild or 'feral' children who were brought up outside of civilised society and in consequence were denied the opportunity to learn language. Two well-known cases of this have subsequently been made the themes of films. The first is the case of Victor, the wild boy of Aveyron who was found in woods in France at the beginning of the nineteenth century. He was brought to Paris and, under the patient care of Dr Itard, learned the rudiments of speech, although he failed to progress beyond the level of a small child. The story of Victor is told in Francois Truffaut's film L'enfant Sauvage. A similar instance is that of Kaspar Hauser who simply turned up in Nuremberg in 1828 aged 16, able only to write his name but making only unintelligible sounds. Under the care of a local teacher he learned to speak a few broken sentences. He became a fine horseman, but showed no interest in sex or money. He was later stabbed to death by an unknown man in a park. His story is told in the film 1993 The Enigma of Kaspar Hauser, directed by Peter Sehr.

Of course Chomsky's assertions have not gone unchallenged. Many attempts have been made by researchers to teach language to apes and monkeys. One of the more successful attempts featured a bonobo or pygmy ape called Kanzi. He acquired a vocabulary of around 200 words by the age of six and was putting together basic sentences of two or three words, often combined with a gesture. He was, however, much more sophisticated at responding to vocal commands and became capable of understanding quite complex tasks he was ordered to carry out. Of course, linguists argue that the important skill in language is performance, or the ability to communicate using it, rather than comprehension, the act of understanding.

Similarly, the wittily named Nim Chimsky (a monkey) learned a vocabulary of around 125 words using sign language. One reason that sign language is more effective for attempting to develop language in monkeys is that the shape of their vocal tracts does not permit the production of sounds is the same way as in humans.

LANGUAGE AND GENDER

Gender, it has been argued, is socially constructed. This idea implies that, although we are born male or female biologically, we learn to behave in a male or female way because of social pressures. Sex and gender are, therefore, two different issues. Sex is biological and anatomical; gender is created by our cultural experiences.

One of the chief ways in which we experience our culture is through the use of language. It follows that language is likely to be a key factor in differentiating the way in which gender is constructed and ultimately how males and females will learn to behave.

In her important book Man Made Language (1998), Dale Spender argues that language reflects the dominance of men in our society. The notion that the power relations in our society favour men is called a patriarchy.

Just as we suggested earlier in this section that language is a tool used in the oppression of cultural minorities, so it can be argued that language is controlled by men and used to support the dominance of men over women. A good example of this is the use of the word 'man' or 'mankind' to signal human beings of both sexes. Another example is the way in which the social status of a woman is often defined by her relation to a man. An unmarried woman is called Miss; a married woman called Mrs, and then takes on her husband's family name. Feminism has achieved significant objectives in the broad acceptance of the term 'Ms' as a title that doesn't signify a woman's social status and in women retaining their own family names rather than taking on their husband's or partner's family name.

Female behaviour that men disapprove of is often spoken of using pejorative or negative words.

Women are far more likely to be described in terms of their physical attributes. A tabloid newspaper is hardly likely to write about an attractive blond man with a gorgeous pair of legs. Such descriptions of women are common. Indeed, the dumb blonde stereotype is exclusively reserved as a way to describe women, despite the number of male celebrities who fit this description. This use of language, a feature of much journalism, suggests that the world is perceived from a male perspective in which women are objects whose desirability is to be evaluated and determined by men.

ACTIVITY . . .

Consider the following pairs of words:

master, mistress   host, hostess   wizard, witch

In what way does the feminine version carry connotations that do not exist in the male equivalent? Can you think of any more examples where the female version carries with it pejorative meanings? How do you think this influences our attitudes to gender?

▼ 2 NON-VERBAL COMMUNICATION

In this section we consider the significance of non-verbal communication.

- We look at the different categories of non-verbal communication, including paralanguage.
- We consider the relationship between verbal and non-verbal communication.

As you will have realised, our verbal behaviour is an important way in which we communicate with one another. However, we also use another large repertoire of skills – non-verbal behaviour.

PARALANGUAGE Communication which is in the form of utterances other than the words themselves, e.g. the volume of one's voice.

KEY TERM

When we communicate we are offering data to the world. In the process of doing so, we also offer information about ourselves, our feelings and attitudes and our relationship to the people we are addressing.

DATA AND INFORMATION The terms 'data' and 'information' are often used as if they were interchangeable; they are not. Data are raw, unprocessed facts, figures, etc. Once data have been processed, information results. When we make a specific enquiry of data, information is produced. The fact that you are 17 is a piece of data, as far as you are concerned. But should a police officer ask your age, and you reply '17', that is information to them. This is because the officer is asking your age for a specific purpose.

KEY TERM

A simple greeting such as 'How ya doing?' or 'Hey?' can carry with it much more about ourselves than seems possible in such a simple utterance. Much of the additional information is transmitted through non-verbal channels. Our tone of voice, the look on our face, or even the way in which we position our body can reveal to the receiver of our message our feelings as we transmit the message. For example, it is possible that the message 'Nice day again' is intended to be a deeply ironic comment on yet another day of bad weather. A sardonic grin or world-weary shake of the head may communicate that the message is intended to be a despairing comment on such depressing weather.

Clearly, verbal and non-verbal communication are closely linked. In the above example we see that the non-verbal message can, and often does, contradict the verbal one to invert the meaning of the message.

But, before we explore this in depth, let us consider the main types of non-verbal signal that people transmit. There are many ways in which people communicate by non-verbal means but the ones we'll focus on here are:

- proxemics
- orientation
- eye contact or gaze
- facial expression and gesture, especially use of hands and arms
- dress
- posture
- paralanguage.

There are other forms of non-verbal behaviour, for example, changes in our skin pigment such as blushing when we are embarrassed. An interesting issue is raised here. How much control do we have over the non-verbal signals we transmit? Blushing is generally seen as an involuntary action that gives away information to another person about our emotional state or even our motives.

We might arguably add smell to this list. In the non-human world smell is a powerful mechanism to send out signals that both attract and repel. The same is true of humans who have created a whole industry to produce synthetic odours that will attract other human animals.

Let's look at each of the forms of non-verbal communication we've identified. From here on in we'll refer to non-verbal communication as NVC.

PROXEMICS

Proxemics, a word coined by E. T. Hall in 1959, is the study of how we handle the space around us, especially in relation to other people. Like most animals, human beings are territorial. Just like a domestic or a feral cat, we create for ourselves spaces that belong to us and to which we try carefully to control access. Our homes and our spaces at work or school or college are examples of these. Consider the rooms in your house. Some are shared by the family, others are 'owned' by specific members of the family. Going into someone else's room is potentially to invade their space.

Consider how spaces are occupied within the classroom.

- How is the teacher's space marked out?
- How are the other spaces occupied?
- Where would a newcomer or visitor to the class sit?

One issue to emerge from your consideration of how space is occupied is about how territory reflects the power relations within groups of people. The more powerful a person, the larger and more impressive the space they will occupy.

There is another, more important type of space; this is the space that we carry with us. Each of us has this individual invisible space that we protect from outside intrusion. It might be compared to an invisible bubble around our body. In a crowded place such as a bus or a train, we can feel uncomfortable if a stranger encroaches on this space. On other occasions, we may welcome certain people to enter this space. Our feelings about this are determined by the situation and by the relationship we have, or might like to have, with the person or people who are near to us.

There are, however, important cultural differences in our attitudes to the proximity, or nearness, of other people. Some people argue that it is typical of British people that they do not encourage physical contact with other people. 'Don't touch' is an admonition we all remember from childhood. We are taught that touching things, other people, or even our own bodies, is socially undesirable. We may be wary of other people who are tactile and touch us. For example, some people like to hold on physically to the person they are talking to, as though to ensure that they have their full attention. In some cultures physical contact with relative strangers is openly encouraged. Watch how continental teenagers greet one another by kissing on both cheeks. In Britain kissing in this way tends to be reserved for close family members and intimacy between sexual partners.

So proxemics can provide us with important information about communication acts between people. It can shed light on the following.

- **The situation they are in** – whether they are whispering intimately to one another or making a public speech.
- **The relationship between two people** – whether they are relative strangers or intimate friends.
- **The relationship they might like to have with each other** – for example, if one person invades another's personal space, the reaction of that person may well suggest whether this is welcome or not.
- **Their cultural background or even their social attitudes** – some people will use the invasion of personal space as a means of intimidating another person. For example, a police officer questioning a suspect will often stand uncomfortably close.

ORIENTATION

Closely linked to the concept of proxemics is the idea of orientation. This means the way in which people place themselves relative to one another. When someone comes to sit next to you, it is generally seen as a much friendlier orientation than someone who sits directly opposite you. The latter position is potentially confrontational while the former suggests closeness and support. Such a technique may well be used by a boss or a teacher wishing to indicate a non-threatening or supportive relationship with a colleague or a student.

ACTIVITY . . .

Consider the significance of orientation at meal times within a social group.

- Does sitting at a table create a relaxed atmosphere and encourage conversation more than eating off a tray?
- Do we trust people more if they sit in certain positions in relation to us?
- Why do we feel uncomfortable when people stand behind us?

EYE CONTACT

Eye contact is one important way in which we communicate our feelings towards other people. Just as we are warned when young about touching, so we are also told that it is 'rude to stare'. Much of our behaviour in terms of eye contact with other people betrays our animal origins. We need to make initial eye contact to assess a stranger, as Erving Goffman (1963) points out. Prolonged staring in the animal world, however, is usually identified as a threatening form of behaviour. Averting the eyes and avoiding someone's gaze can also be seen as a means of avoiding conflict.

In human terms eye contact is obviously not as simple as this, but you may recognise elements of animal behaviour in the way people look at one another. If, for example, you find yourself inadvertently staring at someone, you will notice that their behaviour will change, often becoming either defensive or at the other extreme aggressive towards you. Similarly, we tend to be deeply suspicious of people who 'cannot look us in the eye'. They are seen as shifty or people with something to hide.

Gazing is also to some degree gendered. Men gaze at women, sometimes in an intimidating way. To gaze at another person, or to hold that person in your gaze, may well reflect the power relations between two people. Perhaps men in a patriarchal culture feel freer to gaze than women.

As with proxemics, eye contact, as Michael Argyle (1983) points out, can be an index of the closeness of a relationship that people share. Lovers, at least according to popular music, gaze into each other's eyes. Indeed, there is a popular belief that you can detect the truth in people's eyes. Although people may hide the truth with words, their true feelings will be revealed in their eyes.

It seems clear that, as with many non-verbal signals, eye contact has at least some degree of ambiguity about its meaning. Like many other acts of communication, a lot can depend on the context in which it takes place. For example, we may use eye movement seemingly to negate a verbal message. Take an instance where we use our eyes to indicate that a statement we have made is ironical, i.e. has the opposite meaning of the one that might normally be received. A teacher who says 'You obviously have a profound grasp of communication theory' but accompanies it with a despairing look upwards is most likely telling an unfortunate student just the opposite.

You may also like to consider the way in which people disengage from eye contact. What is the significance of looking away from someone? What signals are being passed when people glance away like this? Later in this section we will consider the role of eye contact in the way in which people make conversation.

Not all NVC that contradicts a verbal message is necessarily deliberate or voluntary. Indeed, non-verbal behaviour may on occasion give away a person's true intentions or state of mind. The term 'leakage' is used to describe the process by which this happens. In interview situations, for example, we may wish to appear relaxed and unconcerned about our chances of getting a job. However, certain aspects of our non-verbal behaviour may reveal the internal tension that we are feeling. Wringing our hands or gripping the seat tightly both indicate stress.

Is it possible to control such tell-tale signs? Is it possible to prevent leakage?

- Think of other instances when someone might try to hide their emotions (a) in a work situation and (b) in a social setting.
- What might give them away (in terms of voice, orientation, eye contact, etc.)?

FACIAL EXPRESSION AND GESTURES

Eye movement or contact is part of the larger system of non-verbal communication of facial expression. Much of the communication we participate in takes place in a face-to-face situation. In general we face the people we are addressing whether it is a formal or an informal situation. Obviously facial expression is bound to be an important indicator to other people of our attitudes, state of mind and relationships to them.

The human face has a complex arrangement of muscles that allows us to produce a whole range of different expressions, most of which are an index of our feelings. Through our facial expression we can indicate whether we are happy or sad or in pain. We can tell them if we are glad to see them or are angry with them or even afraid of them.

One of the most important signals that we can issue through our facial expression is the smile. Smiling is an important facial gesture that indicates to other people that we are ourselves happy and content. It is also used to indicate that we are pleased to see the other person and, most importantly, that we mean them no harm.

Desmond Morris (1994) suggests that two of our most important facial gestures, the smile and the frown, are linked to the facial expressions that we adopt during conflict. When we are angry and feeling aggressive, we tend to tighten our lips around our mouth and lower our eyebrows. This latter action is a means of protecting our eyes in an ensuing fight. We accompany these gestures with an unblinking stare, which we have seen is very much an attempt to intimidate another person.

However, when we become afraid after having committed ourselves to a conflict, we tend to pull back the corners of our mouth exposing the teeth. Morris calls this a typical 'fear face' which is a submissive gesture to suggest to an opponent that we are not a threat. This facial expression is very similar to the smile, which is a uniquely human gesture. A smile, therefore, is in at least one sense a submissive gesture indicating to another person that we are friendly and do not pose a threat to them.

There are many occasions when we may have to smile in a forced way. We are told to say 'cheese' as a way of creating a smile specifically for the camera when a photograph is taken. We may also fake a smile to pretend we are pleased to see someone when we are not. Generally people can detect a false smile – for example, when the camera lingers too long on a smiling television presenter. It seems that we can distinguish between a spontaneous smile and one that is generated for effect. Obviously there are other situations when we may wish to give off false signals with our use of gesture. In a situation such as a card game (e.g. poker), where we do not want an opponent to know what we are really thinking, we will often endeavour to suppress our spontaneous gestures. Indeed, we may even try to give off false signals to stop people reading our body language.

It has been argued that, when people are lying, this can be detected through their body language. For example, it is said that we touch our faces and blink more frequently as though try to cut ourselves off from the lies we are telling.

Desmond Morris's work is important because he used real-life situations to classify the postures and gestures that human beings use. He notes that simple gestures such as the handshake have countless variations. He even argues that there are actual frontiers where different gestures begin and end. Similarly, he suggests that gestures, just like language, are also capable of changing their meanings over a period of time.

ACTIVITY...

The handshake may have its origins in the idea that people meeting are able to demonstrate to one another that they are unarmed by offering an open palm. Clearly, the handshake has developed subsequently as a social greeting, but still is an important means of reassuring both friends and strangers of our friendly intentions towards them.

Observe the handshaking and other greetings rituals that take place between people. Consider how these vary in terms of:

- gender
- ethnicity
- region
- age.

What judgements do you think people make about each other on the basis of handshakes? Why do captains of opposing teams shake hands before a game?

The fact that human beings have adapted to walking on their hind legs has freed their hands, among other things, to be used for making gestures. On occasions these gestures are a replacement for speech. For example, if you are in the quiet working area of a library you may put your finger to your mouth in a gesture to tell someone to be quiet

Similarly, when your voice is otherwise engaged – for example, talking on the phone – you may use hand gestures to tell another person to come in and sit down. You may even be able to indicate that they can help themselves to a drink.

ACTIVITY . . .

Think about situations where gestures are used to achieve objectives that cannot be achieved by language. For example, in sport hand gestures are often used as a code for relaying information without the opposing team being able to decipher it. Financial markets and race-tracks, two gambling arenas, employ extensive use of hand gestures for conveying information.

- Why do you think hand gestures are so important here?
- How do they relate to spoken language?
- What other situations are there where hand gestures can be important?

Some gestures work alongside the words that we utter. It is argued that these hand gestures reveal a good deal about our emotional state as we utter messages to other people. It is interesting to observe that we often make hand gestures even when the receiver of the message is unable to see them – for example, when we are speaking on the telephone. Obviously many of the gestures are automatic. They function to reinforce the message that we are uttering by means of language.

We all have a range of typical gestures that we make for pushing people away or drawing them towards us. Consider what these gestures usually are. What gestures do we use when we want to indicate to people we are pleased with them or we are admonishing them?

Watch a politician or other person addressing a public meeting either on television or, better still, by attending yourself. Make a list of the different types of gesture they use.

- How does each of these gestures relate to the message being spoken?
- How do you, the audience, respond to different hand gestures?
- Are there any gestures that make you more inclined to accept the verbal message?

DRESS

Dress is often identified as an example of a code. As with all codes, there are certain conventions that apply to they way in which things are done. These conventions have to do with the way in which we combine items of clothing and the appropriateness of certain types of styles of dress to specific situations. If we fail to observe the conventions, then we risk giving offence. By the same token, if we choose to ignore these conventions, we may have set out deliberately to challenge convention, perhaps even by seeking to give offence. On the other hand we may just have got it wrong. Imagine a situation in which a good friend invites you to a fancy dress party. You turn up dressed as Batman or Robin to find that everyone else is in normal casual party dress. Your fellow partygoers might enjoy a comic interlude at the sight of your discomfort in failing to conform to the dress code for that occasion.

An extreme example might be to dress in loud and colourful dress for a funeral. Convention demands that people wear black or dark-coloured clothes as a symbol of mourning. To break such a convention might be seen as a provocative act showing disrespect to the dead person and the family of the dead person.

In the same way, most people wear clothes that have at least some kind of congruity. A 'well-dressed' person will wear outfits that match. This will be achieved by avoiding colour clashes and usually by avoiding combining formal and informal garments. However, once dress codes are established, people can choose to ignore, invert or play with those codes. Accordingly some people successfully combine tee-shirts and formal suits, or trainers and formal suits.

- How do you decide what to wear?
- Do you always have a choice?
- Are there clothes that you hate wearing?
- Is your wardrobe organised into 'outfits' – that is, clothes that you know work well together?
- Think through how you might describe your wardrobe as a paradigm and particular outfits as syntagms.

The clothes we wear make a statement about ourselves. Even if we are not the type of person who worries unduly about our dress, people we meet and interact with will still interpret our appearance as though we had deliberately constructed a message. As we have seen, one way in which this is done is through the wearing of clothes inappropriate to a particular situation, by accident or by design.

An interesting example of dress code is the use of uniform. Uniform is used to signify the role or function that a person performs. It distinguishes the wearer from other people. Police officers wear uniform as a means of establishing their power and status as well as making them recognisable to members of the public.

Some uniforms are also signifiers of the rank and status of the person who wears them. In the police and armed forces this may take the form of symbols such as stripes and crowns that can be read by those who understand the code. Generally, the more elaborate the symbols, the higher the rank. Some uniforms may be colour-coded to distinguish people of higher rank.

Uniforms usually have some impact on the behaviour of both the wearer and those with whom they are in contact. A uniform provides a person with a sense of belonging to a group. It also bestows on people a sense of authority. It is interesting to note how the uniforms of security guards imitate those of police officers.

It can be argued, however, that we all wear some sort of a uniform. A uniform is an important method of establishing our allegiance to a group. It can be used to establish to the world that we belong to a particular group and share that group's values. Although less formal and homogeneous than a military uniform, the clothing of different subcultures has served to act as a uniform to identify people with shared values. Hippies, skinheads, punks, crusties, goths and grungers are examples of such subcultures. More recently the vogue for designer labels, sports clothing and trainers has been used to signify allegiances, especially the wearing of football shirts of a particular team.

It can be argued that we are all subject to a pressure to conform and to demonstrate allegiances to different groups within society. Our dress code is an important mechanism by which we signal this conformity to a group.

ACTIVITY ...

- Is it possible to dress in a wholly 'individual' way? What are the 'rules' that, even unconsciously, influence our choice of clothes (e.g. situation, time of day, gender)?
- Do the clothes we wear make a statement about us? Give examples of three very different types of attire and the reactions they are likely to provoke.

A uniform is an extreme example of formal dress. The business suit with its conservative dark shades is worn to distinguish people who have 'important' jobs that require them to meet people and make important decisions. Casual clothes are often seen as inappropriate in a business environment as most companies are keen for employees to reflect a positive, clean-cut image of the firm through their own appearance (efficient, smart and reliable). In some offices, where there is no direct contact with actual customers, management has introduced weekly 'Dress Down Days' when employees can leave their suits behind and are encouraged to wear jeans and tee-shirts or other casual clothes. This practice was first introduced by computer companies in the USA and was designed to help break down barriers between different levels of workers and to encourage teamwork and improve communication on an interpersonal level.

Dressing formally for an interview or even a court appearance is clearly important in the same way. We wear formal clothes to tell the world we have made an effort to look smart. We are also signalling our willingness to conform to the demands of authority, an important gesture to make in both the job market and the magistrates' court.

ACTIVITY . . .

- What is your attitude to school uniform?
- What function do you think it is intended to serve?
- How effectively do you think it serves this function?
- Is uniform generally popular or unpopular with students?

There are situations where dressing casually is more appropriate, such as when we are relaxing or socialising. Casual clothes are generally more comfortable, and this may make us feel more relaxed and behave in a more relaxed way. On occasions, however, a person may wear casual clothes in order to present a reassuring image to another person or group. Some teachers, for example, decide to dress informally perhaps in order to signify a less authoritarian relationship with their class.

It is obvious that we make a lot of initial judgements about people because of their clothes. In the same way, the clothes we choose to wear invite other people to think about us in certain ways.

Dress is just one aspect of the physical appearance that we present to the world. We might also consider such aspects as hairstyle, jewellery, make-up, body adornment and body modification. Each of these is open to interpretation by the people with whom we come into contact. Collectively they make a statement about ourselves and our system of values. Hair length or facial hair in men, for example, can determine the assumptions that people make about the person beneath. The type and style of jewellery worn by men and women is open to interpretation. Similarly, body adornment and decoration in the form of tattoos or face and body piercings can all act as signals to other people. Of course, like all signals they are open to being read in a variety of different ways according to the attitudes, values and background of the 'reader'.

POSTURE

Closely allied to the impact of dress is the impact of our posture. Posture is about the way in which we position our bodies. Much of our early socialisation has taught us the importance of an erect posture, which means holding ourselves upright and straight to our full height. On the other hand slouching is associated with poor posture and by implication laziness or slovenly behaviour. 'Sit up straight', 'shoulders back' or 'chin up' are instructions regularly heard at home and at school.

We associate an upright posture with people who are confident about themselves. The armed forces and the police are drilled into adopting this posture which, in the same way as their uniform, gives them an air of confident authority. Their posture is another sign of the status and role within society.

Contrast this military bearing with a homeless person begging on the streets. Their posture is one of sagging, with their body almost being allowed to collapse into a heap. Their low self-esteem, perhaps combined with cold and hunger, is reflected in their posture. Their body sags to indicate their lack of status and confidence. Indeed, it is common to see people bending their bodies into a foetal position, as though seeking the reassurance they once had in the womb.

Certainly we use posture as one means of indicating to another person our feelings of friendship or hostility. Certain postures such as standing with hands on hips can be construed as confrontational and hostile.

ACTIVITY . . .

Make a list of postures that might be considered hostile. Make a second list of postures that might be considered friendly.

Good posture is something that can be learned. A technique was invented last century by an Australian actor, Frederick Alexander. He argued that adopting good posture by becoming sensitive to the way in which we hold our bodies is beneficial to our physical and mental well-being. Certainly spending time looking at yourself in a full-length mirror from a variety of angles will indicate a good deal about the postures you adopt. It might also provide a useful area of study to consider some of the different postures people adopt when they are communicating with us. Often a person's bodily posture can provide an indication of how comfortable or otherwise they feel about the person they are next to.

Posture is also another aspect of our behaviour when we are together in a group. It is often possible to observe that people unconsciously imitate the postures of the people they are with, sometimes as a couple in larger groups. This process is known by a number of names, but most commonly is called mirroring or, more grandly, postural congruence. An example of this is the way in which people often cross their legs or fold their arms to mirror the postures that people in their immediate circle have adopted.

Part of the function of such actions is to reinforce group identities and to suggest conformity within the group. Just as dress can be used to reinforce the cohesion of the group, so too can posture. This is perhaps another reason why drill is such an important element of training in the armed and police forces.

Consider the ways in which people walk, perhaps using some of the verbs that we use to describe different kinds of walking. What assumptions do we make when we see people:

- strut
- saunter
- swagger
- mince
- march?

PARALANGUAGE

When we speak, we don't just communicate with words: we also make noises that aren't words. We raise and lower our voices. We pause. We stress some words (almost like underlining words when writing by hand or emboldening words when word-processing). We call this paralanguage. It can be defined as those utterances that we make when we are speaking that are not in fact identifiable as language.

If you listen carefully to people speaking, the words they say are punctuated with noises such as 'um' or 'ah'. We also punctuate our speech with pauses, hesitations, little laughs or coughs and splutters. In paralinguistics these phenomena are considered, alongside the words themselves, as an important aspect of the message we are communicating. In addition, people tend to have quite individual speech patterns which can make their voices distinctive and memorable. Such factors as pitch, stress, accent and pace are other aspects of paralanguage that can determine how the messages that we utter are interpreted.

The importance of paralanguage in determining the way in which people respond to our spoken messages is evident from the following example. Imagine you hear the following words:

'The house is on fire.'

If this sentence is spoken, in the absence of any visible punctuation marks, it could be interpreted as a statement or as a question. What would determine the way that we might interpret such an utterance is *how* it is spoken. When we ask a question, the pitch of our voice tends to rise as we near the end of the sentence. This rising pitch is generally interpreted by listeners as an indication that we are asking a question, rather than making a statement. Tone of voice, as it is commonly known, is an important indicator of the intention of the sender in uttering a message. You might like to consider the significance of irony here, where a sender may actually mean the opposite of what is being said. Some people find it almost impossible to detect when other people are being ironical.

Pitch is just one aspect of paralanguage that helps a listener fill in the detail of what we say. If, for example, we were to shout the sentence loudly, it would be readily perceived by anyone in earshot as a warning, an alarm and a plea for help. The volume of our utterances can clearly impact on the way the message is interpreted. We tend to shout when we get angry or excited. Speaking at a particularly low volume, or whispering, usually indicates that we do not wish the message to be overheard. In the same way our speech will tend to speed up when we have a message that is emotionally charged. If someone speaks particularly slowly, we might draw the conclusion that they are patronising us.

ACTIVITY . . .

In the section on language we looked at the issue of accent and dialect. These are also an important aspect of paralanguage as they determine they way we sound to other people. Different regional accents are spoken with unique intonations and rhythms. Many of these accents carry with them connotations of the attitudes behind the voice, many of which are obviously quite stereotypical. You may like to consider what your initial reactions are to the following regional accents, all of which are associated with working-class communities:

- East London
- Liverpool
- Glasgow.

What judgements are you likely to make about the messages that are uttered by people who speak in these accents? You may also like to consider your own sense of linguistic community.

- Do you have an accent?
- How does this make you react to these accents?
- How do you think people from these communities are likely to react to the way in which you speak?
- Are the assumptions they might make correct?

As we suggested in the section on language, 'received pronunciation' is often considered to be the 'correct' way in which to speak the English language. It is interesting to note that elocution lessons are designed to make people speak RP, presumably because this is more desirable than a regional accent.

The function of the sounds that we make in addition to verbal utterances is an important aspect of our exploration of paralanguage. A question that clearly needs to be answered is why we use these sounds and how they contribute to the meaning of our messages.

One function they serve is to stop the flow of speech. This is particularly noticeable when we are listening to someone speak whom we expect to be fluent. A newsreader, for example, rarely hesitates in reading a bulletin. Any hesitation usually indicates that something has gone wrong – the autocue is stuck or a studio director is shouting through the earpiece.

In conversation, however, such hesitation is commonplace and often passes unnoticed. Indeed, we might be suspicious of a person who was too fluent in their speaking. We might think that they had rehearsed it, rather like a salesperson might have practised a pitch to persuade us to fit new double-glazing. In conversation, we hesitate and interject 'ums' and 'ahs' for a number of reasons. Not least of these is to give us more time to consider what we are saying. Typically, if someone asks a difficult or embarrassing question, our immediate response is quite likely to be 'um', not least to give us time to think of an answer or excuse.

If we ask someone a direct question, these hesitations can be interpreted as important signals indicating to us the amount of trust we can put in the response that follows. In a court of law a hesitation may be deemed to tell rather more than the words that follow it.

Figure 4.1 *Truth Machine advertisement*

THE LINK BETWEEN VERBAL AND NON-VERBAL COMMUNICATION

As you will have seen from the above example, there are clear links between verbal and non-verbal communication. Most of the time when we communicate we use a whole repertoire of skills to construct messages. There has been a good deal of debate about the relationship between verbal and non-verbal communication (NVC). One issue that has been frequently revisited asks which of the two is the more important in the construction of a message. You may like to consider your own responses to this complex question and perhaps undertake some research of your own. You can do this by careful observation of how people use both verbal and non-verbal signals in different situations and how other people respond to them. At a more complex level, you may wish to explore the way in which non-verbal and verbal signals relate to one another in the process of conversation.

It is appropriate here to explore this last area. One of the functions of NVC in its different forms is as a regulator. A regulator is a mechanism that helps us to control the flow of conversation. When two people speak to each other, they generally do so in an ordered fashion. Each takes a turn at speaking and contributing to the conversation. This ordered method of communicating is largely achieved as a result of our learning to read different signals that indicate to the other person whether we are intending to continue speaking or wish them to speak.

In conversation with someone, we will indicate that we want them to, for example, listen to us or to react to what we've said. We call these indications cues. Many cues are signalled paralinguistically. Others are achieved by non-verbal behaviours such as eye contact. This is one way in which we invite the person we are addressing to join in conversation. Similarly, they may use eye contact as a method of declining the opportunity to converse. In the middle of a conversation we also use eye contact to signal that we have finished speaking and that we wish them to contribute. Eye contact and facial expression are important methods of encouraging and supporting the person who is speaking. They provide clear feedback signals that help regulate the way in which the person continues to address us.

It has probably occurred to you that one feature of interpersonal communication is that much of what goes on is predictable largely because it is governed by convention. Patterns of greetings tend to work to established formulas. 'How are you?' as a greeting is generally followed by 'Fine, thanks. How are you?' Other responses are of course possible, but social convention determines that this is the most likely exchange. In Part 3 we identified this predictability as redundancy. In interpersonal communication *redundancy* serves at least two key functions.

First, it is an important way of strengthening social bonds. In the example given above, the mutual concern exhibited by both parties suggests that each takes an interest in the other's well-being. Similarly, saying 'Take care' to a departing friend or acquaintance strengthens the relationship by indicating a similar concern.

Second, redundancy is a means of ensuring that a message is accurately received. A good example of this is teaching. Effective teachers use redundancy in a number of ways.

- They plan their classes so they have very predictable shapes to them.
- They use repetition, synopsis and summary to ensure key ideas are understood.
- They wrap up entropic communication with redundant communication (like a sandwich) to ensure students are not disorientated.

In *Key Concepts in Communication and Cultural Studies*, O'Sullivan *et al.* (1994) point out that redundancy is best not seen in a Communication Studies context as 'something unnecessary'. People who send messages with a high degree of redundancy are demonstrating a high degree of concern for their audience in wishing to ensure their messages are accurately and easily decoded.

▼ 3 INTRAPERSONAL COMMUNICATION: SELF AND SELF-CONCEPT

In this section we begin to look at intrapersonal communication.

■ We consider key ideas such as self-concept, self-image, the ideal self and self-esteem.

We have looked at some of the ways in which we communicate with each other by verbal and non-verbal means. We now move to examine what is, for many commentators, the source of all our communicating, our self. Communication within, with and to the self is called intrapersonal communication.

Clearly, intrapersonal communication is vital because it defines who we are.

The existence of the 'self' (the 'inner monologue') may seem self-evident and beyond doubt. We are surely all aware, at some level, of the difference between our inside and outside voices, of the voice that makes the decisions and the one that carries them out. When we look in a mirror, we are immediately aware of two 'selves' – the one seeing, the other seen. Thinking is similar if less obvious. When you are asked a question like 'When was the last time you lied?' or 'What was the most shameful thing you have ever done?' you are immediately aware of a kind of processing going on in your head. This will be partly concerned with recalling various examples of shameful behaviour and rating them for their shamefulness. It is also about examining your sense of self in relation to the context, the audience and your emotional state and gatekeeping the information; modifying or even holding back the 'truth' in order to protect your sense of yourself.

GATEKEEPING A process by which information is selected and modified for inclusion within communication messages. White's Gatekeeping model offers a useful visual representation of this process.

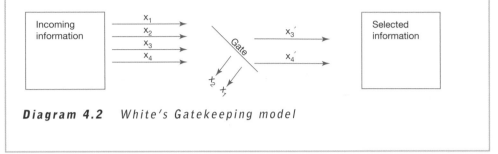

Diagram 4.2 *White's Gatekeeping model*

Gatekeeping is a concept which can be useful at both ends of the communication scale; from helping to explain how our own thoughts become messages to understanding the content of a national newspaper.

Stopping to think about what to reveal about yourself to others is a classic example of what intrapersonal communication is in practice. Non-humans may be conscious of sensations such as hunger, thirst and pain but they lack this self-consciousness, this sense of self within the self. Murphy defines the self as 'the individual known to the individual' (1947). This known individual probably consists of a number of identifiable, if not provable, components and processes, which may include:

- thinking (cognition)
- perception (both sensory [with the senses] and cognitive [with the mind])
- memory
- feelings/desires
- motivation
- personality
- consciousness (that which you are aware of)
- conscience (your moral sense).

Some people would like to add some traditional concepts such as 'heart' and 'soul' or even 'spirit'. These are really answers to the biggest philosophical question 'Who am I?' However, we should equally be aware that above all it is workable definitions we are after; definitions that will help us to understand how communication works. This section will largely provide this by exploring the above list and looking at the impact of these ideas on communication in practice.

SELF-CONCEPT

Let us first look at the ways in which we, as individuals, respond to our individuality. The best place to start is with 'self-concept', the idea we have of ourselves as individuals. Self-concept consists of three elements, each of which makes an important contribution. The first of these is self-image, the opinion or picture we have of ourselves.

Self-image

EITHER (a) answer the question 'Who am I?' 20 times, in each case responding in the form 'I am . . .'.

OR (b) answer the following list of self-probing questions:

- Who are you?
- What do you do?
- What do you do well?
- What do you do badly?
- What is your strongest feeling?
- What is your strongest belief?
- What is your strongest desire?
- What is your oldest memory?
- What is your most shameful lie?
- What has been your greatest triumph?
- What has been your most wretched disaster?
- Who do you love?
- Who do you hate?
- Who do you like?
- Who do you dislike?
- Are you too tall or too short?
- Are you too thin or too fat?
- Are you too clever or too stupid?
- Who would you like to be?
- Which question would you like to be asked?

If you responded to (a), the interesting thing to do is to try to spot trends in the results. If you chose (b), it is valuable to go back and calculate how many of the answers you gave are genuinely honest and thus useful. How many of your answers are really a response to the need to have an answer and/or the need to have a potential audience?

Kuhn and McPartland (1954) conducted this experiment, asking option (a) above, on both seven-year-olds and undergraduates and they reached some interesting conclusions. First they were able to see responses to the 'Who am I?' question falling into two categories which they related to:

- **social roles**: the parts we play, either 'ascribed' (or given) rather like daughter or son, or 'achieved' roles (such as student or part-time worker)

- **personality traits**: statements about what we think we are like, such as 'I am very easy-going' or 'I am very hard-working'.

Kuhn and McPartland also found that the main difference between the seven-year-olds and undergraduates was in the proportions of 'social roles' and 'personality traits'. On average seven-year-olds recorded five social role statements while the undergraduates recorded ten. This suggests that as we get older we progressively describe ourselves in terms of the jobs we do or status we have. This has a convincing ring to it, for on meeting people for the first time the thing adults most often offer, after their names, is what they do.

The other aspects of self-image relate to the various versions of the self which are being imaged. We can distinguish between the intellectual self, the emotional self and the body self (or body image), though we could also add social and physical or physio-logical selves. Body image is a particularly important factor in growing up in a society where stereotyped body images are common. This is the point at which self-image becomes influenced by the other components of self-concept, in particular, the ideal self.

Ideal self

ACTIVITY . . .

Note: this activity is not intended to be a traumatic experience in which you put yourself down. Loosen up – education should be fun!

Ideal self is the kind of person you would like to be at best. Examine the three designations:

- intellectual self
- emotional self
- bodily self.

Sum up the ideal male or female according to society or the media. How far is your ideal self similar or different to these?

Ideal self is an easier concept in theory than it often is in practice. Trying to probe the ideal self in any kind of public context results in the same kind of gatekeeping we spoke of in relation to shameful secrets. In expressing our ideals, we will often resort to projecting these on to other, often public people. To conceive of your ideal self in terms of another person is usually to get role models and ideal selves confused.

Who are your role models and heroes/heroines? What qualities do you admire in them? If you would like to be more like these people, what more than their success (money, fame, sex etc.) do you want?

Carl Rogers would see in role-modelling evidence that we have a number of layers or levels of self-consciousness (1961). The modelling of ourselves in terms of other, often public and famous people, is part of a process that creates, presents and maintains our own 'public self'. This 'public self' is a significantly more superficial version of the self than the one we 'show' to close friends and family, let alone the 'core' self that remains with us at all times. His concentric circle model shows the interconnectedness of these 'selves'.

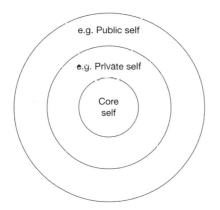

Diagram 4.3 *Roger's Concentric Circle model*

Self-esteem

Rogers (1961) suggests that the gap between self-image and ideal self is likely to be a measure of an individual's self-worth or 'self-esteem', as the third component of self-concept is usually known. Coopersmith (1967) defines self-esteem as 'a personal judgement of worthiness'. In other words self-esteem is a currency of self-regard: it measures and records how good you feel about yourself. High self-esteem is obviously aided by such socially valuable attributes as physical athleticism and/or attractiveness, but it is most significantly helped by the respect of others.

Of the four key factors identified by Dimbleby and Burton (1998) in the creation of a sense of self, three are directly concerned with the relationships we have with others:

- reactions of others
- comparisons with others
- identifications with others.
- The fourth is the roles we play.

'Identifications'

- Who are the significant others for you?
- Whose reactions matter to you?
- Whom do you compare yourself to?
- Who are you compared to?
- With whom do you identify?

We have already to some extent dealt with identifications when we talked about role models. Much research has been done, particularly in the fields of education, management and sports psychology, into the beneficial effects of positive feedback. This is sometimes called the 'Pygmalion effect'. (This is a reference to the play by George Bernard Shaw where Professor Higgins makes a bet that he can turn a Cockney flower girl into the RP-speaking toast of London society. In other words, he believed he could change someone.) Researchers might, for example, privilege schoolchildren according to illogical criteria like eye or hair colour. Most often these children would end up heading the class academically. This suggests that our expectations are a powerful tool for changing attitude, behaviour and perception. This is usually referred to as the self-fulfilling prophecy, a vicious or sometimes beneficial circle.

Here the established expectations cue behaviour, which further supports the expectations. Put another way, you expect laziness from a child who then conforms and confirms your initial expectations. Of course, it can work in a positive way, as a motivational tool where high expectations encourage positive behaviour and achievement follows.

In both cases the issue is essentially self-esteem, which at its positive and negative extremes can have potentially miraculous and/or crippling results. Low self-esteem results in low motivation, a lack of self-confidence, and a lessening in the use of verbal and non-verbal communication. High self-esteem improves all of these, facilitating social interaction, persuasion, and increasing the quality and volume of communication.

Self-esteem is a flexible 'substance', often extremely susceptible to fluctuation. What kinds of thing raise your self-esteem and make you feel good about yourself? What kinds of thing lower your self-esteem and make you feel bad about yourself?

It is likely that your lists were dominated by the influence of other people, those whose responses are likely to make a difference to you. These interested others act as a kind of validation of our behaviour, reflecting (if we're lucky) the kinds of versions of ourselves that we think we are projecting. This is what Cooley (1992) called 'looking-glass theory', the version of the self we find in others' responses. On a superficial level this is evident. When we get dressed up for a night out, we partly see ourselves in other people's reactions to us. The theory is similar to 'the self-fulfilling prophecy' in that expectation is created by response. We receive judgements and evaluations of our behaviour from others and then modify our behaviour accordingly. Cooley was interested in the ways we modify behaviour according to the differences between 'reflections'.

These variations depend very much upon our stability and consistency as *personalities* (for more of this see the next section), our capacity effectively to perceive and interpret feedback, the importance of the responses we are making to others. The depth of our engagement with a person or situation will usually influence the effectiveness of the mirror effect. The looking-glass effect is powerful but only at a fairly superficial level, due to its immediacy. Often this influence is seen in terms of the encouragement of conventional patterns of behaviour and attitudes rather than as infiltrating beliefs and values.

Attitudes, values and beliefs are terms used to describe our various responses to the world. To some extent they represent depth of response and breadth of influence.

ATTITUDES   Our tendency to react favourably or unfavourably to people, objects or situations. Attitudes are created and modified by rewards and punishments (real and implied).

BELIEFS   Our views of existence; what we think is true. Belief includes knowledge and is often given to us by authority figures: we act on our beliefs.

VALUES   The worth you place on things, events and people. Values are the bedrock of all behaviour. Society's values are found in the media.

KEY TERM

Another factor that has bearing on 'looking-glass theory' is the degree to which we are able as individuals to read the often non-verbal feedback. In Gerbner's two-dimensional model, which we encountered on page 128, perception is one of the dimensions. It is a key communication activity. Gerbner suggests that perception is subject to the qualifiers 'selection, context and availability' (what you choose to perceive; where you perceive from physically and psychologically; and how much of the perceived object is available to you). Selection is an interesting criterion as it suggests to some extent that we 'see' what we want to see.

PERCEPTION   A term used to refer to certain human processes and capacities. We gather sensory data from the world about us. We process that data and, in so doing, produce information about the world. We use that information to make sense of the world in the immediate sense and we also carry forward that perception as the capacity to make sense of things we will encounter in the future.

KEY TERM

If the responses of others to us have importance, it is equally important to understand the role interpersonal perception plays in intrapersonal communication. We have already looked at the broad implications of low self-esteem. To these we can surely add 'uncertainty in perception'. If we feel badly about ourselves, we will see this reflected in others. Accurate perception is a precarious business to which all the various elements of the self mentioned earlier in this section contribute. Add to these the various environmental factors which might influence the process (largely what Gerbner calls 'availability' and 'context') and you see the difficulties. Dimbleby and Burton (1998) usefully sum up 'errors of perception' in the following way.

- **We miss out some piece of information.** In other words, we interpret a person or behaviour without all of the relevant information, like when you later discover that the person who appears to have been 'giving you the eye' all night is in fact very short-sighted.
- **We make too much of something**. People often take one feature of a person and for no rational reason amplify this; this is the place where stereotyping and prejudice start.
- **We make false connections between one thing and another.** This is often the outcome of making too much of something; in gender terms, stereotypes make irrational connections between women and certain kinds of behaviour. For example, because women are weak, emotionally fragile and largely moral, you shouldn't swear in front of them.
- **We guess wrongly about the other person by making false association of traits and experience**. Given that perception is invariably partial, it is inevitable that part of the process [and processing] is estimation or guesswork. We take the exhibition of generosity as a character trait as the basis for a positive judgement or we read some other person's bad experience with the police as the basis of 'a dangerous personality'. This is classically the 'halo and horns' effect, privileging one piece of information, positively or negatively, over the rest.

With such potential problems of perception, the self-image has a key role as gatekeeper of the information about the self which is available both from without (the feedback of others) and from within ourselves. This is a balance between intrapersonal and inter-personal communication, between our own influence on the self and the influence of others: between looking-glass self and self-image. To some extent we control the information about ourselves that is made available both to ourselves and to others. What we choose to offer of the self to the world is termed 'self-disclosure', while our responses to what comes back constitutes 'feedback'.

This disclosure/feedback relationship is at the heart of the Johari Window, which is a useful model for setting self-image in the context of the self and other people. Luft and Ingham (1955), the creators of the Johari Window, drew axes that record self-image in terms of information available to the self and others. They then organised the resulting grid into four quadrants.

- **The open area** includes information that is available to all (your gender, race, name are examples).
- **The hidden area** is more intimate and private. Here are those items you choose not to reveal (perhaps the shameful acts we thought about earlier).

- **The blind area** is that which 'looking-glass' theory avoids, that which others can see but not you yourself (perhaps you are too self-critical).
- **The unknown area** is that part of us we cannot easily contact or understand; the sub-conscious, dreams and desires.

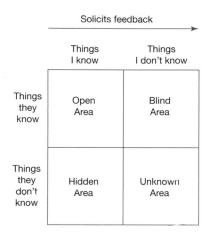

Diagram 4.4 *The Johari Window*

The Johari Window is a flexible model, with areas drawn according to the specific character or situation. Some people can't help but be self-disclosers, whereas others hold on to their private thoughts as if they were gold. You can use the Johari Window to plot these tendencies and to predict outcomes. Engaging in interpersonal communication is, according to this model, about further opening the 'open' frame and at the same time adjusting the 'hidden' and/or 'blind'. It is about self-disclosure as an effective response to feedback. This brings us neatly to the 'looking-glass self', because one thing that we manipulate in our response to others' feedback is information about ourselves that we were only partly aware of.

ACTIVITY...

If we encountered an individual whose hidden quadrant or frame is or was dominant, then that person would likely be secretive or inward-looking. This might be a feature of this person's personality or it might be a response to a particular set of circumstances, such as a bereavement. What sort of situation or individual would you be encountering if the dominant (i.e. largest) frame was:

- open
- blind
- unknown?

Self-disclosure is not the only protective mechanism known to the self-concept and its attendant self-image. We may be theoretically vulnerable to the responses of others, which is why we have strategies through which to counter their effects. This is essentially a *dissonance theory*. The self is faced with two sets of oppositional data – positive information from the self-concept and negative information from the world. These 'informations' are cognitively dissonant (they do not 'rhyme' intellectually; they are difficult to reconcile). Dissonance theory suggests that the likely response to such a conflict of information is for us artificially to weaken one side of the argument. The classic example offered by Richard Gross (1996) is with smokers who believe, know and understand that smoking increases the risk of serious disease. Their response to this cognitive dissonance is often a sort of overreaction.

■   They belittle the evidence.
■   They associate with other smokers.
■   They smoke low-tar cigarettes.
■   They convince themselves that smoking is a highly pleasurable activity.
■   They stress the dangers of smoking and make it a personality feature.

This is exactly what Gergen and Gergen (1981) were dealing with when they identified the various ways in which we protect our selves (ourselves) from negative feedback. These so-called 'self-maintenance strategies' are really a series of dissonant responses for keeping our idea of the self intact. What we do is one or more of the following.

■   Mix with like people. (How many of your closest friends like the same kind of music as you?)
■   Mix with people of lower status or ability. (We go around with our 'inferiors' in order that we look and feel good.)
■   Change our behaviour to conform to norms. (One of the ways that the self protects itself is by changing its 'clothes' and adopting the 'uniform' of accepted ways of behaving in which it will be less likely to attract attention and challenge.)
■   Form low opinion of detractors. (Feedback is effective in proportion to the status of its source; if the source is stupid/unreliable/dishonest, then the feedback will be too.)
■   Disbelieve what others say (which is why we never believe our parents when they tell us our new boy/girlfriend will bring us nothing but trouble).
■   Misunderstand negative feedback. (If we don't fully understand criticism, it can't fully 'hurt' us.)
■   Consciously evoke response. (We behave or dress in a way that will artificially provoke the feedback we want – like dressing smartly for an interview.)
■   Selectively evaluate self (a simple device which stresses some aspects of who we are instead of other less positive aspects).
■   Self-handicapping. (This is a favourite strategy with students of all ages; by not attending or trying or revising, we leave little room for real failure [and no room for success].)

Self-maintenance strategies are employed by us all to a lesser or greater degree: they are designed to keep us comfortable and sane. Spend some time observing your friends and colleagues, and try to collect evidence of Gergen and Gergen's strategies.

Gergen and Gergen offer a useful list of mechanisms which are a mixture of the internally defensive and externally offensive (the best form of defence being attack). We move to discuss the latter as part of self-presentation in Section 5. Meanwhile the next section will try to explore further theories about the self and its internal operations, this self that we are so keen to develop and defend.

▼ 4 INTRAPERSONAL COMMUNICATION: IDEAS ABOUT THE DEVELOPMENT OF THE SELF AND PERSONALITY

In this section we continue to examine intrapersonal communication and move to consider some ideas about the development of the self and personality.

■ We look at the work of Harré, Freud, Laing, Jung, Cattell, Eysenck and Adorno.

The purpose of this section is to stimulate further discussion about the self as communicator and as communicated – in other words, about how the self is not only a primary sender of communication but also part of the message as well. What follows is intended to work in two ways: (a) to provide direct input into your understanding of intrapersonal communication, and (b) to suggest methods of individual research into the self and personality. The section is largely concerned with other people's theories, many of whom have made important contributions to the study of psychology. In Sigmund Freud's case he made vital contributions to the history of twentieth-century thought.

Given that we're going to devote this section to other people's ideas, let's begin by stating some principles of our own. Across the whole of this part our aims are to:

■ define key concepts (such as role, perception, culture and context)
■ identify forms and uses of communication at the level of the individual and the small group (in other words, to recognise what kinds of personal communication there are and what they do)
■ develop useful subject-specific terminology (which will make the communication of the above information more efficient).

If we lose sight of the key elements (the 'what', 'how' and 'why' of personal communication), no amount of theoretical knowledge will help. This section must enhance our understanding of the basic principles developed in the previous section and lay the foundations for the discussion of self as communicated text, which is important to the next section.

We left the self at the end of the last section battling to maintain itself in the face of the assault of the real world and other people. Psychologists identify a series of stages through which this desperate-to-be-maintained self must pass before it enjoys 'autonomy', the capacity to function independently. Jean Piaget (1952), for example, argues that babies have no self-concept and see their own bodies in the same way as they see other objects in the world. There is no sense of self-ownership. As they adapt to their environment, so they find a sense of themselves. This is reinforced by self-recognition (the capacity to recognise your image or reflection) and in self-definition (the capacity to know the difference between 'I /me' and 'you').

Developing alongside this is the child's emerging awareness of the inner self, invisible but clearly communicating and visually localised – even by young children – in the head. This is the beginning of what Margaret Mead (1930) called 'self-interaction', our unique capacity to have discourse with ourselves, through self-perception, through thinking about ourselves and through forms of intrapersonal communication (talking or writing to ourselves). This extended conversation is stimulated by the influence of objective categories like age and gender or by more subjective interpretations like role and personality. All of this is reinforced by the defining discourse (the authoritative voice) of language, through which personality and self are made and then communicated.

Harré has argued that language reflects our attitudes towards selfhood (Harré *et al* 1985). This is essentially a standpoint which can be characterised as 'linguistic relativism'. This approach to language can be efficiently summed up in the philosopher Ludwig Wittgenstein's (1953) famous saying: 'The limits of my language are the limits of my world.' In the case of understanding the self, Harré is saying that what we can say about the self is limited by the vocabulary that we and our culture and language possess. Harré suggests that even the existence and widespread use of the pronouns 'I' and 'me' give the (often false) impression that we are more coherent and unified than we actually are.

ACTIVITY

Look up 'self' in a thesaurus and you'll be directed to two categories of related words.

- **'Identity'**, which includes 'selfness', 'selfsame', 'oneness', 'homogeneity', 'unity' and 'identification'.
- **'Speciality'**, which includes 'I myself', 'ego', 'individuality', 'particularity', 'peculiarity', 'personality', 'singularity', 'special', 'specific', 'personal', 'original' and 'exact'.

What do these associations tell you about our understanding of the self?

Partly Harré is engaged with Roland Barthes' (1973) concept of myth as a level of signification. You will remember that a myth is a sort of collective connotation, a story to explain some aspect of reality which groups of people can buy into. Harré is suggesting that language itself is a mythic structure in which values are enshrined. He is also suggesting that there are only a certain number of 'stories' which can be told about the self. Other cultures will, necessarily, have other stories in which the self is a more or less restricted idea. Moscovici (1985) goes even further to suggest the 'individual' is the greatest invention of modern times; in other words, it is a product of Western culture and language. In a comparative study of Western and non-Western culture, Smith and Bond (1993) found it useful to make a distinction between the independent self (favoured in the West) and the 'interdependent self', between the self as isolated and as part of a 'team'.

Make a list of traditional stories that are told to young European children (for example, 'The Three Little Pigs' or 'Jack and the Beanstalk'). How many of these are centred around what characters do *individually* and how many depend on collective effort (or *teamwork*)?

It is interesting to note that the English language has about 20,000 words which refer to aspects of the human personality, or personality traits as they are commonly called. This is arguably an aspect of the contemporary view in the West that personality is, as *The ABC of Communication Studies* has it, 'an individual's distinctive consistent and patterned methods of relating to the environment', or, more simply, 'individual differences and the typical ways people behave' (Gill and Adams 1998). Clearly, in both senses personality is of interest to the Communication Studies student in that 'distinctive, consistent and patterned methods' can be nothing other than communication. To some extent it could be argued that our personality defines the motivation for, and style and content of, all our conscious acts of communication.

We will certainly want to define and/or dissect the notion of personality if we are fully to understand what communication there is and particularly what it does.

Freud had interesting things to say about human personality and communication. Basically he believed that the development of the self was forged in the conflict between what he called 'the pleasure principle' and 'the reality principle' (Freud 1984). The pleasure principle describes the uncontrolled desire to be physically and immediately satisfied, which is the desire of a foetus in the womb. Growing up, for Freud, is simply the story of the ways in which this instinctive drive is checked by the influence of the real world and other people, which Freud labelled 'the reality principle'. The reality principle provides social roles and responsibility and notions of selfhood that go beyond immediate needs: to include such things as morality (conventions of behaviour) and self-image.

Communication (and language in particular) is implicitly central to Freud's analysis of personality, which in many ways is an impressive model of intrapersonal communication. Freud saw the 'reality–pleasure' contradiction as being contested through the forms of the conscious and unconscious mind. In this, communication in all its forms is a kind of context or even medium. To Freud lapses and slip-ups in spoken and written language are nothing more or less than the intrusion of the subconscious into the conscious (in other words, what we are thinking deep down comes to the surface and interferes with what we are saying). (Freud used the term 'parapraxis' to describe this phenomenon. This is commonly referred to as 'the Freudian slip'). In his book *The Interpretation of Dreams* (1999) he also proposed that a similar case can be made for dreams as an important symbolic intrapersonal code, another way in which one layer of the self communicates with another. 'Words,' Freud claimed, 'are a half-way house to lost things.' In other words, they are properly, in a semiotic sense, symbols, though what is signified is for Freud very like the 'unknown' frame of the Johari Window, that which you barely know yourself.

Freud's analysis of personality dramatises it very effectively, modelling the debate within the self in a coherent and convincing way. For Freud the personality consists of three parts – the id, the ego and the superego (Freud 1984) – and intrapersonal communication is the product of their various relationships. Let us take them in turn.

- **The id** responds directly to the instinct. It is the mouthpiece of needs and desires. As Freud himself pointed out: 'It contains everything that is present at birth . . . above all the instincts.' The id operates according to the pleasure principle: 'I want it now.' Freud dramatises the id to make his point that it is primitive and primal: 'We call it a chaos, a cauldron full of seething excitations.'
- **The ego** represents the conscious self responding to the physical needs of the id and the moral demands of the super-ego. It is the manager of the personality, continually making contingency plans to stave off the next crisis. The ego operates according to the reality principles, bringing the outside world to bear on the desires of the id. The ego is reason, whereas the id is passion. Freud estimated the ego gradually developed, starting at a few months old as the child turned his energies outwards.
- **The super-ego** is the moral aspect of the personality and thus the last fully to develop. It is partly ego-ideal (a sort of ideal ego), which promises rewards for good behaviour, and partly conscience, which threatens punishment for transgressors. The super-ego is in constant conflict with the id, for one is moral and the other is amoral (the id has no sense of morality).

A crude way to demonstrate Freud's argument is to take a simple moral situation and dramatise the roles of id, ego and super-ego. If you were walking home and found a wallet containing some money lying on the ground:

- the id would say, 'Take it, spend it, enjoy yourself; you won't be found out'
- the super-ego would say, 'That would be stealing, and stealing is wrong; you will be caught and punished'
- the ego would have the job of working between these positions in order to make a practical decision. The ego would consider such factors as how much money there is, how much you need it, who's around to see and whose wallet it is.

Try to apply Freud's theory in the same way to the following situation. You find yourself attracted to your best friend's girlfriend/boyfriend, and a string of coincidences has left you alone together at your place. There is no one else at home, and s/he seems 'keen'. What does your id say? What does your ego say? What does your super-ego say?

It is the ego's job to mediate (act as a go-between for) the demands of the id and super-ego. In other words, the ego is a representation of that 'voice' we all listened to in the previous section, when asked about shameful events from our past. The same would be true in a situation where we were asked to reveal something intimate or talk about a taboo subject such as masturbation. The super-ego represents that part of our internal communication which considers the accepted morality. The id represents that part of our internal communication which considers the instinctive reality. The ego acts as a go-between and forges a response. In Gergen and Gergen's (1981) terms, the ego is the self-maintainer. Freud's 'strategies' are unconscious and referred to as defence mechanisms, intrapersonal behaviours designed to (albeit temporarily) resolve the conflict between what we'd like to do and what we should do.

An understanding of defence mechanisms is invaluable for interpreting interpersonal behaviour because it offers a key to decoding a good deal of individual and group communication. A simple list of defence mechanisms would include the following.

- **Repression**: bottling up potentially painful experiences and feelings.
- **Displacement**: transferring your feelings to a substitute object, e.g. being angry with your boss and coming home to pick a row with your partner.
- **Denial**: refusing to accept reality, e.g. that your coursework is late, or that your relationship is over, or that your dog is dead.
- **Rationalisation**: finding acceptable reasons for unacceptable things, like your failure in an examination because you didn't revise.
- **Reaction formation**: consciously thinking the opposite of what you really feel, e.g. being very nice to people you dislike.
- **Sublimation**: working your unacceptable feelings out in a substitute activity, e.g doing the washing up to avoid a vicious argument.
- **Identification**: avoiding conflict by associating yourself with someone else's thoughts or experiences.
- **Projection**: seeing your own faults or problems in other people.
- **Regression**: exhibiting behaviour typical of an earlier stage of your development, e.g. crying or wetting the bed.
- **Isolation**: compartmentalising problems, keeping different thoughts and feelings apart.

How far do you agree with Freud's descriptions of the ways in which we defend ourselves psychologically? Which of the above behaviours can you recognise in your own life and/or the lives of your closest friends and family?

Freud's model of a segmented self overseen by a dominant ego has a validity that can be easily supported by our everyday experiences. We do seem to have an inner voice which, among other things, settles both consciously and subconsciously disputes between what we'd 'like' to do and what we ought to do. In many ways the effectiveness and necessity of defence mechanisms is demonstrated by cases where all forms of defence fail.

R. D. Laing's work on schizophrenia (*The Divided Self*, 1962), for example, offers a model in which the patient's relationship with the world and the self has broken down. Here the patient's communication remains intelligible but only in terms of their own 'divided self' and its relationship with the world. Without the balance and control that Freud would see provided by the ego, schizophrenics, according to Laing, suffer from what he called 'ontological insecurity', an uncertainty which affects even their ability to know and understand anything. This comprises three experiences which Laing labelled as follows.

- **Engulfment**: the fear of being swallowed up, suffocated by others' involvement. This makes love a particular threat.
- **Implosion**: the fear that the world at any moment will come crashing in and obliterate their identity. Schizophrenics feel empty.
- **Petrification/depersonalisation**: the fear of being turned to stone or becoming brainwashed.

Laing's work was an assault on the treatment of schizophrenia as a disease. He came to feel that the way it was being treated made the condition worse, that schizophrenia was something the medical profession did to patients. Writing in the 1960s, which was a period of experimentation, it was not surprising that Laing also came to see schizophrenia as a gateway to a new perception. His 'psychedelic model' sees schizophrenia as an antidote to normality. 'Madness,' he claimed, 'need not be all breakdown . . . it may also be breakthrough.' At a time when access to the unknown self was valued highly, this was a persuasive manifesto.

Laing's theories are interesting now only as an aid; they properly belong to their time. Freud has made a more lasting contribution. Freud offers a challenging analysis of human personality, which we can take or leave but which, either way, stimulates thought about communication. Others have disagreed with Freud's theories of personality, condemning them as abstract and unscientific. However, as tools for analysing the various understandings of intention, they are invaluable.

A one-time colleague of Freud, Carl Jung broke away from Freud's teachings, seeing the personality as a combination of factors: heart, feelings, soul. 'Wholeness' for Jung was both vital and vitally missing from Freud. Jung (1963) identified three elements of the psyche.

- **Consciousness** (thinking, feeling, sensing, intuiting (knowing something without knowing how you know it)). This is the part of the psyche known directly to the individual. For Jung the conscious mind also has two attitudes: either introversion (looking inward) or extroversion (looking outward). The ego is the organisation of the conscious mind, the individual's sense of identity.
- **Personal unconscious** (depressed or forgotten experiences). This is the part of the psyche that is only indirectly available to us by means of therapy or traumatic experience. Sometimes feelings, thoughts and memories cluster together on the personal unconscious and become complexes, significant stand-alone influences within the psyche (these are our 'hang-ups').
- **Collective unconscious** (our genetic heritage, the fruit of evolution). This is the part of the psyche that we have inherited from our ancestors.

For Jung, the collective unconscious is a store of 'primordial images' (a sort of racial memory bank), both human and pre-human. Jung used this to explain various phobias such as fear of spiders or the dark. These images are archetypes, 'original models' of aspects of human behaviour. There are four major archetypes in Jungian psychology:

- **persona**: the outward face we present to the world
- **anima/animus**: our feminine/masculine side
- **shadow**: the dark, primitive source of creativity
- **self**: the unifying force of the personality – selfhood is the aim of the Jungian model and achieved by only a few individuals.

Jung's theories are attractive to students of communication in at least two ways. First, like Freud, Jung offers a provocative set of prompts which are useful as tools of analysis of personal acts of communication. Jung exposes the levels at which communication takes place in a way that is not unlike Barthes's explanation of levels of signification. In this way Jung's archetypes are not unlike Barthes's myths, though for Jung 'ideology' would probably be replaced by 'psychological programming'. Furthermore this allows us to examine the connections between the structure of the self and communication texts, especially in terms of such things as narrative theory. Much of the supportive evidence and informing basis of Jung's theories come from an examination of theories in world mythologies and a recognition of the similarities between these. The stories we tell, much like the dreams we have, may in fact be a 'royal road to the unconscious', a coded version of our intrapersonal structures. Stevens' diagram of the Jungian psyche (cited in Gross 1993) shows the levels at which communication might operate.

The controversy remains with the collective unconscious, the idea of cultural memory. Do we dream our culture at a superficial level because we are immersed in it on a day-to-day basis or as a profound retrieval of inborn and biological information? Certainly the case for archetypal themes in the stories we tell as cultures, in both traditional and contemporary contexts, seems very strong, as the success of the *Star Wars* movies indicates. In the case of George Lucas's nine-part epic story cycle, there is ample room to identify a cast of archetypal characters and themes working out their complexes on an intergalactic scale. After all, what is 'The Force' but Jung's 'shadow' – primal, troubling and creative? In Luke Skywalker and Princess Leia the animus and anima are acknowledged and reconciled, and when the persona of Vadar is eventually breached at least some reflected light is cast on the self.

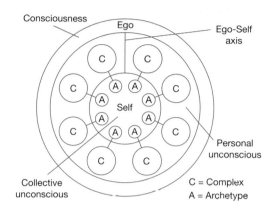

Diagram 4.5 *Jung's psyche (after Stevens)*

Choose any mainstream Hollywood film or well-known novel or play and see if you can identify archetypal elements. Jung's list went well beyond the big four to include birth, rebirth, death, power, magic, the hero, the wise old man, the earth mother, the child, the demon. Remember these are symbolic forms, so, for example, the forty-something central character of a modern film may correspond to the archetype of 'the child'.

Both Jung and Freud offer guides or maps to the interpretation of behaviour. This certainty that all human behaviour can be explained (albeit from the point where the present interprets the past) has generated the criticism that these guides or maps are unscientific. Critics like H. J. Eysenck (1969), whose alternative theories of personality we will look at next, question the validity and usefulness of any theory that is unable either to predict behaviour or to measure it. Freud and Jung are strong on metaphor and symbol. Eysenck (1969) proposes a model through which the personality might be categorised and measured. This psychometric model of personality (in other words, one that hopes to 'measure' the psyche) suggests that there are central aspects of personality (or traits) which can be successfully cross-referenced with others to form clusters (or factors). By analysing these factors, or building blocks, of personality (assuming the tests can be validated) we will be able to build up a picture of the fundamentals of human personality and the range of differences across this idea.

At its crudest this simply identifies a range of character tendencies and asks individuals to plot their own characteristics or those of others on a continuum in order to create an impression of their personality. The problems of this approach are self-evident and have been implicitly addressed in the previous section, where the relationship between self-image, self-esteem and the ideal self were presented. However, systems like Cattell's (1965) do provide a useful starting and talking point. Where would you place yourself and your closest friend (use X and O) on the following model?

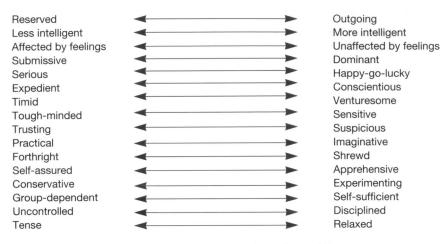

Diagram 4.6 *Psychometric model (after Cattell)*

Using Cattell's list, plot the personalities, as far as you are able, of two of the following 'personalities':

■ footballer Paul 'Gazza' Gascoigne
■ a Spice Girl of your choice (old or new)
■ the Prime Minister/Leader of the Opposition
■ your parent/guardian
■ a respected/feared/despised teacher
■ Chris Tarrant or Anne Robinson.

To 'discover' that Paul Gascoigne is, for example, very outgoing, extremely affected by feelings, always experimenting and too often uncontrolled may be of limited value. However, to have a set of proven tendencies of personality may help us to understand, for example, the different ways in which people are motivated. A drawback with Cattell's approach is that, for the perfectly defensible reason that it is undesirable to specialise any further, there are too many criteria to allow significant classification of individuals. That is to say, once you have made 16 statements about an individual, what you are left with is a convincing statement of their individuality rather than a feeling that they represent a type. Even to schematise Cattell's list into left–right–centre sections would permutate a massive 43 million combinations. (In other words, if we only allowed respondents to be reserved, outgoing or neither, the 16 category system would define more than 43 million personality types.)

Eysenck's approach is bolder for it proposes as a theory that there are a smaller number. He suggests four dimensions which deliver, in all, four distinct character types. Type theories attempt to classify all personalities into a limited number of groups. To some extent the theory of astrology is a type theory, given it assumes that roughly one-twelfth of the population have personalities that are broadly similar and governed by the stars. Eysenck's, in fact, is closer to the ancient Greek theory of the 'Humours'. This stated that human personality was determined by bodily 'chemical' balance; that our feelings and attitudes were aggravated by a predominance of one of the following 'bodily fluids':

too much yellow bile　=　choleric (angry, aggressive, restless)

too much blood　　　 =　sanguine (warm, outgoing, lively)

too much black bile　　=　melancholic (pessimistic, moody, quiet)

too much phlegm　　　=　phlegmatic (thoughtful, calm, reliable).

Galen, a doctor in second century AD Asia Minor, who contrived this theory, may have got the biology wrong but it is interesting that Eysenck incorporates these 'humours' into his own model of personality written some 1,800 years later. Eysenck proposed two axes of personality from which the four 'humours' might be derived. These axes, arrived at by analysing some 700 neurotic soldiers, are extroversion (and its opposite introversion) and neuroticism (and its opposite stability). Extroversion is simply the tendency to be outgoing, with introversion the tendency to direct ourselves inwardly. Neuroticism, or emotionality, describes the tendency to be excitable, changeable and unstable. According to Eysenck, the typical introvert is a quiet, retiring sort of person, introspective, fond of books rather than people, reserved and distant except to intimate friends. The typical extrovert is sociable, likes parties, has many friends, needs to have people to talk to and does not like reading or studying alone; they crave excitement.

ACTIVITY . . .

Which are you? The four designations are:

1　stable – introvert
2　stable – extrovert
3　unstable – introvert
4　unstable – extrovert.

Find examples from public life or your own personal experience for each of the above.

If we look straightforwardly at Eysenck's model, it is easy to see its relevance to our study of communication. First, the qualities that define an individual's position on the axes are chiefly if not exclusively demonstrated in their communication. Second, this implies a conscious or unconscious communicative style for each designated grouping. Finally, if the model proves feasible, it simplifies the business of interpersonal perception and offers hope that we can improve skills of perception and, through this, our capacity to find the most appropriate communication.

Eysenck's dimensions offer us a basis for predicting behaviour, and he and others have pursued investigations into such matters as:

- fatigue (extroverts tire more easily)
- employment (extroverts change jobs more frequently)
- relationships (extroverts divorce more readily)
- pain (introverts have lower pain thresholds)
- drugs (introverts are more difficult to sedate)
- criminality (Eysenck claimed that criminals should classically be 'unstable' extroverts. Research has not confirmed this. Some studies have found criminals as a group to be slightly introverted. Hampson concluded that no verifiable link could be made between personality dimensions and criminality.)

Most useful for us is the work done by Eysenck and others on personality and conditionability, the relative ease or difficulty with which individuals can have the attitudes they hold changed. Eysenck (1947/1999) claimed that introverts were more easily conditioned than extroverts. However, the evidence is inconclusive and Eysenck has been criticised for assuming that any suggestion that introverts are easily conditioned by one kind of stimulus is proof of a general case about a broader range of stimuli.

The twentieth century was the century of Big Brother, so conditioning was always going to be a headline issue (George Orwell proposed in his 1948 novel 1984 a future in which we would be observed in our homes by representatives of the government; Big Brother was the novel's dictator). Partly theorists in the second half of the century were trying to understand and to come to terms with the large-scale political conditioning of the first half of the century, which had led to so many atrocities. Theodor Adorno (1950), who had himself fled Nazi persecution, first made the connection between personality and prejudice and between certain kinds of personality and certain kinds of 'collective ideologies' (such as Fascism). Adorno's research (which started in Nazi Germany and moved, as did he, to the USA) proposed the theory of the 'authoritarian personality'. According to Adorno, the authoritarian personality is:

- hostile to people with inferior status
- servile to those of higher status
- contemptuous of weakness
- rigid and inflexible
- intolerant of uncertainty
- unwilling to face feelings
- an upholder of traditional values and ways of life.

Adorno suggested that these individuals had often experienced a very strict upbringing, which gave them repressed feelings about authority which were re-channelled positively into 'political movements' and negativity into hatred for minorities.

Both Rokeach (1960) and Eysenck (1954) felt that the issue of prejudice (and its consequences) required a specialised scale. Rokeach proposed 'dogmatism' (the degree to which one's mind is open or closed) as a scale by which attitudes might be gauged. Eysenck called this the Toughmindedness and Tendermindedness factor. Both had a political attitudes axis (Eysenck's was radicalism–conservatism; Rokeach used Adorno's 'potentiality for fascism' scale). These allow us to plot a predictive position for various political varieties. The three theorists can be usefully combined in Diagram 4.7.

While Eysenck largely confirmed a relationship between aspects of personality and authoritarianism (where toughmindedness was the significant trait), Rokeach stressed the greater importance of the compatibility of belief systems. Rokeach called this 'belief congruence theory', the idea that we are more positive in attitude towards people whose beliefs are congruent with ours (in other words which are similar in form and content). This will likely determine whom we communicate with, form relationships with, even work with. It was dealt with negatively in terms of cognitive dissonance theory in the previous section.

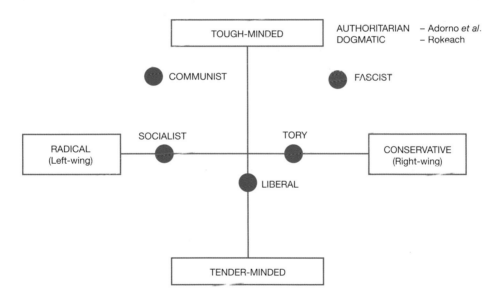

Diagram 4.7 *Example of a political attitudes axis (Gross 1993)*

▼ 5 INTRAPERSONAL COMMUNICATION: SELF AND SELF-PRESENTATION

In this section we conclude our consideration of intrapersonal communication by looking at ideas about the self and self-presentation.

■ We consider the work of Argyle, Goffman and Berne.

Having given self-concept and personality a detailed examination, it is time to come to product and outcome. Intrapersonal communication is all very well in itself, but 'the audience of one' is a demanding one, particularly if you want to try out your range of communication skills. We can think a range of things from the philosophical to the erotic; we can whisper sweet nothings in our own ears (and, if we're desperate, answer in a different voice); we can write notes or a diary or even a poem or a song; but sooner or later we're going to want to communicate with others.

This section is about the influence of what's inside on what comes out. It's about the connections between intrapersonal and interpersonal communication. A common question asked in Communication Studies at all levels is 'What is the relationship between intrapersonal and interpersonal communication?' The first part of the answer is easy: a statement of the strength of this bond which is intimate, essential and significant. The boldest responses would claim that all communication is self-presentation, that the self is all we have to communicate. In this sense the self is both the source and the destination of communication; the motivation, the purpose, the content and the outcome.

Whichever model of motivation we adopt, the self is prominent, either providing us with the energy for pushing us into action or providing us with a set of higher-order needs, such as the need for self-esteem or self-respect, which must be fulfilled. Argyle's (1983) drives ('persistent tendencies to pursue goals') are of three varieties:

■ **social acceptance**: wanting to be a part of various groups
■ **bodily needs**: needing to be fed and watered
■ **specific task goals**: having to do specific things like getting to work on time or putting up a shelf.

Once watered and fed, the self-concept is the driving force, pushing us into relationships, power struggles and good deeds, and all for its identity and self-esteem.

The same is true of the most prominent 'needs' model. Abraham Maslow's (1954) hierarchy is dominated, literally, by *self*-esteem and *self*-actualisation.

Think about all the things you have done so far today, every action and conversation. How far were these done (a) for some significant external reason, for someone else's sake, or (b) for yourself (for your *self*)? How many of those listed in (b) were really necessary?

The more we consider this matter, the more we realise that 'we' are at the mercy of the self, its needs and its desires. So all-controlling is it that it is almost impossible to think of a genuinely selfless act, one that has no reference to our own intrapersonal needs. Even when giving generously to others of time and money, we are often consciously increasing our self-esteem and thinking of our perceived mirror self. Some psychologists identify three forms of motivation for people doing things: egotism, altruism and psychological altruism. To be motivated by egotism is to act in your own interests. To be motivated by altruism is to act in the interests of other people. To be motivated by psychological altruism is to act apparently to meet other people's needs while actually fulfilling your own needs – that is, your need to meet others' needs.

The uncontrollable elements are of course our own personal skills, abilities and understandings. Servicing the self is all very well in theory, but in practice it is fraught with complications: in our ability to understand or know the self (the 'Unknown' frame of the Johari Window); in our capacity successfully to interact with others; in the special problems that reality always brings as a context. To some extent we always talk a better game than we play.

Key to understanding the relationship between the self-concept and the self as communicator is the idea of self-presentation, which Argyle (1983) has defined as 'behaviours designed to create an impression for others'. Self-presentation implies that our interactions with the world are largely conscious attempts to influence other people. In his important book *The Presentation of the Self in Everyday Life* (1990), Erving Goffman offers what is described as a dramaturgical model of self-presentation, in other words one that sees self-presentation as a sort of extended dramatic performance for which we prepare and at which we constantly work. As Goffman himself claims, 'Life itself is a dramatically enacted thing.' His extensive work takes its cues from this understanding and from his assertion that 'we all act better than we know'. Goffman sees self-presentation in six aspects or key elements, all of which are related in some way to the idea of life as drama:

- persona
- performance
- staging
- teams

- role
- personal style.

PERSONA

The first aspect, similar to one of Jung's key archetypes, is persona, the various personality 'masks' we might wear when undertaking roles. While these personae are to some extent selected or encouraged by their respective roles or contexts, they are not bound to them (persona is the singular form and personae is the plural form). The idea is that we have a number of viable selves, or variations on the self, and that we select the version that best fits the situation or role. In extremes it is easy to see this as a viable argument. The persona adopted for a Sunday afternoon picnic with your family may be very different from the one you need for your job as a prison warder or for your journey through the early morning rush hour or even your attendance with friends at a heavy metal concert. In between these there is a grey area in which such aspects as your mood, the setting or your simple lack of engagement or interest work against any coherent 'character' persona. Persona in fact works best as an explanation of formal situations, where conscious performance is an issue – at work, in an interview, even in an examination. Here the way you play is a matter of choice; it is about strategy. Elsewhere it is often not a real issue.

ACTIVITY . . .

How far is Goffman's theory realistic? If it works, we should notice a difference in the way we communicate in different situations. Try to identify some of your personae and suggest some of the differences in the ways they communicate.

To some extent we see persona most at work in the world of the media, where presentation is a matter of marketing. The Spice Girls are a classic case of created personae, with each 'girl' representing a subset of attitudes and characteristics. When the presentation of the persona is professional, as in film acting, some people are better at it than others. Some actors present a range of personae across a range of roles, while others cannot (or do not).

Performance

If personae are masks, performance describes the different ways in which they can be worn. These ways range crudely from 'for real' to 'ironically/for laughs/ for reward'. This partly describes the degree to which the self is honestly and wholeheartedly engaged in the act of self-presentation. At the 'sincere' end of the scale, the persona is a device that allows us to be ourselves, or as close to this as is possible. It is worth reminding ourselves why this is not an attainable goal. We have dealt with too much evidence that suggests that the self is ultimately unknowable. Hopefully, most of the time we are working on the 'sincere' end of the scale, trying as we might to present ourselves as we really are. This, after all, is the key even in formal (and fake) situations like interviews and examinations.

However, on occasion, we also need to 'play the game', to put on a show merely to fulfil the demands of a situation. This is what Goffman calls 'cynical' performance, where the persona you employ is disconnected from the self and simply 'exhibited'. The 'cynical' self in performance represents us rather than presents us, for it is largely dealing with the audience's rather than our own needs. (We are literally giving the audience what it wants.) This is very like a theatrical performance.

ACTIVITY . . .

Suggest how you would be likely to perform on the sincere–cynical axis in the following situations.

Sincere ⟵————————⟶ **Cynical**

1   On a first date.
2   In your Communication Studies examination.
3   At your wedding/on the day you move in with your partner.
4   In an Internet chatroom.
5   Visiting a sick relative.
6   Listening to your best friend's problems.

Clearly, there cannot be a definitive answer, but in most of the above there will probably be pressures from both ends of the line.

STAGING

Obviously performances need a context, and Goffman suggests that for our self-presentations these are carefully constructed and controlled. 'Staging' is the term he uses for all of the ways our self-presentation is 'set' – the physical locations, the props, the costume. Here he makes a distinction between that which he refers to as front, which is the routine combinations of location and costume we come to expect, and those stagings which are more spontaneous or infrequent. Front then might cover those aspects of a male teacher's self-presentation that you see on a day-to-day basis – his classroom, his limited wardrobe of style-less clothes, his supermarket carrier bags full of student work. The staging might be very different if the same teacher were called in to staff a school or college disco or gig. The physical setting is a dimly lit hall, the costume an unfortunate attempt at trendy gear, and the significant 'prop' an overbearing smell of an ancient aftershave.

The best examples of active staging are probably to be found in what the research rather archaically calls 'courting rituals', the sometimes ridiculous lengths we go to in order to attract prospective partners. Men and women in pubs and clubs on the lookout for a companion or a date often use extravagantly artificial stagings, presenting themselves in strategic locations and in supposedly appropriate postures. In a more modest way staging is also important when we meet and greet someone. Rising from your chair and moving towards someone you are greeting is clearly about staging, fixing the physical relationship between you and your audience. Taking this kind of initiative is a particularly good way of beginning to dismantle the barriers that are often put up in formal communication contexts like interviews by their own staging.

ACTIVITY . . .

A common assessment activity in Communication Studies is the formal or semi-formal oral presentation, in which you are asked to deliver an illustrated talk to a small group audience you invite. You are invariably asked for your own staging. In other words, you are allowed to arrange the room and your audience as you wish. Assuming your own presence, the need to use visual aids, and an audience of five friends, suggest two contrasting stagings for this talk. Evaluate the strengths and weaknesses of each, e.g.

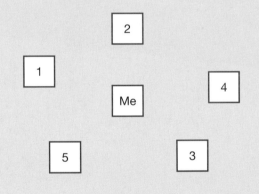

Strengths:

- self is central
- element of surprise.

Weaknesses:

- intimidating for all
- limits use of visual aids
- difficult to address members equally.

How might 'costume' affect the success or failure of your two 'models'? What would it be best to wear in each case? Do different stagings suit different cos-tumes? (If you have them sitting on the floor on beanbags, will informal clothing be a necessity?)

TEAMS

What is also implied by the oral presentation scenario is what Goffman described as teams, in other words the company we keep – our friends and fellow actors 1963. These teams may be part of what we have identified as front, 'that part of the individual's performance which regularly functions in a general and fixed fashion to define the situation for those who observe the performance'. Staging is often shared or enhanced by the participation of others who form the groups (Goffman's 'teams'), which will be the focus of the next three sections. The teams that Goffman refers to range from the structured and specialised sets of people (who, for example, allow television presenters to do their job) to the small (as small as one other person) friendship groups which form a context for much of our communication.

If you're selling burgers at a major fast food chain the notion of teamwork will not be unfamiliar. Those people who are part of your team support your self-presentation as a competent employee or undermine it by making you wait too long for chicken nuggets. Goffman argues that the situation is the same even if the context is very much more informal. First, teams are part of your front, they are part of the furniture of your staging, reflecting aspects of your personal front (your age, your fashion sense, your attitudes). This can turn out to be a considerable psychological barrier in terms of the in-group/out-group dynamics (where people are mildly put off by the presence of other people who already know one another). Add to this the characteristic costume of a youth subcultural group (nose ring, make-up, Marilyn Manson tee-shirt), and a team becomes a gang and the cause of a minor moral panic.

ACTIVITY . . .

Gender is assumed to play a significant part in explaining the differences between kinds of team. What team behaviour is expected from the following teams? (What sort of context will they create for an individual's self-presentation?)

- A boy band.
- A girl band.
- Five girls/women 'out on the town'.
- Five boys/men 'out on the town'.

Your team may be only one other person. This does not detract from a theory that sees observed relationships as a significant context. The very ease we have with our closest friends makes the notion of team performance very persuasive. In this sense, getting to know someone is to become part of their team, to communicate with them and alongside them. If you think of the smallest group (of two), it is useful to think theatrically in terms of 'double acts' and then of your own 'work' with your closest friend.

If we consider high-profile comedy pairings (for example Morecombe and Wise, the Two Ronnies, Smith and Jones, French and Saunders, Newman and Baddiel), we are immediately aware of the front that is being established. We are being 'sold' physical differences as an index (a connection is being made) of character differences. These are used consciously to create a context for comedy, a staging for humour. The team-work is often slick and professional but the principles are the same as for our own two-person performances. We play off other people, and that play begins with appearance and goes from there.

Choose three friends whom you might see individually. Briefly describe the 'teamplay' in each of the three pairs you form when you're with them individually. How does it differ and what difference, if any, does it make to you as a presented self?

ROLE

Given that Goffman uses a theatrical metaphor, it seems surprising that it should have taken us so long to come to role. Role refers to the parts we play and is, in essence, the focus of Goffman's model. Though Goffman admits that 'All the world is not, of course, a stage', he also points out that 'the crucial ways in which it is not are not easy to specify'. When we considered the business of defining who we are, when we first looked at intrapersonal communication, we identified 'social role' as a significant theme of the responses. The research, by Kuhn and McPartland (1954), also indicated that 'definition by role' becomes more prominent as we mature (undergraduates referred to the idea of role twice as often as 7-year-olds did).

What is the role we play when we are alone? For example, 7.36 am: Woke up. Thought about the day ahead. This is what Mead (1930) called 'self-interaction'. Is this the meta-role, the role of roles? Is this the maskless self? Is it, in fact, the 'casting' role: who will I be today?

Goffman sees the parts we play as an organising principle of our self-presentation. He would see most of us moving from role to role across the day. We may wake up as a wife or husband, walk downstairs into the role of father or mother, before playing the commuter in the early morning rush hour. We may arrive at work to the unexpected role of friend or confidante before we assume the role of employee or employer. The workplace is alive with role differentiation, and potentially role conflict, where the role of 'mother of a sick child' conflicts with the role of 'full-time worker'. Work is often obsessed with rank and status. This makes offices and staffrooms settings for conflicting and overlapping roles. The evening may produce a new set of roles; you may be the guest at a party, a diner at an expensive restaurant, or a part-time worker in a pub (though these may not be the roles of an average student).

Keep a fanatically accurate record of one day's interaction with other people (take a notebook with you). For each of the listed interactions, try to define the role you were playing (either consciously or subconsciously).

That leaves only personal style. How can this be last on the list? It almost seems an afterthought, as if Goffman isn't entirely convinced it exists. More than this, personal style is marginalised simply because Goffman's extensive model has left very little space in which this style can operate. Surely we'd like to believe our individuality counts for more than that? Surely, to extend the metaphor, we are more like actor-managers than actors. After all, we provide the script and allow the show to be put on.

We may provide the script but that does not mean that in any significant way we 'write' it. Script is the unspoken element in all of this. Goffman would see it as intimately connected to each of the other aspects. Personae bring language or at least register and tone; performance gives clues as to how language might be used; staging sets the idiom more precisely in the way that foreign words in a phrase book might be clustered around 'the tobacconist' or 'the swimming baths'; teams sensitise or desensitise language to audience needs and expectation; roles often have their own dialects, or at least registers (technical, specialist and restricted). The more fragmented the analysis becomes, the harder it is to see a place for the personal voice, the authorial voice, even personal style.

This is perhaps the function, even the justification, of creative or aesthetic communication. When we write something personal or imaginative – a story, a poem, even a memoir – we are in fact writing ourselves, and for ourselves. The same is true of our drawing, painting, performing, sculpting, singing and some of our speaking. We are imposing our personal experiences and personal style and in doing so are emphasising the unity rather than fragmentation of the self. Poetically this could be described as a healing process, a mending. This idea is central to Jungian psychology and a potential role for Goffman's notion of personal style as a sort of 'synoptic' element (one that unites the others). Personal style is therefore that which gives coherence to self-presentation, that which lends it its voice. Without personal style (or if this element is underdeveloped or stilted), performance has no fluidity, no coherence; we are merely 'rude mechanicals', bad actors. With a mature personal style we can be artists, authors of our own 'stories', *auteurs* (the French term used to signify those film directors who stamp their own identity on their work).

Choose an artist or musician or writer or film-maker whose work has an individual or personal style. Try to define this 'style' as a bullet-point list. Now do the same for someone you know very well (close friend or family member), looking at the key characteristics of their personal communication.

The strengths of Goffman lie in the detailed way he has worked through the elements of self-presentation and the coherence with which he has brought them together. Goffman offers a set of prompts which act as a useful starting point for examining interpersonal behaviour. It is not an approach that dwells too long on the self as such, but rather as it is demonstrated in performance, as it appears 'dressed' in the world. An alternative approach, which pays greater attention to the state of the self and which offers an alternative metaphor for the relationships between individuals and the world of others, is Transactional Analysis.

The writer most frequently associated with Transactional Analysis (or TA as it is known) is Eric Berne (1968). At the heart of Berne's theories is the notion that communication is transactional, that it consists of innumerable 'transactions' (or interpersonal deals). A transaction is an exchange of communication. It might be an acknowledged smile of greeting or part of an involved and sophisticated negotiation. Berne argues that when we communicate with others we are involved in negotiations and in game-playing with the intention of either reaching a compromise or outplaying our opponent in order to overcome them. This is an interesting view, if not a startling one, but Berne goes further to relate these transactions and these games to what he called ego-states, conditions of the self.

KEY TERM

> **TRANSACTIONAL ANALYSIS** An approach to understanding and ultimately improving interpersonal communication introduced by Eric Berne in his book *Games People Play* (1968). Berne proposes three 'ego states': child, parent and adult.

The essence of Eric Berne's theories of personality is that each of us is really three people. These are identified as 'the child', 'the parent' and 'the adult'. These are not stages of maturity, they are options within all of us. They have their own patterns of behaviour and particular uses of speech and body language. In the course of normal communication each will become dominant in its own contexts. The idea is that when we are communicating we choose from which ego-state to speak and our receiver does the same. When we get recognition for our communication, in the form perhaps of a smile or a nod, we receive what Berne called a 'stroke'. A stroke is a form of positive reinforcement, a boost to our self-esteem and for Berne it is the most important reason we communicate. We transact to receive strokes. With small children strokes are literally physical, whereas with adults strokes tend to take a verbal form. Berne claimed that without strokes 'the spinal cord will shrivel up'. Clearly, negative recognition produces negative strokes and everything deteriorates.

According to Berne, there are three ego-states.

- **The child**: the child state is emotional and poorly controlled but also creative and affectionate. The child is prey to its emotions; it is sulky, physical and inconsistent. When drunk or hyped up on emotion of any kind, we often retreat to the child state.

- **The parent**: Claude Steiner describes the parent ego-state as 'like a tape-recorder . . . it is a collection of pre-recorded, prejudged and prejudiced codes for living'. When we are in our parent state we become our parents or the people who raised us. Berne distinguishes between the 'Critical Parent' and the 'Nurturing Parent'. For Steiner, 'The parent uses old tapes to solve problems and is therefore at least 25 years behind.' We probably have all known teachers who are stuck fast in their 'Critical Parent' state.
- **The adult**: the adult uses reason and logic to solve problems. It thinks and feels in relation to experience. In Steiner's words, 'The adult is a human computer.' The adult has its emotions under control.

Berne's work is useful as a tool for analysing interpersonal exchanges and the role of the self in these. It is widely used in counselling as a therapeutic tool. In his book *Games People Play* (1968), Berne motivated discussion on TA by offering compelling and often amusing examples of the way the ego-states interact and literally of the 'games people play'. Steiner identifies, for example, five ways in which people can get strokes.

- **Rituals**: 'a pre-set exchange of recognition strokes'. For example, you might pass a friend in the corridor early in the morning and take part in this kind of exchange:

   'Alright, Chloe?'
   'How are you?'
   'Great.'
   'See you later, then.'

This would be described as a 'four-stroke ritual'.

- **Pastimes**: 'a pre-set conversation around a certain subject'. These might include the weather, old friends, school/college/work, television, music.
- **Games**: 'a repetitive, devious series of transactions'. Games are a risk. They can be won; they can also be lost. We are not always aware we are playing.
- **Intimacy**: 'a direct and powerful exchange of strokes'. This is about touching and being close. It may involve sex, but sex may also feature in all the other categories.
- **Work**: 'an activity which has a product as its result'. Along with intimacy, this is the most satisfying way of getting strokes. Without meaningful work, people resort to rituals, pastimes and games.

Berne's work gives a satisfying new angle on behaviour and potentially a fresh way to look at communication problems. Berne would put down many of the disruptions in communication we experience on a day-to-day basis to a mismatching of ego-states. Berne conceived of two significant sorts of transaction:

- **the complementary,** where the ego-states of the participants are matched.
- **the crossed,** where the ego-states are mismatched. This is where problems start.

Consider, for example, a teacher–student relationship in two versions.

   TEACHER: 'What do you think the issue is here?' (Adult–Adult)
   STUDENT: 'Depends where you're looking from.' (Adult–Adult)

This is a complementary transaction. Compare this to the following.

TEACHER: 'What do you think the issue is here?' (Adult–Adult)
STUDENT: 'Just get off my back, will you?' (Child–Parent)

This is a crossed transaction, and communication has already deteriorated.

Although the language of TA is simple, and deliberately so, its insights are certainly not superficial. Berne developed the approach as a practical way to make a difference. He was interested in empowering people, in allowing them to see that they have choices, in promoting thinking and self-respect. TA is about understanding the factors that got us to where we are and then using this understanding to inform a better future. On one level it is about de-parenting, for the Parent is the significantly poorest ego-state and Berne himself has suggested that most parents take princes and princesses and turn them into frogs. TA is also a model for understanding the smallest groups, the dyad or group of two. Group communication is what we'll consider next.

▼ 6 GROUP COMMUNICATION: WHAT GROUPS ARE AND WHAT THEY DO

We now move to consider group communication.

■   We begin by looking at a range of definitions of what constitutes a group.

The most common approach to the study of group communication is to begin by attempting some kind of definition of what a group is, or to line up a number of competing definitions. Before we load 'group' with all manner of theoretical baggage, it is important that we see it for what it is, an important label for the place where we experience a large amount of communication on a day-to-day level. This section will locate the practice of group communication within the practice of day-to-day communication of which it forms a significant proportion and then use that experience to attempt to reconcile various academic definitions of 'group'.

ACTIVITY...

Imagine the communication that usually happens across your average student or work day. List the people you usually talk to or with whom you interact.

The list you have made is a crude list of the groups to which you belong. These are collections of people you habitually communicate with, often in limited and specific contexts. Hartley (1997) identified three types of these, all of which may be included in your list:

■   family groups
■   friendship groups
■   work groups.

If we consider these three types of group, we can begin to describe the dimensions of our experience of significant others. We may, for example, conclude that there are certain general differences across these three designations. Work groups tend to be rather more formal than the other types. Some groups are 'ascribed' (like our families) and others 'achieved' (like the membership of teams). Some groups are large and others are small. Moreover, within friendship groups there is considerable variation of intensity and commitment which may result partly from how well established these groups are.

ACTIVITY . . .

Answer the following questions in the order they are given.

1   Who were your FIVE best friends at the end of junior school?
2   Which of these people went on as friends to secondary school?
3   Who were your FIVE friends in Year Nine (at age 14)?
4   Which of these remained by the end of secondary school?
5   How many of these went on with you to college?
6   How many of these (in question 4) do you still keep as friends?
7   Who are your FIVE best friends now?
8   Are any of these those you listed in answer to question 1?

Clearly, a dimension of groups is their longevity, whether they are short term or long term. Another dimension is their significance to us and the resulting frequency of interaction that entails. Those groups that you spend most time with are referred to as primary groups, with secondary groups as those with which you have intermittent contact. In terms of friendship, this is directly related to the level at which you have bonded with the other person or people. Burton and Dimbleby (1995) suggests four levels of companionship:

- close friend
- other friend
- associate
- acquaintance.

If these are the starting point for the designation of 'kinds of friendship groups', it is clear that any definition of a group must range in size from the dyadic one-to-one, which is the staple unit of interpersonal communication, to the reasonably large social groupings which are a natural spin-off of work groups and sports groups. Stanton has suggested that in all cases there is an optimum number. This is dependent on such variables as context, task and personality, and stands somewhere between the need for participation and the need for a breadth of knowledge and experience. An example might be discussions about the optimum size of teaching groups in a school or college. Too many students means some will be unable fully to participate in the work of the group; too few students will limit the range of opinions and responses available.

Compare two groups of which you are a member. They could be family, friendship or work groups. Consider the extent to which size is a factor in their success or lack of it.

Douglas (1979) includes number in his extensive list of criteria by which groups may be assessed, with size as its classification. It would be useful to carry the two groups you have just considered through this substantial list of classifications.

Criterion	Classification
1 Nature	natural/artificial
2 Origin	spontaneous/created
3 Leader	directive/non-directive
4 Location	environmental influences
5 Members	selection criteria
6 Outcome	group purpose
7 Number	size
8 Throughput	open/closed
9 Orientation	approach
10 Programme	choice of activity
11 Duration	time factor

A one-year Communication AS group would in this way be described as artificial, created, directive, based in the room ET30, largely self-selecting, determined to pass AS Communication Studies, of a specific size, closed, enthusiastic, studying Communication Studies, and lasting one year. Each of these is a useful prompt, not only for understanding this or any specific group, but also for uncovering the paradigms of 'group' as an idea. In identifying a specific group as artificial, we are being prompted to consider what a natural group would be like.

Find examples of groups which can be classified in the following ways according to Douglas's criteria.

(a) Natural   (nature)
(b) Spontaneous   (origin)
(c) Non-directive (leader)
(d) Open   (throughput)
(e) Short term   (duration)

We began with a deliberate non-definition of what group was – a vague term that describes all of the habitual communication we have with significant others. By merely pricking the surface of our experience, we have exposed the immense variety in these contexts, what could be termed units of communication practice. We are now ready, in the light of this experience, to construct and test out definitions of 'group'.

Clearly, group is a descriptive term that can be applied to a wide variety of communication practices. In terms of personal communication, it is fair to say that we are mostly engaged in group communication, communication with or within groups. There is a significant amount of redundancy or predictability in personal communication in groups – established routines, patterns, even networks of communication that we occupy. What this entails can be clarified if we bring together a number of academic explanations.

What is a group? In order for a group to exist, the following must apply.

- **Individual members must exist in some kind of relationship**. According to Burton and Dimbleby (1995), 'If there is no interaction between the individuals, then a group cannot be formed.' Hartley talks of a regular pattern or structure of interaction. Judy Gahagan (1975) asserts, 'A group should be conceived of as a system whose parts interrelate.'
- **Groups share common interests, goals and purposes**. In *Between Ourselves*, Burton and Dimbleby define a group as 'a collection of individuals who interact in some way and share some common goals or interests'.
- **Groups share common values and norms**. O'Sullivan *et al.* (1994) define norms as 'those sets of social rules, standards and expectations that both generate and regulate social interaction and communication'. In most groups these norms are unwritten and unspoken.
- **Groups develop set roles of behaviour which members accept**. O'Sullivan *et al.* (1994) define roles as 'socially defined positions and patterns of behaviour which are characterised by specific sets of rules, norms and expectation'. To some extent these developed roles are the manifestations of the values and norms of the group; in other words the theory is put into practice.
- **Group members have an identity**. Hartley (1997) talks about the existence of a group depending on the perception that it exists, logically both inside and outside the group. Turner (1991) categorised this effectively when he claimed, 'A group exists when two or more people define themselves as members of it and when its existence is recognised by at least one other.'

A handy summary of these descriptions of group is provided by Douglas (1979), who declared that a group was 'the largest set of two or more individuals who are jointly characterised by a network of relevant communications, a shared sense of collective identity and one or more of shared goal dispositions with associated normative strengths'. Or as Gahagan (1975) more succinctly puts it, 'A group of people is significantly more than the sum of its parts.' In mathematical terms it is not about addition but about integration.

So far we have established what kind of groups we are in and what kind of things they are. In doing so we have recognised a distinction between those groups that we are 'assigned' to (those which are ascribed to us) and those which we join of our own free will. In terms of the latter we might reasonably ask why we join these groups. Douglas lists seven reasons beyond 'the individual is born into the group'.

- They choose to do it.
- It is part of doing something else (e.g. a job).
- They are compelled to do so.
- They are compelled to do so by specific changes in circumstances (e.g. an accident).
- They drift into it over a period of time.
- They are invited to do so.
- They are proud to do so (this is the 'achieved' idea, for example gaining entry to a prestigious sports team).

Douglas adopts a pragmatic approach to the business of joining groups; others have adopted a more psychological one. Maslow (1954), for example, offered social needs as one level of his hierarchy, suggesting that companionship in whatever configuration was a basic human necessity. Dimbleby and Burton (1998), similarly, define the reasons people join groups in terms of two simple socio-emotional and task-orientated criteria. In other words, in terms of intrinsic social and emotional needs, and extrinsic instrumental needs; the need to support and protect the self, and the need to get things done. Their twin criteria were to:

- achieve a shared goal or resist a common threat
- have a sense of belonging and security.

These have a primal feel, as if all groups were essential and extreme. It may be difficult to square the interactions within your work social group with 'shared goal' and 'common threat' or even 'belonging' and 'security'. Many viable groups are more mundanely constructed. A more tentative list was compiled by Nicholson (1977) who set out to establish the factors that had bearing on the formation of friendships. His list is less striking but perhaps more realistic.

- The need for stimulation.
- The need for reassurance.
- The attraction of similarity (mixing with People Like Us).
- The recognition that friendships are expendable (we are prompted into relationships by the knowledge that some, and potentially all, will fail).
- The fact of proximity (we join with people we constantly see).
- Physical attractiveness.

Nicholson suggests that relationships and the joining of groups are primarily about finding something to do and less to do with those factors that influence other personal relationships like love. Clearly, though, there are the same intrinsic and extrinsic motivations: the desire to be whole and strong; to have a sense of group identity; and a desire to do things, to complete tasks and achieve goals. Stanton (1996) has related these primary functions of groups to roles members play within them. Stanton describes these as Task Roles (functions required in carrying out a group task) and Group Building and Maintenance Roles (functions required in strengthening group life and activities).

▼ 7 GROUP COMMUNICATION: INSIDE GROUPS

In this section we look at how groups form and function.

- We will consider how groups communicate internally.
- We will examine the roles group members perform when in groups.
- We will look at Moreno's work on sociometrics and at Douglas's work on group processes.

The previous section ended by suggesting some of the reasons why people join groups either formally or informally. This section will take that process a step further by exploring how groups form, how they function, and how they are structured. As with all of this work, it is useful to test the theories offered against your own experience in groups.

ACTIVITY . . .

Choose two groups to which you consider you belong, one informal group (a friendship or family group perhaps) and one formal group (a work or school/college group). For each group respond to the following prompts.

- Status of group: family/friendship/work/other?
- Who?
- When?
- Where?
- Why did this group form?
- How did this group form?

Any explanation of how groups form and how they work needs to ring true with your experience of groups.

Tuckman (1965) and others have suggested that there are four stages in the life and work of groups. Argyle described them as 'formation', 'rebellion', 'norming' and 'co-operation'. In Tuckman they are more dramatically and memorably termed 'forming', 'storming', 'norming' and 'performing'.

- **Forming** is the initial stage of basic interaction in which a number of people come together and communicate regularly.
- **Storming** is the crucial stage of disorder and sometimes conflict through which relationships are forged; the testing stage, which determines whether a group will develop.
- **Norming** is the explicit result of storming, the establishment of group 'rules', ways of working, thinking, communicating and self-presentation.
- **Performing** is the stage at which a functioning group emerges as a significant communicator, complete with its own 'personality' and patterns of behaviour.

In practice groups do not conform neatly to this evolutionary plan and it is more useful to see these stages as fluid, dynamic aspects of the life of groups rather than successive phases of development. It is likely that this pattern will be repeated often across the life of a group as the group develops. As a general guide, however, these are accurate descriptions of the life of most groups.

Within these general descriptors of the stages through which groups are continually working or ceasing to work, two factors are constantly at play – the roles of individual members, and the patterns and processes of intra-group communication

Burton and Dimbleby (1995) have described the roles we undertake in relation to the three kinds of group we have considered as interdependent. The model they offer suggests that the role we play in one sort of group influences the roles we play in other groups.

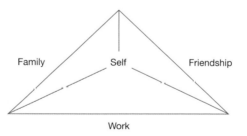

Diagram 4.8 *Burton and Dimbleby's group communication model*

What Dimbleby and Burton are suggesting is that role is an organising concept of our behaviour in groups: that if our roles within our family are relatively passive, then that fact will make our likely roles within our work groups more or less passive. We may conform to our given or chosen role stereotype or react against it. Either way there is a significant influence. When considering role as a concept, it is important to distinguish between roles that are 'ascribed' or 'assigned' (like membership of a family) and those that are 'achieved' or 'assumed' through being earned (like membership of a team).

'Assigned' carries with it connotations of the group being 'directive'; 'assumed' might imply initiative or the lack of it. All four descriptors are useful for indicating the complexity and subtlety of role as an idea and clarifying some of the differences between one situation and another. For example, is the role of 'father' 'ascribed' or 'achieved'? All we can really say is that this is a good question, and good questions are what education is about.

ACTIVITY . . .

List the roles you perceive yourself to have, from son/daughter to college member or sportsperson. Describe each role using one or more of the following descriptions:

- achieved
- ascribed
- assigned
- assumed.

The 'perceive yourself' part of the last activity introduces another variable or, to put it another way, complication. Shaw (1981) has argued that it is vital to distinguish between three versions of any role:

- perceived role
- enacted role
- expected role.

In other words, Shaw makes an interesting distinction between the role we think we're filling, the role we fill, and the role others expect us to fill. Much in-group conflict might be seen to derive from these discrepancies. The 'storming' process, which we discussed earlier, is partly about ironing out critical differences between these three ideally harmonious 'states'.

ACTIVITY . . .

Choose a group you feel happy and confident in, ideally your Communication Studies group, and write down:

- what you think your role in the group is
- the roles of three others in that group.

Ask others in the group to do the same and compare results.

At the end of the previous section we briefly considered Stanton's (1996) description of two types of role in groups: Task roles, and Group Building and Maintenance roles. Stanton relates these to types of behaviour and communication skills, suggesting that being a group member is about having a portfolio of skills. 'Task roles' includes such things as initiating activity, seeking information and co-ordinating, whilst 'Group Building and Maintenance roles' includes encouraging, gatekeeping and standard setting. Kurt Albrecht, on the other hand, is much more rigid in his designations of the specific role needs of groups. He describes five kinds of group member.

- **Energisers**: those who provide group motivation.
- **Ideas people**: those who think what to do.
- **Action people**: those who get things done.
- **Organisers**: those who make sure things are done efficiently.
- **Uncommitted**: those who make no real contribution.

These can easily and more flexibly be seen as four group functions and one group dysfunction. At a general level they probably do offer recognisable character generalisations but they also constitute those elements that every group needs.

ACTIVITY . . .

For the two groups you identified in the first activity in this section, complete the following.

Who are the:

- energisers
- ideas people
- action people
- organisers
- uncommitted?

It is likely that in most groups these functions will vary according to such variables as task (what the group are doing), personnel (who the group are) and environment (where the group are). Knowing this, it may be more satisfactory to see intra-group communication in terms of skills or processes rather than in terms of roles, in terms of in-group activities rather than personal specialism.

Dimbleby and Burton (1998) identify a number of interpersonal communication skills, which are valuable to group members. The implication is that these might and will be developed and will be present in group members to varying degrees. Being in healthy groups will presumably help these develop, just as possessing these skills will help groups be healthy. The Dimbleby and Burton list of group skills runs as follows.

- To be able to offer praise for ideas and actions.
- To be able to show agreement with group ideas.
- To be able to offer information and ideas.

- To be able to evaluate ideas and information.
- To be able to invite opinions and involvement.
- To be able to bring together ideas and opinions.
- To be able to suggest actions involving the groups.

In your opinion rank these group skills according to their significance to groups. In your own contexts, which of these skills can you identify and which do your fellow group members lack?

Albrecht, and Dimbleby and Burton essentially offer differently focused accounts of what goes on in groups. Albrecht is concerned primarily with individual members and their specific functions; Dimbleby and Burton with individual behaviour and performance. A third approach focuses on the group itself and the processes within it. Bales's Interaction Process Analysis (1950) is an attempt systematically to describe what goes on in groups.

Bales identifies socio-emotional and task-orientated needs as the basis of group motivation and then proceeds to clarify the specific ways in which these are made evident in group behaviour. He labels these 'ways' as 'interaction processes', a series of specific responses individuals make in groups.

Bales offers a sophisticated model of the implications of certain kinds of group behaviour, both positive and negative. He identifies six significant levels at which problems might occur, in other words six points at which barriers might impede communication. Like Albrecht he identifies negative factors in the interaction of group members, replacing 'uncommitted' with 'socio-emotional behaviour: negative'. Bales has clipped them down to 'disagrees', 'shows tension' and 'shows antagonism' and in all cases connected them to the dynamic of the group. Bales sees these negative elements as essential to the active processes through which groups work. The problems are all subtly couched in positive terms: 'reintegration', 'tension reduction' and 'decision'.

Stanton (1996) is less convinced about the value of dissident elements in groups. She sees certain member characteristics as potentially harmful to the functioning and long-term future of some groups. She talks of the 'hidden agendas' of some group members, whereby what these members want and need is often at odds with what the rest of the group wants and needs. Her examples of 'hidden agenda' behaviour include trying to impress; defending vested interests; responding negatively to other group members; and using the group for amusement.

Stanton lists types of non-functional behaviour as follows.

1 Being aggressive.
2 Blocking.

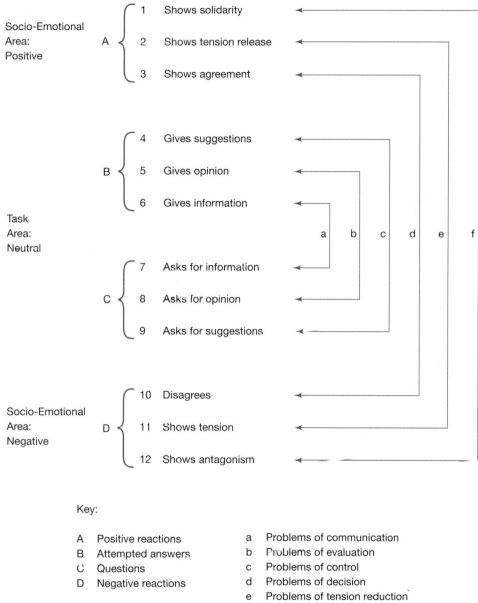

Socio-Emotional
Area:
Positive

A { 1 Shows solidarity
    2 Shows tension release
    3 Shows agreement

B { 4 Gives suggestions
    5 Gives opinion
    6 Gives information

Task
Area:
Neutral

C { 7 Asks for information
    8 Asks for opinion
    9 Asks for suggestions

Socio-Emotional
Area:
Negative

D { 10 Disagrees
    11 Shows tension
    12 Shows antagonism

a b c d e f

Key:

A Positive reactions
B Attempted answers
C Questions
D Negative reactions

a Problems of communication
b Problems of evaluation
c Problems of control
d Problems of decision
e Problems of tension reduction
f Problems of reintegration.

Diagram 4.9 *Bales's Interaction Process Analysis (IPA) model*

3 Self-confessing.
4 Competing.
5 Seeking sympathy.
6 Special pleading.
7 Horsing around.
8 Seeking recognition.
9 Withdrawal.

You may already recognise some of these behaviours in yourself or in others. One of the things to which they relate is the degree to which members commit themselves to groups. The problems of interaction which Bales elegantly identifies are often less elegant and less identifiable in practice. The very essence of 'hidden agendas' is the fact that they are hidden. If we are to understand how group members interact, we will need to back up this theory with some practice.

ACTIVITY . . .

Arrange to observe a group in action, perhaps one of your own, and simply tally the number of times each member of the group makes a contribution to what the group is saying or doing. Observe over a significant period (for example, 30 minutes) and on more than one occasion. Look at the results and see how far they match your expectation and experience. Could you have predicted the most frequent contributor and the least frequent?

If you take your tally evidence and relate it to relative group positions, you may arrive at something like this.

In a group such as a teaching group, there may be something to be learned from the relationship between positioning in relation to the teacher and group interaction. Some positions may in fact be inherently stronger than others and may as a result be occupied by those who have the greatest influence. Similarly, those who are not so keen to interact may occupy weak positions. The arrangement of a group around a single desk may or may not tell us much about their interaction but it does offer likely variables.

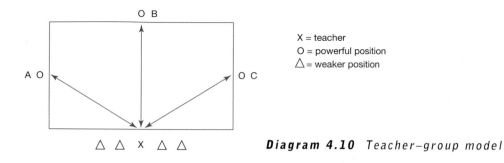

Diagram 4.10 Teacher–group model

In these kinds of 'directive' groups, member positioning is rarely uninformative. Members might on occasion find weak positions by default (by arriving late for example) but across a significant period of 'storming', weaker positions will usually go to the uncommitted or communicatively reluctant. In the example above, it would be unsurprising that in an interaction tally A, B and C will enjoy a significant share. This is a statement of power not structure. To understand what goes on beyond these simple axes we need a more sophisticated tool, a measurement of the way individuals react to and with others.

Moreno's work on sociometrics, literally the measurement of social relationships, offers a handy next step. If we are trying to discover how a group is patterned, structured or aligned, Moreno would argue that we must look at more than the behavioural evidence of their frequency of interaction and their physical interaction. We need to consider the alignments they are playing out with other people in the group (in other words who in the group likes/respects/admires who else). Sociometrics asks how socially inclined we are towards others, how keen we are to interact with them. For example, members of a small group might be asked to express their preference for working with any two other group members. To be effective the question would stress the context, whether it be work or social. Their decisions would then be plotted in this way:

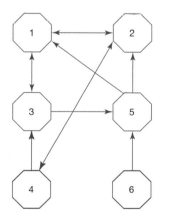

Diagram 4.11 Network of group interactions I

This simple mechanism offers a significant confirmation or challenge to practical observation. To a limited extent it goes beneath the surface to explore the underlying relationships within any group. What the diagram above reveals is a significant network of interactions which can be quickly 'read'. There are clear bonds between members 1 and 3, 1 and 2, 2 and 4, and a basic solidity about most of the group. Members 1 through 5 conform to what Moreno called a 'cluster', a series of significantly interacting individuals, who clearly constitute a subgroup. On the other hand, member 6 shows signs of being an 'isolate', an individual not significantly bonded with the rest of the group. The suspicion that member 6 is an isolate could be followed up through observation or, with sensitivity, by couching a negative question: 'Which group member would you be least likely to work with?' It is always interesting to relate these social 'maps' to the physical ways in which groups behave. The individuals plotted above sat in this configuration.

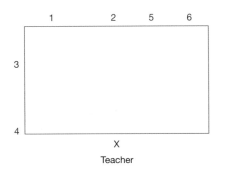

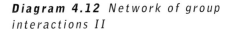

Diagram 4.12 *Network of group interactions II*

The focus of this small group is easy to see and it would not be difficult to predict the results of an analysis of the frequency of interaction. One of the crudest group norms relates to members' 'territory' within the group 'lands', whether it be a seat in a classroom or a place in the car park. In most established groups, changing this pattern is likely to prompt a significant response. This is partly to do with habit and an innate conservatism (wanting things to stay the same) but Moreno would argue that it is also to do with the fact that changing your position may in effect be changing your whole social outlook. If in any of the group situations you are habitually in you have a set place to stand or sit, try a change of position. You will be surprised how radically different the group looks from your new perspective. What you are in fact doing is disrupting patterns of social behaviour, those norms that time and experience have generated and reinforced.

ACTIVITY . . .

Conduct a sociometric survey on a group you know, confidentially asking a simple question about preferences for small group or paired work. Predict the shape of this group and then anonymously plot your results. Ask members of the group to comment on your sociometric plan.

The task might read something like:

'You have been invited to select from this group the *three* other people with whom you would choose to work. Please rank these below.'

1 . . . .

2 . . . .

3 . . . .

The shape of groups tells us a lot about them, and sociometry is one of the ways in which we might get a picture of how groups are intrinsically organised. In this respect all groups are subtly different. One aspect of any group's sociometric layout which is worth considering is the extent to which the revealed structure is centred around either an internal or external influence. To put it another way: does the group have leaders? Teaching groups, for example, are good examples of centralised groups while friendship groups are more often decentralised.

The importance of group structure is emphasised by Douglas's model of group processes which usefully pulls together many of the ideas contained in this section. Douglas (1979) identifies four kinds of processes, or categories, which also mark four stages in group development.

Category	1 Basic	Interaction
	2 Structural	Group development
		Social structure
		Subgroup formation
	3 Locomotive	Decision-making
		Purpose and goal formation
	4 Motor	Formation of norms, standards, values
		Development of cohesion
		Development of group influence
		Development of 'climate' (this refers to a group's specific 'atmosphere' or 'character')

Having arrived at structure and subgroup formation and predicted the progress from here, we will leave the final section to deal with 'locomotive' and 'motor' processes.

▼ 8 GROUP COMMUNICATION: HOW GROUPS WORK AND WHEN THEY DON'T – LEADERSHIP AND LETHARGY

In this last section we will bring our consideration of group communication and of personal communication to a close by looking at how groups work, what motivates them to work, and what happens when they don't work.

■ We will look at the notion of conformity within groups, and the positive and negative outcomes this may lead to.
■ We will examine ideas about leadership.

This section will look at fully operational groups as they move into action and how they are directed. As groups develop, so the benefits and obligations of individual members develop, too. We enjoy being part of the group but also feel responsible to it. Hartley has expressed this two-sided experience in terms of 'liberation' and 'conformity', suggesting that membership of functioning groups both sets you free and in a strange way confines you:

> On the one hand a group can develop norms which restrict its members' behaviour and communication; on the other hand a group can provide support and under-standing for its members and allow them to express themselves in ways that they otherwise would not have done.
>
> (Hartley 1997)

We can all think of groups that especially restrict or support us, but most do both to different degrees at different times. Moreover, we are ourselves differently committed to different groups, and so our 'conformity' is itself subject to variation.

KEY TERM

CONFORMITY This might usefully be defined as the tendency of individuals to adhere to or follow the conventions or norms of a particular group or situation. It refers to the way we fit in with the expectations of a particular group or situation.

Conformity in fact operates at a number of levels or depths. In some groups our 'fitting in' is only skin deep; it is put on to keep face or to avoid conflict. This level of conformity is described as 'compliance'; there may be many occasions with our families where we conform at this level because it's easier.

Conformity at a more significant level might see the recognition that certain situations or groups provoke certain kinds of response. In other words, we begin to associate certain kinds of attitudes and behaviour with certain situations. This is 'identification'; the willingness to use the group concerned as a cue for certain types of behaviour, attitude and communication. This is still some way from a sincere performance but it does offer a coherent set of responses tied to a particular context. In more significant cases a third, and potentially disturbing and/or enriching, stage is reached whereby the group's norms sincerely become those of the individual members. The goal of all advertisers, propagandists and cults is 'internalisation', the stage at which the values, attitudes and beliefs of others become part of the self.

ACTIVITY . . .

Try to identify situations where you have 'conformed' at the three levels suggested:

- compliance
- identification
- internalisation.

What are the benefits and problems of conformity at each of these stages?

Conformity as an idea is a sort of inverse measurement of group influence on individuals; the lower the level, the less 'pull' the group has. In all cases it has significant positive and negative elements.

Allen (1965) suggests that conformity is a complex idea which is subject to a series of pressures and that these, both individually and collectively, dictate the level of conformity. Allen's factors are:

- level of commitment to group
- level of attractiveness of the group
- status of the group
- degree of interdependence within the group
- composition of the group
- size and unanimity of the group
- the extent to which group norms are extreme
- whether the group is task-competent
- level of task confidence
- difficulty and importance of task.

Much of Allen's work focuses on the coherence and quality of the group to whose norms the individual is conforming. It is tempting simply to break down groups into 'good' and 'bad' ones or, more academically, into functional and dysfunctional ones. Kell and Costs (1980) have refined this in their identifications of group maturity. The following is a checklist against which you can measure your own groups. A mature group:

- offers the facility for individual growth
- offers an atmosphere of trust
- offers equality of membership
- adapts to points of disagreement
- encourages participation
- encourages sacrifice for group benefit
- has a good time.

What Kell and Costs are essentially suggesting is that a mature group functions like a rich soil; it allows individual members to grow. Immature groups thus function like the proverbial 'stony ground', offering little in terms of support and harming rather than helping individual members.

We began this section by addressing the balance between what groups allow and what they restrict. Restriction in the extreme case can have harmful implications whereby a group becomes an unhealthy context for individual work. Marilyn Brewer and Norman Miller begin their book *Intergroup Relations* (1996) with this description of where unhealthy, immature groups can lead ultimately:

> On November 18 1978, more than 900 men, women and children committed suicide at Jonestown in Guyana. Told that their group was under siege, members of the Reverend Jim Jones's People's Temple lined up to receive glasses of red Kool Aid laced with cyanide. All drank the liquid as they were told, and almost all died within 30 minutes.

This is a shocking description of a real-life group. It is shocking, too, that, on the limited evidence offered, the Jim Jones's People's Temple seems to demonstrate some signs of group maturity – the atmosphere of trust, the encouragement of participation, the sacrifices for the group's benefit. However, it is difficult to see how mass suicide offers genuine evidence of a facility for individual growth.

The extract gives much clearer evidence for what Irving Janis in 1972 labelled 'GroupThink', a sort of psychological disease associated with some groups. GroupThink was identified by Janis as the psychological degenerative condition which afflicts group members, undermining their facility for individual response.

KEY TERM

GROUPTHINK This is described by Janis (1972) as 'a deterioration of mental efficiency, reality testing and moral judgement which results from in-group pressure'.

These three areas of deterioration – mental efficiency, reality testing and moral judgement – all seem particularly pertinent to the Jim Jones tragedy. Janis published a list of symptoms of GroupThink which might function as an early-warning list:

- illusion of invulnerability (thinking you can't be harmed)
- collective rationalisation (explaining things away as a group)
- belief in inherent morality of group (irrespective of others)
- stereotypes of out-groups
- direct pressure on dissenters (taking action against those who disagree)
- self-censorship (removing the bits they don't like)
- illusion of unanimity (imagining the whole group thinks the same)
- self-appointed mind-guard (someone to keep reality out).

Much of what GroupThink consists of amounts to what Zimbardo (1988) has called 'de-individuation', the undermining of individuality for the good of the group. Most of us will have experienced this first hand or observed it in our political leaders or celebrities. The behaviour of the members of successful pop groups read like a casebook on GroupThink – the illusion of invulnerability, the direct pressure on dissenters, the illusion of unanimity. Perhaps in the context of international super stardom, mental efficiency, moral judgement and especially reality testing are always going to take a battering.

More disturbing examples are found in the context of criminality, where groups can provide a sometimes murderous reinforcement of deviant behaviour. Certain criminal acts would appear to result from the way in which groups generate a 'collective rationalisation' which finds reasons for the unreasonable.

GroupThink, as a dysfunction of group, is a complex combination of factors – membership, context, task. Stanton (1996) has defined group effectiveness in terms of two sets of variables – those that cannot be controlled and those that can. In the 'uncontrollable' set he lists three sets – group variables, environmental variables and task variables (all of which might be seen to contribute also to the ineffectiveness which GroupThink essentially is).

These variables in fact correspond to the questions 'Who?', 'Where?' and 'What?'. By implication Stanton is saying that the effectiveness of your Communication Studies group is dependent on:

- who's in it
- where it is – physically and structurally
- what it's doing.

These are uncontrollable in the sense that they are largely given.

ACTIVITY ...

If these factors are 'uncontrollable', what sort of elements can we influence in groups? Try to construct a list of controllable variables.

What is always available as an influence is member activity and motivation. The size and shape of a group might be largely set whereas the behaviour is open to amendment. Motivation may vary from task to task and members may be more or less able to participate. Often this motivating role becomes a function of the group or the motivator becomes something like a group leader. Stanton in fact lists 'leadership style' as his first controllable variable, underlining its importance. The problem is that across a range of different groups leadership does not appear to be a consistent feature. It is relatively easy to define in a formal context like a work or educational situation but rather more difficult in personal and social contexts.

What differences are there between the 'leadership' of these kinds of group?

■ Family.
■ Friendship.
■ Work.

Think of groups to which you belong. Who are the leaders?

Leadership is something that is communicated through the form and style of messages. It works on individuals and motivates them to the achievement of certain goals. How it operates and what forms it takes has been addressed by Myers and Myers (1992), who suggested four 'approaches' to the understanding of leadership.

KEY TERM

LEADERSHIP Tedeschi and Lindskold (1976) have defined leadership with reference to three factors – social influence, behaviour and authority. They suggest that leadership, when we experience it, consists of an impact on the way people interact, a set of actions and a sense of power. Tannenbaum has more formally defined leadership as 'interpersonal influence exercised in a situation and directed through the communication process toward the attainment of a specialised goal or goals'.

The first approach identified by Myers and Myers is the 'trait' approach. This great person theory approaches leadership through personality. Leaders are those with special character 'traits' or excess of quality. Leaders are born, not made.

This approach is supported by Stogdill (1981), who proposed a substantial list of those qualities that leaders might possess in greater abundance than the rest of us. It might be useful to think how far you can find leaders to match each of these categories or how far your own teachers excel or excelled in any of these:

- intelligence
- scholarship
- dependability
- activity
- social status
- initiative
- persistence
- self-confidence
- insight
- popularity
- adaptability
- verbal facility.

Stodgill proposes that leaders are those who are more intelligent, more dependable, more persistent and so on.

The second approach identified by Myers and Myers (1992) is the 'situational' approach. Contexts make leaders. Leadership is simply a particular response to a particular situation.

It might be argued that each situation has its own character. This character arises out of the sometimes opposed factors of the need for quality and the need for acceptance or content. Leadership styles are responses to this relationship between quality and acceptance. A range of leadership styles could be mapped as follows.

- If quality is more important than acceptance: preferred decision style = COMMAND (leadership style is 'autocratic').
- If acceptance is more important than quality: preferred decision style = CONSENSUS (leadership style is 'collective').
- If quality and acceptance are both important: preferred decision style – CONSULTATION (leadership style is 'democratic').
- If neither quality nor acceptance is important: preferred decision style = CONVENIENCE (leadership style is *laissez-faire*).

KEY TERM

LEADERSHIP STYLES   Four styles are often identified.

- **Autocratic (authoritarian)**: leadership by command; the leader is sole source of decisions.
- **Democratic**: leadership by consultation; decisions are made by group or its elected representatives.
- *Laissez-faire*: leadership by instinct; decisions are made by whoever can make them.
- **Collective**: leadership by consensus; decisions are made by whole group together.

Which leadership or decision-making style might be appropriate in the following situations?

- *Millionaire.*
- Electing a member of parliament.
- Electing a student council representative.
- Selecting a venue for a special celebration.
- Choosing where to go next Friday night.
- Choosing your A Level subjects.
- Appointing the captain of a sports team.
- Awarding a promotion to a member of staff.
- Choosing a friend to share a 'Holiday of a Lifetime' prize.
- Choosing an audience for an oral presentation.

This is a flexible enough approach to allow a range of answers, though research often attempts to discover which works best. When Lewin, Lippett and White (1939) set children to make soap models under various kinds of supervision, they found that the 'autocratic' approach produced most models while the 'democratic' created best group morale; *laissez-faire* simply let things go, and little was achieved. In a modern welfare state the 'collective' of some models is replaced by 'bureaucratic'; leadership by faceless administration and written justification.

The third approach identified by Myers and Myers (1992) is the 'functional' approach. Leadership is a collection of jobs a group needs doing. These jobs might be done collectively. Myers and Myers identify three sorts of job:

- **procedural**: running the group
- **substantive**: giving input
- **maintenance**: keeping the group going.

There is no reason why different members of the group might not offer these very different kinds of function. The key to successful leadership might in fact be appropriate skills rather than talented individuals – for example, openness, information and persuasion.

The fourth approach identified by Myers and Myers is the 'contingency' approach. Leadership is a mixture of the other approaches. Argyle (1983) offers a good example of contingency in his checklist of the sources of leadership:

- Personality
- Composition of group
- Context
- Group structure
- Character of task
- Ability to motivate.

Leadership is a factor of all groups from the group of two to the largest organisations. It may be explicit or implicit, formal or informal. It affects us all either as leader or as led; it shapes the character of our experience of much communication. We see it in action in our political leaders, our work and social environments, even in our family situations. What kind of leaders we make depends largely on the groups we are in and the attitudes we have.

A study of political leaders by the American Psychological Association, presented to their 2000 conference, suggested that leaders fall crudely into eight types. These might also function as an alternative list of leadership styles. They were derived from a large-scale critical analysis of the first 41 American presidents but might easily be applied to leaders in a range of situations from managers to opinion leaders.

Eight types of leader (Rubenzer 2000):

- Dominators
- Introverts
- Good guys
- Innocents
- Actors
- Philosophers
- Maintainers
- Extroverts.

ACTIVITY . . .

Identify leaders, either public or personal, who might fit each of these types.

FURTHER WORK . . .

1   Verbal/non-verbal communication:
    a   Non-verbal communicative behaviour appears to be governed by unwritten 'rules' which regulate such behaviour in a particular culture. List ten such unwritten rules which appear to regulate public behaviour in Britain today.
    b   How might the regulation of social encounters be influenced by body movement and the use of body adornment?
    c   Conventions such as punctuation, spelling and grammar serve to regulate written communication. To what extent are conventions used to regulate face-to-face oral communication?
    d   Outline the uses and limitations of language as a means of communication.

continued

e   Assess the importance of non-verbal communication in social interaction.

f   'Women are better communicators than men.' Discuss.

g   'Language most shows a man. Speak that I may see thee.' How far is this true?

h   To what extent can you rely upon non-verbal communication alone?

i   'Actions speak louder than words.' Discuss.

j   'The limits of my language are the limits of my world.' Discuss.

k   Evaluate the ways in which purpose, role and context affect body language.

l   How do people use verbal and non-verbal communication to regulate their interpersonal exchanges?

m   Language is man-made. Discuss.

2   Intrapersonal communication:

a   Analyse the importance of self-image and self-esteem in interpersonal communication.

b   How useful and accurate is Maslow's 'Hierarchy of Needs' in analysing the motivation of communicative behaviour?

c   Evaluate the factors that affect the playing of roles.

d   How does intrapersonal communication influence interpersonal communication?

e   To what extent does our own self-image influence the way we communicate with other people?

3   Group communication:

a   Choose any contrasting groups or organisations with which you are familiar. How do they use communication to (i) achieve goals, (ii) reinforce norms, and (iii) display identity?

b   How important is leadership to the successful functioning of a group? Answer with reference to two groups of which you are a member.

c   To what extent is a knowledge of role useful in understanding group communication?

d   Analyse the ways in which groups communicate either externally and internally.

e   Evaluate the reasons people join groups.

f   How might a knowledge of group dynamics help someone to lead a meeting?

All of the above questions are taken from past papers of the pioneering AEB (now AQA) Communication Studies A Level (1976–2001).

FURTHER READING

Burton, G. and Dimbleby, R. (1995) *Between Ourselves*, London: Edward Arnold.

Hartley, P. (1997) *Group Communication*, London: Routledge.

Hartley, P. (1999) *Interpersonal Communication*, 2nd edn, London: Routledge.

FURTHER VIEWING

Morris, D. (1994) *The Human Animal*, London: BBC Worldwide.

PART 5: USING YOUR COMMUNICATION SKILLS TO PASS EXAMINATIONS

In this part we will look at how your communication skills can be used to help you prepare for and to sit examinations.

- We will explore approaches to revision.
- We will look at how you can be more personally effective when preparing for, and sitting, examinations.
- We will offer you useful techniques to assist you when taking examinations.

The purpose of this part is to offer both general and specific advice on how to improve your chances of gaining high marks in the examinations you may sit in Communication Studies (and elsewhere). Its rather clumsy title is a deliberate attempt to develop this process from the start. Communication Studies is a discipline which encourages effective communication and a personal critical response to all manner of contexts and texts. Examinations, and particularly examination advice, cannot be immune to the need to be both rigorously criticised and effectively communicated.

The skills we need in examinations will of course include reading and writing, speaking and listening, drafting and dealing with questions. It is equally important to practise critical skills to deal with the examination as yet another text, and to plan in both a general and specific sense. There will also be a need for common sense. This is not a skill but all too sadly and too often it isn't demonstrated in the examination room.

It is easily said but examinations should not be feared. It is likely that you will have worked hard all year on your Communication Studies course. In truth it would be very frustrating if the knowledge you acquired there was never tested or called upon. Exams are merely the rather artificial opportunity you get to demonstrate what you know and to receive some, hopefully much, credit for it. They are a time- and money-saving alternative to having a visiting examiner come to your house to quiz you in depth on your knowledge of the subject. Positively, examinations usually ask you about what you know rather than what you don't know: after all, to 'examine' means 'to look at in detail', not 'to catch out'.

EXAMINATIONS

There are lots of places to go for advice on examination preparation and technique: study skills guides, websites, your teachers/fellow students, Radio One's annual series of radio and television revision programmes. What common sense tells you is that there can be no single definitive answer any more than there can be a single effective general model of communication. At the centre of the examination process is the examinee, just as at the centre of the revision process is the reviser – in other words, you! What helps is whatever helps you to be relaxed, to be confident, to be clear-headed and clear-sighted. If, for you, this means eating garlic harvested at a full moon with a platinum sickle, then so be it!

What follows is a debate between received wisdom and an individual approach; not a contest, but a conversation. It partly rehearses the advice which everybody knows to give to prospective students; it is largely the advice which you would give to yourself if you were writing this part of this book. It also challenges that advice to suggest that there are a large number of potential 'negotiated' readings, or even 'oppositional' readings, of this advice. This is partly meant to function as a viable alternative to the all-too-common position of knowing what you should do both to revise and to prepare for your examinations and equally knowing that you will never actually do this. Too many students buy into the self-fulfilling 'prophecy' which begins with despair, moves to an unrealistically extensive revision plan, and ends with no revision (and despair).

Some of the advice that follows is deliberately provocative because its very purpose is to make you all as individual learners think about how you learn best and how you might best prepare for examinations which judge your quality as learners. Nothing here is advocated, save the need for individual students to make rational and personal decisions about their own revision and preparation. All too often the most important lesson of education is that 'you shouldn't let other people get your kicks for you'.

Communication Studies is not a subject that lends itself to 'right answers'. You are mostly asked for analysis and evaluation in contexts where the choice of evidence and treatment is yours. Much of what has been covered in this textbook remains a matter for debate, and it is your job to join these debates rather than attempt to bring them to a satisfactory conclusion. What is often being marked is your ability to fashion a convincing argument and support it with relevant evidence: it is the quality of your argument not the character of your argument that is important here.

Advice on examination practice, or rather examinations in practice, falls into three phases.

1   **Revision**: which looks at the various ways in which the knowledge gained from a course of study can be recalled, marshalled and reorganised so as to be useful in the examination.
2   **Preparation**: which covers the period from the arrival in the examination room to the first time your pen is used.
3   **Technique**: which deals with how different forms of question might be approached – from design to realisation.

Let's look at these three phases in more detail.

REVISION

Literally 'the act of seeing again', revision is a taboo word for many students, describing a process they only vaguely understand and one that, even when done thoroughly, offers questionable results. Revision has a dubious reputation; stereotypically it involves sitting still for long periods of time and suffering. There is a profound moral dimension to this. In fact it is treated by society at large and by the educational community specifically as a kind of moral performance indicator. Good students do revision in the same way that they don't do sex or drugs. Bad students on the other hand spend their time doing the last two and thus have no time for the former. For, above all things, revision takes time.

Every institution, whether it be school, college or self-help guide, has its own timescale: 'start at Easter', 'at least three months' or 'Christmas is a good time to start'. Courses are cut short, curtailed to allow for the 'revision period', the part of the course where the dynamic that is learning is brought to a standstill. At some point the revision timetable must be drawn up – provided by your school or college, or constructed with a sharp pencil and 30cm ruler. This is a statement of intent, an attempt formally to engage in a self-fulfilling prophecy.

A good example is found in our sister volume AS *Media Studies: The Essential Introduction* (Rayner *et al.* 2004).

Drawing up a revision plan

A revision plan is the essential first step towards preparing yourself for your Media Studies exam. You may find the following steps a useful way to guide you in drawing up such a plan.

1 Make sure you know what you need to revise. Either check with the specification or syllabus yourself, or ask your teacher what you need to do. In some cases you may find that there is a choice of topic areas and you may have to decide how many of these you are going to prepare for the exam.

2 Make a list of the topics you have decided you need to cover. Check where you can best find the information you need on these topics. Start with your own notes and then look at how textbooks, such as this one, may be able to help you.

3 Draw up a revision timetable devoting a suitable amount of time to each topic. Be realistic about how many hours you can devote to this. There will almost certainly be other subjects making demands on your time, as well as all of those diversions you will have to succumb to.

4 Put together a list of up-to-date examples that you can draw upon to illustrate your answers. If you have made good notes throughout your course, you should have a good range of texts such as films, television and radio programmes, newspaper and magazine articles you can call upon. It is also worth thinking in advance about how you may be able to use these in the exam. Remember, too, to keep an eye on such sources as the *Media Guardian* for up-to-date information on key media issues and debates.

5 Remember that revision you do at the very last minute may be of little use. Revising is like preparing yourself for a sporting event. A sustained programme of preparation will always be more effective than a last-minute panic.

This is sensible advice but it is not the only approach to revision. One problem with revising in this semi-formal way is that you run the risk of putting unwanted pressure on knowledge that has been organically and contextually acquired. You also simply put pressure on yourself over a significant period of time and stress the skills of recalling information instead of the skills of analysis and evaluation.

An alternative approach is to see revision as both a more general and more focused activity. First, this would see revision as a course-long activity and would see the regular activity pattern of this book as a reasonable representation of most teaching within the area. In applying knowledge in practical and semi-practical situations, we are in fact revising our understanding of the key concepts of topics and particularly of our singular central topic, communication itself. This process may regularly lead to topic summary sheets on which you record the key ideas of some topic, but these are merely the regular reminders of how the course is to be assessed.

ACTIVITY . . .

Do you know how the course you are currently doing is assessed?

■ How many examinations?
■ How long are they?
■ What is the mark breakdown across papers/units?
■ What does the mark scheme for each paper reward?

Too often the course is seen as something to remember when in fact it is something to experience. The principle of 'study leave' is well established in this country but not well founded on any significant evidence. Letting students leave school or college to revise reinforces the separation between the course and the examination and restresses the importance of memory over analysis. Examinations need not be viewed like this. They are a small but significant part of the course and one of the 'audiences' that any course must have. Most often the courses we do are defined by the qualifications we seek, in other words by the examinations we sit.

This fact can be approached sincerely or cynically. Partly we must dismiss the need for specific revision altogether, for if we have engaged with intrapersonal communication what question can we fear? More practically we might think early about the amount of knowledge necessary to 'fill' an answer planned and written within as little as 30 minutes. We may in fact 'knock up' our own revision plan which will serve as a gloss to the previous one or perhaps define a continuum within which we all can work.

A substantial engagement with the course, its form and its content, is the essential first step towards preparing yourself for your Communication Studies examination. Revision is all very well but 'vision' is actually much more important. Make sure you 'see' it clearly first time around so you won't struggle to recall it. The following steps may form a useful guide.

AN ALTERNATIVE REVISION PLAN

1   Make sure you know how you are to be assessed. Get hold of past questions and mark schemes. Check the range of topics to be assessed and the number of questions to be attempted. Calculate the minimum number of topics to be prepared for the examination and the frequency with which they occur. Give yourself an amount of security according to your temperament (if you are by temperament cautious, revise extra topics).

(NB: The new specifications at AS and A Level are by their design easier to predict because they specify not only what you must know but also that this knowledge must be tested.)

2   Consider each topic you cover in terms of (a) its most important content and (b) the amount of information you could reasonably use, if known, in between 30 and 45 minutes. Compile the essential information, together with quotations and/or notes, on no more than one side of A4 paper for each topic. This is an indication of the amount of knowledge you can need or use in an examination. Given that no examination is longer than two hours, and that three questions is the maximum request, revision cannot consist of more than six sheets of paper or six sides of A4 paper.

(Psychologically and symbolically the information and content knowledge that you need for any formal examination should be able to be comfortably located on your table/desk. You should end up sitting with no more than six separated and organised A4 sides, perhaps fewer. In this way 'what is to be known' is put in its place and you are in a position to think about what you are being asked and how your response will be structured.)

3   If you have clarified the significant content for each topic and reduced it to a single side of A4, the fixing of content detail is in fact best done close to the examination. If there are things you feel you need to remember, two days is a much more sensible timescale than two months. Try as far as you can to think about one examination at a time and to concentrate your knowledge-fixing on the two days before the examination. This may seem like a heresy but remember we are not here talking about things you don't know but rather about things you do. Obviously other examinations in other subjects will interfere, but ideally you should deal with one examination at a time and not begin to revise the second paper until the first is over.

What this approach advocates is that knowledge of assessment – of what examinations are and what they do – is as important as knowledge of subject. Study at Advanced Level must involve more than the regurgitation of knowledge, and the more that is crammed in, the more likely it is to emerge in an unprocessed fashion. In Communication Studies in particular there is an established equality between theory as such and the evidence of communication in practice. The latter can be rehearsed across the course but there must ideally be room for 'live' performance, the act of coming to an examination question in an examination room and drawing freshly upon your experience as a communicator. This is the first lure of the subject: we are all experienced and mainly skilful communicators. This subject asks us to draw on that experience and skill. The more that we try to learn this 'experience', the less like experience it becomes.

Knowledge of assessment begins with the classification of your exams which you attempted earlier. Different kinds of examination require different kinds of preparation as well as different kinds of skills. However, there are simple statements to be made which cover general features of the examination experience.

PREPARATION

However much good advice you're given and take, the problems of the examination room come down to a simple problem: you need to be calm, relaxed and clear-headed – and you're not! However cool you are in the face of a formal examination, by the time you've stood around for 10 minutes outside the exam room with 25 to 50 fellow students who are bombarding you with trivial questions about the coming examination, you are likely to be a little wound up. The way you behave in the first 5 minutes of the examination is therefore vital.

Unfortunately it is not uncommon to find candidates filling this vital opening 5 minutes with frantic writing. No sooner has the invigilator's 'The time is 9.30, you may now begin' died in the air than the first task response is finding an introduction. This is simply an impossibility if you are interested in maximising your achievement. Clearly, the first 5 minutes are for reading, for getting to know the paper, and for discovering across a couple of readings at least the opportunities that the paper offers. Better not to open the paper at all for the first 5 minutes than attempt an immediate answer to the first question.

You are partly allowing yourself time to acclimatise to the examination environment, making yourself familiar with the overall picture before the real work begins. This may give you ideas, albeit crude ones, about which questions are most demanding and about which questions should be tackled first. Often in this initial assessment questions are clarified and what appeared easy and attractive at first sight now seems problematic and confusing. This is not the only safeguard against poor question selection but it is the first of a number of filters.

You are also moving into 'examination time', the medium of examinations. Being asked to perform to time is the essence of the examination experience and thus nothing is more important than keeping to time. Do not be fooled by the theory that two good answers are better than three mediocre ones; siphoning time from one question to another rarely allows a significantly greater performance. Unfinished papers simply and literally wipe marks and thus grades off a candidate's achievement. Your performance in the questions you attempt can never compensate for the question you have missed. In fact the latter dilutes the former. Hear this loud and clear: you must attempt the number of questions you're asked to. This is the ugly reality of examinations: if you attempt a three-question AS paper but in fact only manage two questions, the level of performance required in these two answers, just to reach a basic pass mark of, say, 40 per cent, is in fact 60 per cent (this may be the difference between a B grade and an E grade).

The great myth of examination time is the suggestion that, to arrive at your time allocation for each question, you divide the number of questions to answer into the time allowed. This in fact overlooks all the other advice that we are giving about the psychology of doing examinations. What you are asked to do is write *in* 3 hours (or two examinations of 1½ hours) not write *for* 3 hours. In the new 1½ hour AS examination you must allow at least 10 to 15 minutes for examination management time – reading the paper in a considered way; moving from one topic area to the next; and checking that all words have been successfully transferred from your head via your pen to the page (and that most of them are spelled correctly). This leaves 25 minutes to plan and execute your answer, not 30. This seems a minor point but if you don't time realistically and 10 minutes are spent reading followed by lots of 30 minutes, then the final question may be squeezed down to next to nothing.

SCORING AND EXPLODING: PAPER VANDALISM APPROVED

The other thing you must do, and this can start pretty much with the first reading, is to make the examination paper your own. You do this in a primitive way by defacing it, leaving your own marks on it. These marks are the evidence that you have ruthlessly explored the questions' potential and have identified any potential problems with them. If you do not do this, you have not justified your entry. If your paper can be handed back and reused, or even effectively photocopied, you really haven't made the examination your own – it still belongs to the examiner and the examining body.

The longer you stay in the examination system the more likely you are to have a tragic examination story – about the friend of yours who read 'First World War' when it said 'Second World War' or answered eight questions when the instructions said 'choose ONE'. These stories are told up and down the country in the lead-up to examinations, and much fun is had at the expense of these buffoons who could not be us. Yet the catalogue is added to every year without fail. Candidates answer on books they haven't read, attempt six hours' work in three hours or even sit the wrong examination. If defacing the paper does nothing else, it reduces this risk. Educationists and psychologists frequently assert that the most effective learning is active – and not passive – learning. Taking your pen to the examination paper is a sound extension of this principle. You claim and maintain your status as an active examination candidate; you will not settle for being a passive examination candidate for whom examinations are something that happens to them.

Underachievement in public examinations is in fact rarely the result of a hideous lack of ability, skill or knowledge but more often a result of a hideous lack of relevance. Most examiners report that most papers they mark are hampered by the fact that the candidate, even if the paper is complete, has not responded to questions in their entirety and thus has made it impossible for the paper to access the upper range of marks available. To get full marks is unlikely, but to put yourself in the game and get a mark out of the full allocation must be a primary goal. In some scripts (this is examiner-speak for a candidate's examination answer book) the answers are so negligent of the questions that the final mark is low because only a third or even less of the question's scope has been addressed. Let's say this again: physically marking the paper makes this broader response to specific questions significantly more likely.

Looking for key words is part of your starting point, but even so it is vital to be aware that there are two sets of key words:

■ words that instruct, direct or govern (e.g. 'analyse', 'describe', 'state', 'evaluate', 'consider', 'compare')
■ subject-specific words (e.g. 'self-concept', 'feedback', 'semiotic').

If you can discover what it is you have to do and what is the precise focus of subject content of your examination, you are well on the way to success. Be careful you don't make the identification of key words your only goal; the next stage is necessary, too. Successfully identifying the key words of a question should always clarify the question but it may lead you to conclude that this is a question you should avoid.

Once the key words have been 'scored' they then should be 'exploded' into the margins of your question paper for note-form explanation. If the question addresses 'feedback', it is important that you should be able to write in your own words what 'feedback' is. Similarly, if the question asks you to consider the effectiveness of a text for its intended audience of 'eight-year-olds', it is important that you are able to understand not only that 'eight-year-olds' is an important part of the question but also what that phrase might mean. In this case your exploded notes might include words and phrases like 'restricted code', 'highly visual', 'energetic'.

ACTIVITY . . .

Consider (a) the key words and (b) their implications in the following sample examination questions (NB do *not* answer the questions themselves).

1   Explain how and why individuals often reject evidence that appears to contradict their self-image.
2   Using material from EITHER or BOTH of the documents, prepare a revision sheet for your fellow A Level students on 'what signs are and what form they take'. The revision sheet should contain no more than 250 words of text. (*You will be rewarded for your organisation of the revision sheet, for your clarification of key semiotic ideas and for your choice of accurate and appropriate examples.*)

Once you've dealt with the paper in this way, you're ready to offer your responses. Here the advice we offer must take account of the different kinds of examination that Communication Studies favours.

UNSEEN PAPERS

Most examining bodies set a paper that requires you to write about a communication text that you will see for the first time in the examination itself. This is often called the unseen paper. Typically the examination will consist of a print-based text, such as a magazine article, which you will be asked to consider in the examination room. Usually you are asked to respond to the text in around 1½ to 2 hours. The type of text – video, sound, print – may vary, as will the precise instructions telling you what to do. The principles for approaching this type of exercise, however, remain very similar. In fact it is likely you will have had a go at some practice papers in class to help you get the hang of it. Moreover this examination task is also probably very close to the sorts of activities you'll have experienced in Communication Studies classes, when your teacher has brought in a communication text and has asked everyone to discuss and analyse it.

A good way of practising for the unseen paper is to look at texts you have chosen yourself. Magazine covers, advertisements, extracts from television programmes, cinema trailers and CD covers are all good examples. Then try to get down some notes as quickly as you can on what specific aspects of the text you would want to point out if you were writing an analysis. In this way you will help prepare yourself mentally for the task of unseen analysis in the examination itself.

The current trend in unseen papers is to provide fairly detailed information advising you what you should look for in your commentary on the text. This guidance provides a useful checklist of points to cover. It is important to bear in mind that it may not be a good idea to work mechanically through the list trying to get something down under each heading. Each text that you will be asked to consider is unique. As such it needs an individual response. Your potential to identify the unique qualities of the text and base your commentary on these is the real test of your performance in such a paper. The checklist is, however, a useful mechanism for ensuring that you have not ignored a key element of the analysis which is important.

Organising your response is an important aspect of this question. A brilliantly perceptive textual analysis is of little use if it is confused and difficult to follow. The guidance or checklist may come in useful here as a way of suggesting to you headings under which to organise your response. However you decide to organise what you have to say, make sure that it is both logical and user-friendly for the examiner. The easier it is for someone to digest what you have to say, the more likely you are to be rewarded for it.

It is important that you also spend some time thinking before you start to write your response. This is true for all examinations, but it is especially important for an unseen paper. This is probably the first time you will have seen the text you are to deal with. You need, therefore, to spend time getting familiar with it and preparing yourself to develop your idea on the text. If the examination rubric permits, by all means start scribbling down some notes to help remind you of the important points; but, whatever you do, do not try to start writing your analysis straightaway. Give yourself time to see the text as a whole before you look at the individual parts.

RUBRIC These are the instructions that appear on the cover of the examination paper and at the head of each section of the examination paper. Typical rubrics are: 'Answer two questions' or 'Answer one question from each section'.

Analysing texts is a test of your skill in applying key Communication Studies concepts. It follows that if you can use the technical terminology of the discipline with accuracy and authority you will produce a convincing analysis. Understanding key terms such as connotation, anchorage, paradigm or ideology is important. Using them appropriately to describe how the text functions is even more important.

The mistake that many students make in this sort of paper is that they focus too much on simply describing the text itself. You can safely assume that the examiner has already seen the text. Your job is to analyse. This means you should be able to explain how the text works by exposing some of the underlying thinking that has gone into its construction. It is the complexities of the text that you should attempt to reveal; simply describing what is in front of you goes little way to achieving this.

ESSAY PAPERS

The other type of paper you are most likely to encounter is the essay paper. In this you are expected to write a number of essays in a given period of time. It is always a good idea to make yourself familiar with the type of paper you are sitting in advance of the examination. It is common for a paper to be split into sections, each reflecting an area of the specification you have studied. For example, there may be a section on verbal and non-verbal communication, another on intrapersonal communication and a third on group communication. If you are sitting such a paper, two things are important. One is to make sure just what questions you are supposed to attempt. Look out for an instruction on the paper telling you what to do. For example, it may say: 'Attempt one question from any two sections.' Clearly, you will not do well in the examination if you disregard such an instruction. The second important issue is about preparing yourself for an examination of this sort. If you know that you are to answer two questions on two different topics from a choice of four, how are you going to prepare? Some students will only prepare for the questions in two sections, while others may prepare three or even four topics to give themselves the widest choice on the day.

There are arguments for and against both approaches, and your teacher may be the best person to advise you on a strategy. However, do be absolutely certain that you follow the instructions on the paper and answer the specified number of questions.

Much of the advice that we can offer about dealing with essay papers is relevant to most other subjects. However, the problem of repeating advice you may already have been given is much outweighed by the advantages you will get in the examination by hearing it a second time.

Once you have decided what the question is asking you to do, it is important that you then try to answer this question. Clearly, essays at this level must be planned and planned realistically with reference to the reasonable expectations of what might be achieved within as little as 25 minutes and never more than 40. What follows is an approach to these limitations, which also includes a final 'poor question selection' filter.

A PRACTICAL APPROACH TO ESSAY PAPERS

An A/AS essay is a five-paragraph essay. The paragraphs will normally function as follows.

1 **Introduction**: address key words; set the essay's agenda.
2 First main point and evidence.
3 Second main point and evidence.
4 Third main point and evidence.
5 **Conclusion**: air other points; leave the reader with something to think about.

No essay can be attempted without three main points (at least). If you can't find three, choose again.

Do not decide that the question is close to an answer you have already prepared and write that down without regard for what the question is actually demanding. Be aware of the scale of the response required; be modest and realistic.

Once you have decided which questions you are going to attempt, you need to consider the order in which you are going to tackle them. Experience of marking examination papers suggests that the last answer that candidates attempt is often their weakest.

One strategy you might like to consider is to spend time planning all the questions you are to answer as soon as you have chosen them. This means mapping out your response to each in note form before you actually start writing the first one. This will mean that you can then use your notes as the basis for each response and allocate the remaining time equally between the questions. It also means that if other points occur to you as you are working on another question, it is simple to note it down ready for use later on.

Rough notes are an invaluable help in producing a good essay response. One approach that many students find effective is to use a sheet of paper and write down in note form all the relevant points that come into their head. Once this has been done, it is a good idea to put together points that have an obvious link between them. You can use the five-paragraph plan to impose a structure on what you are going to write. It is surprising how often you will find that there will be five or six points that you want to make. If you number these in order of importance, this can form a useful route through your essay.

ACTIVITY . . .

Using one of the questions at the end of Part 4, try noting down and numbering the points you would want to make as your response.

Your style of writing is an important element of how well your essay is received. Rambling, unstructured or disorganised responses full of waffle do not get good marks in examinations. Examiners are not easy people to fool. The best approach is a simple and straightforward style of writing. Try to avoid seeming pretentious, for example by trying to use words that you do not properly understand but which you think sound impressive.

A good essay answer will also start in an interesting way. Do not think that the first paragraph has to be a mere rehash of the question. If you can think of a bright attractive introduction, perhaps a quotation or even something controversial, then do not be afraid to use it. Similarly, try to end on a high note. Do not just let your essay trail off at the end but try to find a positive ending that will help sum up what has gone before.

A particularly important point to bear in mind is to support your arguments. This can be done specifically in two ways. The first is by drawing on published authorities to give weight to the point you are making.

Similarly, you should refer to practical examples of communication or communication texts that you have considered to support your point of view. For example, you may allude to a particular communication context with which you are familiar to support an answer on the importance of paralanguage to interpersonal communication. The best examples are generally those you have found for yourself, rather than texts that the whole class has studied and which all students are likely to refer to in the same examination.

Finally, it is to be hoped that you will have had a lot of enthusiasm for your Communication Studies course. Do not be afraid to let this shine through in the examination. Examiners do enjoy reading scripts that demonstrate genuine engagement and commitment on the part of students and always try to reward this.

FURTHER WORK: TEXTS AND MEANINGS

In this section we consider in some detail how to approach a textual analysis paper by selecting a couple of representative questions from the AS unit exam, entitled 'Texts and Meanings in Communication (CMS2)', to show both the nature of analytical tasks and exemplify the format of the exam.

Text analysis is prompted in two ways, which correspond to the two compulsory tasks in the CMS2 exam. You will see that they represent approaches which are 'open' and 'closed' or, more precisely, 'undirected' and 'directed'. In the former you are asked to employ your critical tools freely on a text, while the latter identifies specific tools which it wants you to use on the task, from general issues like 'representation' to the specific focus of ideas like 'myth' and 'ideology'. The key is both to understand the prompts offered by the tasks and to connect the tasks to the content of Part 3, which has provided you with the requisite analytical tools.

Each 'Texts and Meanings in Communication' paper presents two documents for analysis and offers two compulsory tasks. Task 1 constitutes a classic text analysis task: 'Here is a text: analyse it!' or, in the slightly more refined context of a public examination:

'Through a detailed textual analysis explore the ways in which this text communicates with its audiences.' (June 2003)

In other words, 'Using the stuff you've learnt in preparation for this exam analyse this text.' This task can, of course, be applied to any text and you can expect in

Communication Studies to be asked to address an enormous range of texts from book jacket designs to greetings cards. For example in the summer of 2002 candidates were offered this highly motivated text, taken from The *Cartoon Network Annual* 2001.

DOCUMENT 1

Figure 5.1 Document 1: Summer 2002

Task 1 leads us straight into a critical analysis and a set of 'hand-holds' to encourage uncertain candidates. It is important that you, as candidates, are able to identify the key words.

Task 1

> In response to Document 1 use techniques of textual analysis to explore in detail how this text operates and what meanings it might contain.
>
> (*You may wish to consider*:
>
> ■ mode of address
> ■ narrative
> ■ genre
> ■ audiences.)

It may be conventional to assume that the legend 'You may wish to consider' should be read as 'You MUST of course consider', but if you're not careful that in itself might be a limitation. You get marks in a text analysis paper from a combination of your ability to use appropriately and efficiently the technical and critical tools and from your independent personal response to the text. The cynical approach to 'hand-holds' (those bits in italic which are meant to help you) will certainly go some way to ensuring the first objective is met but can lead the unwary to simply see the 'answer' as four paragraphs, one on each of the bullet points. It is better to see any set of prompts as simply a reminder of the nature and the level of this task, as the start of a list of tools you can use.

Given that the ability to make sense of a variety of texts is also a 'lay' activity, a very normal part of a normal life, this reminder of the technical nature of work in public examinations is perhaps the most important 'clue'. Examinations, as it has been suggested, are the extremely artificial way we have of testing the success students can achieve on a given course. In this way all examinations, though here it's more important than most, carry an assumed but largely invisible warning/statement, which runs: 'In this exam you will be particularly/specifically rewarded for knowledge and under-standings that have been acquired from studying Unit X of course Y.'

In this particular case this means using those techniques and ideas that you learned from Part 3 of this book (and inevitably from your teachers). What this amounts to is a set of key concepts like representation, mode of address, narrative and genre, and then two sets of tools gathered around the Process and Semiotic approaches. At this level you are not asked to privilege one approach but rather to choose those tools that you find useful in a given context (for a given text).

Typically then you might use a process model, like Laswell's, to identify the text and then adopt a semiotic approach to ensure that your response is appropriately (and valuably) technical. You will also want to evidence your independent personal response by being selective about what you decide to 'talk' about. One of the primary differences between a 'competent' and 'good' exam response is the ability of the latter work to be selective whereas the former simply and indiscriminately analyses everything.

This must inform your preparation (or 'paper vandalism'). In 45 minutes you are asked to read, annotate and respond to an unseen text: much of this work will have to be done on the text itself. If you can identify four or five 'issues' or significant components and rank them in order of importance you are well on the way to cracking this task. It is then only a matter of selecting the most useful tools with which to address them. Some of these issues have been prompted by the hand-hold.

For 'Johnny Bravo', for example, the process might go a little like this.

1. Identify significant 'issues' (in no particular order).
   - Genre/format (highly colourful cartoon).
   - Layout/sequence/narrative.
   - The Bravo character.
   - The representation of the female characters.
   - The question of purpose/intention/audience.

2. Select 'useful' tools.
   - Conventions of cartoons/connotations of cartoon format.
   - Theories of narrative (rather than narration)/triangular structure 1:2:3 which undermines rather than builds up Johnny's superiority.
   - The dominant Bravo syntagms and significant paradigms (key signifiers).
   - The status of signs (icon/index/symbol)/ levels of signification/stereotyping.
   - Dominant hegemonic/negotiated/oppositional readings.

3. Structure response.
   - Introduction: identify text and its initial 'issues' (Laswell would reveal 'says what?' and 'to whom?' as 'interesting'. Speculate on message and audience.
   - Identify the dominant formal syntagm (its component parts) and key signifiers (this will always be an open discussion). Address the key issue for you, using the formula, 'The key to understanding this text is . . .' Most texts will furnish at least three of these which can be used as the backbone, as they will lead the three or four paragraphs which are the heart of your response. In this case, it would be easy to go for any of the following.
   - 'The key to understanding this text is the Johnny Bravo character.'
   - 'The key to understanding this text is its genre.'
   - 'The key to understanding this text is its narrative technique.'

Interestingly three of the bullet points are already being addressed and 'mode of address' will implicitly be addressed by all three of these major points.

The other common text analysis task offers you the tools and a text, and asks you to demonstrate your knowledge and understanding and skill. A good example, and one which caused some problems, was sat in summer 2003 and offered the following text.

DOCUMENT 2

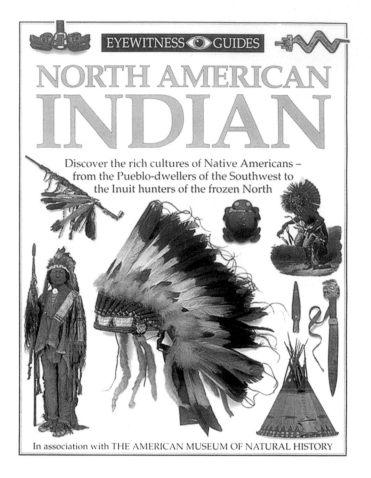

Figure 5.2 *Document 2: Summer 2003*

This was accompanied by a classic CMS2 Task 2.

Task 2

Document 2

Barthes suggested that signs signify (operate) on a number of levels, which he called 'levels of signification' (denotation, connotation, myth and ideology). Explore in detail the levels of signification at which this text operates

Here you are forced to abandon the formats that you may have developed to deal with open analysis tasks (that of course is partly the point of this kind of task). Instead you have to allow the question to set the agenda for you and then respond to its prompts. In many ways this makes these tasks more straightforward but at the same time your specific knowledge and understanding of the tools of textual analysis is being tested.

It is useful to offer an overview of the text, for example by applying a process model to clarify the issues. For this text Laswell's model might reveal the following.

- Eyewitness Guides
- say 'Here is some information on North American Indians'
- to interested older teenagers/adults (?)
- on the cover of a factual book
- with primarily a phatic function: 'Open me'/'Buy me'.

At the same time, using the tools of semiotic analysis we note a familiar syntagm consisting of:

- a significant white background
- some largely anchoring symbols (words)
- a collection of variously sized and styled images taken from an identified paradigm
- an animated logo.

You are then prepared for a simple journey from the relatively gentle denotation and connotation to the rather more challenging myth and ideology. This journey can be as broad and expansive as time and your knowledge allows but it must reach its destination. The first thing to remember is that this is not a trick and the text will have been matched to the question (or vice versa). There will be good examples of myth and ideology at work in the text. In fact a clear-headed straightforward look at the text will realise that confronting Western ideas about 'Indians' (even the word is ideologically charged) is essentially the agenda of this cover. It gives us the expected set: feathered headdress, tepee, ghost dancer, pipe of peace, warrior 'brave'. Thus it confronts 'myth' in both an enabling and misleading way, though the latter is clearly meant to function as an obvious warning. The cover does address 'myth' in the 'King Arthur' non-specialist sense, by offering evidence of the simple existence of this Indian paraphernalia. It also though, in the Barthesian sense, addresses 'myth' as a collective connotation, a set of shared assumptions. The way these myths are informed and their functions lead us then naturally to ideological issues.

Once we have realised this, it is simply a matter of working through the examples. An obvious place to start might be the impassively staring Indian chief on the left of the page as we look.

- DENOTES an elderly man dressed in skins and feathers holding a spear.
- CONNOTES all manner of things associated with 'Red Indians': their warlike nature, their primitive society, their tribal organisation.
- MYTHS include that of the 'noble savage' communicated by the facial expression which speaks of wisdom and 'honour' and the big spear!

■ IDEOLOGICALLY these myths are informed by a white eurocentric view of the world where 'savagery' is a contrast to our 'civilisation'. 'They' are defined by their difference to 'us' and their representation improves ours by default.

THEMES IN PERSONAL COMMUNICATION

One of the key tests for any course, and any book that claims it is suitable for that course, is the degree to which the work you have done before the inevitable examination prepares you for it when it comes. We have said a lot about Personal Communication in Part 4, but it is worthless if you are not able to use it to pursue a qualification in the subject. This is not to suggest that the examination is more important than the course, but rather to point out that as a simple test of knowledge and understanding of the subject the examination should be a natural end point and 'no big deal'. Given that public examinations are rigorously evaluated, assessed and scrutinised, it is likely that if you cannot recognise the exam as something you can do (or could have done if you'd done more work), then something has gone wrong with your course (or your course text).

AS Communication Studies Unit 3 is such an examination: a straightforward test of knowledge and understanding of what they and we have called 'Themes in Personal Communication'. These themes are organised into three sets:

■ verbal and non-verbal communication
■ intrapersonal communication
■ group communication

The key issue here is that you have 90 minutes in which to make three answers based on three areas you have explicitly studied. In other words, it is a test against the clock of what you know. In such a limited amount of time there is hardly room for anything more than a demonstration of knowledge of key concepts and the application of these to real-life communication. The first choice was as follows.

SECTION A

Answer **one** question from this section.

Verbal and Non-verbal Communication

1   It has been claimed that language is the most sophisticated form of communication ever developed but that only human beings have the capacity to learn and use language. What are the arguments for and against this point of view?
2   Explain the role which paralanguage can play in a conversation between two people.

Keywords are our first priority. Question 1 offers 'claimed' (denoting a point of view), 'language . . . most sophisticated form of communication' (which begs the question, 'Is it?'), 'only human beings' (which rules out other animals) and 'learn and use' (which may be separate issues). It goes on to ask for 'arguments' (series of linked reasoned statements) 'for and against' (though not necessarily balanced). If we adopt the five-paragraph essay plan suggested earlier in this section, it might look like this.

1 Introduction: which generally addresses the details of the claim by defining/commenting on terms of reference: language, sophisticated, humans/non-humans.
2 Arguments for.
3 Arguments against.
4 Your own view in the light of these.
5 Final thoughts: comment on unresolved elements.

Question 2 is much more practical, applying knowledge to practical situations. The keywords are 'Explain' (suggests detail and analysis), 'role' (the part played/function discharged), 'paralanguage' (the non-verbal aspect of speech) and 'conversation' (the classic model of dyadic communication). A plan might look like this.

1 Introduction: define paralanguage and outline its vital role.
2 Main point 1: 'it expresses attitudes and emotions' with two or three good examples.
3 Main point 2: 'it regulates communication'. pitch and intonation punctuate communication and assign functions to language (e.g. questioning by rising intonation).
4 Main point 3: 'it emphasises/supports verbal communication': volume and speed do this especially.
5 Final thoughts: on the importance of paralanguage.

Having negotiated the first section, it is time to tackle 'intra'.

SECTION B

Answer **one** question from this section.

Intrapersonal Communication

3 How helpful is Transactional Analysis in explaining the relationship between ego-states and acts of communication?
4 Explain how and why individuals often reject evidence which appears to contradict their self-image.

'How helpful' is a question which, daft as it sounds, does require you to come to some sort of decision on the scale 'totally helpful', 'very helpful', 'quite helpful', 'not very helpful' or 'totally unhelpful'. This is a classic theory question in that it deals with the most important criterion: how useful (in this case 'helpful') the theory is when applied to practical situations. Given the range of possible responses, the structure, too, will be variable. You might structure your three central points/paragraphs around TA's ego states (parent, child and adult) or conversely around evidence of TA's advantages and deficiencies.

Question 4 is more directed, although the explanations themselves are up for grabs. The 'trick' is in 'how *and* why', which demands two lists; the 'how' list led by the preposition 'by' (e.g. by discrediting the source); the 'why' list led by the phrase 'in order to' (e.g. in order to undermine the criticism they are making). 'Self-image' is clearly a key term that will need defining in the introduction, a paragraph that should also site the question where it belongs, in the discussion of 'self-maintenance strategies' and/or 'defence mechanisms'. Gergen and Gergen, as well as Freud, will be useful here as a theoretical foundation which then can be tested against experience.

Group comes last in the sequence but do remember you can attempt these sections in any order you wish. Altering the printed order is once again a way of showing your control over the exam time and experience. In this case the group questions were perhaps the most straightforward, whatever order the questions were attempted in.

SECTION C

Answer **one** question from this section.

Group Communication

5   Why do groups develop in different ways?
6   Some groups are more successful than others in achieving their goals. Discuss the key factors which contribute to the success of these groups.

The first group question is deceptively simple and as such makes particular demands on the candidate. Common sense must be your guide here; for, while the question appears simply to ask for your opinion, in the context of the exam what it is really asking for is a response that surveys critically the opinions of others. This is not to prescribe your response: good answers might focus on any or all of group variables, group motivation, group functions, group dynamics and intra- and intergroup communication.

The above list of content is also a starting point for uncovering potential factors in response to question 6. A very useful piece of theory here might be Kell and Corts (1980) on 'group maturity', which offers a checklist of criteria for defining 'mature' groups (for 'mature' read 'successful'). This list of factors would likely form the basis of a very competent answer.

The section titles, indicating the three sections of the paper, become very useful guides, a list of opportunities to write about specified key issues like 'NVC', 'the self' and 'groups'. The summer 2003 paper demonstrates these principles.

SECTION A

Answer **one** question from this section

Verbal and non-verbal Communication

1   It has been claimed that the ability to acquire and use language is an innate capacity unique to human beings. What are the arguments for and against this point of view?
2   Using examples explain how both culture and context influence the ways that people interpret non-verbal communication.

Here is the mainstream for Section A: invitations to look either at verbal or non-verbal communication. The first of these is as straightforward a question as you can get, asking only for a set of arguments supporting and disputing the 'special' linguistic capabilities of human beings. You will find these in Part 4, Section 1 (see pages 167–169).

The NVC question is a little more challenging offering as it does a couple of 'key concepts' alongside a familiar content. Like most NVC questions it offers little room (and even less reward) for mere description, asking as much for sound practical examples as for theoretical arguments. Of course context and culture will influence the reading of NVC, but your preparation should furnish well thought-out practical examples rather than simply lists and quotes.

SECTION B

Answer **one** question from this section.

Intrapersonal Communication

3   Explain and assess the significance of ONE of the following approaches to the self in the context of communication:

   (a) Freud and theories of personality development
   (b) Jung and the psyche
   (c) Transactional Analysis
   (d) The split or divided self.

continued

4   Why is it often difficult for a person to change his or her self concept? What advice could be given to someone who wished to alter his or her self concept?

Here some rather more specialist work on theories is offered alongside a mainstream question on 'self concept'. Again the first question is probably the more straightforward, with marks readily available for simply understanding Messieurs Freud, Jung, Berne and Lang. 'Significance' here suggests value, credibility, even usefulness. 'Self concept' also requires basic knowledge as a stepping stone to speculation: identifying the component parts of self concept should remind you of their interdependence and thus why self concept is difficult to change. The practical advice section is asking for practical application of the theoretical positions you adopted in the first part of the question. 'Don't bother!' is unlikely on its own to be considered to be an adequate response!

SECTION C

Answer **one** question from this section.

Group Communication

5   Using examples discuss the various ways in which membership of social groups can influence the lives of young people.

6   It is often the case that individual members of groups have goals that are different from the goals of the group as a whole. How could a successful group leader in a work, school or college situation overcome problems that arise from these differences?

Group communication can cause most problems for Communications candidates. Both of these excellent questions require good quality practical examples, preferably individually chosen. The first is an open question, which in an accessible way asks the most fundamental 'group' question: 'What are groups and what do they do for/to us?' There is room for a range of benefits and 'damages', theoretically supported, for example, by Kell and Costs, and Janis (GroupThink). There is also room for a number of perspectives: the young people themselves might have different answers to their parents or the media.

The final question is more involved, largely because it is a problem-solving exercise which needs an explicit problem. Here the theory is largely based in three ideas: 'goals', 'intragroup conflict' and 'leadership styles' and the answer is always, 'It depends . . .'. The quality of your variables often equates to the quality of your answer.

▼ GLOSSARY

actor synonym for communicator

anchorage the process by which the meaning of a text is fixed, usually by means of a caption or voice-over to visual images

archetype an ideal or model after which others are patterned

attitudes tendencies to react favourably or unfavourably to things

audience the receiver(s) of a message

autonomy the ability to act independently

barrier anything that interferes with the communication process

beliefs things you know but which can't be proved

broadcast to communicate to a mass audience

channel a communication route or connection

closed text a message that is capable of being read in a limited number of ways, sometimes only the one way

codes systems of communication using agreed rules and meaning shared by the participants

cognitive dissonance a state of conflict between a person's belief system and the way in which they may choose to act

communicate to share experiences

communication barrier see *barrier*

communication text anything that has the potential to communicate (see also *text*)

competence the capacity to perform an act, e.g. speaking a language

complexes ideas or impulses that compel habitual or obsessive behaviour (psychological barriers to communication)

conformity the tendency to go along with the majority view

connotation   the meanings in a text that are revealed through the receiver's own cultural experience

conscience   our moral self

consciousness   the state of being conscious

consumer   the receiver of a message

content analysis   a quantitative methodology that involves counting and the analysis of large amounts of data contained within communication texts

convention   the accepted, or commonly used, method for producing a text

critical thinking   the process of arriving at an objective and reasoned assessment or evaluation, e.g. of your own work

cue   a prompt

culture   shared beliefs, knowledge and experiences which form and reinforce communities

data   raw, unprocessed facts; once data have been processed, information results

decode   to convert an encoded message into a form that can be understood

deconstruction   the process of taking apart a text in order to analyse its parts

defence mechanisms   anything that seeks to protect the self from harm

denotation   the specific, direct or obvious meaning of a sign rather than its associated meanings

determinant   something that exerts influence in communication, e.g. social class, economics, technology

dialect   a type of speech specific to a particular area within a country

disclosure   the act of opening oneself up

discourse   a particular type of language associated with communication between groups with common interests, e.g. the discourse of the law

discourse analysis   a branch of linguistics that concerns itself with the analysis of conversations between two or more people

displacement   the capacity of language to refer to things removed in place and time

dissonance theory   the idea that, when faced with conflicting information about ourselves, we subconsciously handicap those parts of the argument that are most unacceptable to us

ego   the conscious self (Freud)

elaborated code   communication that allows the expression of individuality, identified particularly through the use of a wide vocabulary

elite   a privileged group of people

empathy the capacity to experience imaginatively someone else's feelings and emotions

encode to convert a message into a form capable of being transmitted, e.g. words

entropy a measure of the uncertainty or randomness contained within a message

extrovert an outward-looking person

feedback the response received by the sender to a message

foil overhead projector transparency (see *overhead transparency*)

front what is offered by a first impression

gatekeeping the process that controls the flow of information

genre a means of classifying texts into groups that share common characteristics, e.g. documentaries

grammar the conventions governing our use of language

group a collection of individuals

GroupThink a disease of groups whereby individual performance is inhibited by the priorities of the group as a whole

halo effect the tendency to overpraise

Harvard referencing system a method of acknowledging quotation or reference from other published sources

horns effect the tendency to demonise or to overcriticise

icon a sign that works by its similarity to the thing it represents

id the unconscious, animal urge (Freud)

ideal self the kind of person we would like to be

index a sign that works by reminding us of the existence of something else, e.g. smoke is an index of fire

information data that has been subjected to specific enquiry

intention purpose

intergroup communication communication between different groups of people

interpersonal communication communication between people at an individual level

intertextuality reference within one text to another text, often across different media or genres (e.g. a television advertisement may parody a scene from a famous film)

intragroup communication communication within a group

intrapersonal communication communication within the self, e.g. thinking

introvert   an inward-looking person

jargon   vocabulary specific to a particular group

Johari Window   a formula for analysing intrapersonal communication

kinesics   the study of the ways meanings are communicated by bodily movement

language   an abstract system of communication using words and sentences to convey meaning

langue   the shared system which all speakers of a language use

leakage   see *non-verbal leakage*

linguistic relativism   the process by which language can influence or control one's view of the world

linguistics   the scientific study of language

looking-glass theory   the idea that we develop ourselves in response to how others see us

medium   the method we use to communicate (e.g. speech)

mirror self   the tendency to see oneself through a reflection of how others see one

moral panic   a scare, often ill-founded, spread by the media which shocks people into calling for action

mode of address   the means by which a text speaks to its audience

motivation   in addition to the everyday meaning of 'a force that drives us', motivation is a term used in semiotics to refer to the relationship between a sign and what it represents: the higher the motivation of the sign (be it word, symbol, drawing or photograph), the closer the resemblance to whatever it is representing

narrative   the way in which a text reveals information to the audience in order to create a 'story'

narrowcast   texts that are intended for transmission to a limited (as opposed to mass) audience

negotiation   a relationship between sender and receiver that shapes meaning

netiquette   the conventions for using e-mail, derived from a contraction of the two words 'network' and 'etiquette'

noise source   the origin of any barrier to communication

non-verbal communication (NVC)   messages, such as body movements and facial expression, which do not use language to communicate

non-verbal leakage   the tendency of non-verbal codes to contradict or undermine intentional and verbal communication, e.g. lack of eye contact may betray the telling of a lie

open text a text that is capable of a wide range of different interpretations

overhead projector (OHP) equipment designed to show an image or text to a roomful of people

overhead transparency (OHT) a clear plastic sheet used with an OHP on which information for projection is displayed

paradigm a set of signs from which choices can be made

paralanguage communication that is in the form of utterances other than the words themselves, e.g. the volume of one's voice

parole the everyday use of language as opposed to the system of language and the conventions that govern it

patriarchy social organisation in which men occupy the key positions of power

perception the process of making sense of sensory data

performance communicative behaviour

persona an adopted form of the self/identity

personality what we are like

phatic communication aspects of language that serve to reinforce social relationships rather than communicate information, e.g. saying 'Have a nice day' when meeting someone

phonetics the study of the sounds used in speaking a language

phonology the study of sounds and their role in language

pitch the intonation of speech which determines the way in which our voice may rise and fall

polysemy the capacity of a text to have more than one meaning or to be open to a range of different readings

postural congruence the tendency to mirror another person's body language by adopting similar postures

PowerPoint computer software for creating visual aids, such as OHTs

preferred reading the reading of a message that the producer guides the receiver towards, the reading they would like the reader to make

process school a school of thought in which communication is conceived as a process whereby information is transmitted

producer the sender of a message

prompt a cue

proxemics the study of how we handle the space around us, especially in relation to other people

psyche the soul, the inner being

psychometry a scheme for measuring psychological behaviour

Pygmalion effect a byproduct of selective perception

Q&A (question and answer technique) the phase in a presentation in which the audience are able to ask questions

reading can be categorised as being of three different types:

(a) **dominant-hegemonic:** the 'intended' message contained within a text that the majority of readers are likely to accept

(b) **negotiated:** an interpretation of a text that identifies the dominant reading but seeks to question its validity

(c) **oppositional:** an interpretation of a text that rejects the 'intended' message and makes a different or contrary interpretation

received pronunciation (RP) 'standard English' or the generally accepted means of speaking without regional accent

receiver someone who gets a message

register adopting a specific use of language appropriate to the situation in which communication is taking place and the audience being addressed

regulator a controller

report a formal account of something that has taken place, either written or verbal

representation the act of presenting the world again

restricted code communication that reinforces the shared values of a group, characterised by a limited vocabulary

role a part we play

rubric written instructions usually found on an examination paper

school of thought where groups of academics come together because they feel the same way about particular issues

self what we are

self-concept the idea we have of ourselves

self-definition the capacity to know the difference between 'I/me' and 'you'

self-disclosure the act of revealing ourselves, consciously or otherwise

self-esteem what we think of ourselves

self-fulfilling prophecy the concept that the way in which we treat people (because of our expectations of them) may influence their behaviour in such a way that they fulfil these expectations

self-image   how we see ourselves

self-maintenance strategies   the ways in which we keep ourselves going

self-presentation   the conscious process through which self becomes text

self-recognition   the capacity to recognise an image or reflection of oneself

self-reflexivity   the act of consciously thinking about oneself or one's behaviour

semantics   the study of the relationship between signs and meanings

semiotics (**semiology**)   the study of signs and how they communicate

sender   the originator of a message

sign   that which stands for or represents an object, idea or mental concept

signification   the process of signifying (see *signify*)

signifier/signified   the two components of a sign: the physical aspect such as a sound or word, and the mental concept

signify   to use a sign in order to represent an object, idea or concept

skill   a capacity that can be learned, practised and refined

slide   see *overhead transparency*

sociometrics   the study of personal interrelationships within a social group

stereotype   to represent a person by attributing to them simple characteristics supposedly shared by a larger group

superego   the controlling part of the self (Freud)

symbol   an arbitrary sign that works by the agreement among people as to what it represents

syntagm   an ordered sequence of signs

syntax   the conventions governing the use of language

text   any form of communication that can be read/interpreted, e.g. advertisement, film, book

Transactional Analysis (TA)   theory in which interpersonal communication can be studied in relation to different ego states adopted by people

typography   the use of different types and styles of lettering in printed texts

values   fundamental responses to reality

▼ RESOURCES

COMMUNICATION, CULTURAL AND MEDIA STUDIES INFOBASE

www.cultsock.ndirect.co.uk/MUHome/cshtml/
A really useful resource for the student of Communication Studies. A helpful index provides access to key terms and concepts which are considered in an accessible manner. Provides useful links to further reading and information.

THE MEDIA AND COMMUNICATION STUDIES SITE

www.aber.ac.uk/media/index.html
Another useful site that breaks the disciplines down into useful topic areas. Provides links to articles, some of which students will find more accessible than others.

CRITICAL THEORY AND CULTURAL STUDIES

http://eserver.org/theory/
Generally quite a high-powered site, although with a searchable database.

www.theory.org.uk
A lively and challenging site with an interesting focus on popular culture.

www.popcultures.com/
A searchable site with useful links to articles by and about key theorists.

VOICE OF THE SHUTTLE

http://vos.ucsb.edu/browse.asp?id=2720
Generally a site focused on Media Studies but containing material on broader cultural issues.

▼ BIBLIOGRAPHY

Adorno, T. (1950) *The Authoritarian Personality*, New York: Harper & Row.

Allen, R. E. (1990) *Oxford Writers' Dictionary*, Oxford: Oxford University Press.

Allen, V. L. (1965) 'Situational factors in conformity', in L. Berkowitz (ed.) *Advances in Experimental Social Psychology*, Vol. 2, New York and London: Academic Press.

Argyle, M. (1983) *The Psychology of Interpersonal Behaviour*, 4th edn, Harmondsworth: Penguin.

Bales, R. F. (1950) *Interaction Process Analysis*, New York: Addison-Wesley.

Barrass, R. (1984) *Study! A Guide to Effective Study, Revision and Examination Techniques*, London: Chapman & Hall.

Barthes, R. (1967) *Elements of Semiology*, London: Cape.

Barthes, R. (1973) *Mythologies*, selected and translated by A. Lavers, New York: Hill & Wang.

Berne, E. (1968) *Games People Play: The Psychology of Human Relationships*, Harmondsworth: Penguin.

Bernstein, B. (1971) *Class, Codes and Control*, London: Routledge & Kegan Paul.

Birtwhistell, R. (1970) *Kinesics and Context: Essays in Body Movement Communication*, Philadelphia, PA: University of Pennsylvania Press.

Brewer, M. and Miller, N. (1996) *Intergroup Relations*, Milton Keynes: Open University Press.

Burton, G. and Dimbleby, R. (1995) *Between Ourselves: An Introduction to Interpersonal Communication*, 2nd edn, London: Edward Arnold.

Carey, G. V. (1971) *Mind the Stop*, Harmondsworth: Penguin.

Cattell, R. B. (1965) *The Scientific Analysis of Personality*, Harmondsworth: Penguin.

Chambers, E. and Northedge, A. (1997) *The Arts Good Study Guide*, Milton Keynes: Open University Press.

Cherry, C. (1978) *On Human Communication: A Review, a Survey and a Criticism*, 3rd edn, Cambridge, Mass./London: MIT Press.

Chomsky, N. (1968) *Language and Mind*, New York: Harcourt Brace & World.

Cobley, P. (ed.) (1996) *The Communication Theory Reader*, London: Routledge.

Cohen, S. (1980) *Folk Devils and Moral Panics*, Oxford: Blackwell.

Cooley, C. H. (1992) *Human Nature and the Social Order*, New York: Transaction Publishers.

Coopersmith, S. (1967) *The Antecedents of Self-Esteem*, San Francisco: Freeman.

de Saussure, F. (1983) *Course in General Linguistics*, trans. R. Harris, ed. C. Bally and A. Sechehaye, London: Duckworth.

Dimbleby, R. and Burton, G. (1998) *More than Words: An Introduction to Communication*, 3rd edn, London: Routledge.

Douglas, W. D. (1979) *Groups: Understanding People Gathered Together*, London: Tavistock.

Drew, S. and Bingham, R. (1997) *The Student Skills Guide*, Aldershot: Gower.

Eco, U. (1973) 'Social life as a sign system', in D. Robey (ed.) *Structuralism: An Introduction*, Oxford: Clarendon Press.

Eco, U. (1979) *The Role of the Reader: Explorations in the Semiotics of Texts*, Bloomington, Ind.: Indiana University Press.

Eysenck, H. J. (1947/1999) *Dimensions of Personality*, London: Routledge.

Eysenck, H. J. (1954) *The Psychology of Politics*, London: Routledge & Kegan Paul.

Eysenck, H. J. and Eysenck, S. B. G. (1969) *Personality Structure and Measurement*, London: Routledge.

Fiske, J. (1990) *Introduction to Communication Studies*, 2nd edn, London: Routledge.

Fiske, J. and Hartley, J. (1978) *Reading Television*, London: Methuen.

Fowler, H. W. (1983) *A Dictionary of Modern English Usage*, Oxford: Oxford University Press.

Freud, S. (1984) *On Metaphysics: the Theory of Psychoanalysis. 'Beyond the pleasure principle', 'The ego and the id' and Other Works*, ed. J. Strachey and A. Richards, The Pelican Freud Library Vol. 11, Harmondsworth: Penguin.

Freud, S. (1999) *The Interpretation of Dreams*, trans. J. Crick, Oxford: Oxford University Press.

Fry, R. (1997) *How to Study*, London: Kogan Page.

Gahagan, J. (1975) *Interpersonal and Group Behaviour*, London: Methuen.

Gerbner, G. (1970) 'Cultural Indicators: the case of violence in television drama', *Annals of the American Association of Political and Social Science*, 338.

Gergen, K. J. and Gergen, M. M. (1981) *Social Psychology*, New York: Harcourt Brace Jovanovich.

Gill, D. and Adams, B. (1998) *The ABC of Communication Studies*, Walton-on-Thames: Nelson.

Goffman, E. (1963) *Behaviour in Public Places*, New York: Free Press.

Goffman, E. (1990) *The Presentation of the Self in Everyday Life*, Harmondsworth: Penguin.

Gowers, E. (1987) *The Complete Plain Words*, 3rd edn, Harmondsworth: Penguin.

Gramsci, A. (1971) *Selections from the Prison Notebooks*, ed. and trans. Q. Hoare and G. Nowell Smith, London: Lawrence & Wishart.

Gross, R. (1996) *Psychology: The Science of Mind and Behaviour*, London: Hodder & Stoughton.

Guiraud, P. (1975) *Semiology*, trans. G. Gross, London: Routledge & Kegan Paul.

Hall, E. T. (1959) *The Silent Language*, New York: Doubleday.

Hall, S. (ed.) (1980) *Culture, Media, Language*, London: Hutchinson.

Halliday, M. A. K. (1978) *Language as Social Semiotic*, London: Edward Arnold.

Harré, R., Clarke, D. and de Carlo, N. (1985) *Motives and Mechanisms*, London: Methuen.

Hartley, P. (1997) *Group Communication*, London: Routledge.

Hartley, P. (1999) *Interpersonal Communication*, 2nd edn, London: Routledge.

Hawkes, T. (1977) *Structuralism and Semiotics*, London: Routledge.

Jakobson, R. (1962) *Selected Writings*, The Hague: Mouton.

Janis, I. L. (1982) *Groupthink: Psychological Studies of Policy Decisions and Fiascoes*, 2nd edn, Boston: Houghton Mifflin.

Jung, C. G. (1963) *Memories, Dreams, Reflections*, ed. A. Jaffé, trans. R. and C. Winston, London: Collins/Routledge.

Kell, C. L. and Corts, P. R. (1980) *Fundamentals of Effective Group Communication*, New York: Macmillan.

Kuhn, H. H. and McPartland, T. S. (1954) 'An empirical investigation of self-attitudes', *American Sociological Review*, 47.

Laing, R. D. (1962) *The Divided Self*, London: Routledge.

Lasswell, H. (1948) 'The structure and function of communication in society', in L. Bryson (ed.) *The Communication of Ideas*, New York.

Lewin, K., Lippett, R. and White, R. (1939) 'Patterns of aggressive behaviour in experimentally created social climates', in *Journal of Social Psychology*, 10.

Luft, J. (1969) *Of Human Interaction*, Palo Alto, Calif.: National Press Books.

Luft, J. and Ingham, H. (1955) 'The Johari Window: a graphic model for interpersonal relations', University of California Western Training Lab.

MacDougall, J. (2000) 'Finding the "ism" of the real', in *itp Film Reader* 2, ed. Stafford.

McEwan, I. (1987) *The Child in Time*, London: Cape.

McLuhan, M. (1964) *Understanding Media*, London: Routledge.

Maslow, A. (1954) *Motivation and Personality*, New York: Harper & Row.

Mead, M. (1930) *Growing up in New Guinea: A Comparative Study of Primitive Education*, London: G. Routledge & Sons.

Mepham, J. (1974) 'The theory of ideology in capital', W.P.C.S. no. 6, University of Birmingham.

Moreno, J. L. (1951) *Sociometry, Experimental Method and the Science Society*, Beacon House.

Morris, D. (1994) *The Human Animal*, London: BBC Books.

Moscovici, S. (1985) 'Social influence and conformity', in D.T. Gilbert, S.T. Fiske and G. Lindzey (eds) *The Handbook of Social Psychology*, Westminster, Md.: Random House.

Murphy, G. (1947) *Personality*, New York: Harper & Row.

Myers, G. and Myers, M. (1992) *The Dynamics of Human Communication*, 6th edn, New York: McGraw-Hill.

Nicholson, J. (1977) *Habits*, London: Macmillan.

Orwell, G. (1948) *1984*, London: Penguin.

Orwell, G. (2000) 'Politics and the English language', in *Essays*, Harmondsworth: Penguin.

O'Sullivan, T., Hartley, J., Saunders, D., Montgomery, M. and Fiske, J. (1994) *Key Concepts in Communication and Cultural Studies*, London/New York: Routledge.

Partridge, E. (1999) *Usage and Abusage*, Harmondsworth: Penguin.

Piaget, J. (1952) *The Child's Conception of Numbers*, London: Routledge.

Peirce, C. S. (1966) *Collected Papers of Charles Sanders Peirce*, Cambridge, Mass.: Belknap Press of Harvard University Press.

Potter, D. (1996) *'Karaoke' and 'Cold Lazarus'*, London: Faber.

Pound, E. (1951) *ABC of Reading*, London: Faber.

Roget's Thesaurus of English Words and Phrases (2000) ed. B. Kirkpatrick, Harmondsworth: Penguin.

Rayner, P., Wall, P. and Kruger, S. (2004) *AS Media Studies: The Essential Introduction*, London and New York: Routledge.

Rogers, C. R. (1961) *On Becoming a Person*, Boston: Houghton Mifflin.

Rokeach, M. (1960) *The Open and Closed Mind*, New York: Basic Books.

Rubenzer, S. (2000) Paper given to the American Psychological Association, reported in *The Independent*.

Sapir, E. (1956) *Language, Culture and Personality*, ed. E. G. Mandelbaum, Berkeley, Calif.: University of California Press.

Shannon, C. and Weaver, W. (1949) *The Mathematical Theory of Communication*, Champaign, IL: University of Illinois Press.

Shaw, M. (1981) *Group Dynamics*, 3rd edn, New York: McGraw-Hill.

Smith, P. B. and Bond, M. H. (1993) *Social Psychology across Cultures*, Brighton: Harvester Wheatsheaf.

Spender, D. (1998) *Man Made Language*, 4th edn, London: Pandora.

Stanton, N. (1996) *Mastering Communication*, 3rd edn, Basingstoke: Macmillan.

Stogdill, R. M. (1981) *Stogdill's Handbook of Leadership*, 2nd edn, New York: Free Press and London: Collier Macmillan.

Strinati, D. (2000) *An Introduction to Studying Popular Culture*, London and New York: Routledge.

Tedeschi, J. T. and Lindskold, S. (1976) *Social Psychology: Interdependence, Interaction and Influence*, New York: Wiley.

Tuckman, B. W. (1965) 'Developmental sequence in small groups', *Psychological Bulletin*, 63.

Turner, J. C. (1991) *Social Influence*, Oxford: Oxford University Press.

Watzlawick, P., Beavin, J. H., Jackson, D. D. (1967) *Pragmatics of Human Communication. A Study of Interactional Patterns, Pathologies, and Paradoxes*, New York: Norton.

Whorf, B. L. (1956) *Language, Thought and Reality*, ed. J. B. Carroll, Cambridge, Mass.: MIT Press.

Williams, R. (1962) *Communications*, Harmondsworth: Penguin.

Wittgenstein, L. (1953) *Philosophical Investigations*, Oxford: Blackwell.

Zimbardo, P. G. (1988) *Psychology and Life*, 12th edn, Glenview, Ill.: Scott, Foresman.

▼ INDEX

e-mail 38; accounts 38; addresses 38, 39; attachments 41; blind carbon copies (bcc) 39; carbon copies (cc) 39; empathy 40; getting connected 38–41; netiquette 40–1, 272; onscreen forms 39, 39f; organisation 41; programmes 38–9; replying 40; security 41; subject 39–40

Eco, U. 11, 98

effective communication 19, 21

effective reading 52–4

ego 201–3, 204, 270

ego-states 218–19

egotism 211

elaborated codes 163–4, 270

elements of communication 136, 136f

Eliot, T. S. 1, 23

elite 270

Elizabeth (film) 117–19, 117f

emotive function 136

empathy 21, 29, 40, 70, 71, 271

enacted roles 228

encode/encoding 8, 271

energisers 229

engulfment 203

Enigma of Kaspar Hauser, The (film) 169

entropy 119, 121–2, 271

essays: bibliography 53–4, 55–6; examination papers 256–7; five-paragraph essays 68–9, 144–5, 257–8; writing style 257–8

evaluation writing 57

examinations 247; A level questions 8, 243–4, 258–68, 259f, 262f; annotation 253–4; argument 248; assessment 250, 251–2; essay papers 256–7; exploding (note-taking) 254; key terms 256; note-taking 254, 257; number of questions 252; preparation 252–3; relevance 253–4; revision 249–52; rubrics 255, 274; skills 22, 247; technique 248; textual analysis (closed) 98, 261–4, 262f, 269; textual analysis (open) 98, 258–61, 259f; Themes in Personal Communication 264–8; time 252–3; unseen papers 254–6; writing style 257–8; *see also* Communication Practice; presentations

existence 94

expected roles 228

extroversion 204, 207–8

extroverts 271

eye contact 49; cues 71, 185; disengagement 175; eye movement 175; gazing 174; observation data 64, 65; power relations 174, 176; staring 174

Eysenck, H. J. 205–6, 207–8, 209

facial expression 175–6, 185

family life 62

Fawlty Towers 69–70, 84–5

'fear face' 176

feedback 21, 30, 194, 271; Internet 134; mass media 133; non-verbal communication 29–30, 185; perception 193; 'Pygmalion effect' 192; verbal communication 29–30

feminism 96, 170

feral children 169

figures of speech 23

FilmFour 117–19, 117f

films 134–6; *Blair Witch Project* 134–6, 134f; *Cruel Intentions* 87; *Elizabeth* 117–19, 117f; *Enigma of Kaspar Hauser* 169; *Girl Interrupted* 72–3; *Iris* 86; *L'Enfant Sauvage* 169; *Once We Were Warriors* 10f; *Titanic* 135; *Tomb Raider* 120f; *Trainspotting* 77–8, 81f, 107f, 108; *Zulu* 166

Finney, Albert 166

Fiske, J. 15, 108, 118, 144

flip charts 87

flyers 113–15, 114f, 115f, 155

foils 271

football 6, 8–9

form 7, 132

formal communication 19, 21

forming (groups) 227

Fowler, H. W. 22

French 162, 165

French and Saunders 215

Freud, S. 198, 200–3

Freudian slip 201

friendship 11, 215, 216, 222, 225, 235

front 213, 215, 271

frowning 176

function 7

functions of communication 136–7, 136f

functions of language 159–60

Gahagan, J. 224

Galen 207

271; intention 24; jargon 13, 23, 24–5, 272; letters 26–7, 37; note-taking 50, 52, 254, 259; paragraphs 25, 35–6; process 22; punctuation 56; purpose 24; register 24, 25; revising 23, 36; sentences 23; spelling 36; structure 25–6, 35; style 23, 257–8; *see also* computers; e-mail

youth subculture 12, 215

Zimbardo, P. G. 239
Zulu (film) 166